GRAPHIC FREUD

HYSTERIA

TEXT BY RICHARD APPIGNANESI

DRAWINGS BY OSCAR ZARATE

SELF MADE HERO

DEDICATIONS

To Helen (from R.A.)

To Mrs. Cooper and Hazel (from O.Z.)

First published 2015
by SelfMadeHero
139–141 Pancras Road
London NW1 1UN
www.selfmadehero.com

© SelfMadeHero, 2015

Text by Richard Appignanesi
Drawings by Oscar Zarate
Designed by Txabi Jones

Publishing Assistant: Guillaume Rater
Sales & Marketing Manager: Sam Humphrey
Publishing Director: Emma Hayley
UK Publicist: Paul Smith
US Publicist: Maya Bradford
With thanks to: Kate McLauchlan, Nick de Somogyi and
Deborah Levy

A CIP record for this book is available from the British Library

ISBN: 978-1-906838-99-7

10 9 8 7 6 5 4 3 2 1

Printed and bound in Slovenia

FOREWORD

We owe a great deal to the grandly expressive female hysterics of the late 19th and early 20th centuries. Their apparently inexplicable symptoms (loss of voice, paralysis of limbs, anorexia, bulimia, chronic fatigue, fainting fits, indifference to life) were asking subversive questions about femininity: What does it mean to be a woman? What should a woman be? Who is her body supposed to please and what is it for? Does she construct her femininity through being an object of male desire? If she is required to cancel her own desires, what is she supposed to do with them? Hysteria is the language of the protesting body.

You will meet some of these women in this incredible graphic novel, magically brought to life with delicacy and complexity in the drawings of Oscar Zarate.

At the start of Freud's career in patriarchal Vienna, he was under the impression that there was one sexuality and that it was male. Fortunately he changed his mind, but he humbly confessed that after thirty years of professional practice, he still did not know what women wanted. Yet Freud was witness to the most modern of female questions and conflicts. Unlike his mentor, the pioneering French neurologist Jean-Martin Charcot, nicknamed the Napoleon of Neuroses (you will also meet him here, along with his pet monkey who roamed through the wards at the Salpêtrière hospital), Freud encouraged his patients to speak freely and without censorship. This was no small matter considering how callously women had been silenced by the societal restrictions of their day and not least by their families, many of whom were sexual predators. Richard Appignanesi unfolds for readers some of their incredible stories, as told to Freud in his consulting room in Bergstrasse 19.

Anna O., Elisabeth von R., Dora, and Jane Avril (a dancer at the Moulin Rouge who was painted by Toulouse-Lautrec) all struggled with myths about female character and destiny. In their attempt to find words for disabling despair, Freud tuned in to their most awkward and shaming memories or reminiscences. Psychoanalysis was born when he discovered that it was possible to interpret rather than medicate symptoms that had no biological or neurological cause. As Freud describes in his *Introductory Lectures on Psychoanalysis*, the task of a psychoanalytic treatment "is to make conscious everything that is pathogenically unconscious". He never promised that the Talking Cure would make us happy but he believed it might make us less miserable. If words are so powerful that they can make us pregnant (as Anna O. believed), it is not surprising that psychoanalysis has always paid the closest attention to the structure of language. Freud wanted to find the truths that had been dodged.

The diagnosis of hysteria which began with Hippocrates in the 5th century B.C. has now been erased from the *Diagnostic and Statistical Manual of Mental Disorders* ("DSM"). Yet we all know that trauma (the Greek for "wound") has not gone away, and neither have the girls and women who self-harm. As Appignanesi astutely argues in this compelling history of how the birth of psychoanalysis offered methods to investigate the unconscious mind, there is no doubt that personal and political conflicts, and above all rage and hopelessness, continue to speak through the body in our own turbulent century. Hysteria is not about "them", it is about all of us.

Hysteria is dead! Long live hysteria!

Deborah Levy

Deborah Levy's most recent novel, *Swimming Home*, was shortlisted for the Man Booker Prize. Levy dramatized two of Freud's most iconic case histories for BBC Radio 4, *The Wolf Man* and *Dora*. The acclaimed artist Andrzej Klimowski is currently adapting her short story, *Stardust Nation*, into a graphic novel, to be published by SelfMadeHero in 2016.

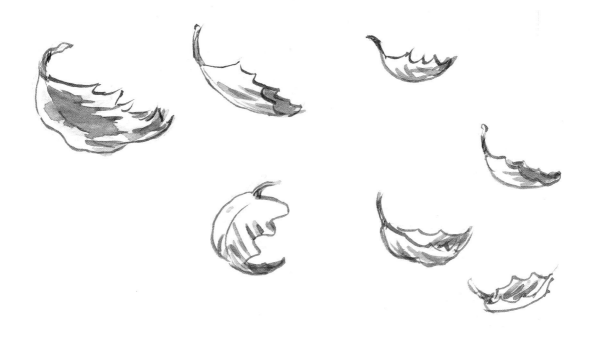

LONDON, SEPTEMBER 1938.
I REST IN MY HAMPSTEAD GARDEN.

A GUST OF WIND...

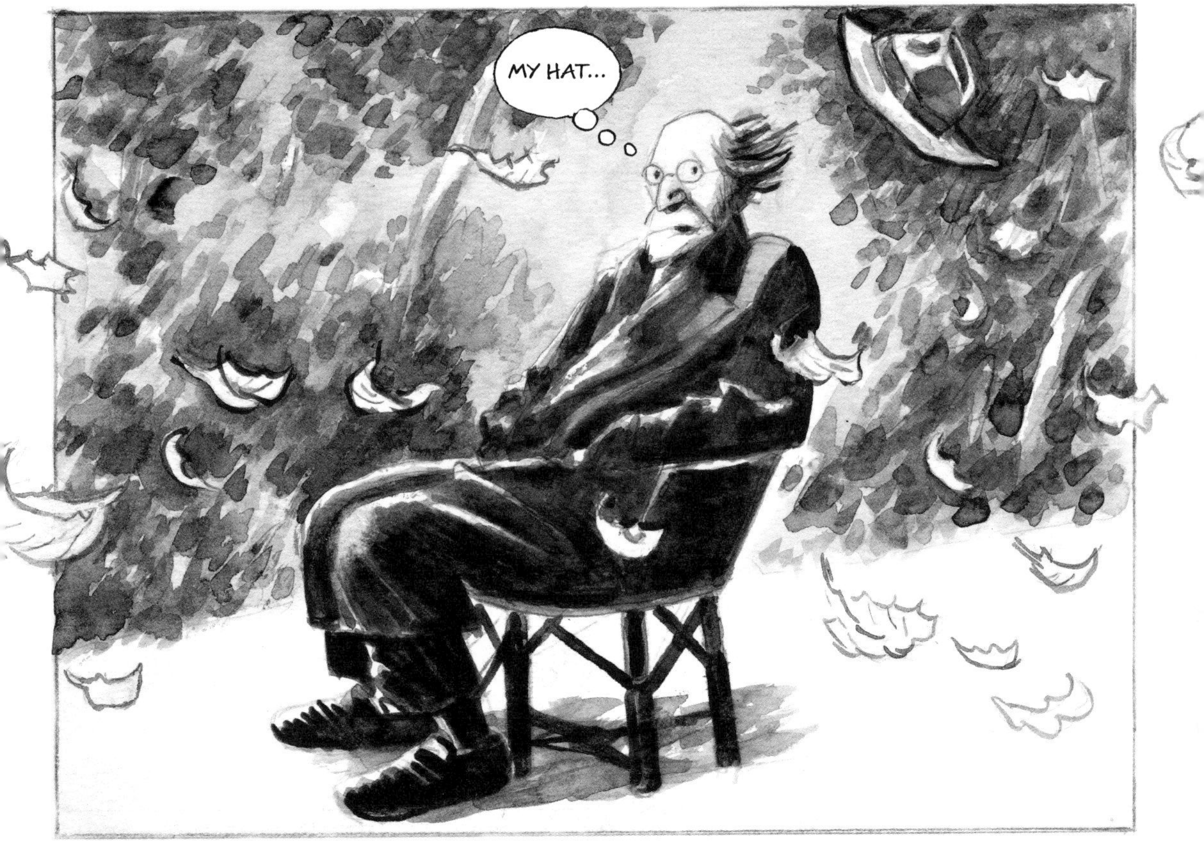
MY HAT...

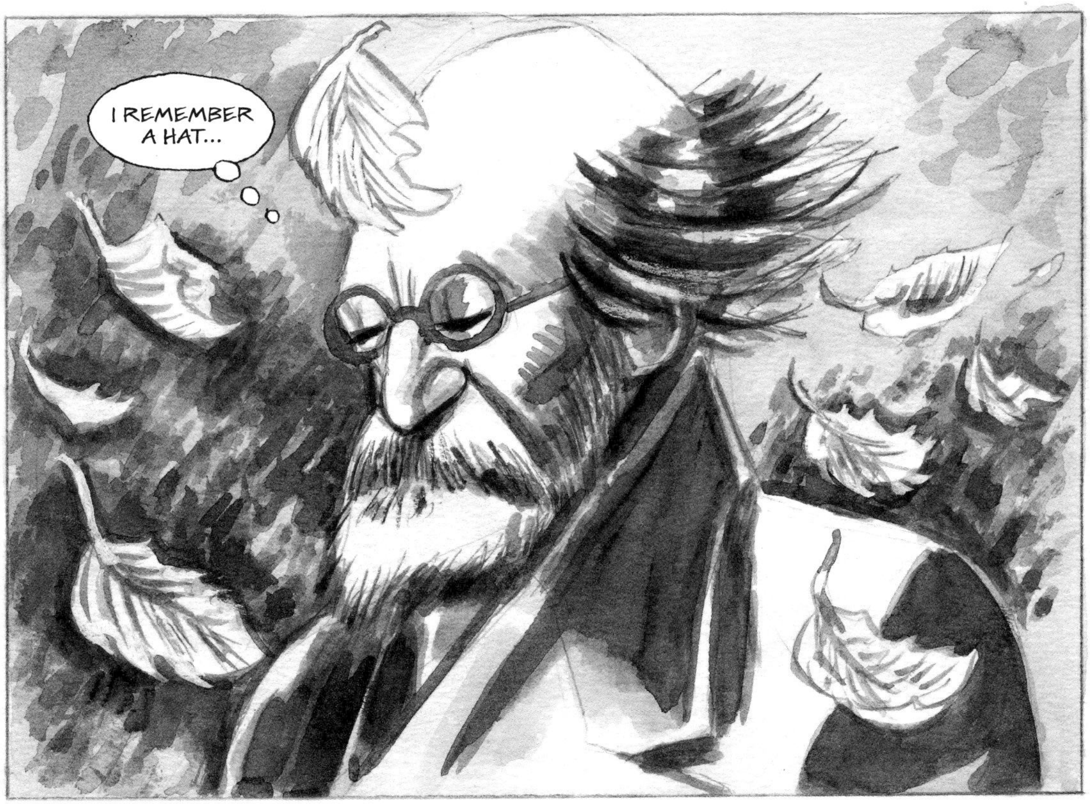
I REMEMBER A HAT...

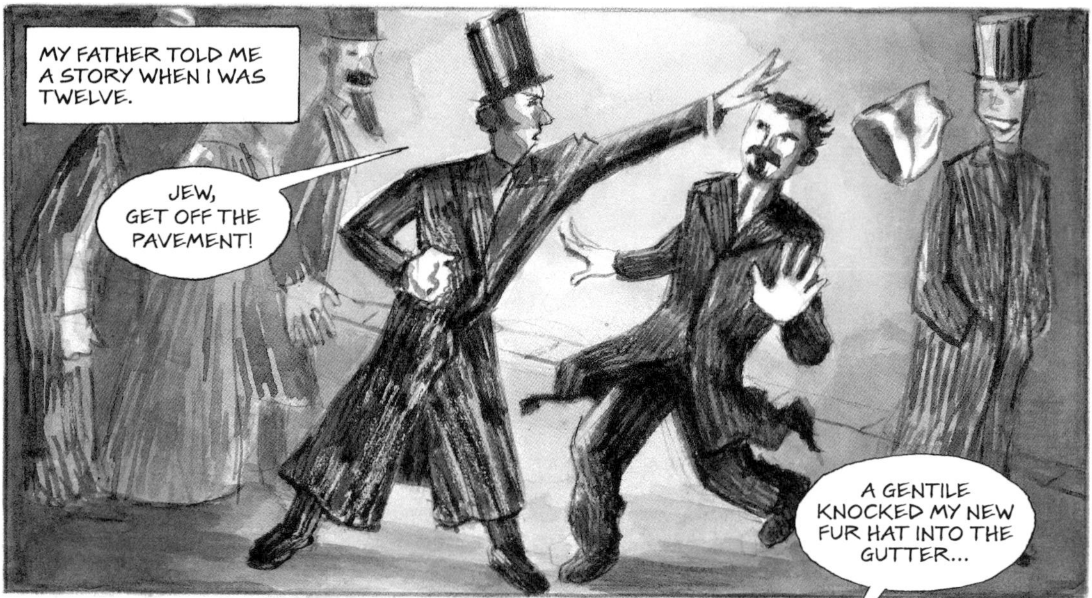
MY FATHER TOLD ME A STORY WHEN I WAS TWELVE.
JEW, GET OFF THE PAVEMENT!
A GENTILE KNOCKED MY NEW FUR HAT INTO THE GUTTER...

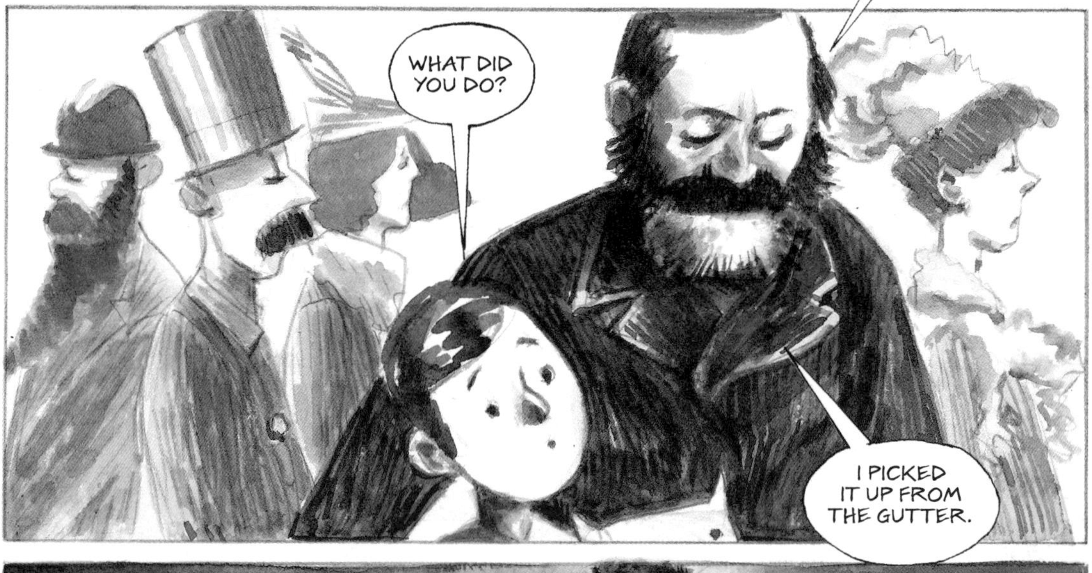
WHAT DID YOU DO?
I PICKED IT UP FROM THE GUTTER.

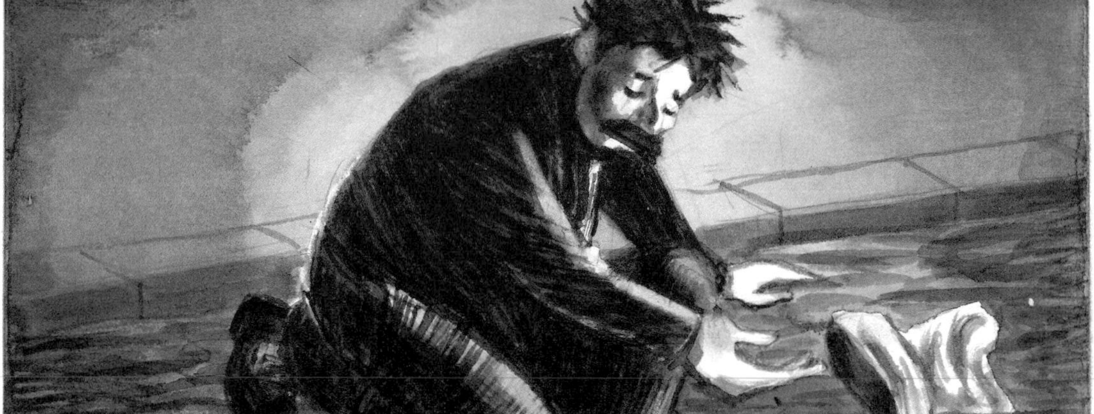

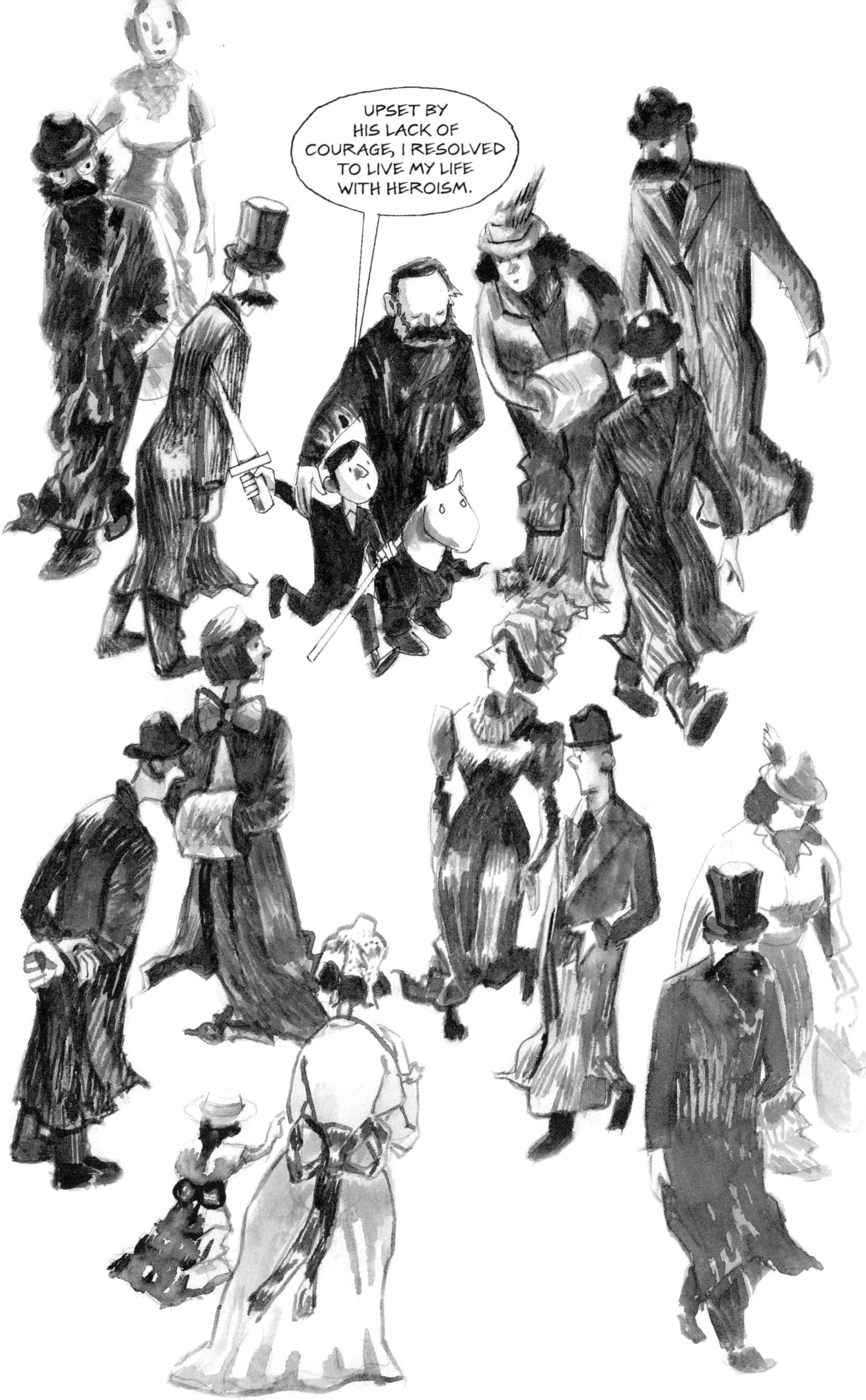
UPSET BY HIS LACK OF COURAGE, I RESOLVED TO LIVE MY LIFE WITH HEROISM.

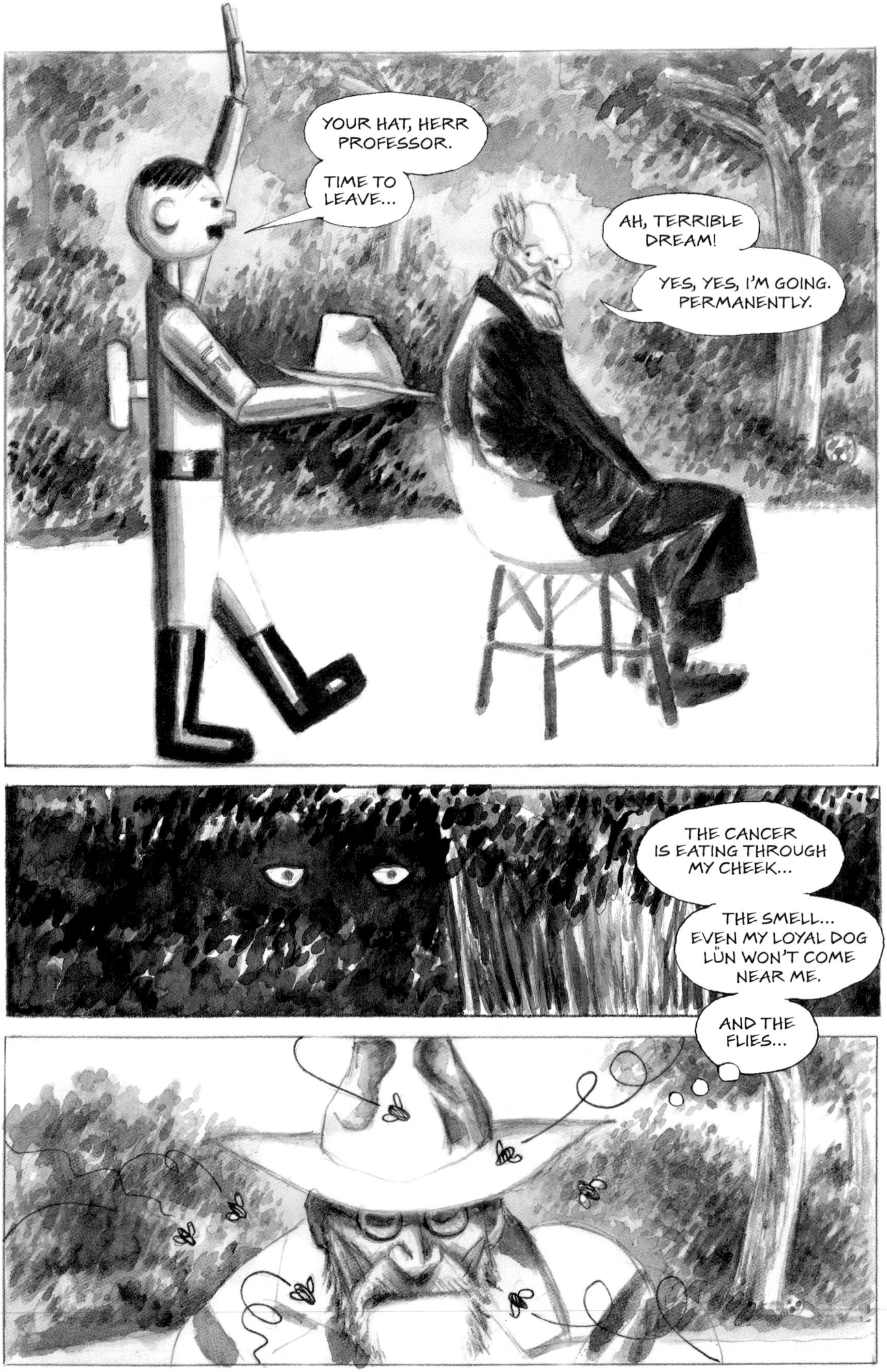
YOUR HAT, HERR PROFESSOR.
TIME TO LEAVE...
AH, TERRIBLE DREAM!
YES, YES, I'M GOING. PERMANENTLY.
THE CANCER IS EATING THROUGH MY CHEEK...
THE SMELL... EVEN MY LOYAL DOG LÜN WON'T COME NEAR ME.
AND THE FLIES...

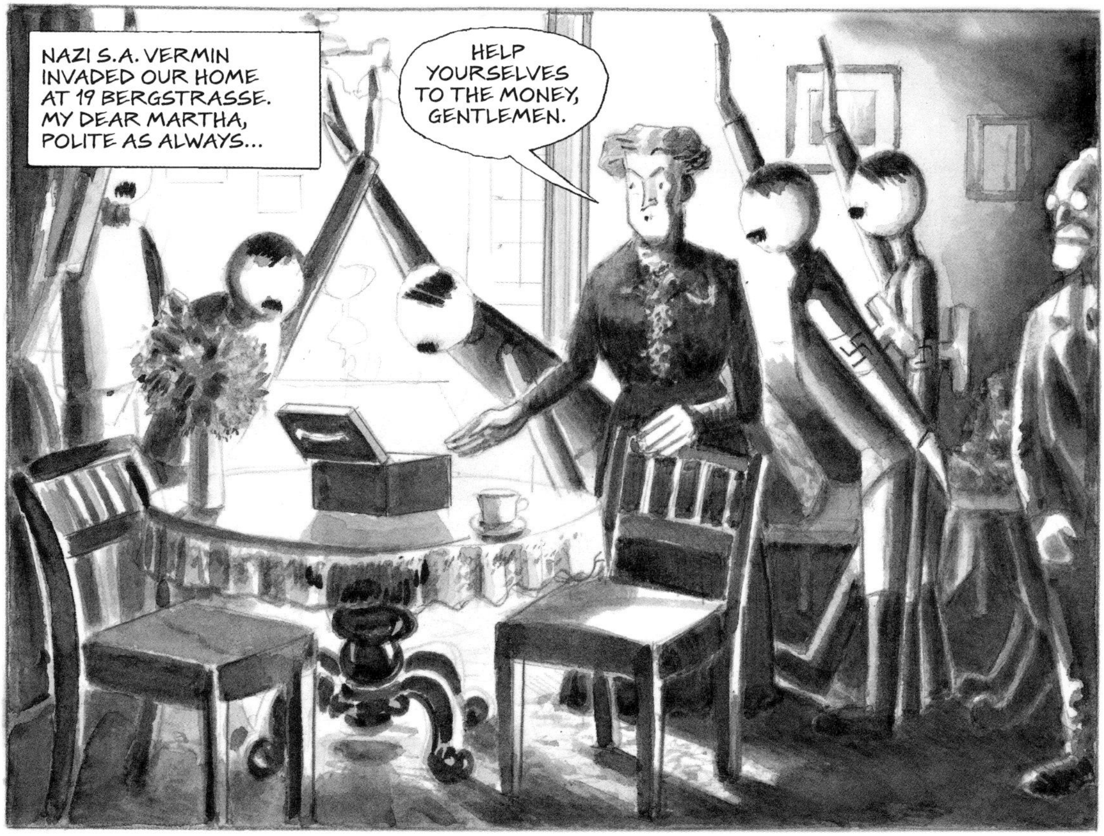
NAZI S.A. VERMIN INVADED OUR HOME AT 19 BERGSTRASSE. MY DEAR MARTHA, POLITE AS ALWAYS...
HELP YOURSELVES TO THE MONEY, GENTLEMEN.

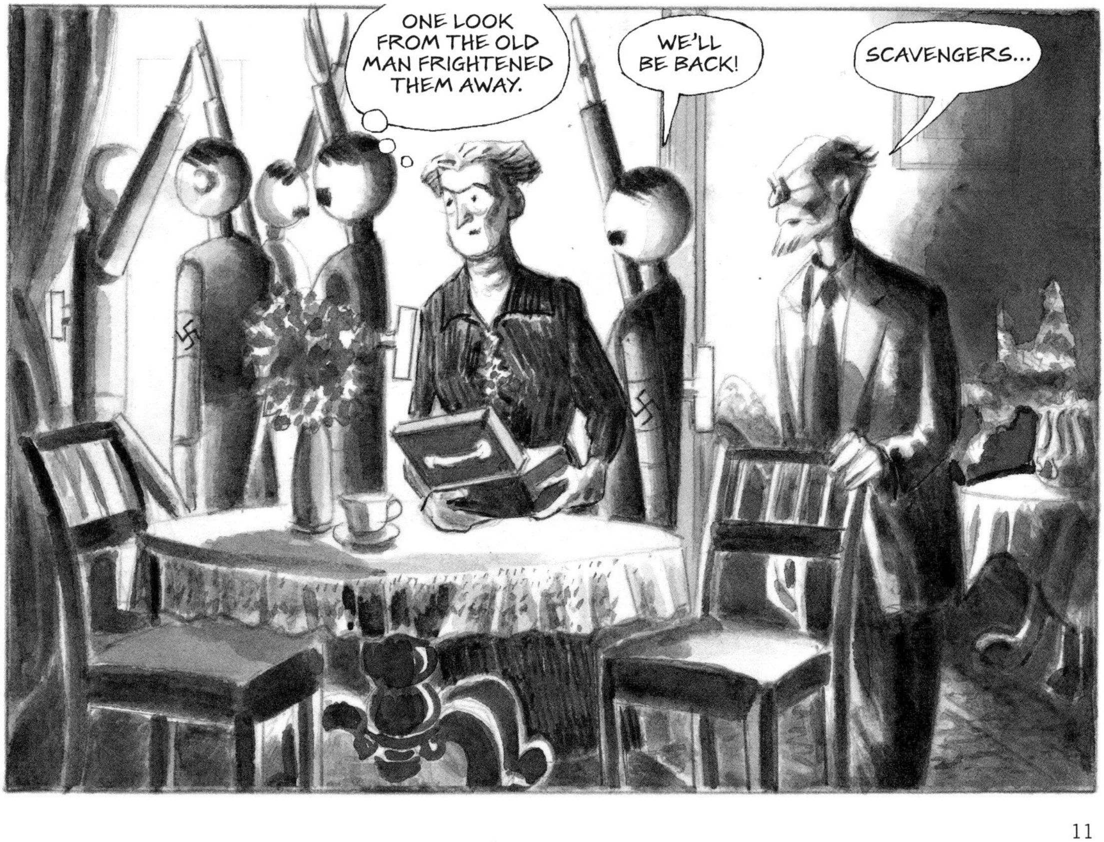
ONE LOOK FROM THE OLD MAN FRIGHTENED THEM AWAY.
WE'LL BE BACK!
SCAVENGERS...

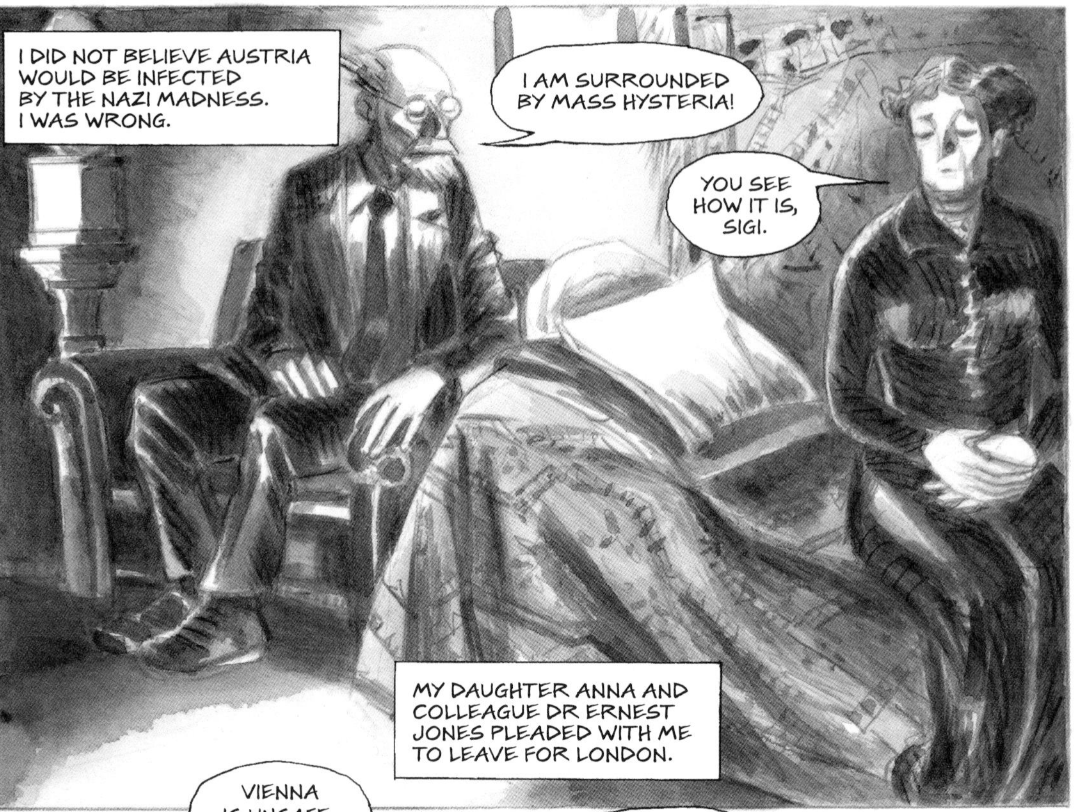
I DID NOT BELIEVE AUSTRIA WOULD BE INFECTED BY THE NAZI MADNESS. I WAS WRONG.
I AM SURROUNDED BY MASS HYSTERIA!
YOU SEE HOW IT IS, SIGI.
MY DAUGHTER ANNA AND COLLEAGUE DR ERNEST JONES PLEADED WITH ME TO LEAVE FOR LONDON.

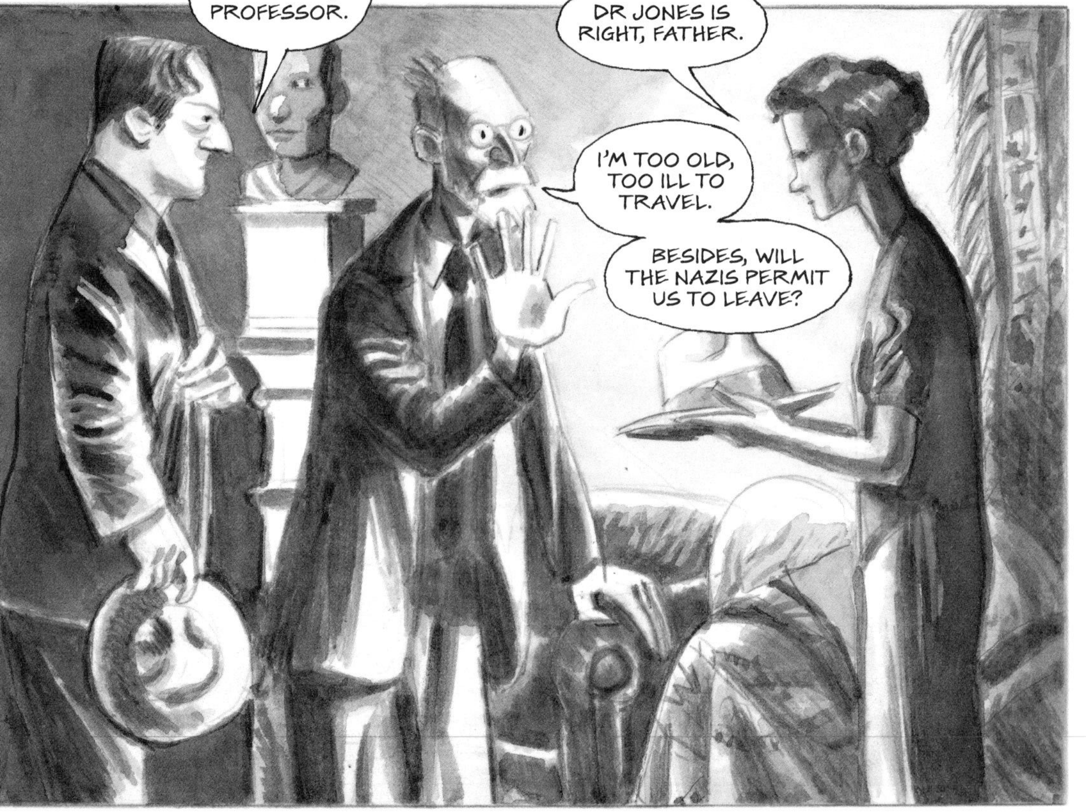
VIENNA IS UNSAFE, PROFESSOR.
DR JONES IS RIGHT, FATHER.
I'M TOO OLD, TOO ILL TO TRAVEL.
BESIDES, WILL THE NAZIS PERMIT US TO LEAVE?

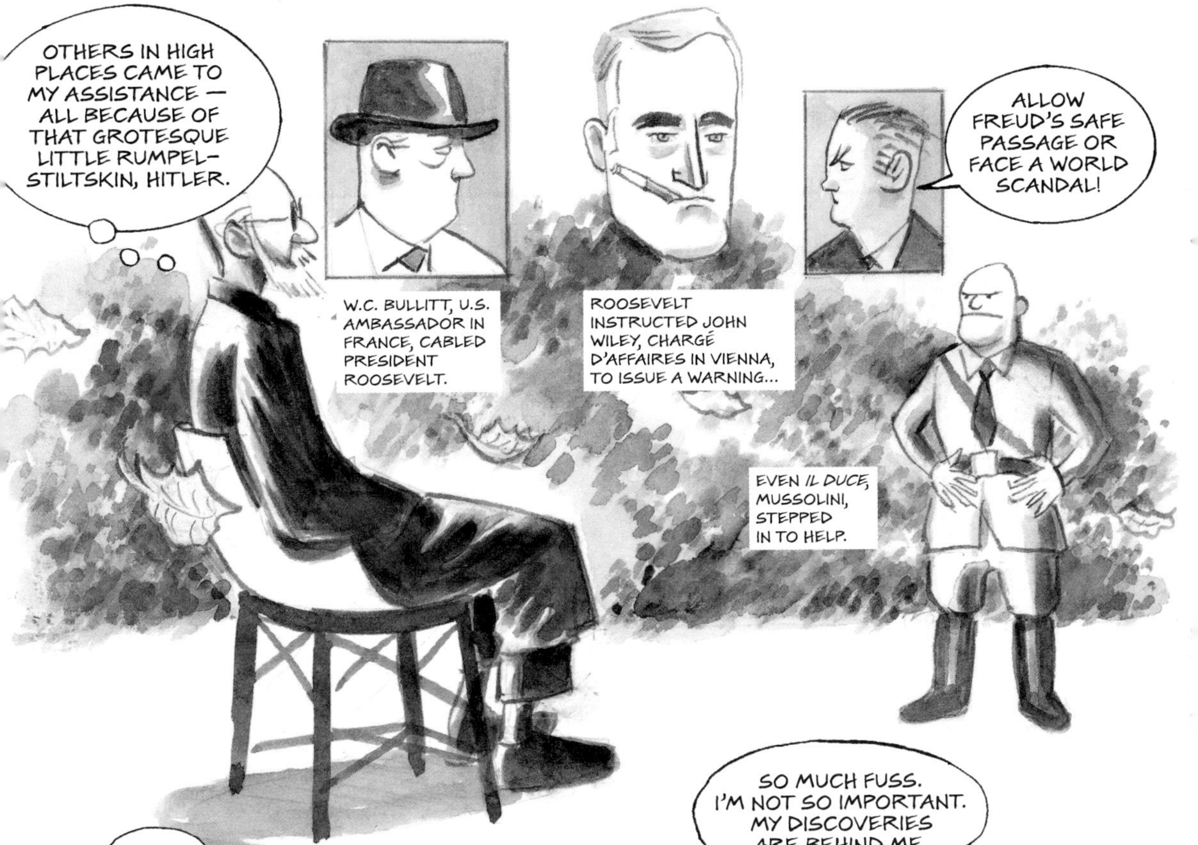
OTHERS IN HIGH PLACES CAME TO MY ASSISTANCE — ALL BECAUSE OF THAT GROTESQUE LITTLE RUMPEL-STILTSKIN, HITLER.
W.C. BULLITT, U.S. AMBASSADOR IN FRANCE, CABLED PRESIDENT ROOSEVELT.
ROOSEVELT INSTRUCTED JOHN WILEY, CHARGÉ D'AFFAIRES IN VIENNA, TO ISSUE A WARNING...
ALLOW FREUD'S SAFE PASSAGE OR FACE A WORLD SCANDAL!
EVEN *IL DUCE*, MUSSOLINI, STEPPED IN TO HELP.

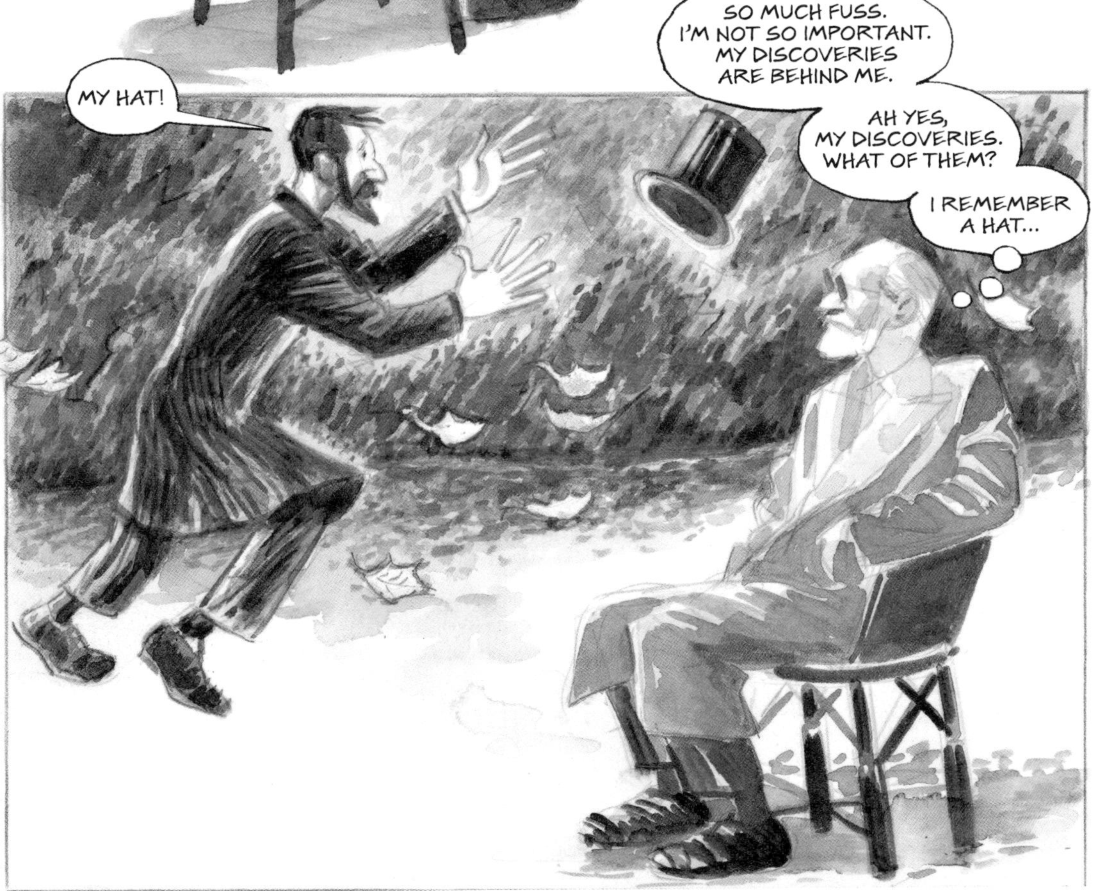
SO MUCH FUSS. I'M NOT SO IMPORTANT. MY DISCOVERIES ARE BEHIND ME.
MY HAT!
AH YES, MY DISCOVERIES. WHAT OF THEM?
I REMEMBER A HAT...

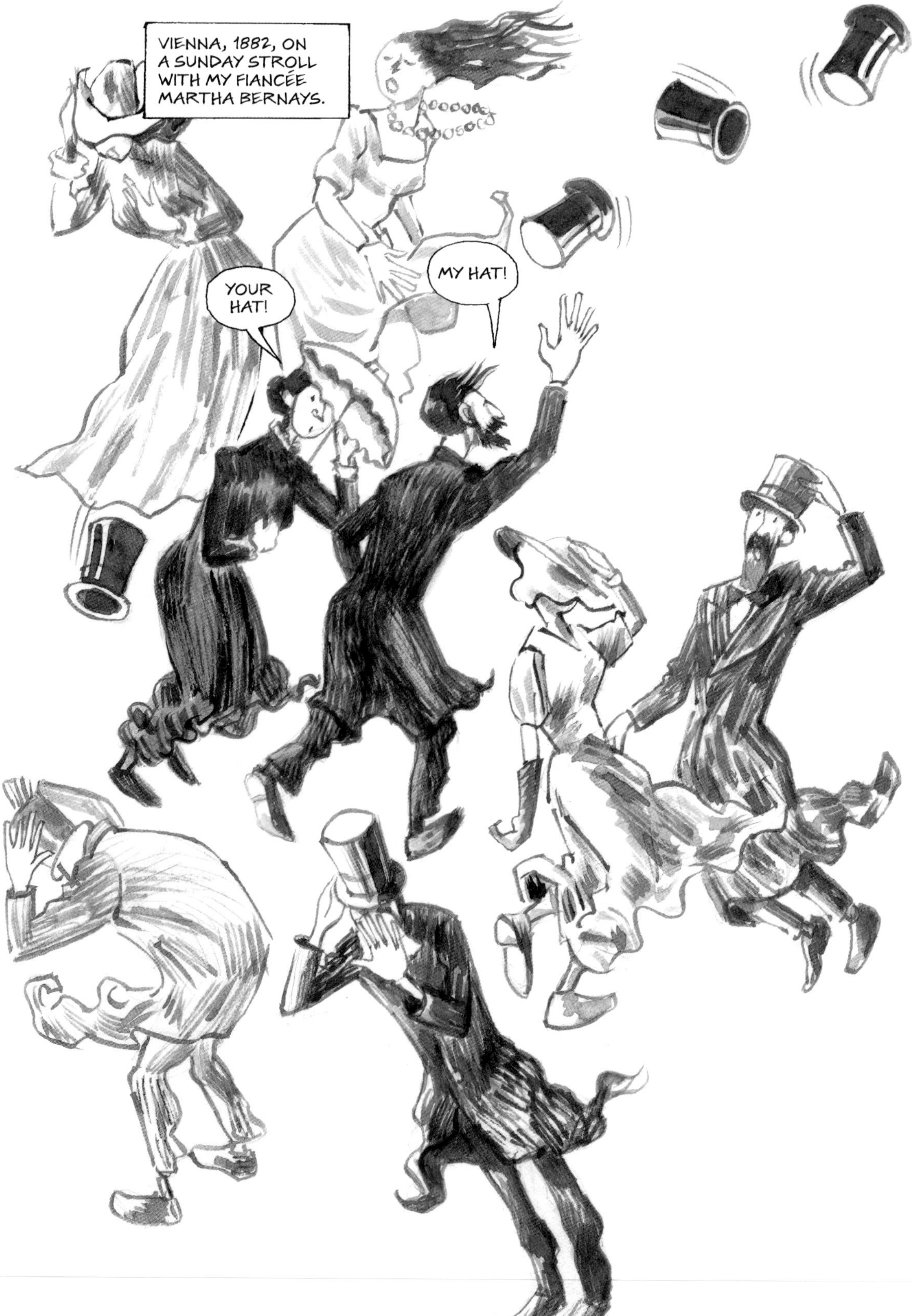
VIENNA, 1882, ON A SUNDAY STROLL WITH MY FIANCÉE MARTHA BERNAYS.
YOUR HAT!
MY HAT!

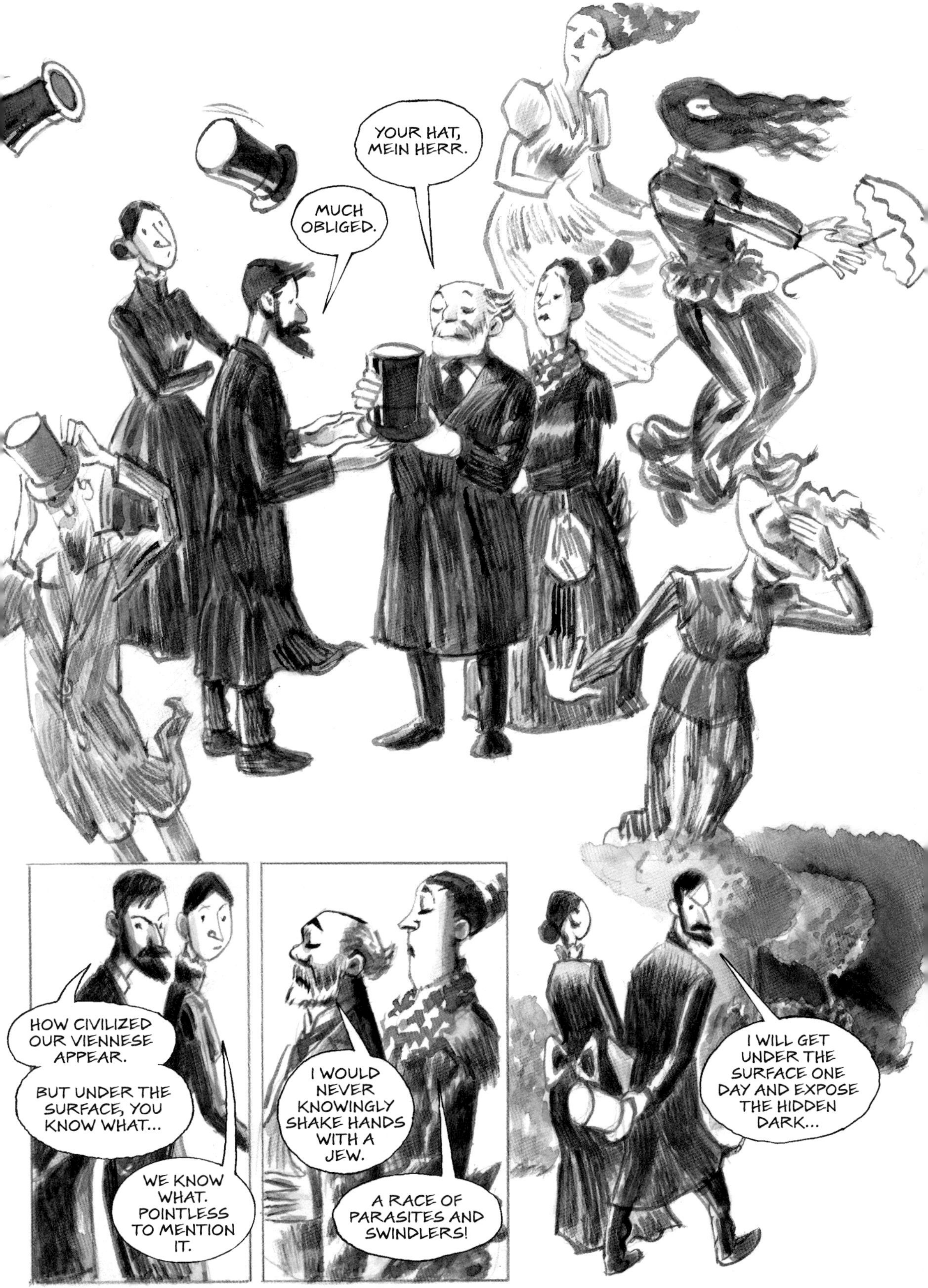
MUCH OBLIGED.
YOUR HAT, MEIN HERR.
HOW CIVILIZED OUR VIENNESE APPEAR.
BUT UNDER THE SURFACE, YOU KNOW WHAT...
WE KNOW WHAT. POINTLESS TO MENTION IT.
I WOULD NEVER KNOWINGLY SHAKE HANDS WITH A JEW.
A RACE OF PARASITES AND SWINDLERS!
I WILL GET UNDER THE SURFACE ONE DAY AND EXPOSE THE HIDDEN DARK...

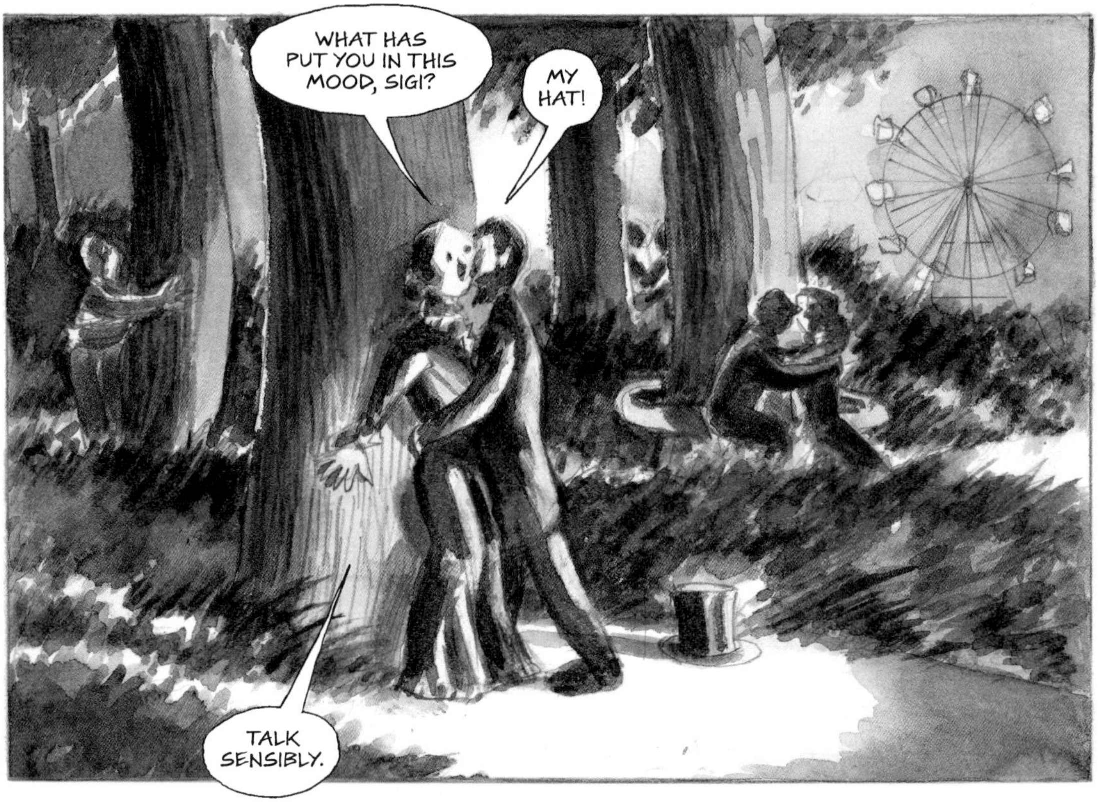
WHAT HAS PUT YOU IN THIS MOOD, SIGI?
MY HAT!
TALK SENSIBLY.

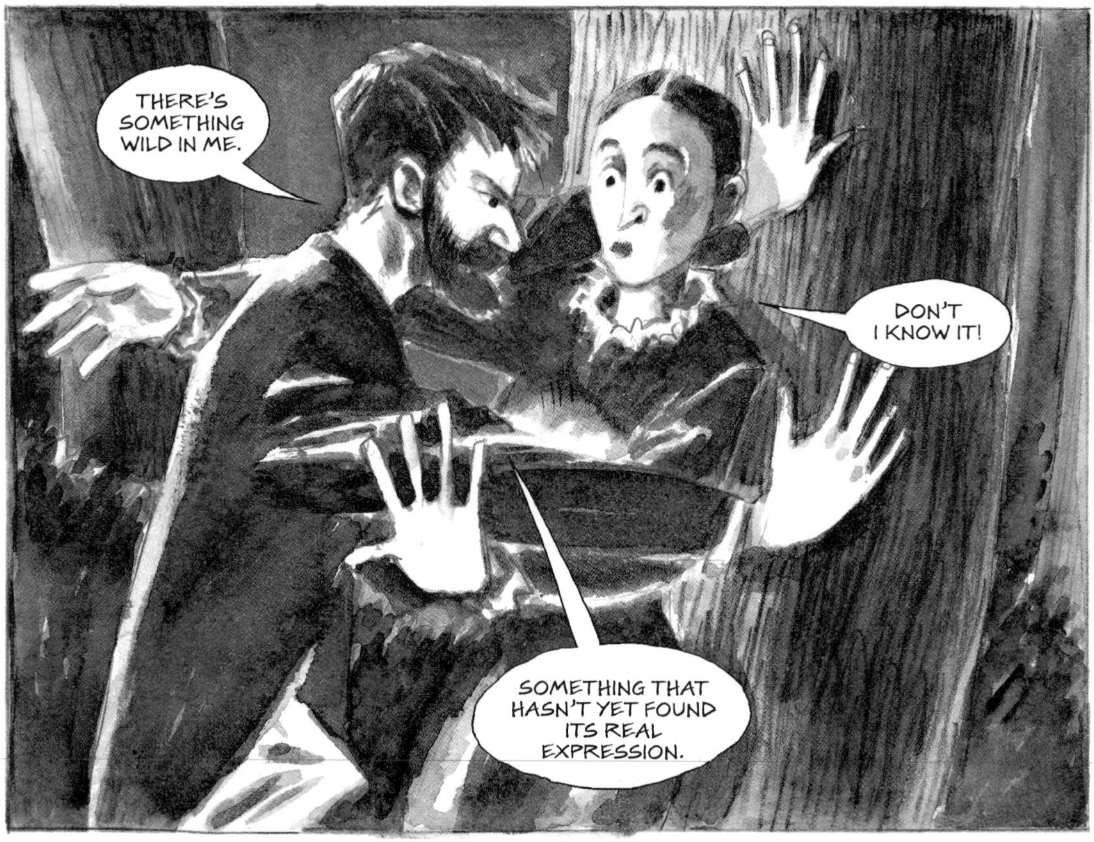
THERE'S SOMETHING WILD IN ME.
DON'T I KNOW IT!
SOMETHING THAT HASN'T YET FOUND ITS REAL EXPRESSION.

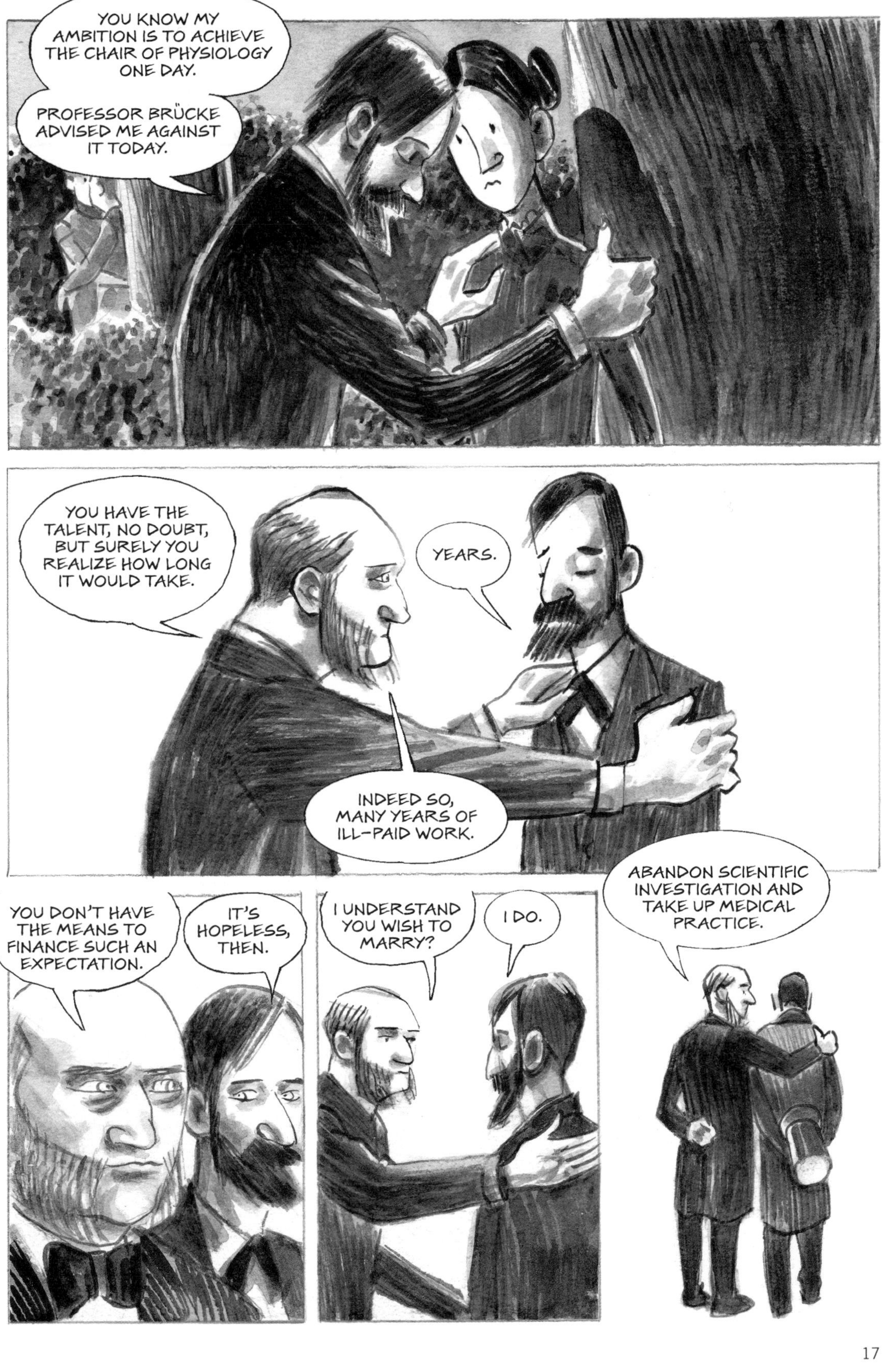
YOU KNOW MY AMBITION IS TO ACHIEVE THE CHAIR OF PHYSIOLOGY ONE DAY.
PROFESSOR BRÜCKE ADVISED ME AGAINST IT TODAY.
YOU HAVE THE TALENT, NO DOUBT, BUT SURELY YOU REALIZE HOW LONG IT WOULD TAKE.
YEARS.
INDEED SO, MANY YEARS OF ILL-PAID WORK.
YOU DON'T HAVE THE MEANS TO FINANCE SUCH AN EXPECTATION.
IT'S HOPELESS, THEN.
I UNDERSTAND YOU WISH TO MARRY?
I DO.
ABANDON SCIENTIFIC INVESTIGATION AND TAKE UP MEDICAL PRACTICE.

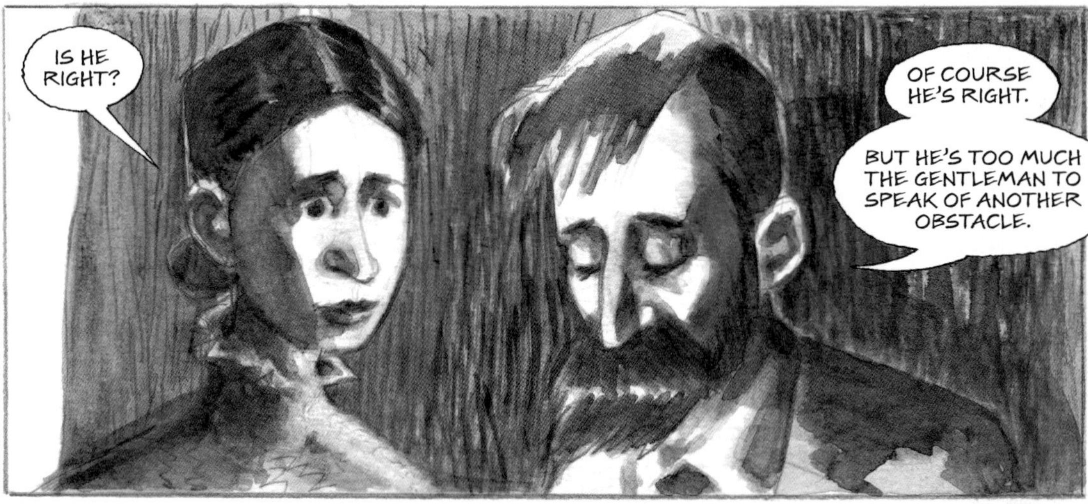
IS HE RIGHT?
OF COURSE HE'S RIGHT.
BUT HE'S TOO MUCH THE GENTLEMAN TO SPEAK OF ANOTHER OBSTACLE.

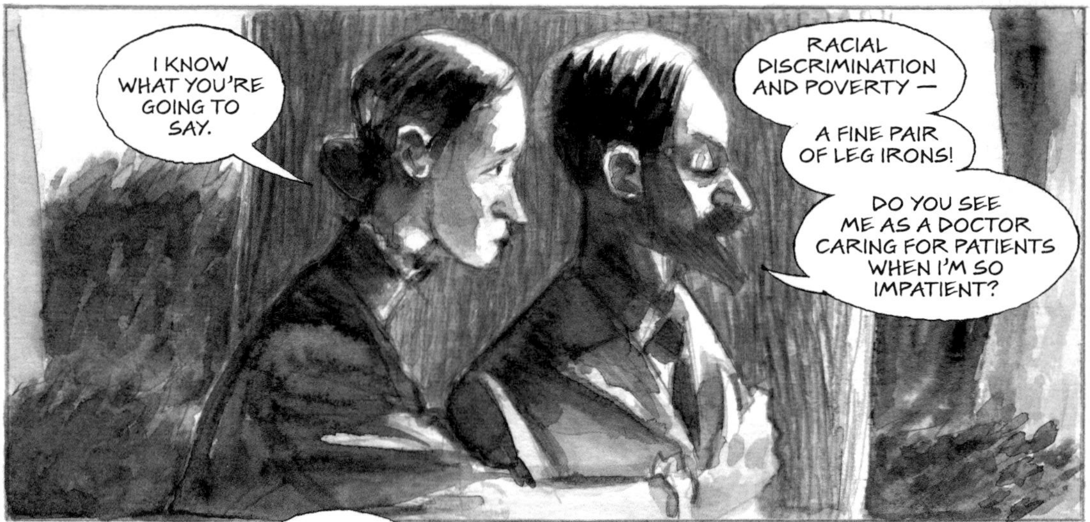
I KNOW WHAT YOU'RE GOING TO SAY.
RACIAL DISCRIMINATION AND POVERTY —
A FINE PAIR OF LEG IRONS!
DO YOU SEE ME AS A DOCTOR CARING FOR PATIENTS WHEN I'M SO IMPATIENT?

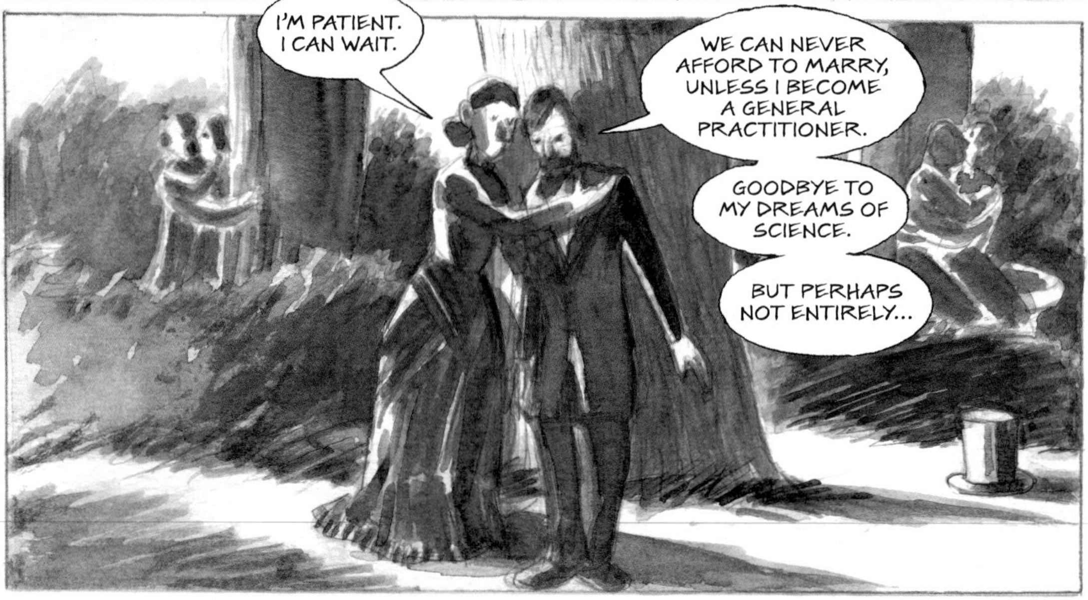
I'M PATIENT. I CAN WAIT.
WE CAN NEVER AFFORD TO MARRY, UNLESS I BECOME A GENERAL PRACTITIONER.
GOODBYE TO MY DREAMS OF SCIENCE.
BUT PERHAPS NOT ENTIRELY...

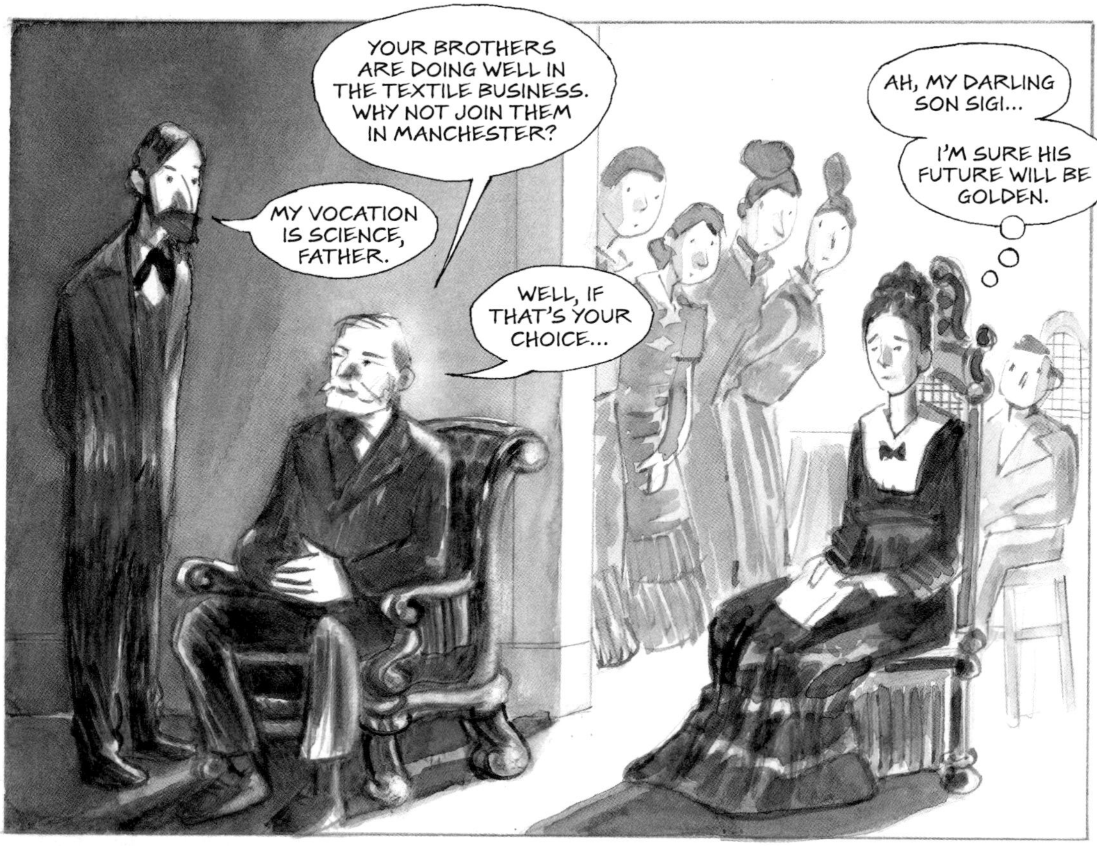
YOUR BROTHERS ARE DOING WELL IN THE TEXTILE BUSINESS. WHY NOT JOIN THEM IN MANCHESTER?
MY VOCATION IS SCIENCE, FATHER.
WELL, IF THAT'S YOUR CHOICE...
AH, MY DARLING SON SIGI...
I'M SURE HIS FUTURE WILL BE GOLDEN.

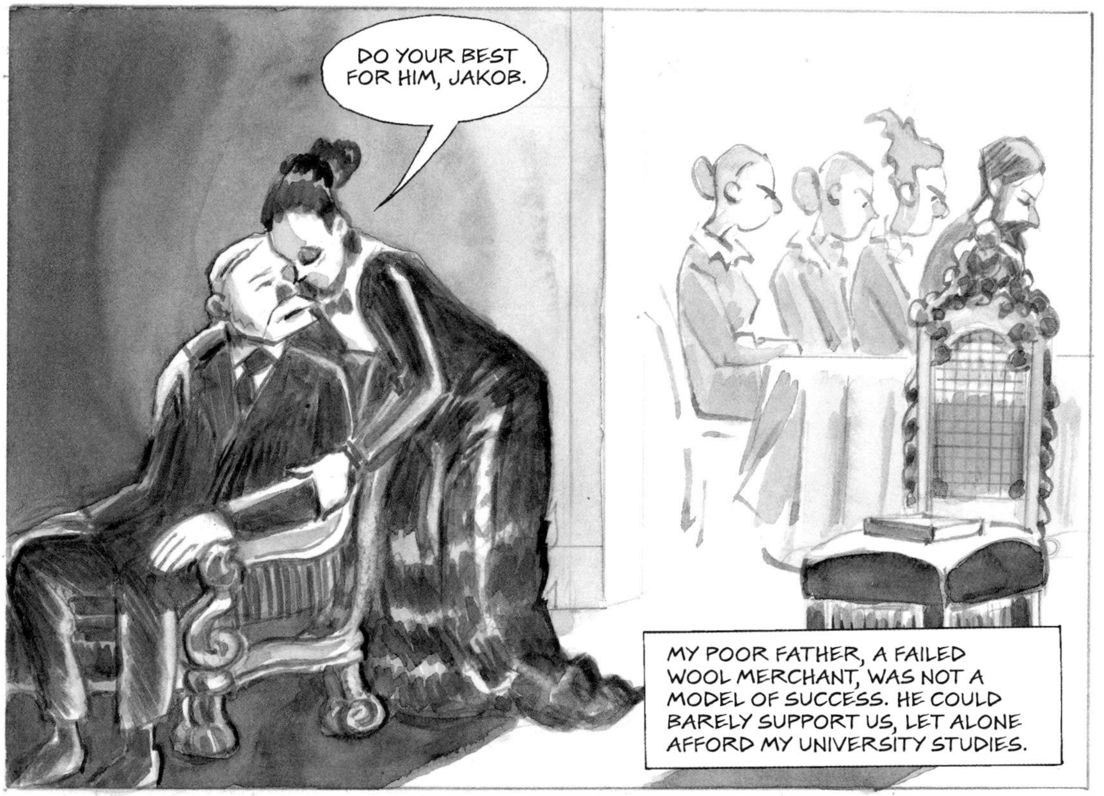
DO YOUR BEST FOR HIM, JAKOB.
MY POOR FATHER, A FAILED WOOL MERCHANT, WAS NOT A MODEL OF SUCCESS. HE COULD BARELY SUPPORT US, LET ALONE AFFORD MY UNIVERSITY STUDIES.

I WAS 17 IN 1873 WHEN I ENTERED THE VIENNA UNIVERSITY MEDICAL SCHOOL, MY ONLY POSSIBLE ROAD TO SCIENCE. CARL CLAUS, HEAD OF COMPARATIVE ANATOMY, GRANTED ME A RESEARCH PROJECT IN TRIESTE AT THE ZOOLOGICAL EXPERIMENTAL STATION.

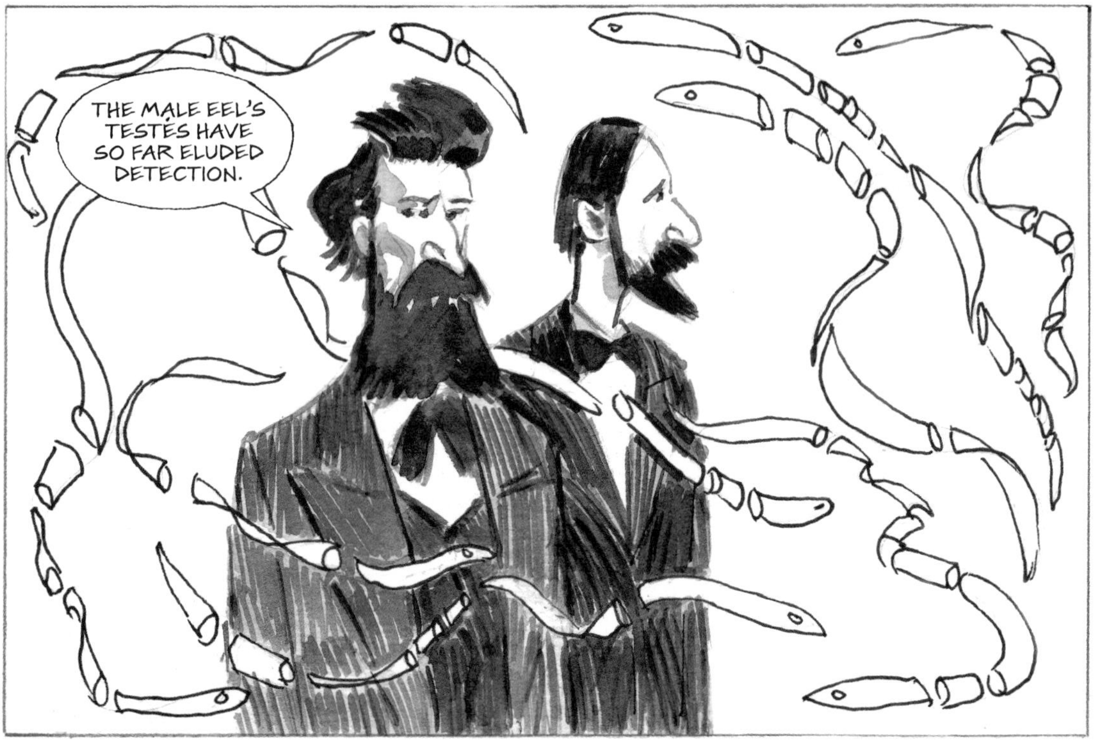
THE MALE EEL'S TESTES HAVE SO FAR ELUDED DETECTION.

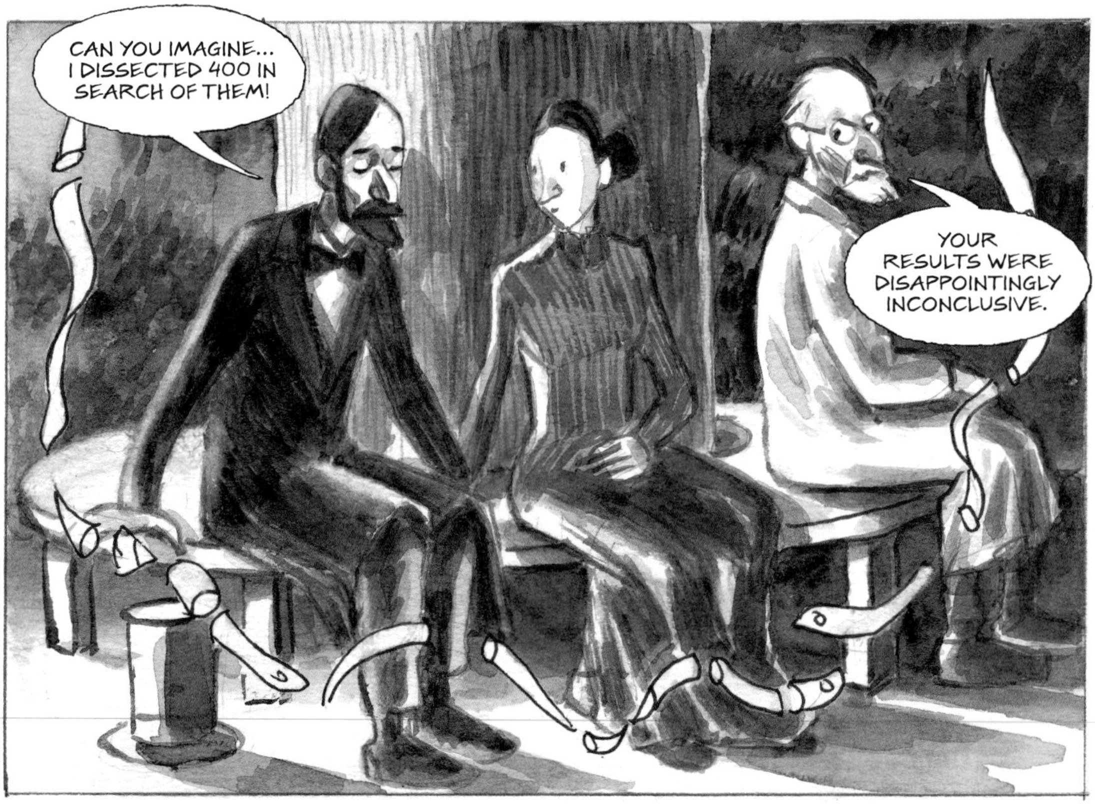
CAN YOU IMAGINE... I DISSECTED 400 IN SEARCH OF THEM!
YOUR RESULTS WERE DISAPPOINTINGLY INCONCLUSIVE.

I FOUND MY HOME IN PROFESSOR ERNST BRÜCKE'S INSTITUTE OF PHYSIOLOGY IN 1876. I WILL NEVER FORGET BRÜCKE'S TERRIFYING PRUSSIAN BLUE EYES AND HIS CONTEMPT FOR VIENNESE FRIVOLITY.

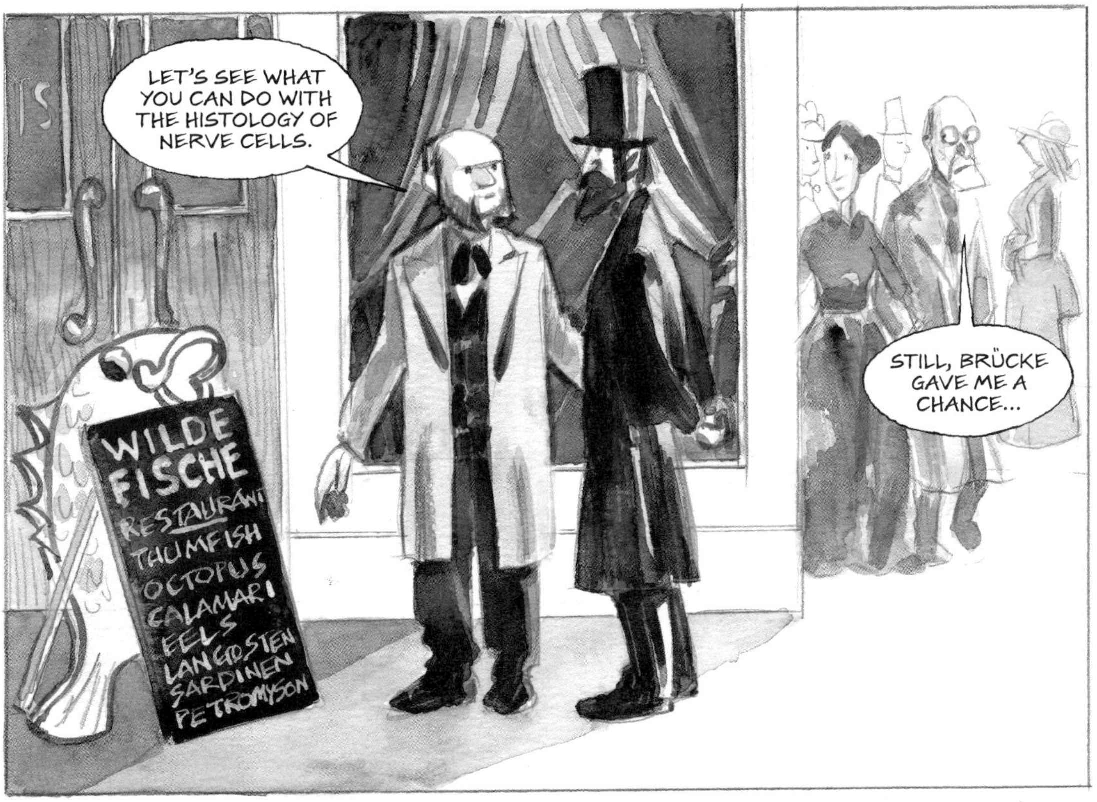
LET'S SEE WHAT YOU CAN DO WITH THE HISTOLOGY OF NERVE CELLS.
WILDE FISCHE
RESTAURANT
THUMFISH
OCTOPUS
CALAMARI
EELS
LANGOSTEN
SARDINEN
PETROMYSON
STILL, BRÜCKE GAVE ME A CHANCE...

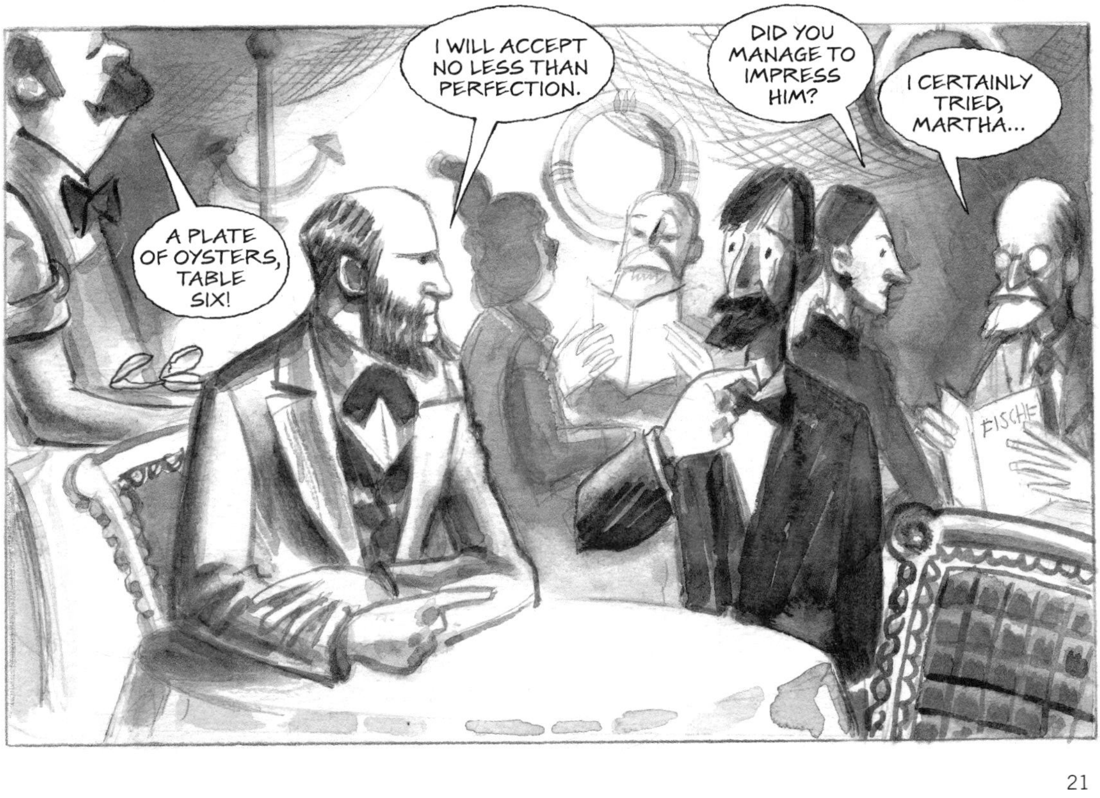
A PLATE OF OYSTERS, TABLE SIX!
I WILL ACCEPT NO LESS THAN PERFECTION.
DID YOU MANAGE TO IMPRESS HIM?
I CERTAINLY TRIED, MARTHA...
FISCHE

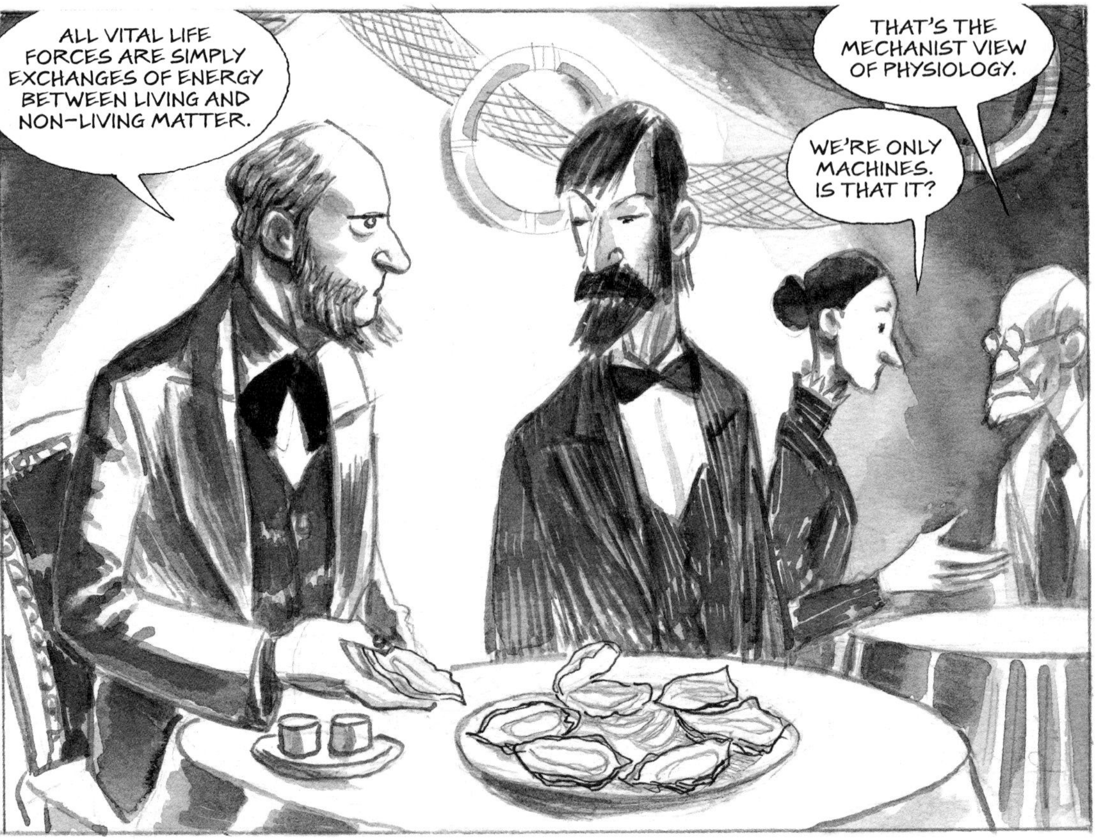
ALL VITAL LIFE FORCES ARE SIMPLY EXCHANGES OF ENERGY BETWEEN LIVING AND NON-LIVING MATTER.
THAT'S THE MECHANIST VIEW OF PHYSIOLOGY.
WE'RE ONLY MACHINES. IS THAT IT?

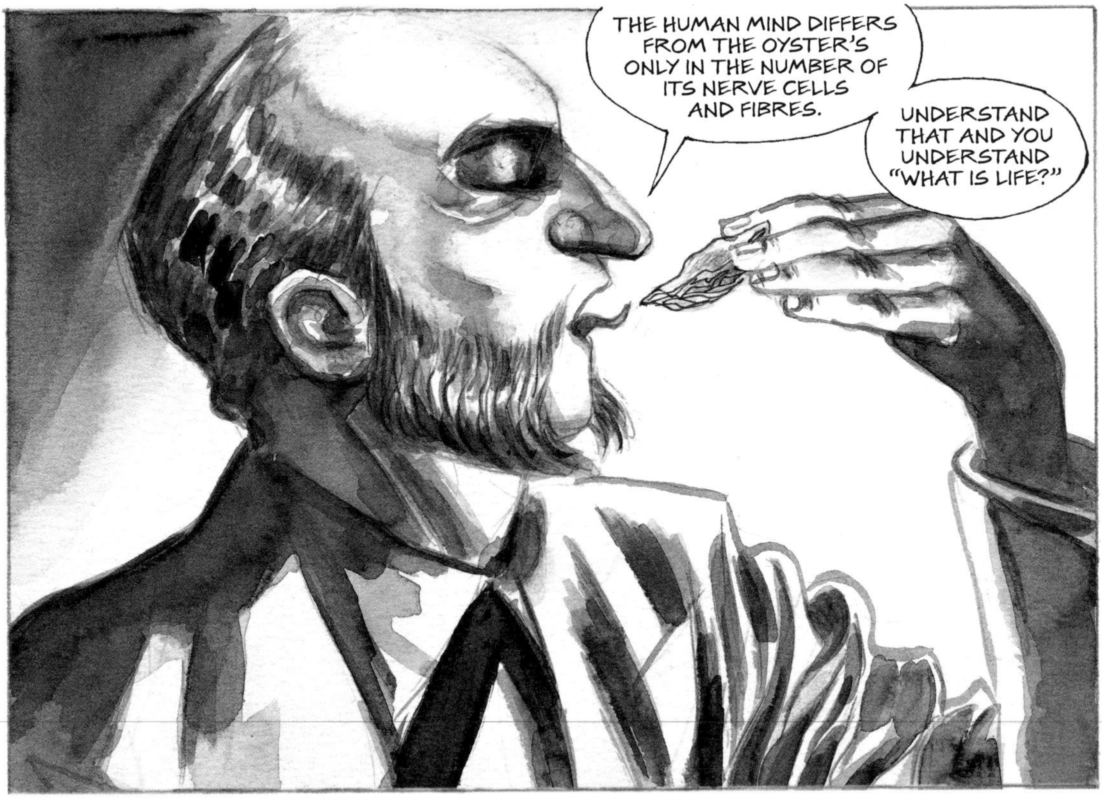
THE HUMAN MIND DIFFERS FROM THE OYSTER'S ONLY IN THE NUMBER OF ITS NERVE CELLS AND FIBRES.
UNDERSTAND THAT AND YOU UNDERSTAND "WHAT IS LIFE?"

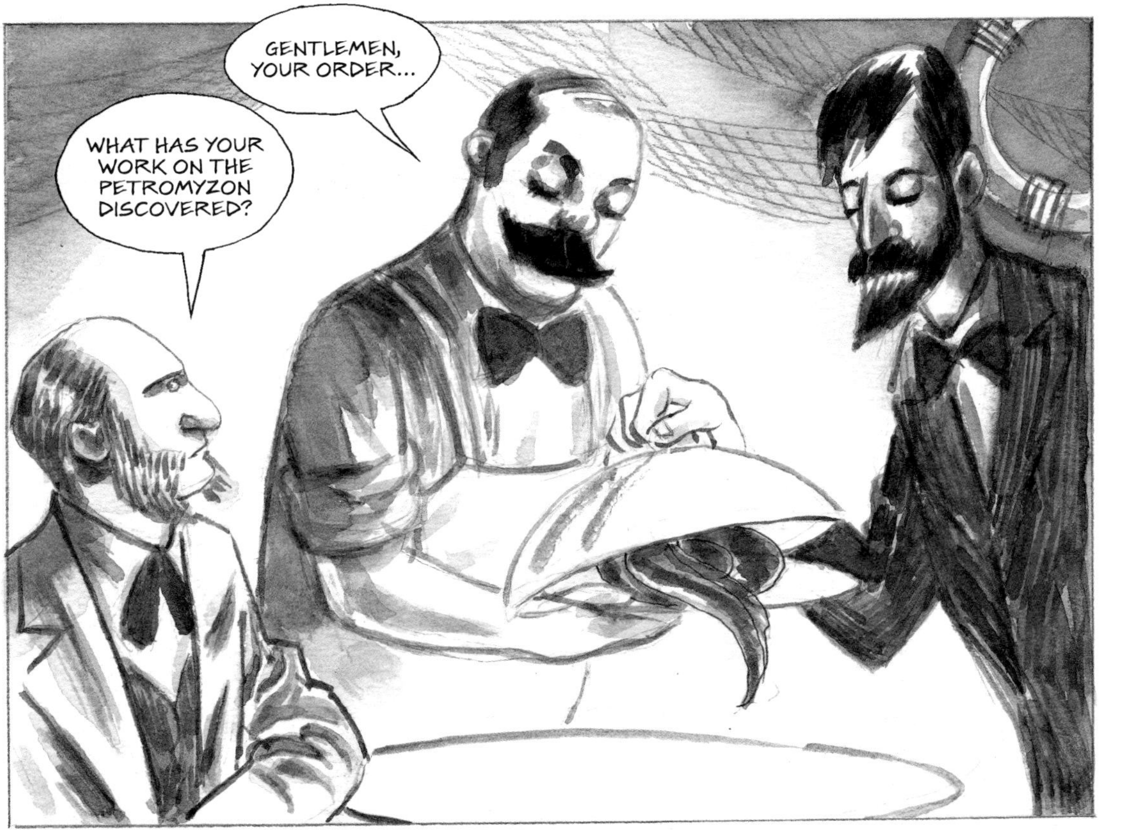
GENTLEMEN, YOUR ORDER...
WHAT HAS YOUR WORK ON THE PETROMYZON DISCOVERED?

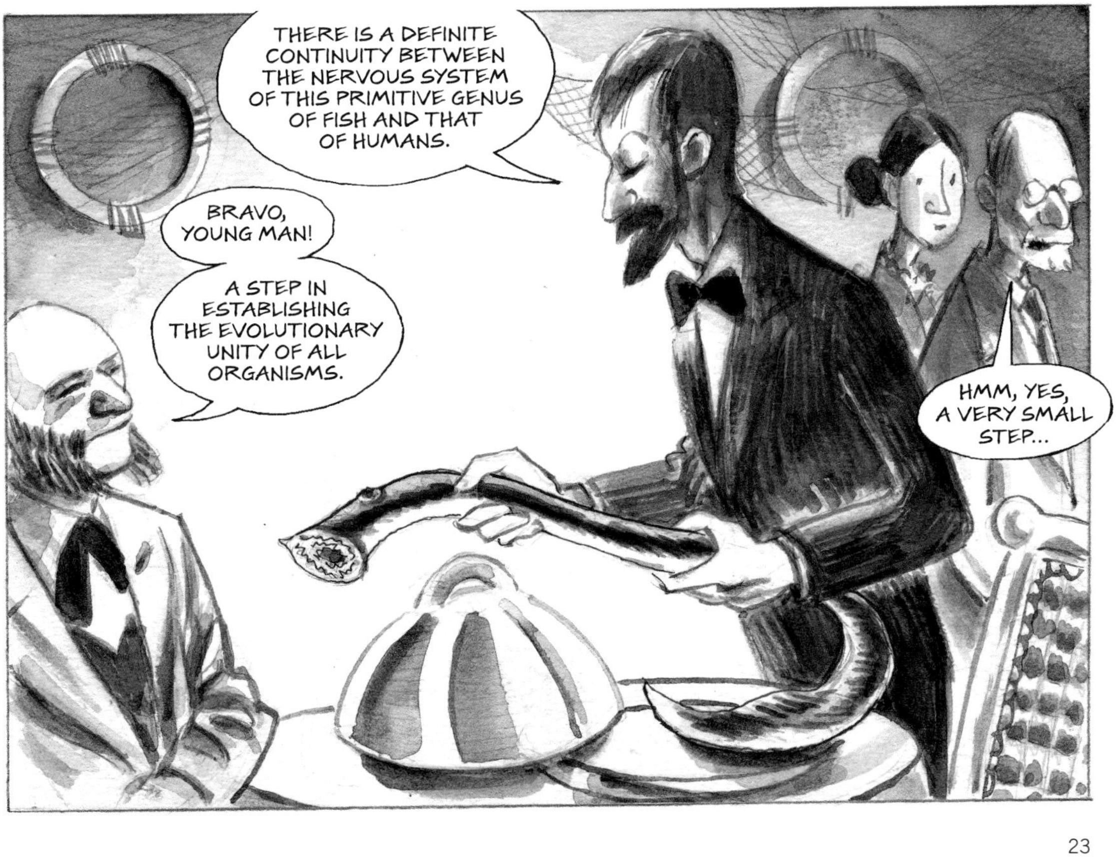
THERE IS A DEFINITE CONTINUITY BETWEEN THE NERVOUS SYSTEM OF THIS PRIMITIVE GENUS OF FISH AND THAT OF HUMANS.
BRAVO, YOUNG MAN!
A STEP IN ESTABLISHING THE EVOLUTIONARY UNITY OF ALL ORGANISMS.
HMM, YES, A VERY SMALL STEP...

I WENT ON IN 1881 TO EXAMINE THE NERVOUS TISSUE OF CRAYFISH "IN VIVO" UNDER THE HARNACK NO.8 MICROSCOPE LENS.

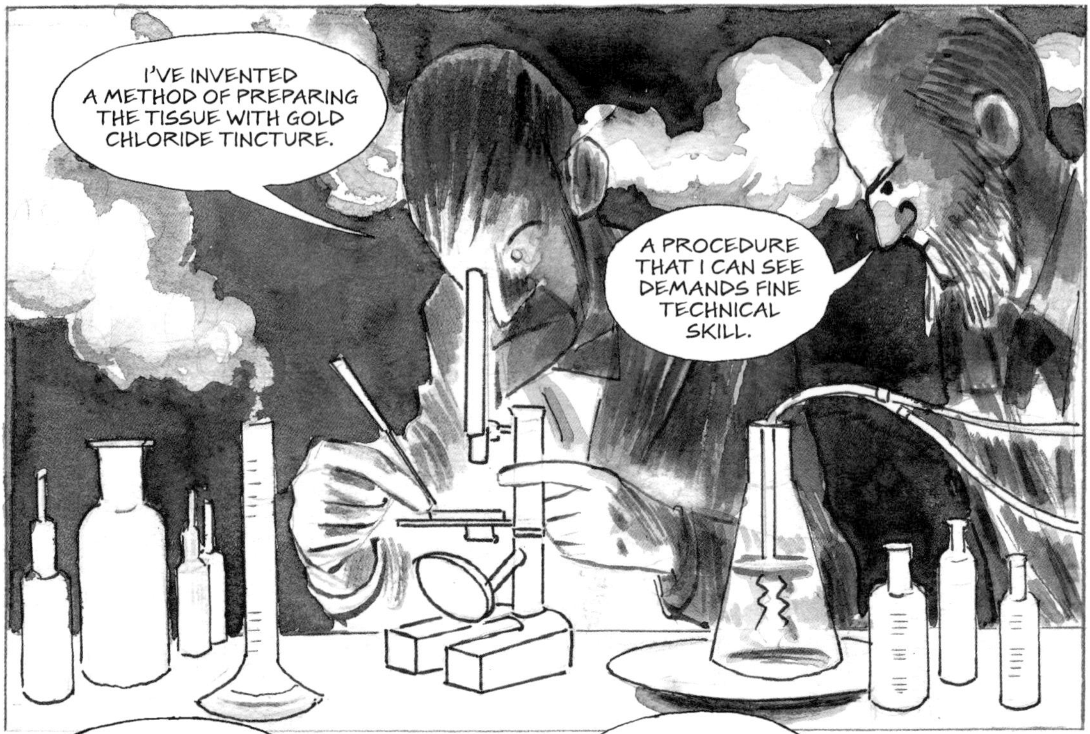
I'VE INVENTED A METHOD OF PREPARING THE TISSUE WITH GOLD CHLORIDE TINCTURE.
A PROCEDURE THAT I CAN SEE DEMANDS FINE TECHNICAL SKILL.

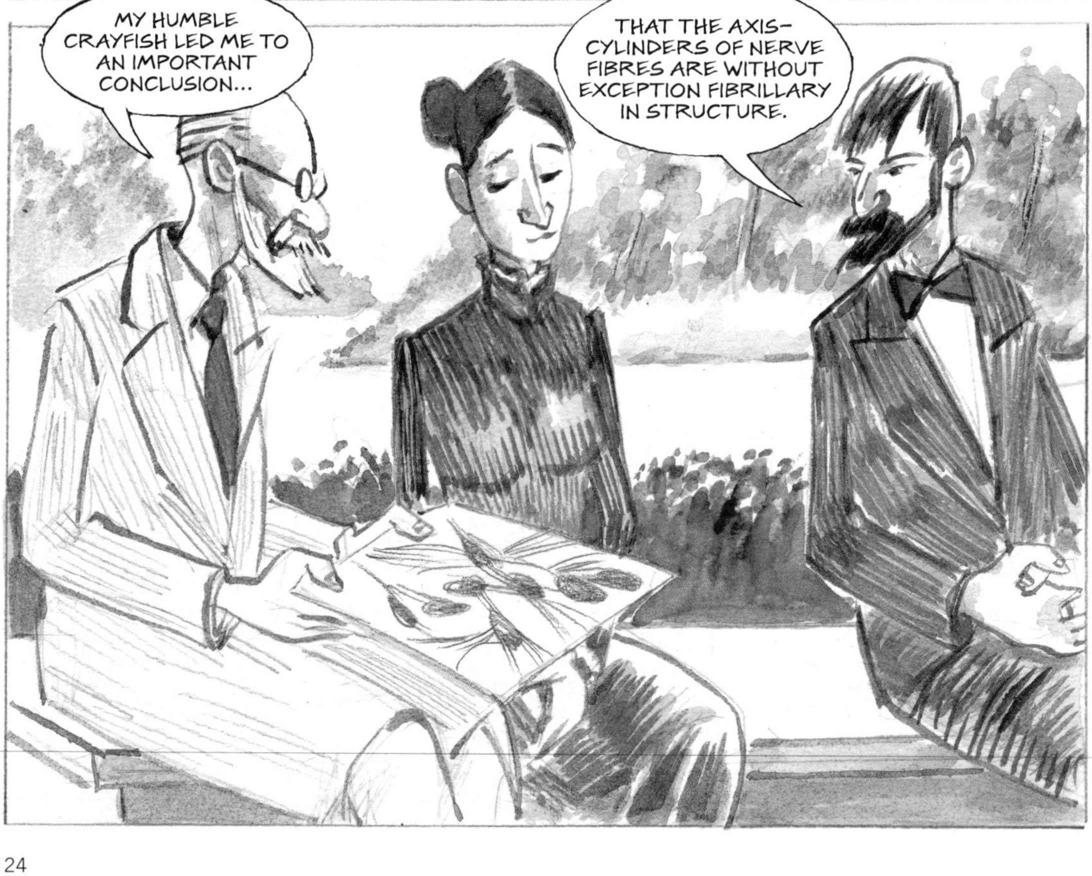
MY HUMBLE CRAYFISH LED ME TO AN IMPORTANT CONCLUSION...
THAT THE AXIS-CYLINDERS OF NERVE FIBRES ARE WITHOUT EXCEPTION FIBRILLARY IN STRUCTURE.

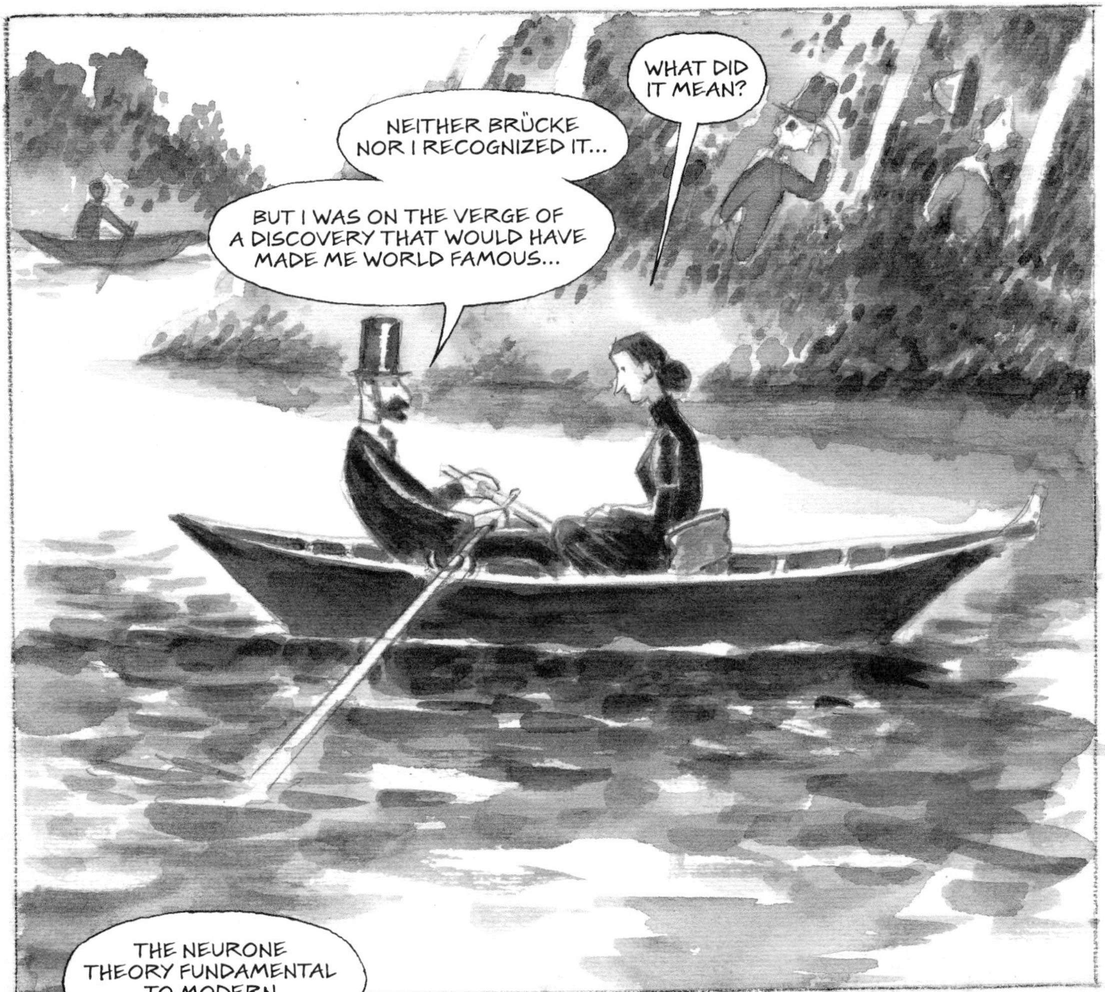
NEITHER BRÜCKE NOR I RECOGNIZED IT...
BUT I WAS ON THE VERGE OF A DISCOVERY THAT WOULD HAVE MADE ME WORLD FAMOUS...
WHAT DID IT MEAN?

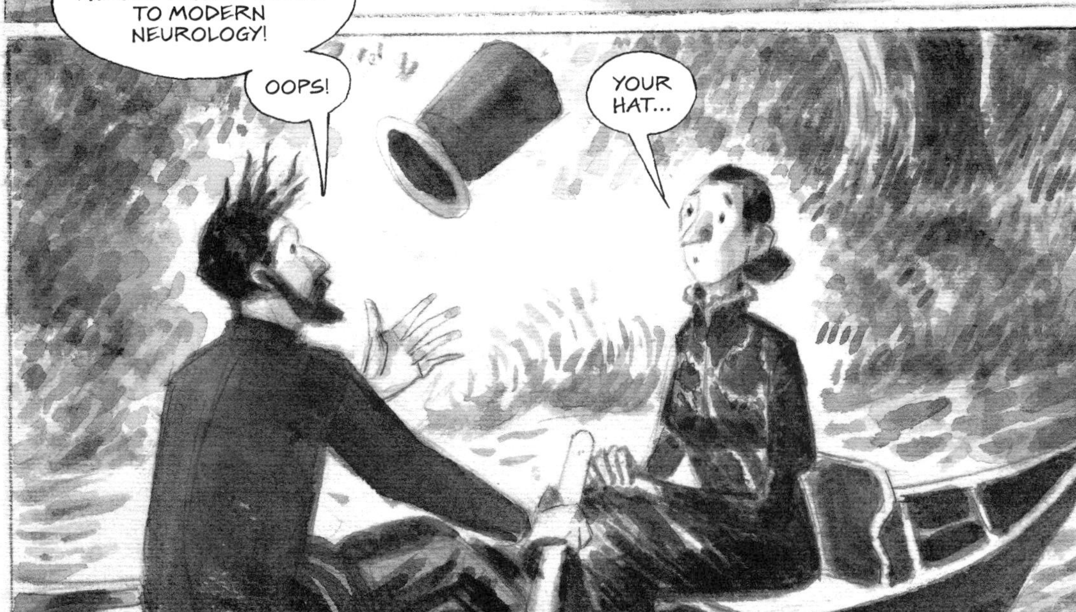
THE NEURONE THEORY FUNDAMENTAL TO MODERN NEUROLOGY!
OOPS!
YOUR HAT...

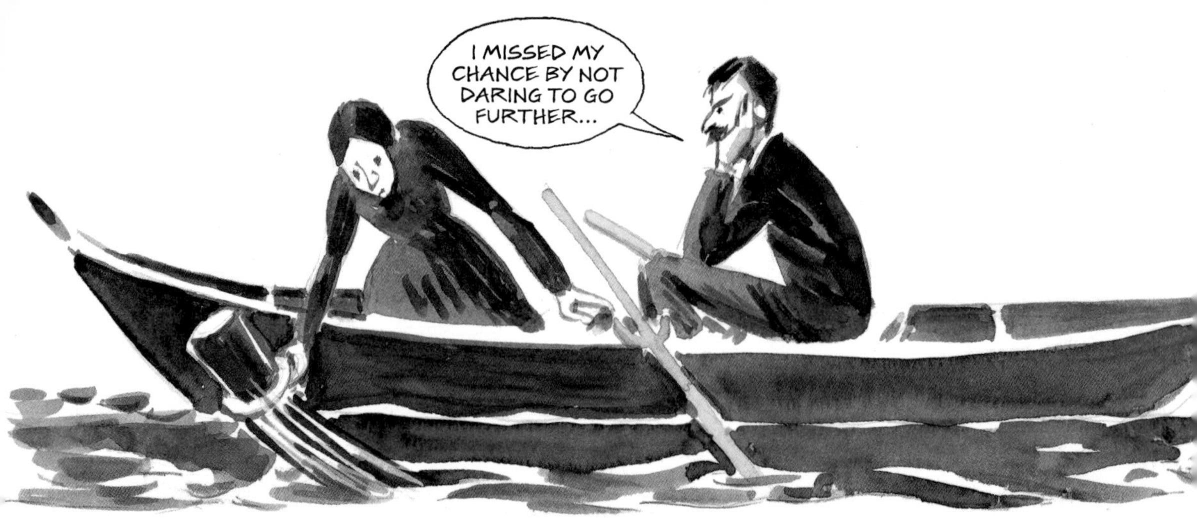
I MISSED MY CHANCE BY NOT DARING TO GO FURTHER...

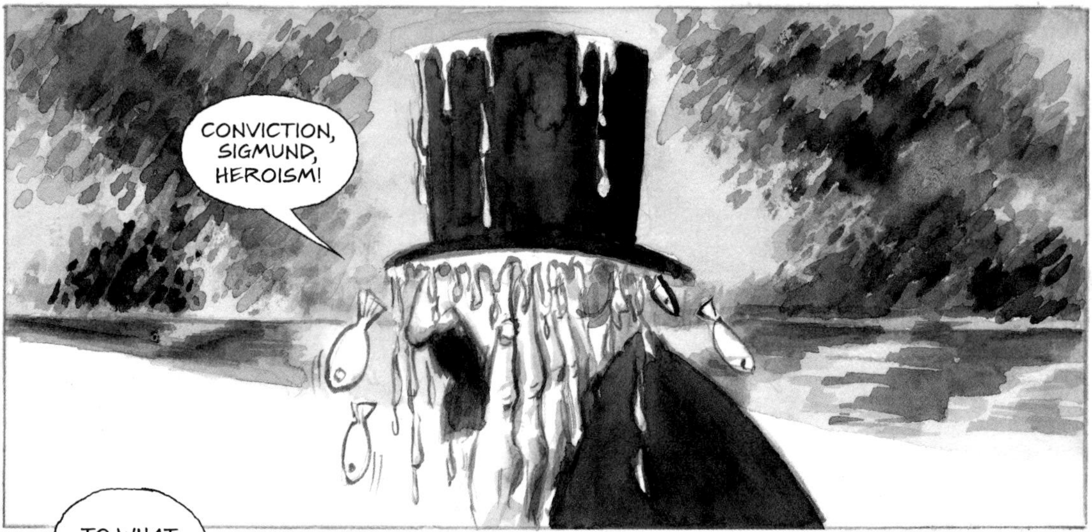
CONVICTION, SIGMUND, HEROISM!

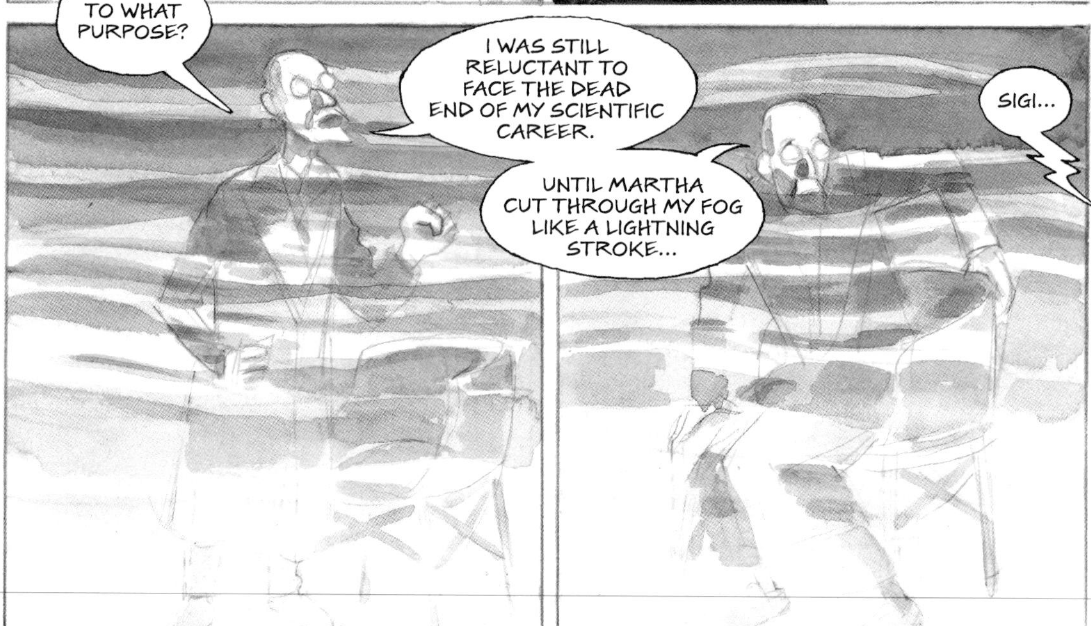
TO WHAT PURPOSE?
I WAS STILL RELUCTANT TO FACE THE DEAD END OF MY SCIENTIFIC CAREER.
UNTIL MARTHA CUT THROUGH MY FOG LIKE A LIGHTNING STROKE...
SIGI...

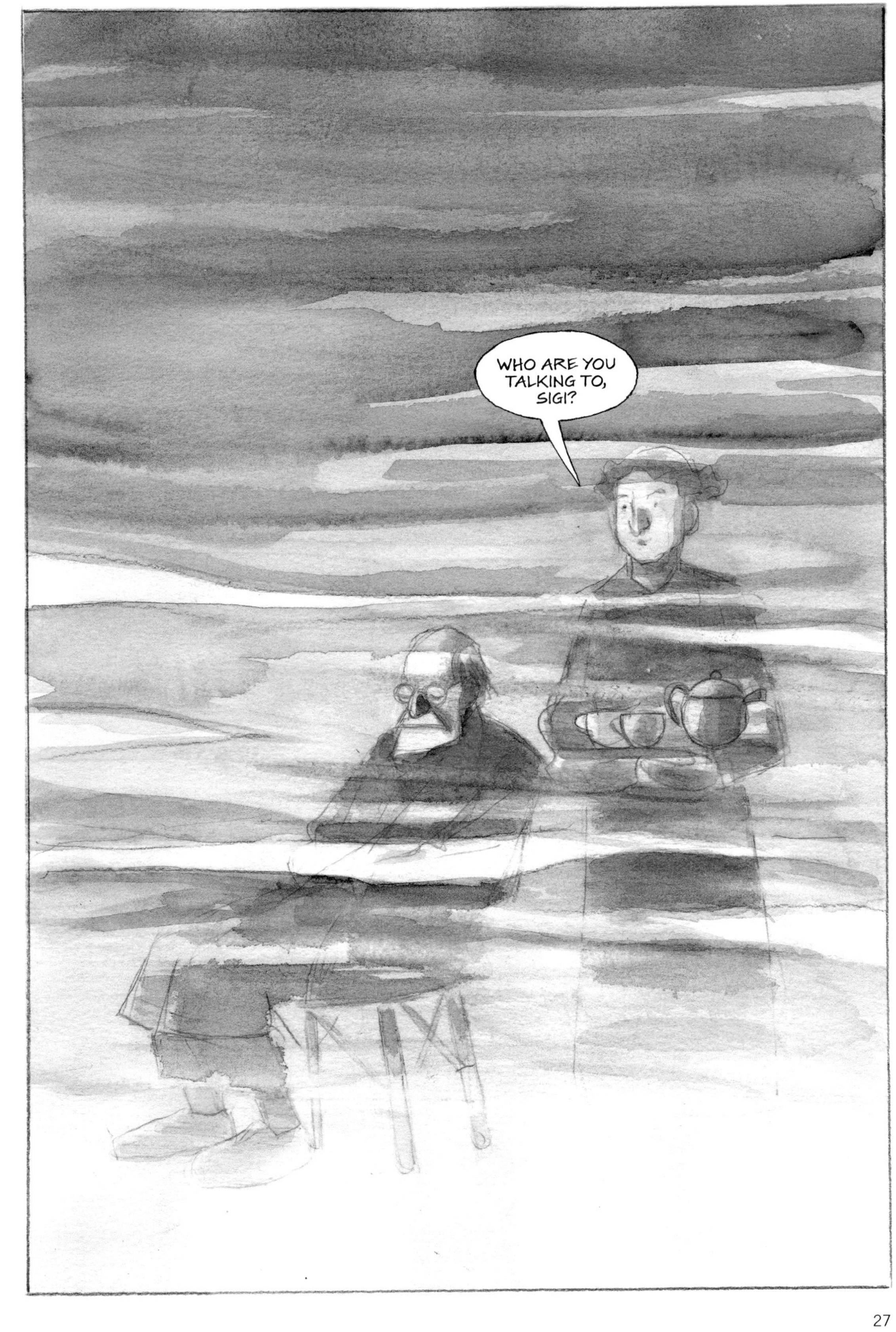
WHO ARE YOU TALKING TO, SIGI?

I GOT MY M.D. DEGREE IN 1881 BUT NEEDED PRACTICAL CLINICAL EXPERIENCE. I DID THREE YEARS OF PRACTICE IN THE DEPARTMENTS OF THE GENERAL HOSPITAL.

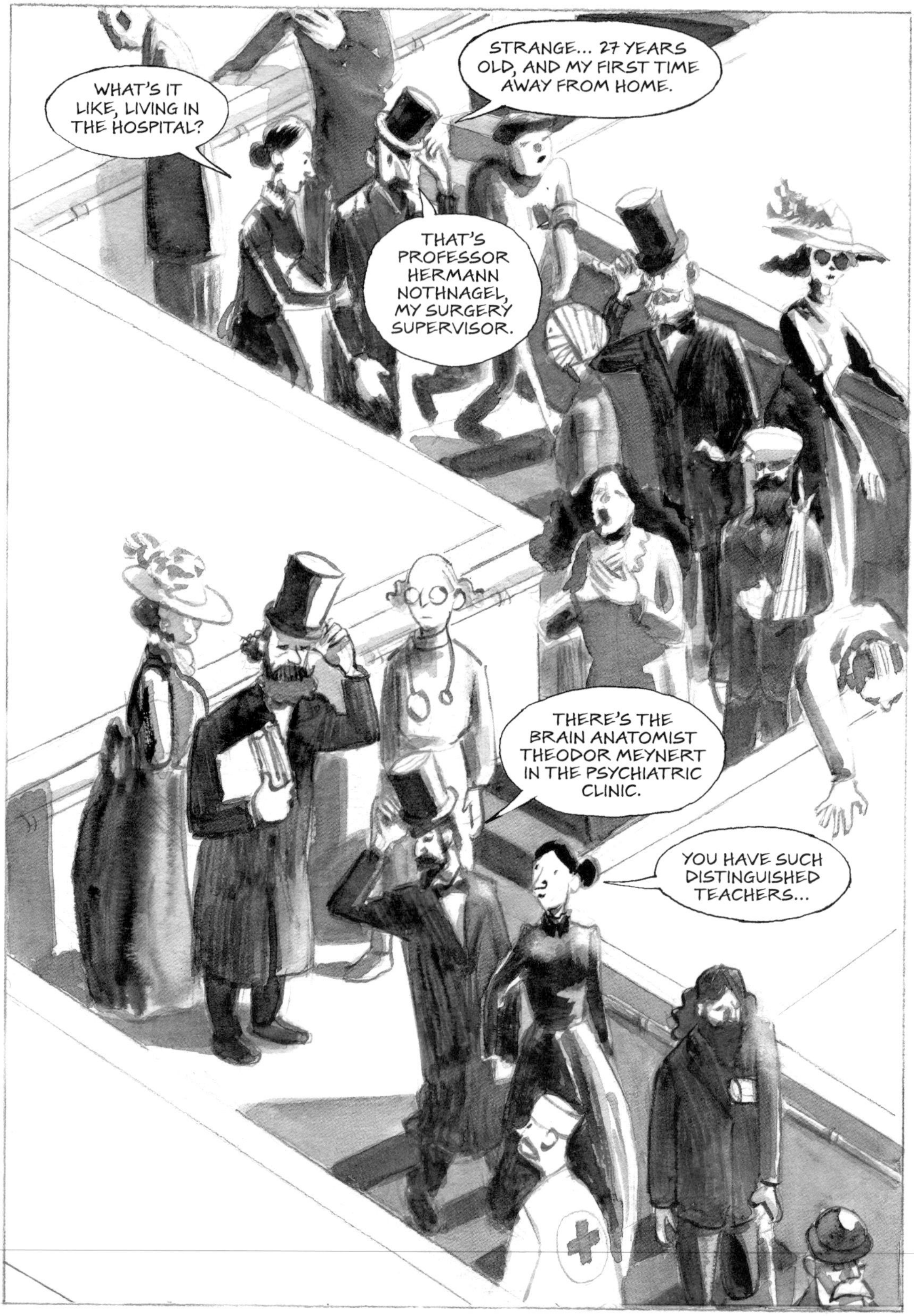
WHAT'S IT LIKE, LIVING IN THE HOSPITAL?
STRANGE... 27 YEARS OLD, AND MY FIRST TIME AWAY FROM HOME.
THAT'S PROFESSOR HERMANN NOTHNAGEL, MY SURGERY SUPERVISOR.
THERE'S THE BRAIN ANATOMIST THEODOR MEYNERT IN THE PSYCHIATRIC CLINIC.
YOU HAVE SUCH DISTINGUISHED TEACHERS...

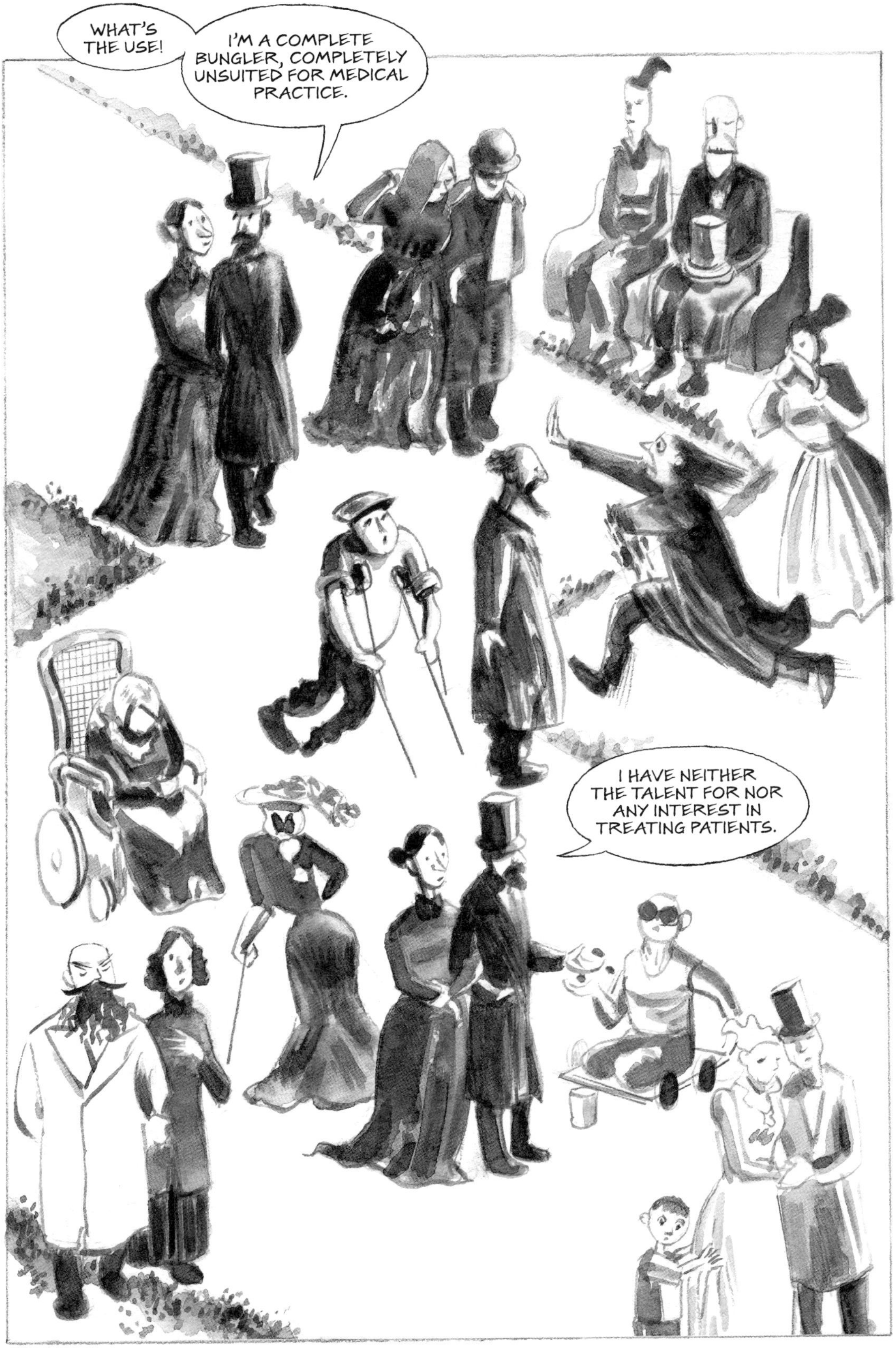
WHAT'S THE USE!
I'M A COMPLETE BUNGLER, COMPLETELY UNSUITED FOR MEDICAL PRACTICE.
I HAVE NEITHER THE TALENT FOR NOR ANY INTEREST IN TREATING PATIENTS.

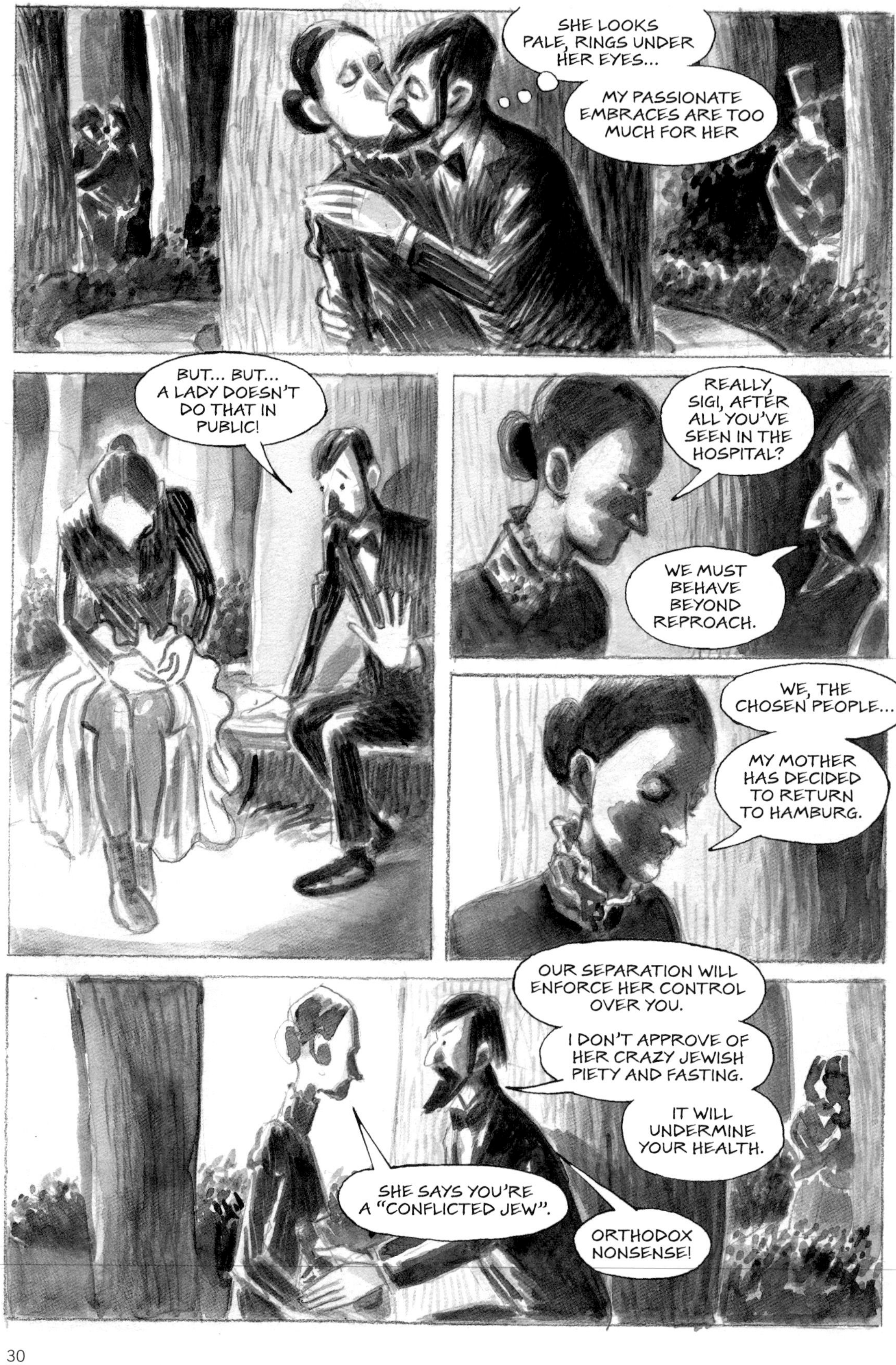
SHE LOOKS PALE, RINGS UNDER HER EYES...
MY PASSIONATE EMBRACES ARE TOO MUCH FOR HER
BUT... BUT... A LADY DOESN'T DO THAT IN PUBLIC!
REALLY, SIGI, AFTER ALL YOU'VE SEEN IN THE HOSPITAL?
WE MUST BEHAVE BEYOND REPROACH.
WE, THE CHOSEN PEOPLE...
MY MOTHER HAS DECIDED TO RETURN TO HAMBURG.
OUR SEPARATION WILL ENFORCE HER CONTROL OVER YOU.
I DON'T APPROVE OF HER CRAZY JEWISH PIETY AND FASTING.
IT WILL UNDERMINE YOUR HEALTH.
SHE SAYS YOU'RE A "CONFLICTED JEW".
ORTHODOX NONSENSE!

I WAS APPOINTED SUPERINTENDENT IN 1884 AND FOR SIX WEEKS HAD CHARGE OF THE DEPARTMENT OF NERVOUS DISEASES. CONDITIONS WERE TERRIBLE.

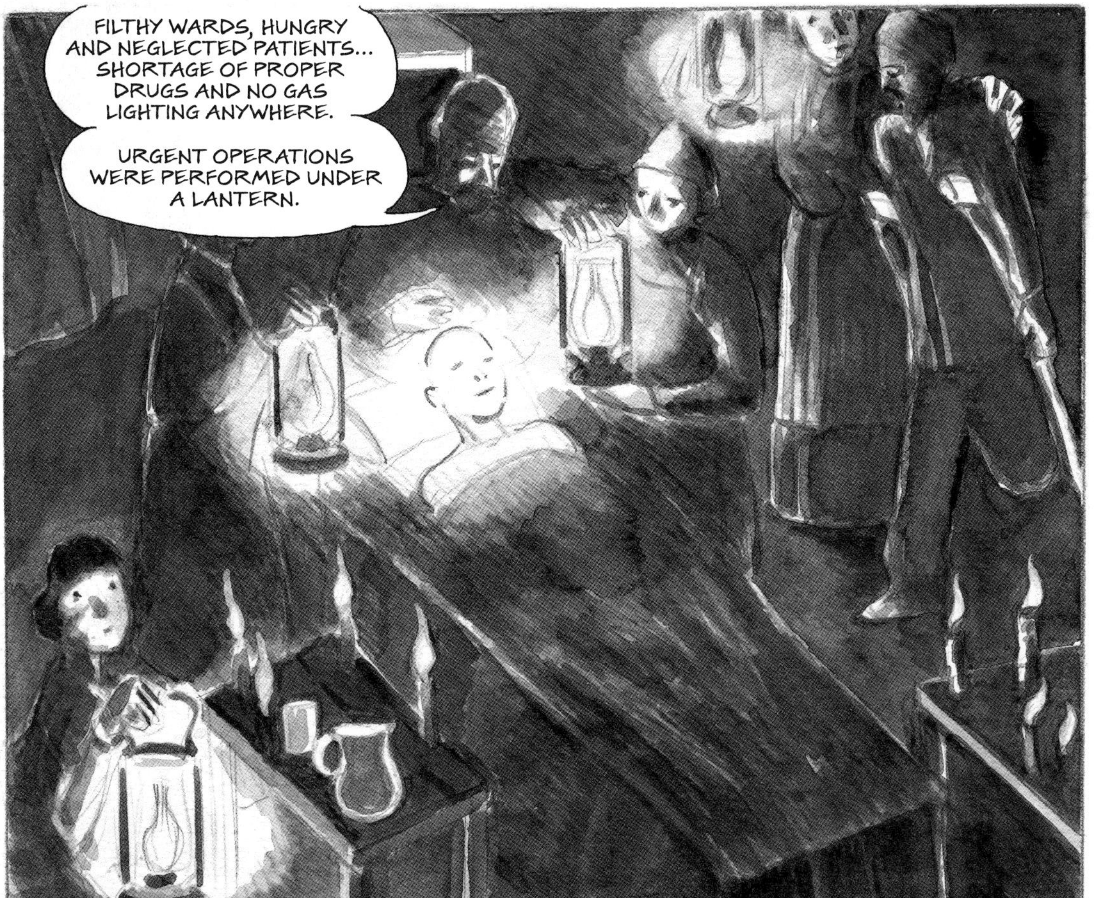

FILTHY WARDS, HUNGRY AND NEGLECTED PATIENTS... SHORTAGE OF PROPER DRUGS AND NO GAS LIGHTING ANYWHERE.
URGENT OPERATIONS WERE PERFORMED UNDER A LANTERN.

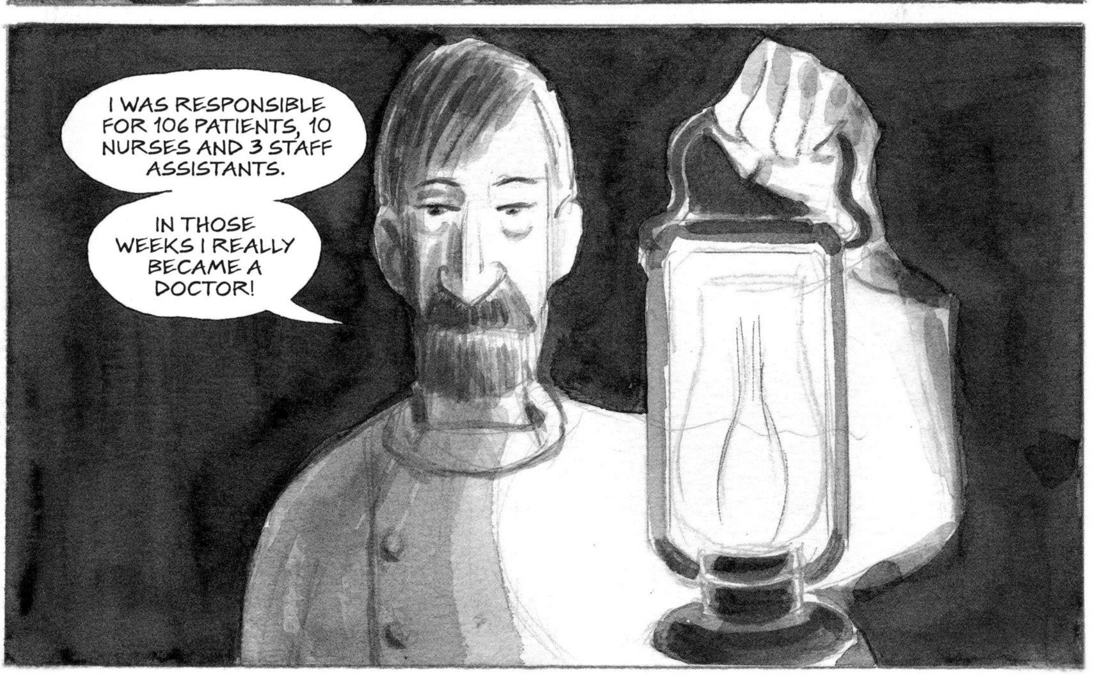

I WAS RESPONSIBLE FOR 106 PATIENTS, 10 NURSES AND 3 STAFF ASSISTANTS.
IN THOSE WEEKS I REALLY BECAME A DOCTOR!

WE COULDN'T MARRY ON MY SUPERINTENDENT'S SALARY OF 45 GULDEN. I HAD TO FIND SOMETHING QUICKLY TO MAKE MY NAME. THE OPPORTUNITY AROSE WHEN I READ A REPORT ON A NEW UNTESTED DRUG.

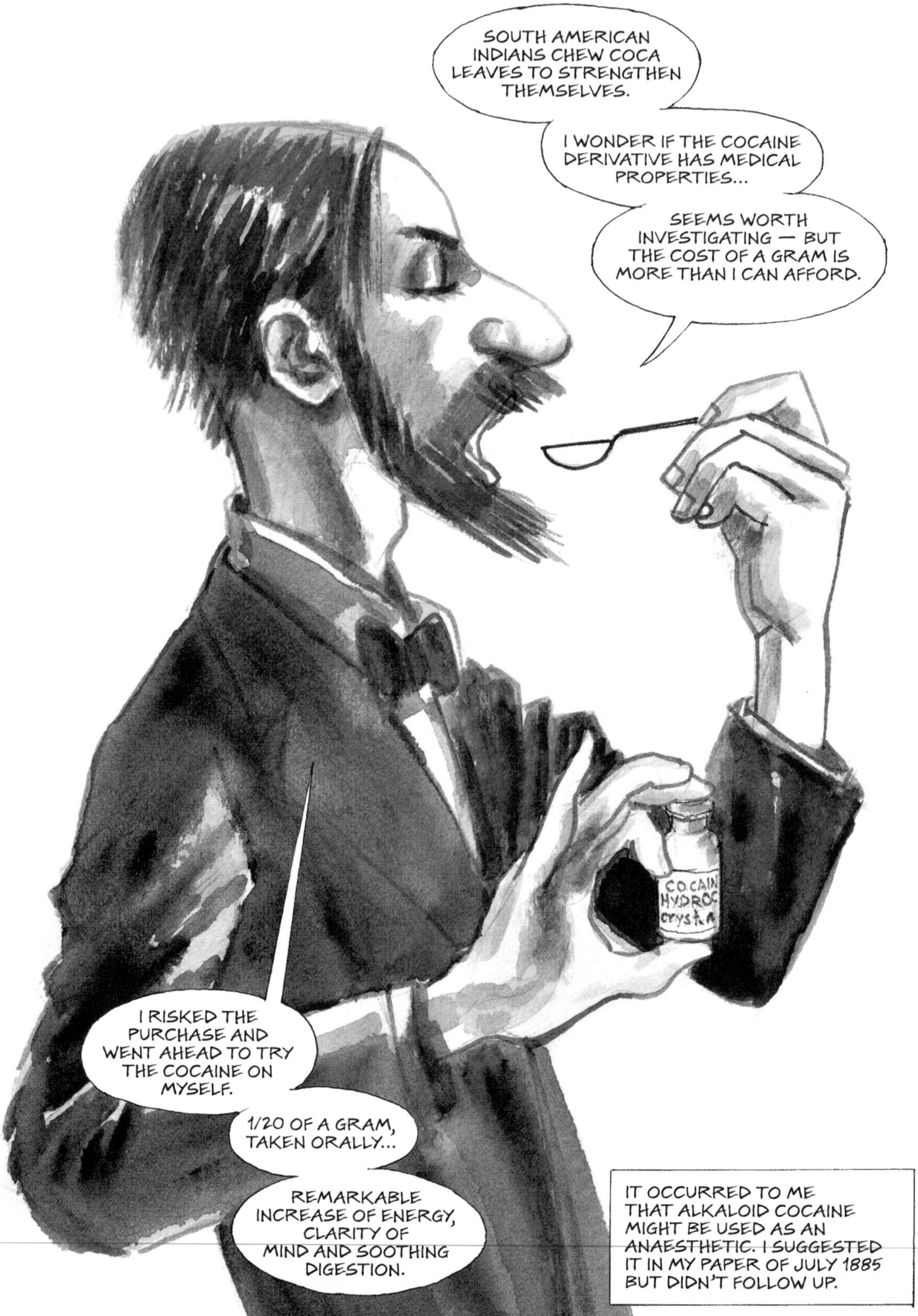
SOUTH AMERICAN INDIANS CHEW COCA LEAVES TO STRENGTHEN THEMSELVES.
I WONDER IF THE COCAINE DERIVATIVE HAS MEDICAL PROPERTIES...
SEEMS WORTH INVESTIGATING — BUT THE COST OF A GRAM IS MORE THAN I CAN AFFORD.
CO.CAIN
HYDROC
cryst. A
I RISKED THE PURCHASE AND WENT AHEAD TO TRY THE COCAINE ON MYSELF.
1/20 OF A GRAM, TAKEN ORALLY...
REMARKABLE INCREASE OF ENERGY, CLARITY OF MIND AND SOOTHING DIGESTION.
IT OCCURRED TO ME THAT ALKALOID COCAINE MIGHT BE USED AS AN ANAESTHETIC. I SUGGESTED IT IN MY PAPER OF JULY 1885 BUT DIDN'T FOLLOW UP.

INSTEAD I RUSHED TO VISIT MARTHA IN HAMBURG AFTER TWO YEARS' SEPARATION. VERY FOOLISH OF ME. I SHOULD HAVE TAKEN MORE TIME TO EXPERIMENT WITH THE ANAESTHETIC PROPERTIES OF COCAINE. BUT I WAS MORE EAGER TO SEE MARTHA.

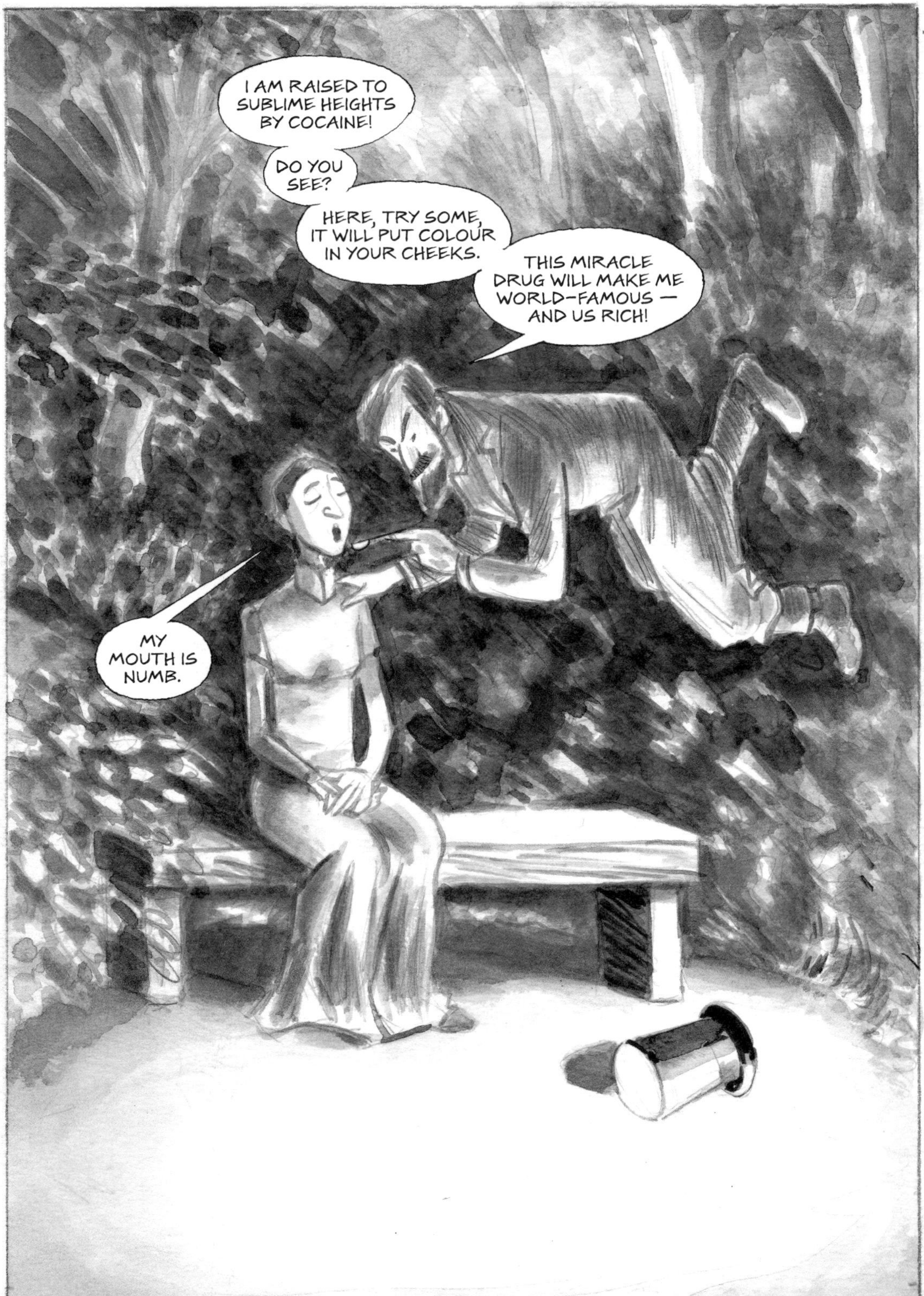
I AM RAISED TO SUBLIME HEIGHTS BY COCAINE!
DO YOU SEE?
HERE, TRY SOME, IT WILL PUT COLOUR IN YOUR CHEEKS.
THIS MIRACLE DRUG WILL MAKE ME WORLD-FAMOUS — AND US RICH!
MY MOUTH IS NUMB.

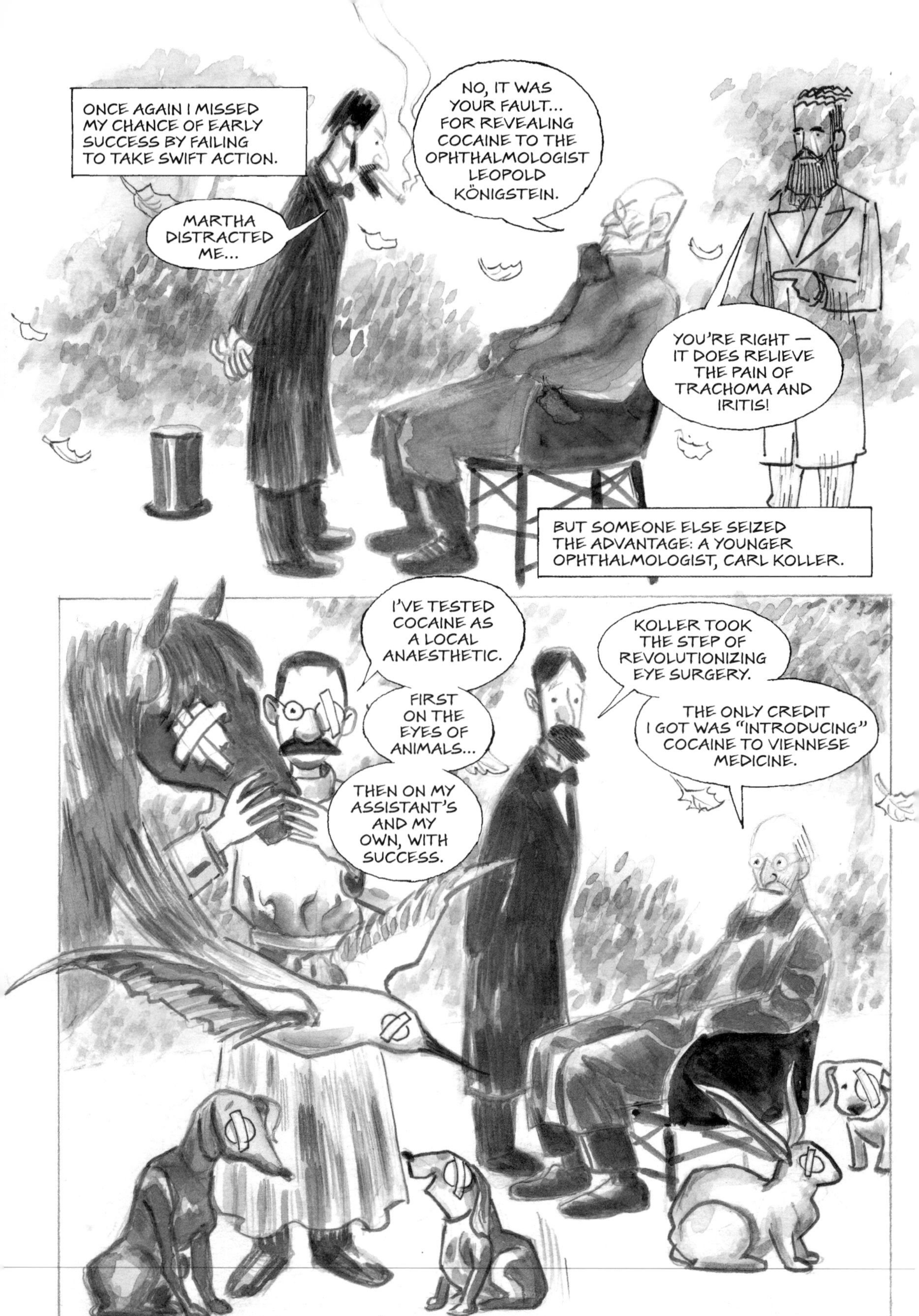
ONCE AGAIN I MISSED MY CHANCE OF EARLY SUCCESS BY FAILING TO TAKE SWIFT ACTION.
MARTHA DISTRACTED ME...
NO, IT WAS YOUR FAULT... FOR REVEALING COCAINE TO THE OPHTHALMOLOGIST LEOPOLD KÖNIGSTEIN.
YOU'RE RIGHT — IT DOES RELIEVE THE PAIN OF TRACHOMA AND IRITIS!
BUT SOMEONE ELSE SEIZED THE ADVANTAGE: A YOUNGER OPHTHALMOLOGIST, CARL KOLLER.
I'VE TESTED COCAINE AS A LOCAL ANAESTHETIC.
FIRST ON THE EYES OF ANIMALS...
THEN ON MY ASSISTANT'S AND MY OWN, WITH SUCCESS.
KOLLER TOOK THE STEP OF REVOLUTIONIZING EYE SURGERY.
THE ONLY CREDIT I GOT WAS "INTRODUCING" COCAINE TO VIENNESE MEDICINE.

I DIDN'T RESENT KOLLER'S COMPETITION. I OWED HIM FOR CORRECTLY DIAGNOSING MY FATHER'S GLAUCOMA.

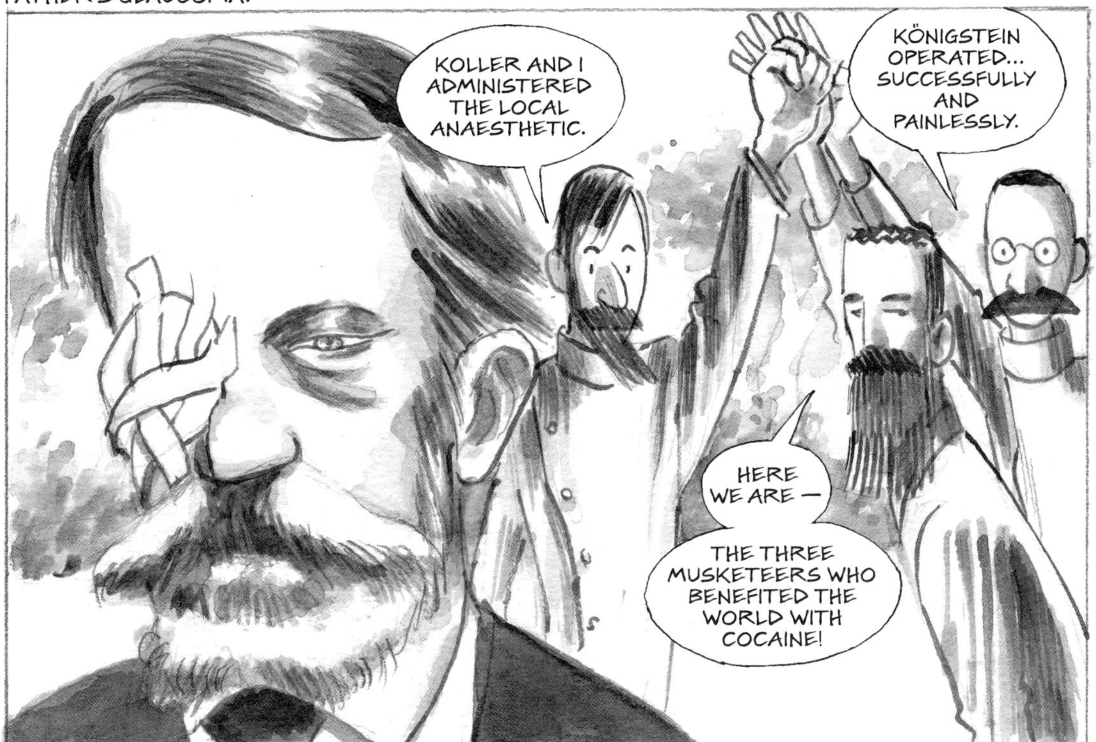
KOLLER AND I ADMINISTERED THE LOCAL ANAESTHETIC.
KÖNIGSTEIN OPERATED... SUCCESSFULLY AND PAINLESSLY.
HERE WE ARE —
THE THREE MUSKETEERS WHO BENEFITED THE WORLD WITH COCAINE!

MY CLOSE FRIEND, ERNST VON FLEISCHL-MARXOW, INFECTED HIS HAND DURING PATHOLOGY RESEARCH. AMPUTATION OF HIS RIGHT THUMB DID NOT PREVENT THE SPREAD OF NERVE-TISSUE TUMOURS.

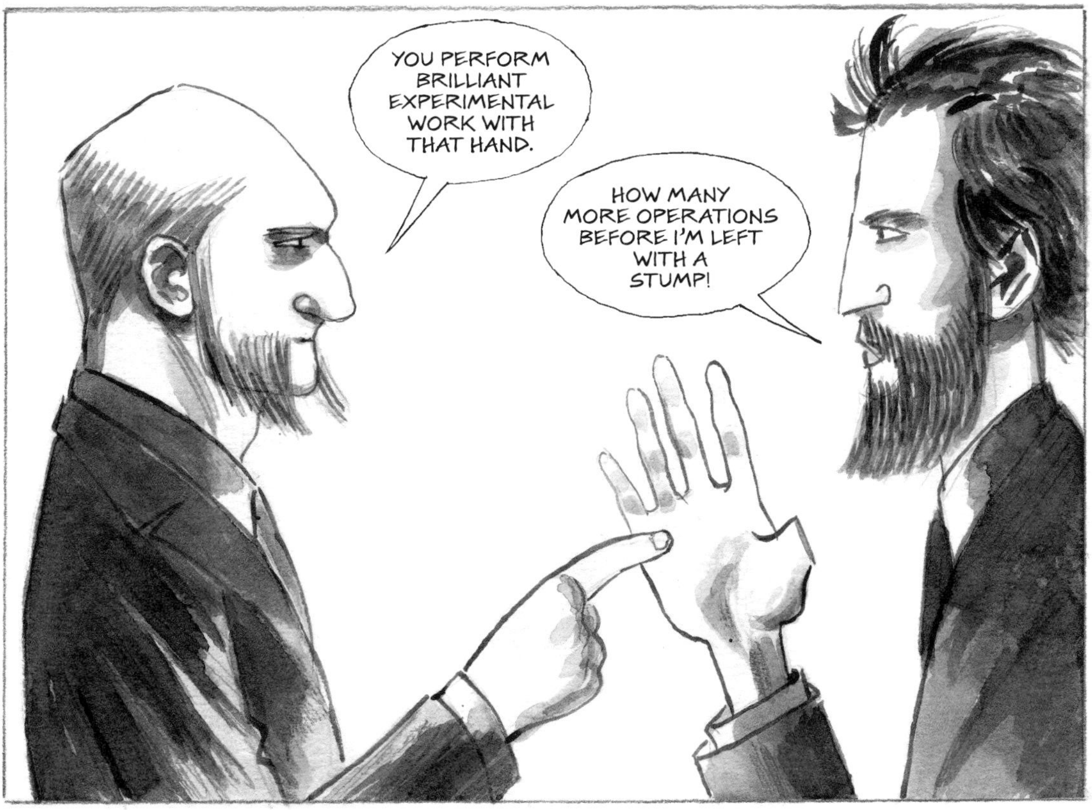
YOU PERFORM BRILLIANT EXPERIMENTAL WORK WITH THAT HAND.
HOW MANY MORE OPERATIONS BEFORE I'M LEFT WITH A STUMP!

ERNST BECAME ADDICTED TO MORPHINE TO RELIEVE HIS UNENDURABLE PAIN. I REMEMBER TERRIBLE NIGHTS WITH HIM IN HIS AGONY.

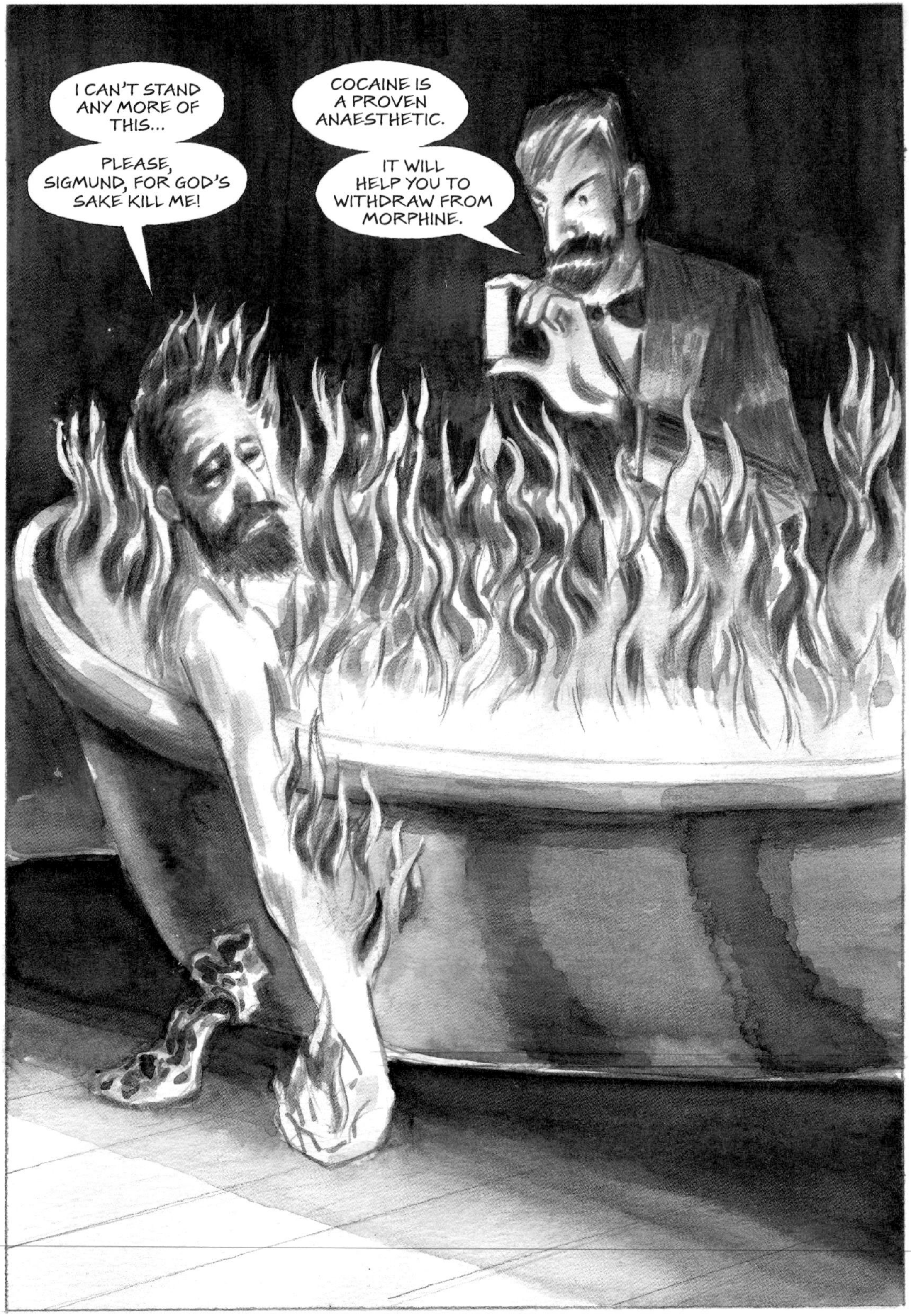

I CAN'T STAND ANY MORE OF THIS...
PLEASE, SIGMUND, FOR GOD'S SAKE KILL ME!
COCAINE IS A PROVEN ANAESTHETIC.
IT WILL HELP YOU TO WITHDRAW FROM MORPHINE.

ERNST AND I MISTAKENLY BELIEVED THAT COCAINE WOULD COUNTERACT MORPHINE ADDICTION. HE SEEMED TO IMPROVE AT FIRST BUT SOON BECAME HOPELESSLY ADDICTED TO COCAINE.

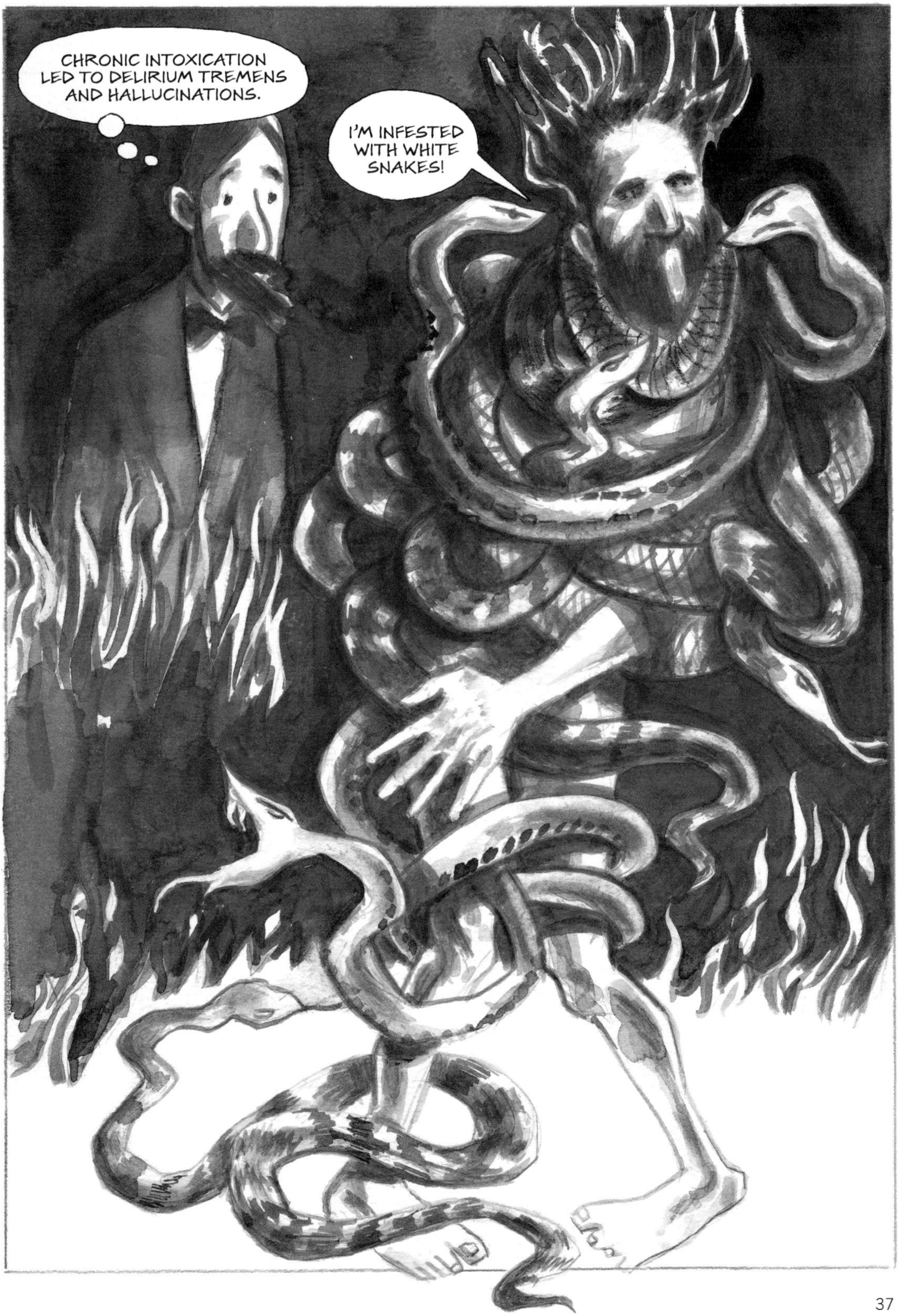
CHRONIC INTOXICATION LED TO DELIRIUM TREMENS AND HALLUCINATIONS.
I'M INFESTED WITH WHITE SNAKES!

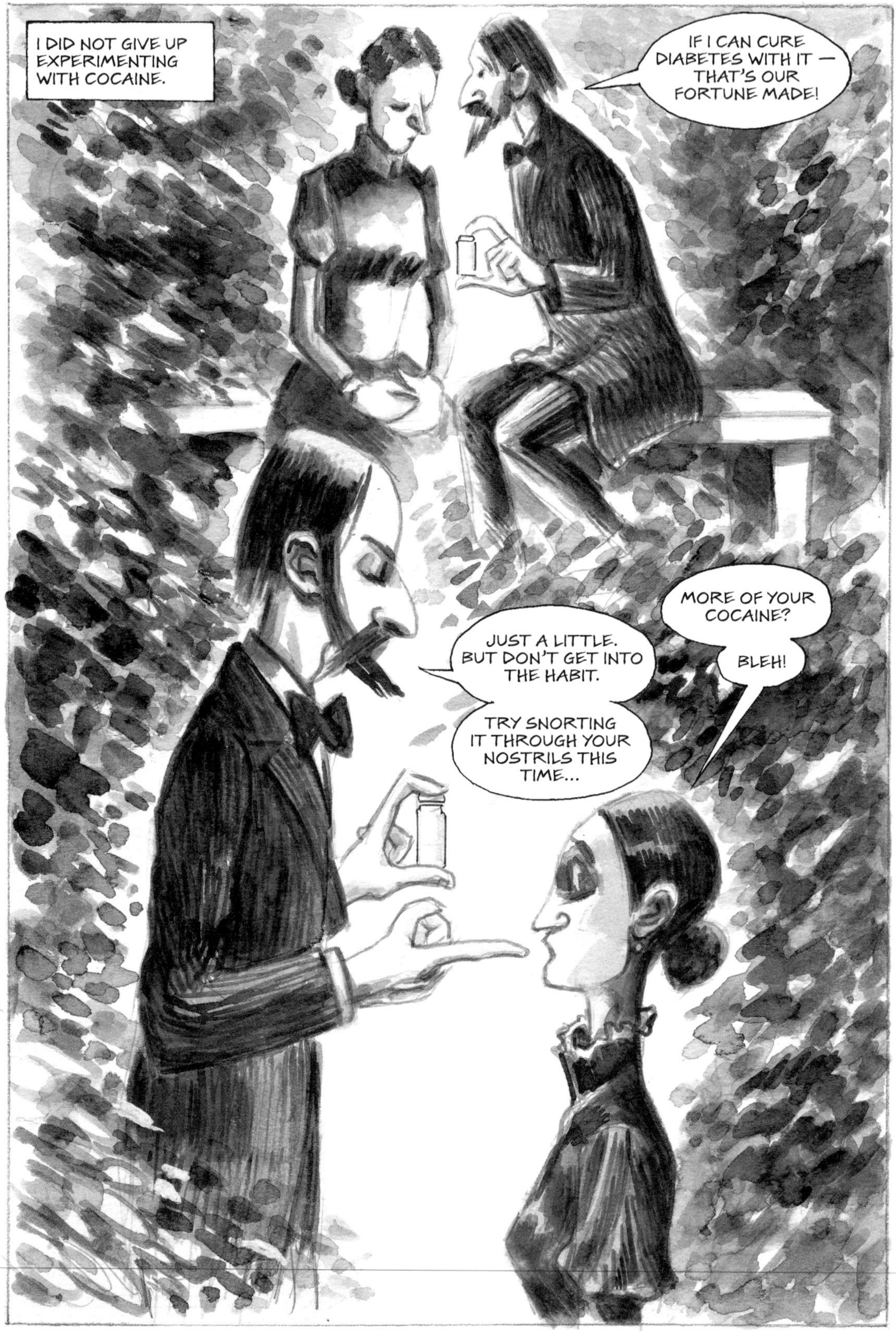
I DID NOT GIVE UP EXPERIMENTING WITH COCAINE.
IF I CAN CURE DIABETES WITH IT — THAT'S OUR FORTUNE MADE!
MORE OF YOUR COCAINE?
BLEH!
JUST A LITTLE. BUT DON'T GET INTO THE HABIT.
TRY SNORTING IT THROUGH YOUR NOSTRILS THIS TIME...

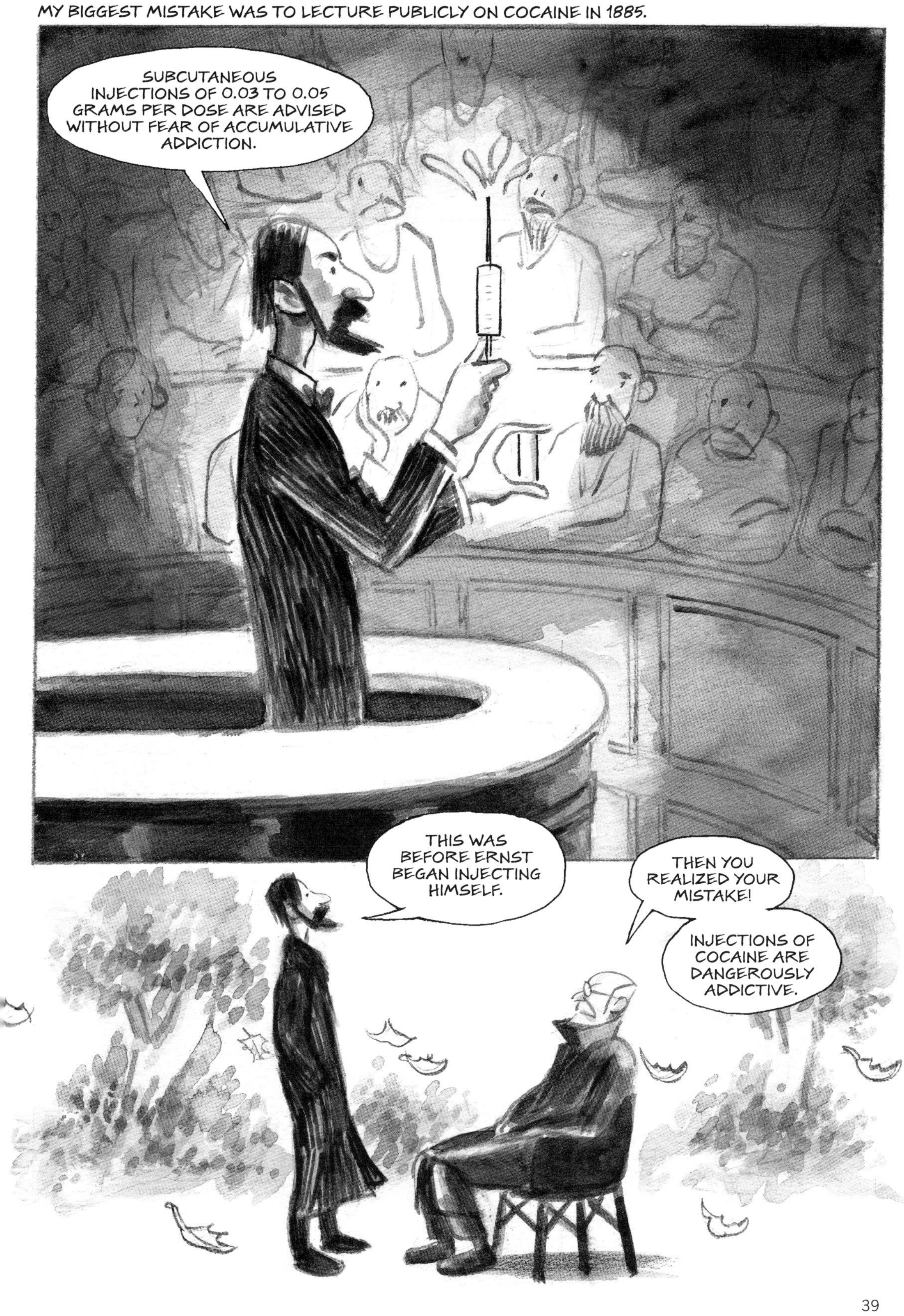
MY BIGGEST MISTAKE WAS TO LECTURE PUBLICLY ON COCAINE IN 1885.
SUBCUTANEOUS INJECTIONS OF 0.03 TO 0.05 GRAMS PER DOSE ARE ADVISED WITHOUT FEAR OF ACCUMULATIVE ADDICTION.
THIS WAS BEFORE ERNST BEGAN INJECTING HIMSELF.
THEN YOU REALIZED YOUR MISTAKE!
INJECTIONS OF COCAINE ARE DANGEROUSLY ADDICTIVE.

THE PSYCHIATRIST FRIEDRICH ALBRECHT ERLENMEYER REPORTED ALARMING INCREASES OF COCAINE ADDICTION IN 1886.

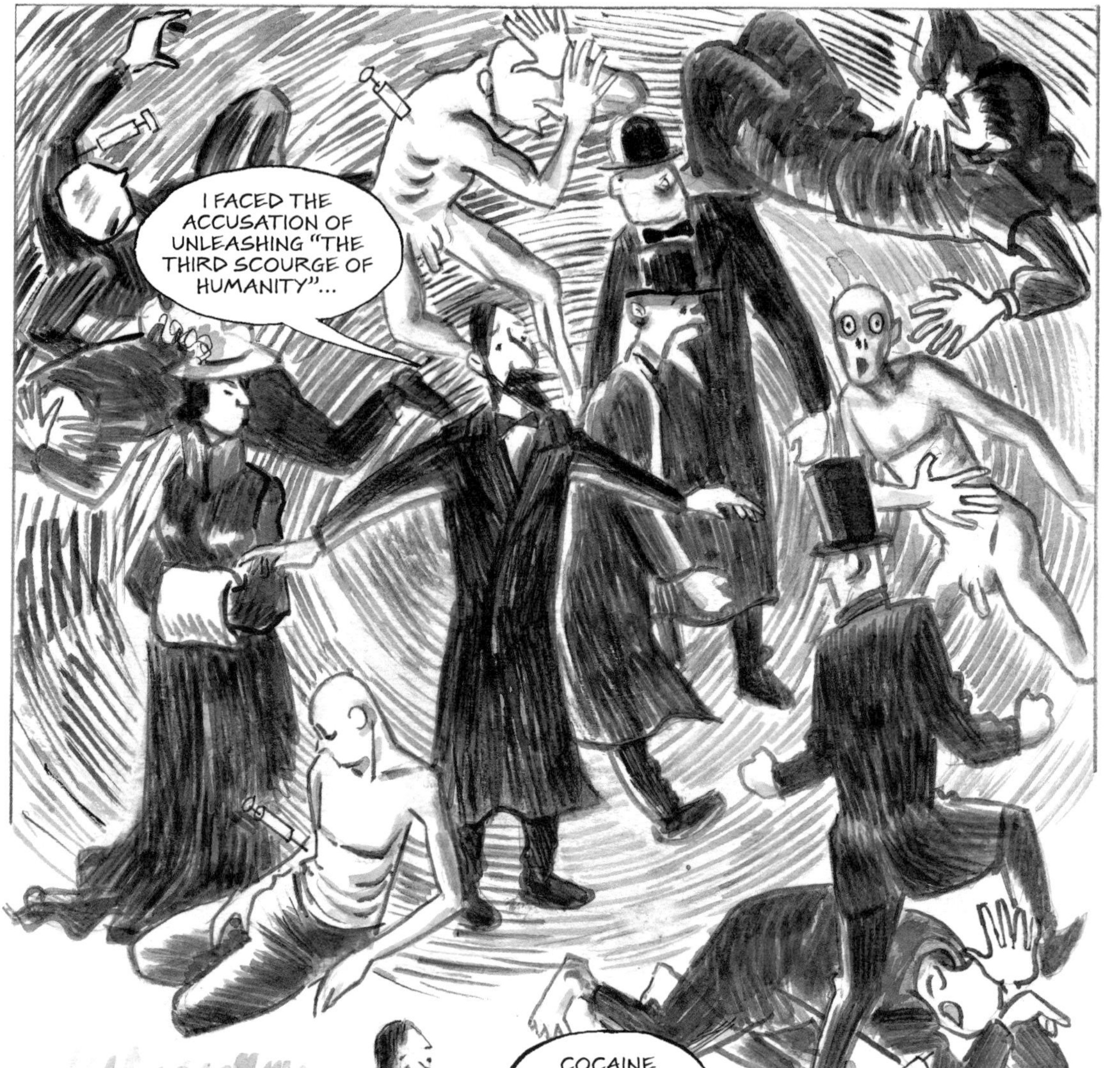
I FACED THE ACCUSATION OF UNLEASHING "THE THIRD SCOURGE OF HUMANITY"...

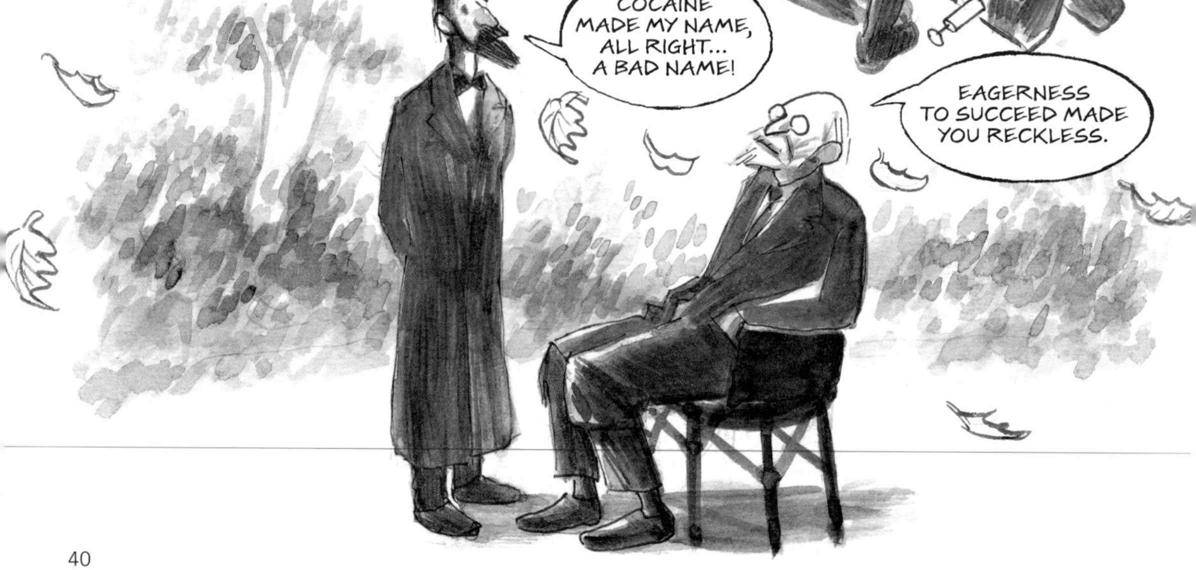
COCAINE MADE MY NAME, ALL RIGHT... A BAD NAME!
EAGERNESS TO SUCCEED MADE YOU RECKLESS.

FORTUNATELY I DID NOT LOSE THE SUPPORT OF BRÜCKE, NOTHNAGEL AND MEYNERT, WHO CAMPAIGNED FOR MY GRANT TO STUDY IN PARIS WITH THE GREAT NEUROLOGIST JEAN-MARTIN CHARCOT.

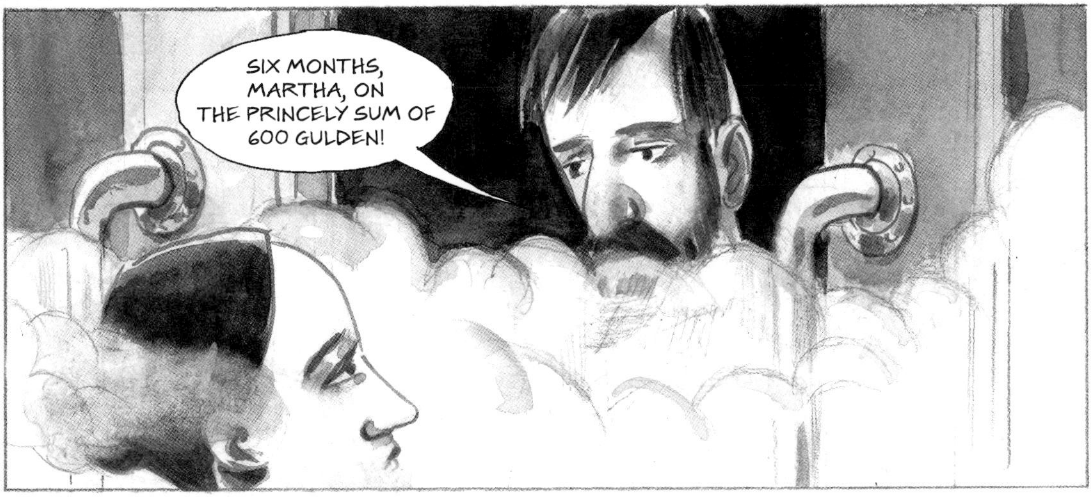
SIX MONTHS, MARTHA, ON THE PRINCELY SUM OF 600 GULDEN!

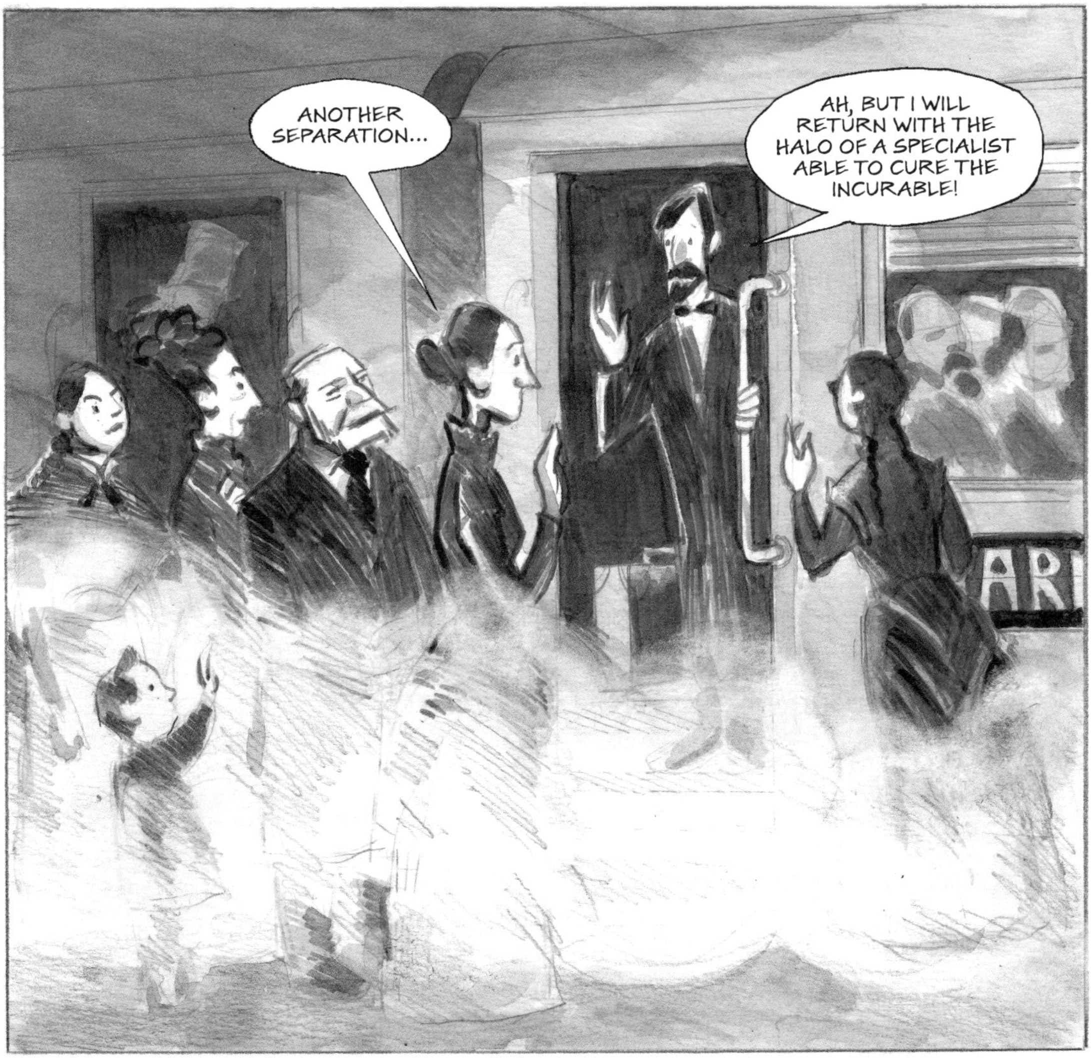
ANOTHER SEPARATION...
AH, BUT I WILL RETURN WITH THE HALO OF A SPECIALIST ABLE TO CURE THE INCURABLE!

MY VOYAGE OF DISCOVERY REALLY BEGAN WITH CHARCOT AT LA SALPÊTRIÈRE HOSPITAL. MORE THAN A HOSPITAL, IT WAS A SELF-SUFFICIENT MINIATURE CITY OF 5,000 MOSTLY FEMALE INMATES, WITH ITS OWN MARKET, BAKERY, LAUNDRY, VEGETABLE GARDENS, CHURCHES, SCHOOL, GYMNASIUM, LIBRARY, POST OFFICE, FIRE STATION AND CEMETERY. IT EVEN HELD PUBLIC CONCERTS AND DANCES.

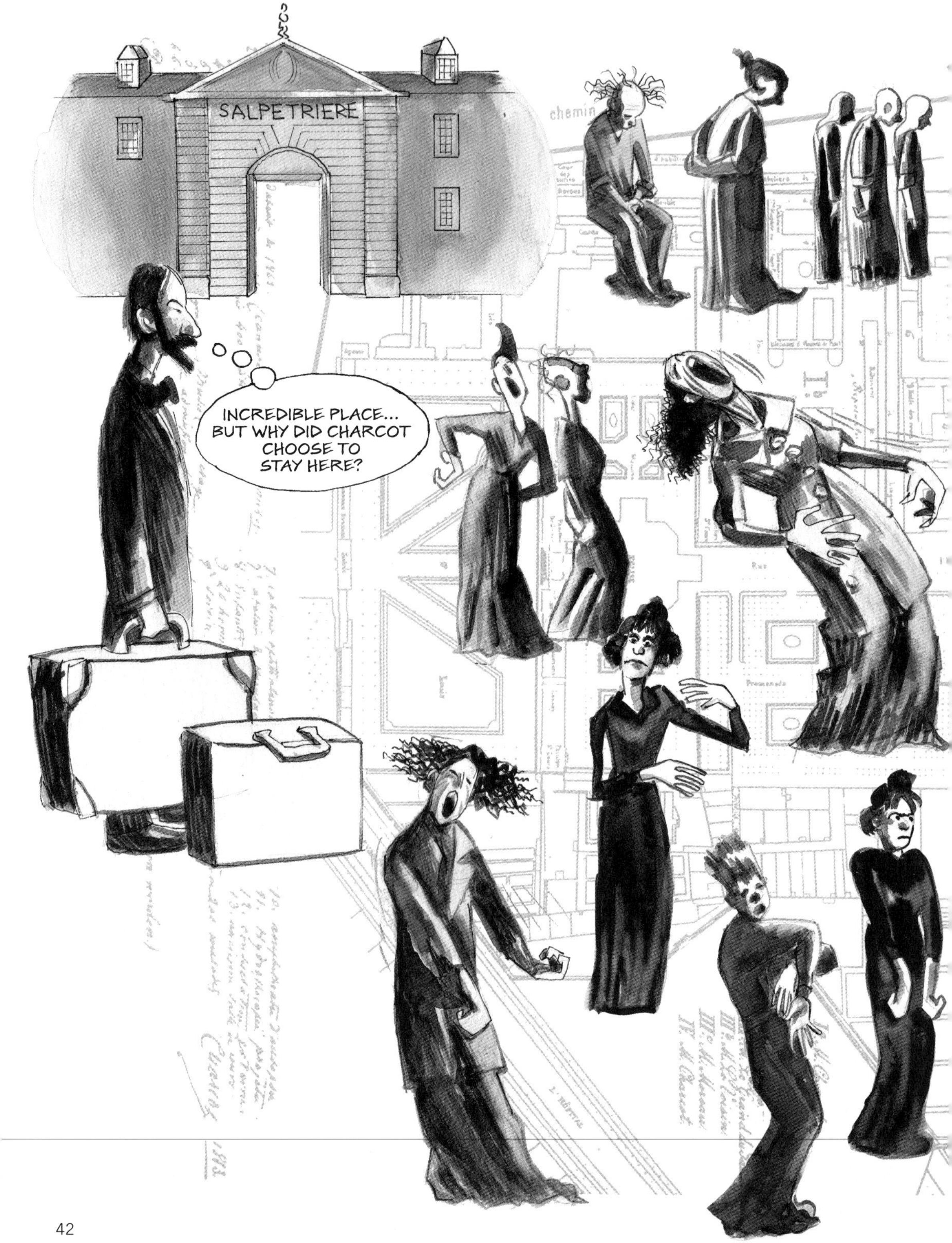
SALPETRIERE
INCREDIBLE PLACE... BUT WHY DID CHARCOT CHOOSE TO STAY HERE?

LA SALPÊTRIÈRE HAD SERVED FOR TWO CENTURIES AS A REPOSITORY FOR INCURABLES — THE INSANE, EPILEPTICS, PARALYTICS, DISEASED PROSTITUTES AND SENILE WOMEN. IT WAS CONSIDERED OUTDATED, A PROFESSIONAL DEAD END FOR AN AMBITIOUS CAREER DOCTOR. BUT CHARCOT DECIDED TO REMAIN AFTER HE SERVED HIS INTERNSHIP THERE.

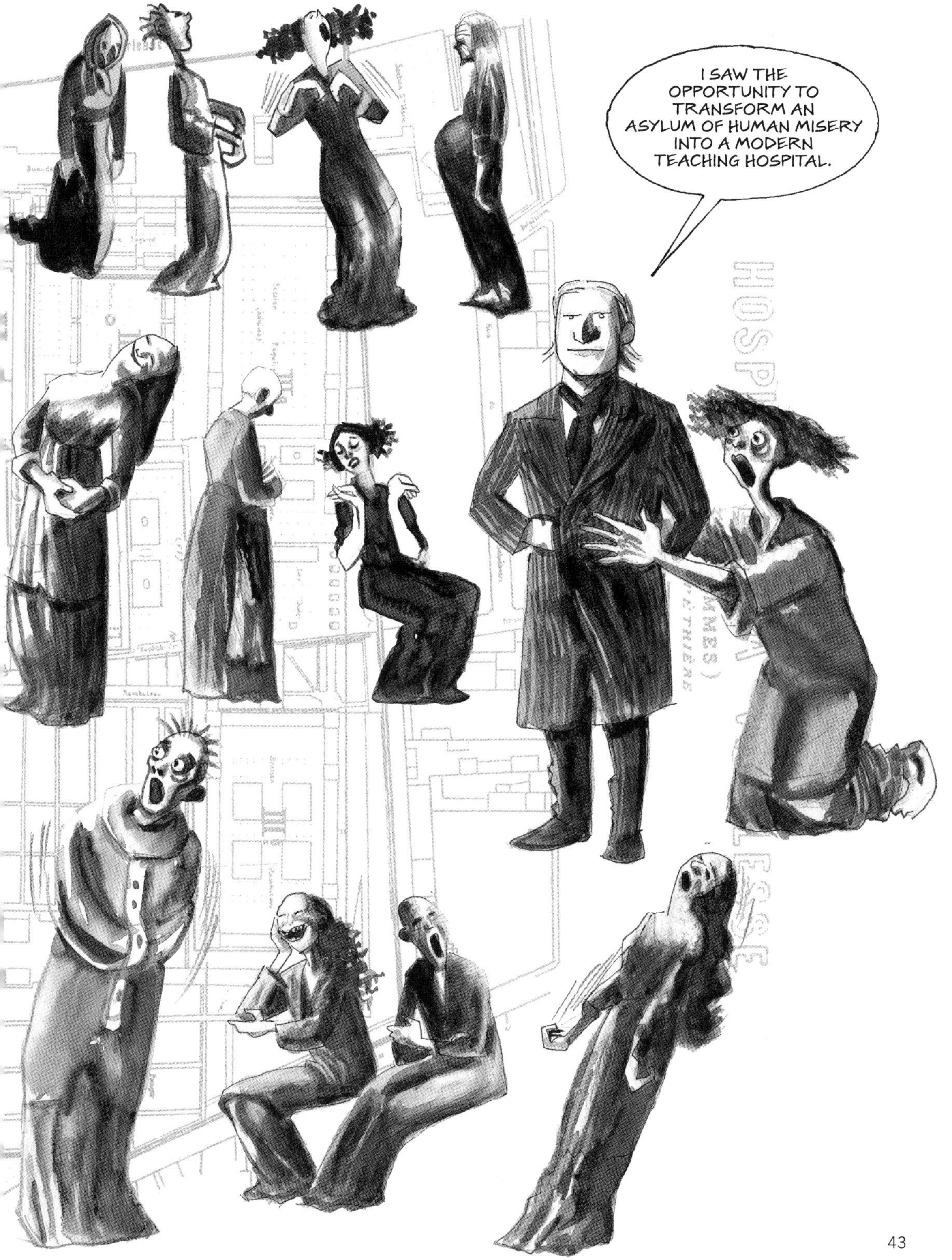
I SAW THE OPPORTUNITY TO TRANSFORM AN ASYLUM OF HUMAN MISERY INTO A MODERN TEACHING HOSPITAL.

SUCCESS INDEED! CHARCOT HELD LAVISH TUESDAY SOIRÉES AT HIS MANSION ON THE BOULEVARD SAINT-GERMAIN. HE HAD MARRIED A WEALTHY WIDOW AND COULD AFFORD EXTRAVAGANT ENTERTAINMENTS OF THE MOST DISTINGUISHED GUESTS, FROM ARTISTS, SCHOLARS AND SCIENTISTS TO HEADS OF STATE.

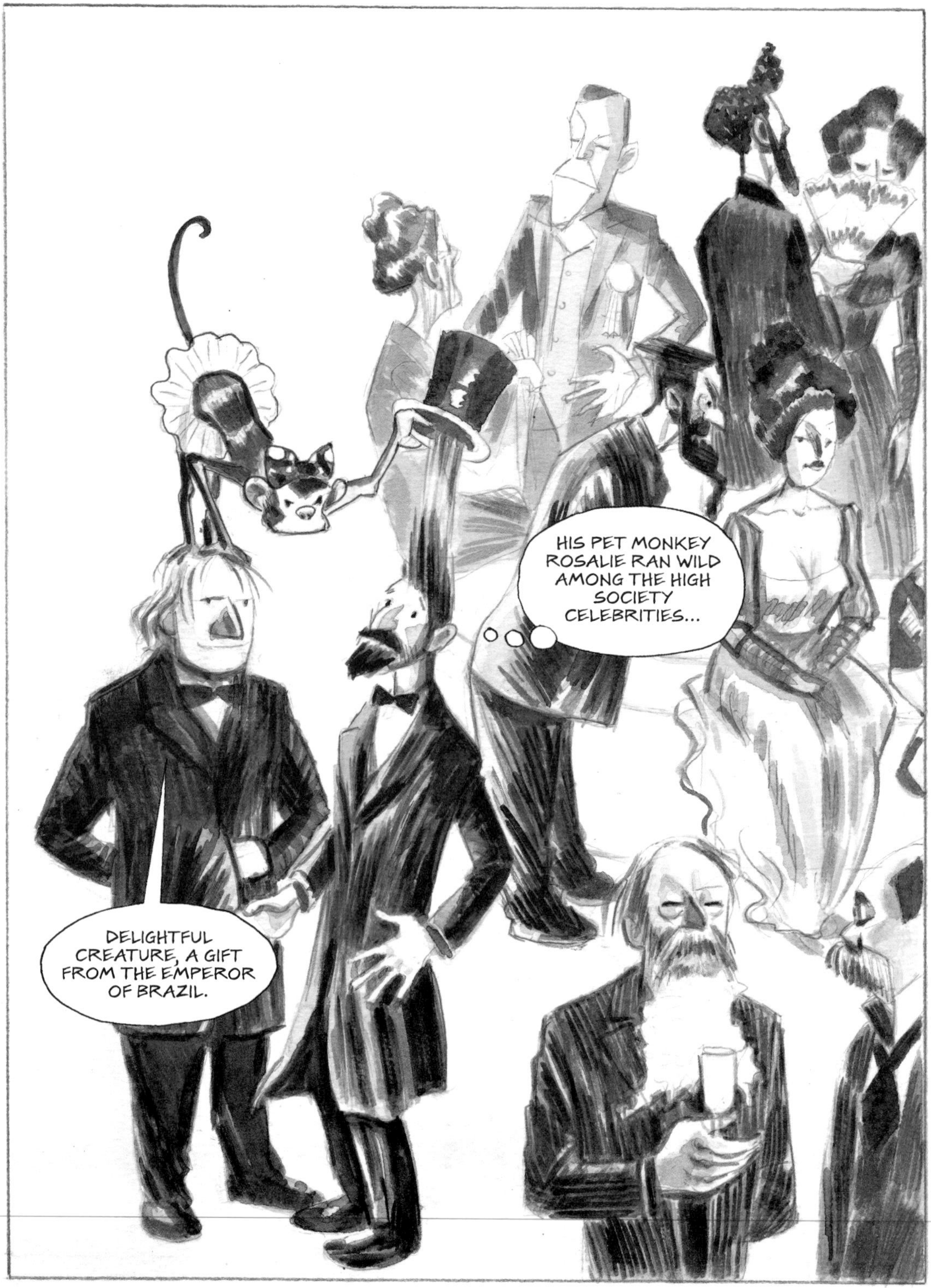
HIS PET MONKEY ROSALIE RAN WILD AMONG THE HIGH SOCIETY CELEBRITIES...
DELIGHTFUL CREATURE, A GIFT FROM THE EMPEROR OF BRAZIL.

I FELT OUT OF PLACE. HOW COULD I, A SHABBY YOUNG FOREIGNER, IMPRESS HIM? WHAT COULD I DO TO ATTRACT HIS ATTENTION AMONG ALL HIS OTHER TALENTED JUNIOR DOCTORS? THEN I HAD AN IDEA. AND A GOOD DOSE OF COCAINE LOOSENED MY TONGUE.

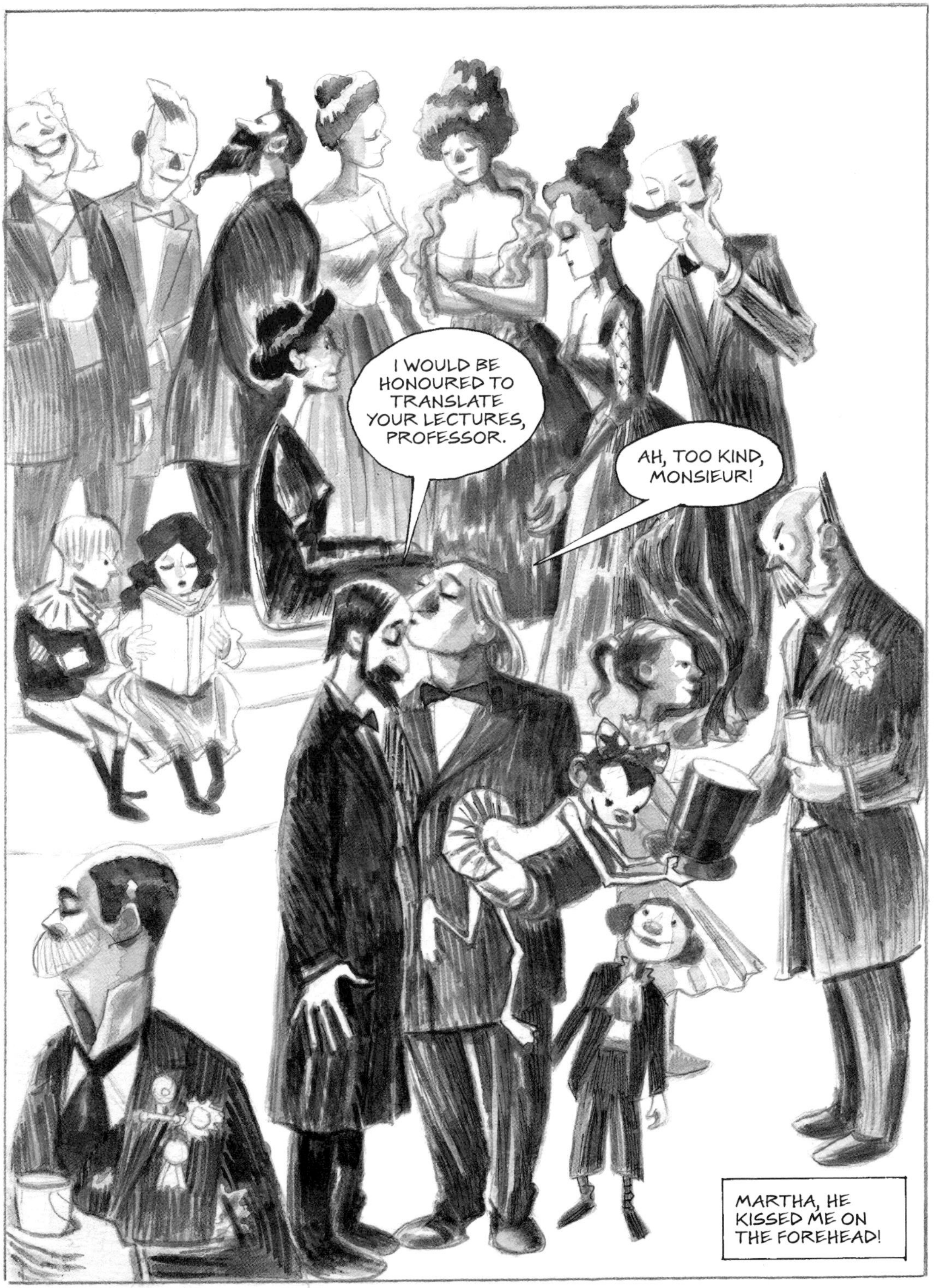
I WOULD BE HONOURED TO TRANSLATE YOUR LECTURES, PROFESSOR.
AH, TOO KIND, MONSIEUR!
MARTHA, HE KISSED ME ON THE FOREHEAD!

CHARCOT EARNED HIS WORLD RENOWN AS THE FOUNDER OF NEUROLOGY BY INVESTIGATING HITHERTO UNCLASSIFIED PATHOLOGIES. GERIATRIC DISEASES, CEREBRAL HAEMORRHAGES, EXOPHTHALMIC GOITRES, AMYOTROPHIC LATERAL SCLEROSIS, MULTIPLE SCLEROSIS, TABETIC ATAXIA, APHASIA... THERE WAS NO END TO HIS CURIOSITY.

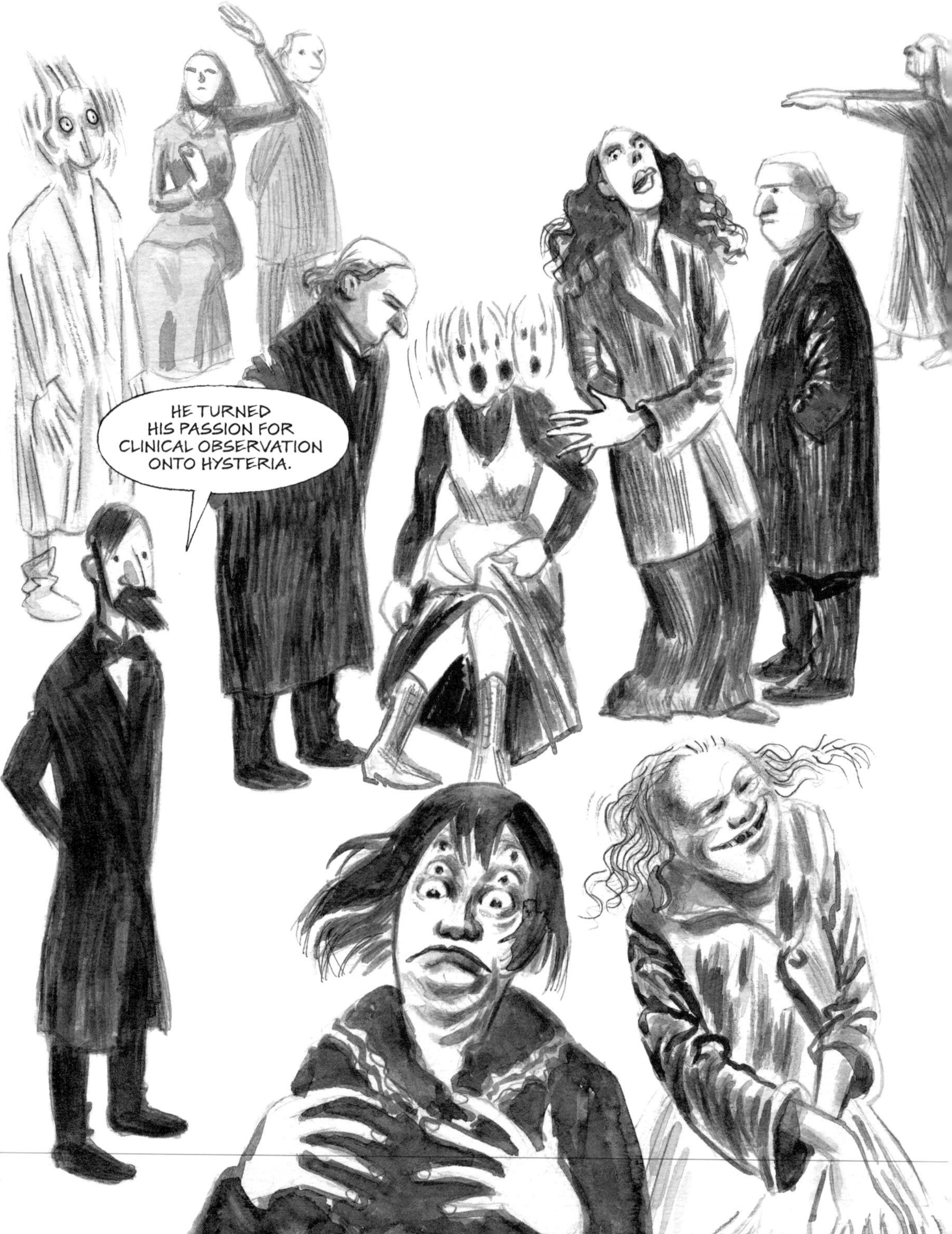
HE TURNED HIS PASSION FOR CLINICAL OBSERVATION ONTO HYSTERIA.

CHARCOT WAS NOT AT FIRST INTERESTED IN HYSTERIA... UNTIL A CHANCE RE-ARRANGEMENT OF THE WARDS PLACED EPILEPTICS AND HYSTERICS IN HIS CARE.

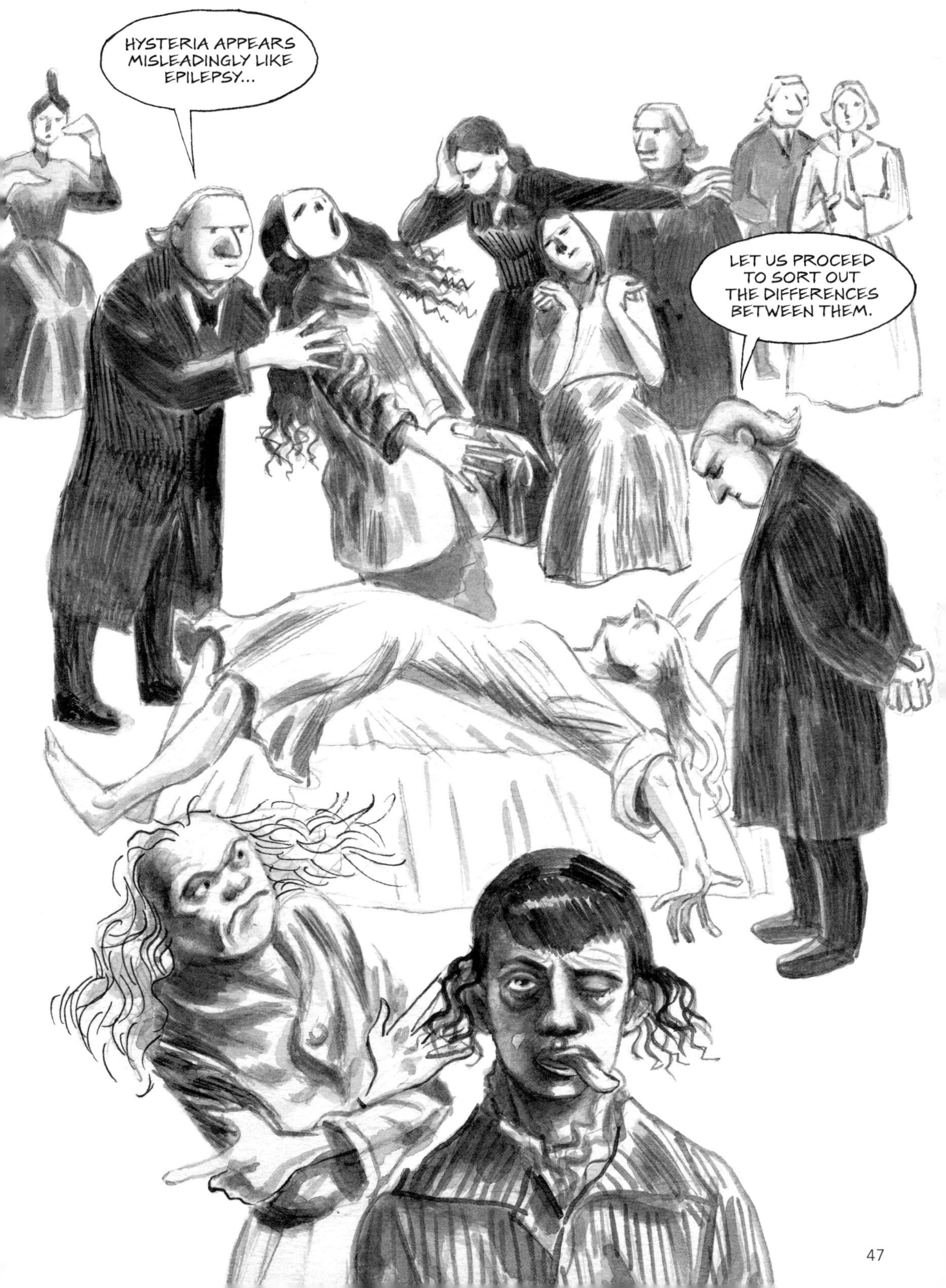
HYSTERIA APPEARS MISLEADINGLY LIKE EPILEPSY...
LET US PROCEED TO SORT OUT THE DIFFERENCES BETWEEN THEM.

HYSTERIA, FROM THE GREEK "HUSTERA", THE UTERUS, HAD ALWAYS BEEN ASSUMED EXCLUSIVELY FEMALE, A "UTERINE FRENZY" OF BAFFLING SYMPTOMS THAT DEFEATED MEDICAL DIAGNOSIS.

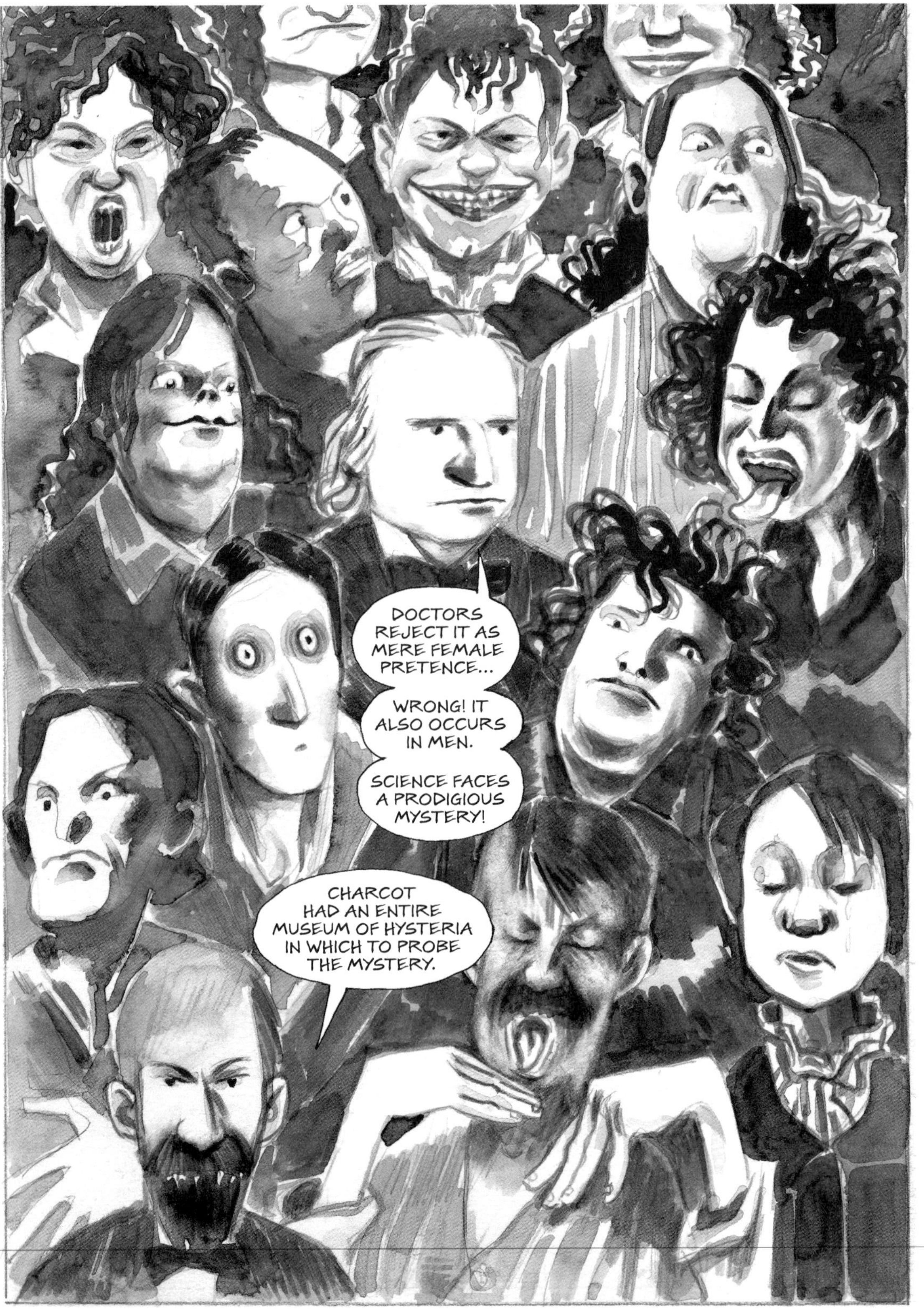
DOCTORS REJECT IT AS MERE FEMALE PRETENCE...
WRONG! IT ALSO OCCURS IN MEN.
SCIENCE FACES A PRODIGIOUS MYSTERY!
CHARCOT HAD AN ENTIRE MUSEUM OF HYSTERIA IN WHICH TO PROBE THE MYSTERY.

WHERE OTHERS HAD SUSPECTED FRAUD IN DISPLAYS OF HYSTERIA, CHARCOT DETECTED CLASSIFIABLE SYMPTOMS.

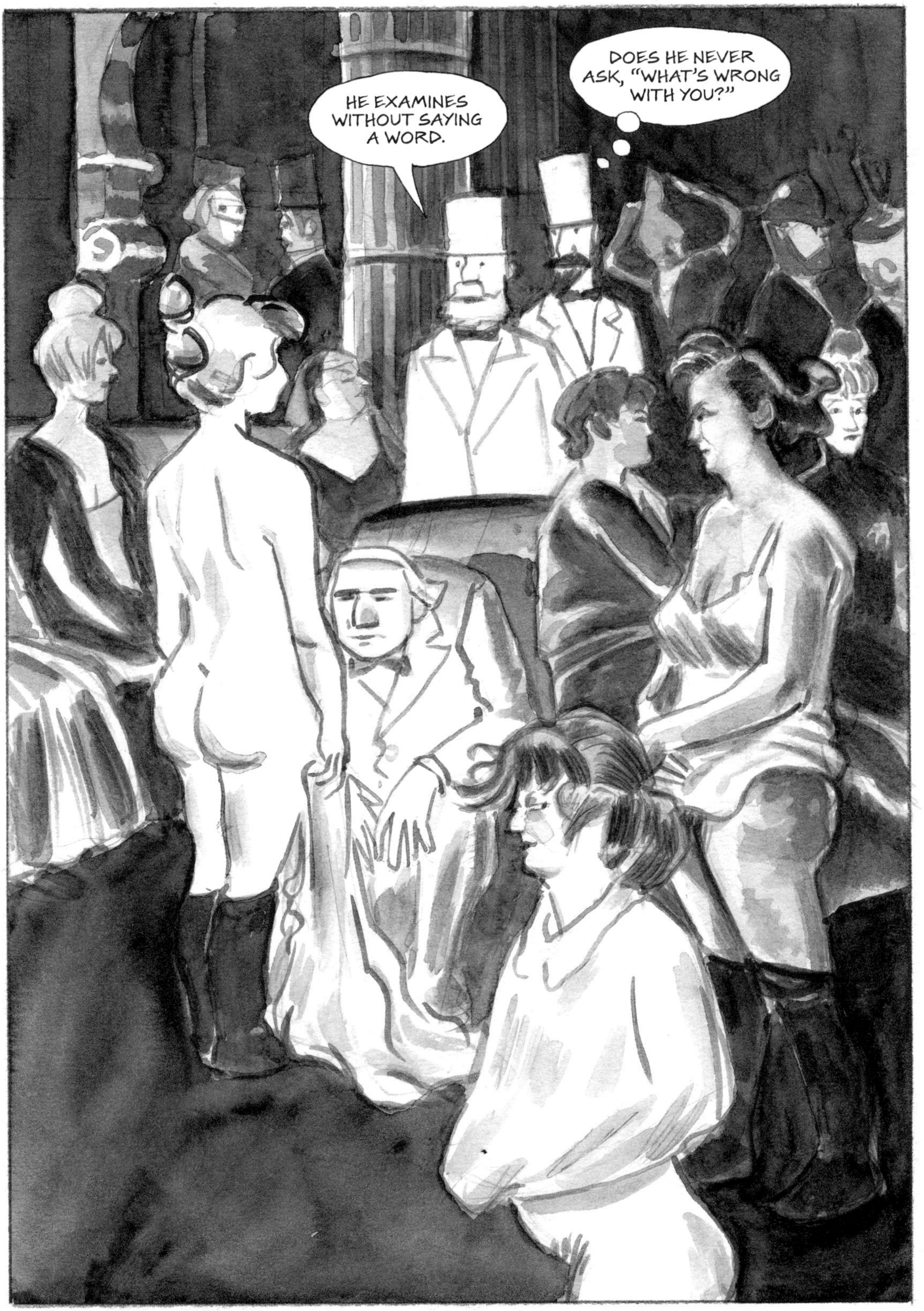
HE EXAMINES WITHOUT SAYING A WORD.
DOES HE NEVER ASK, "WHAT'S WRONG WITH YOU?"

CHARCOT HAD AN ARTIST'S KEEN EYE. HE CONSTANTLY PAINTED AND DREW, SOMETIMES UNDER THE INFLUENCE OF HASHISH.

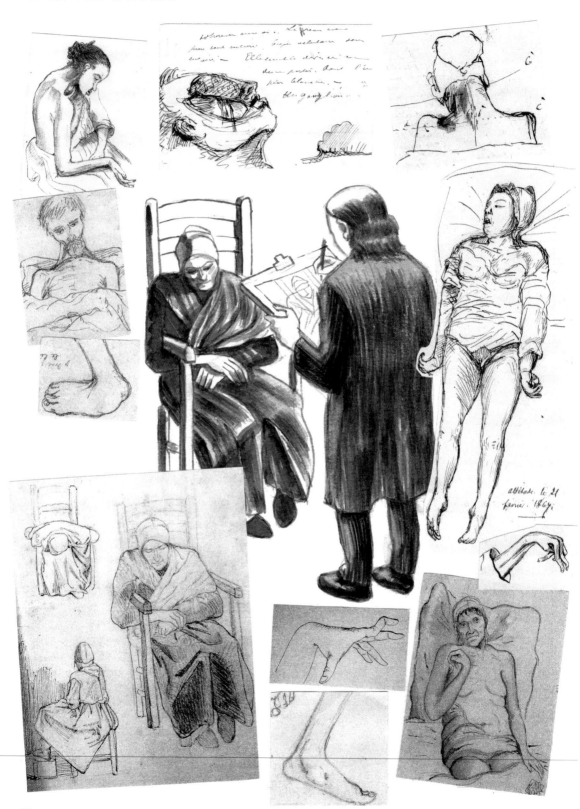

I WAS SET THE TASK OF CONDUCTING AN AUTOPSY ON THE HYSTERIC JOSÉPHINE DELET. ALLEGED CAUSE OF DEATH: CEREBRAL ATROPHY. CHARCOT HAD AN IDEA THAT MY INVESTIGATIONS WOULD REVEAL SOME NEUROPHYSIOLOGICAL CAUSE FOR HER HYSTERIA.

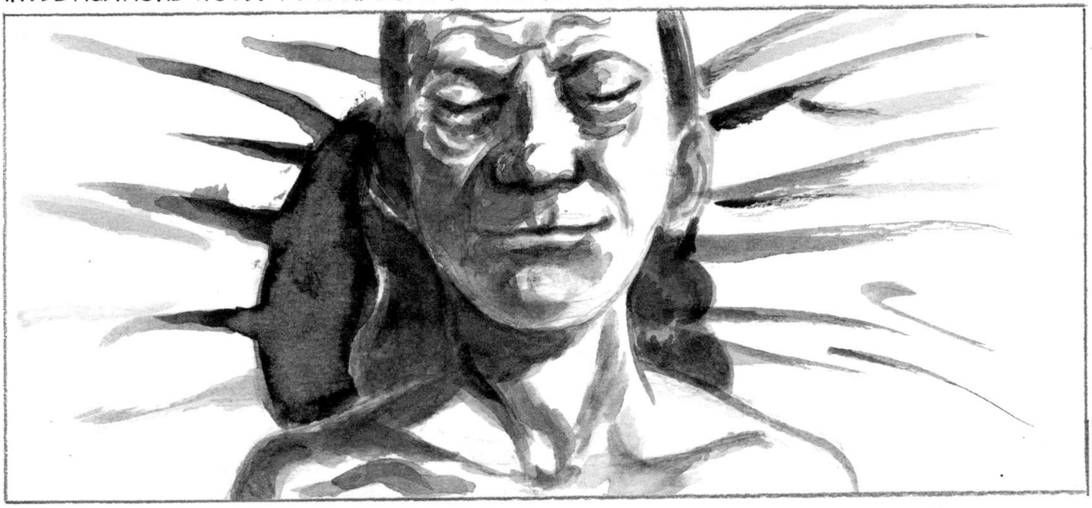

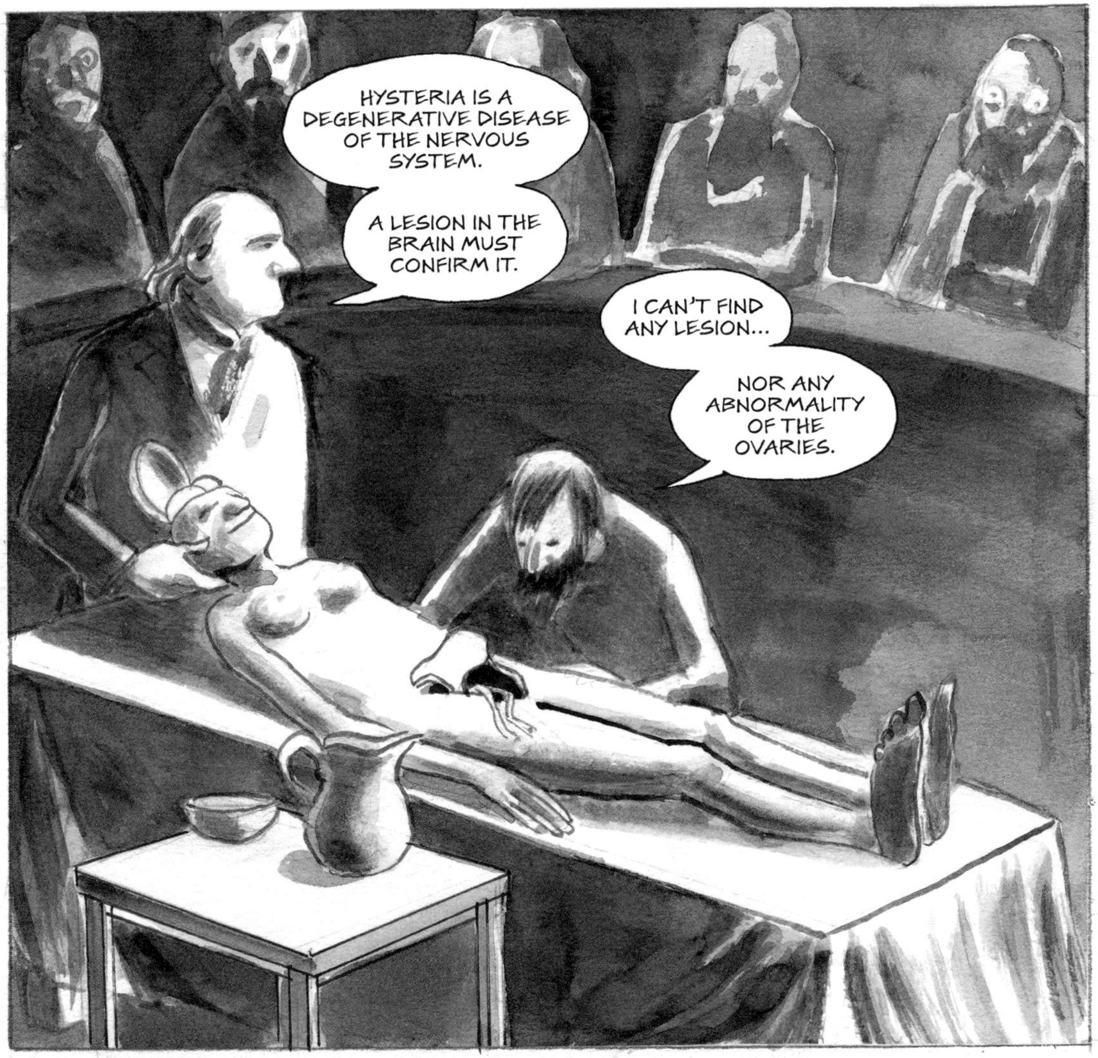

HYSTERIA IS A DEGENERATIVE DISEASE OF THE NERVOUS SYSTEM.
A LESION IN THE BRAIN MUST CONFIRM IT.
I CAN'T FIND ANY LESION...
NOR ANY ABNORMALITY OF THE OVARIES.

SIMILAR NECROPSIES HAD TIME AND AGAIN PROVED FUTILE. CONVULSIVE SEIZURES, HEMIPLEGIC PARALYSIS, VIOLENT HALLUCINATIONS — ALL SUCH EXHIBITIONS OF HYSTERIC SYMPTOMS ELUDED ORGANIC LOCALIZATION.

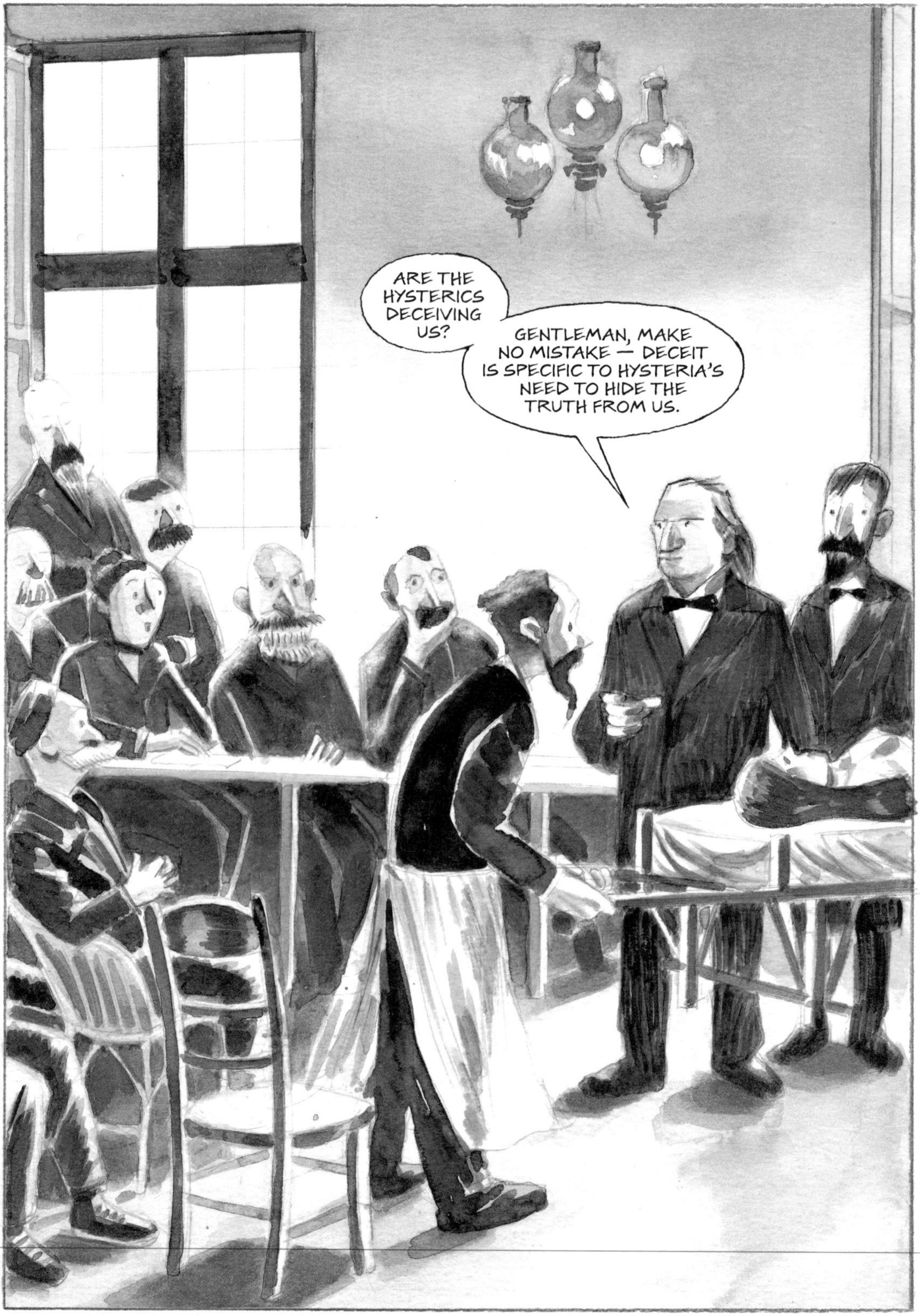

ARE THE HYSTERICS DECEIVING US?
GENTLEMAN, MAKE NO MISTAKE — DECEIT IS SPECIFIC TO HYSTERIA'S NEED TO HIDE THE TRUTH FROM US.

COULD IT BE THESE WOMEN WERE LYING WITH THEIR BODIES? WAS HYSTERIA A SPECTACULAR FAKE? CHARCOT GAVE PUBLIC DEMONSTRATIONS TO CONVINCE THE SCEPTICS.

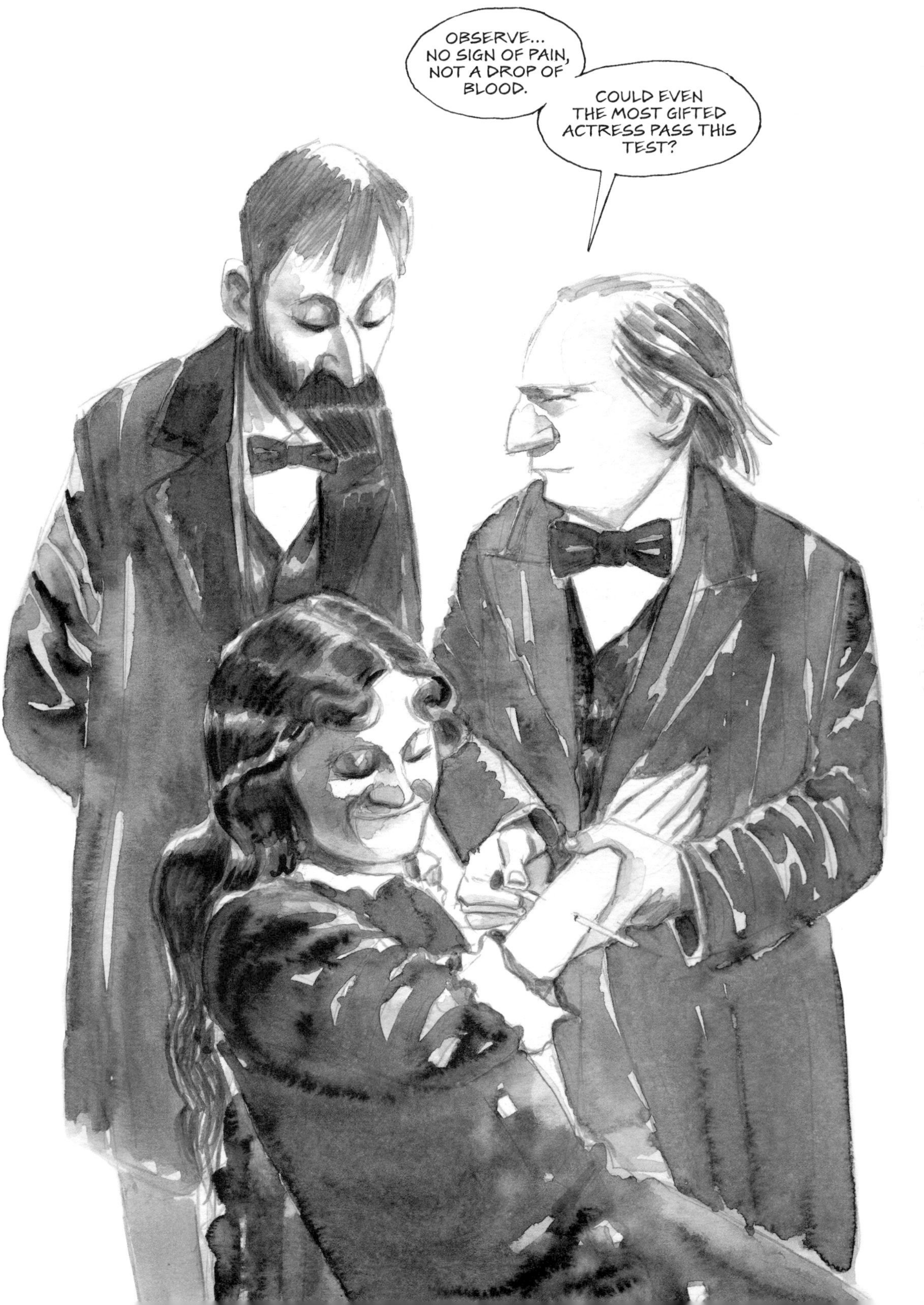
OBSERVE... NO SIGN OF PAIN, NOT A DROP OF BLOOD.
COULD EVEN THE MOST GIFTED ACTRESS PASS THIS TEST?

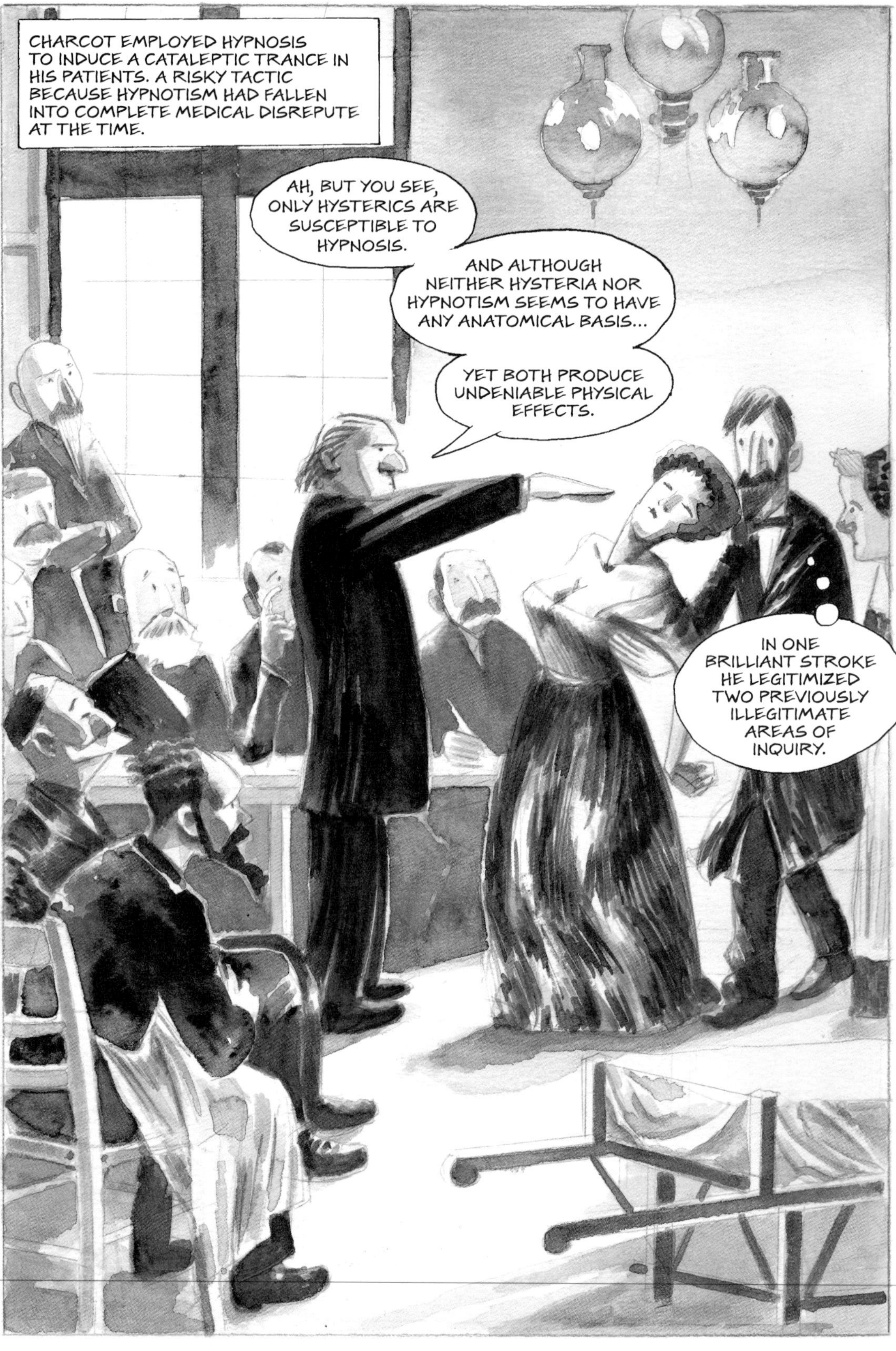
CHARCOT EMPLOYED HYPNOSIS TO INDUCE A CATALEPTIC TRANCE IN HIS PATIENTS. A RISKY TACTIC BECAUSE HYPNOTISM HAD FALLEN INTO COMPLETE MEDICAL DISREPUTE AT THE TIME.
AH, BUT YOU SEE, ONLY HYSTERICS ARE SUSCEPTIBLE TO HYPNOSIS.
AND ALTHOUGH NEITHER HYSTERIA NOR HYPNOTISM SEEMS TO HAVE ANY ANATOMICAL BASIS...
YET BOTH PRODUCE UNDENIABLE PHYSICAL EFFECTS.
IN ONE BRILLIANT STROKE HE LEGITIMIZED TWO PREVIOUSLY ILLEGITIMATE AREAS OF INQUIRY.

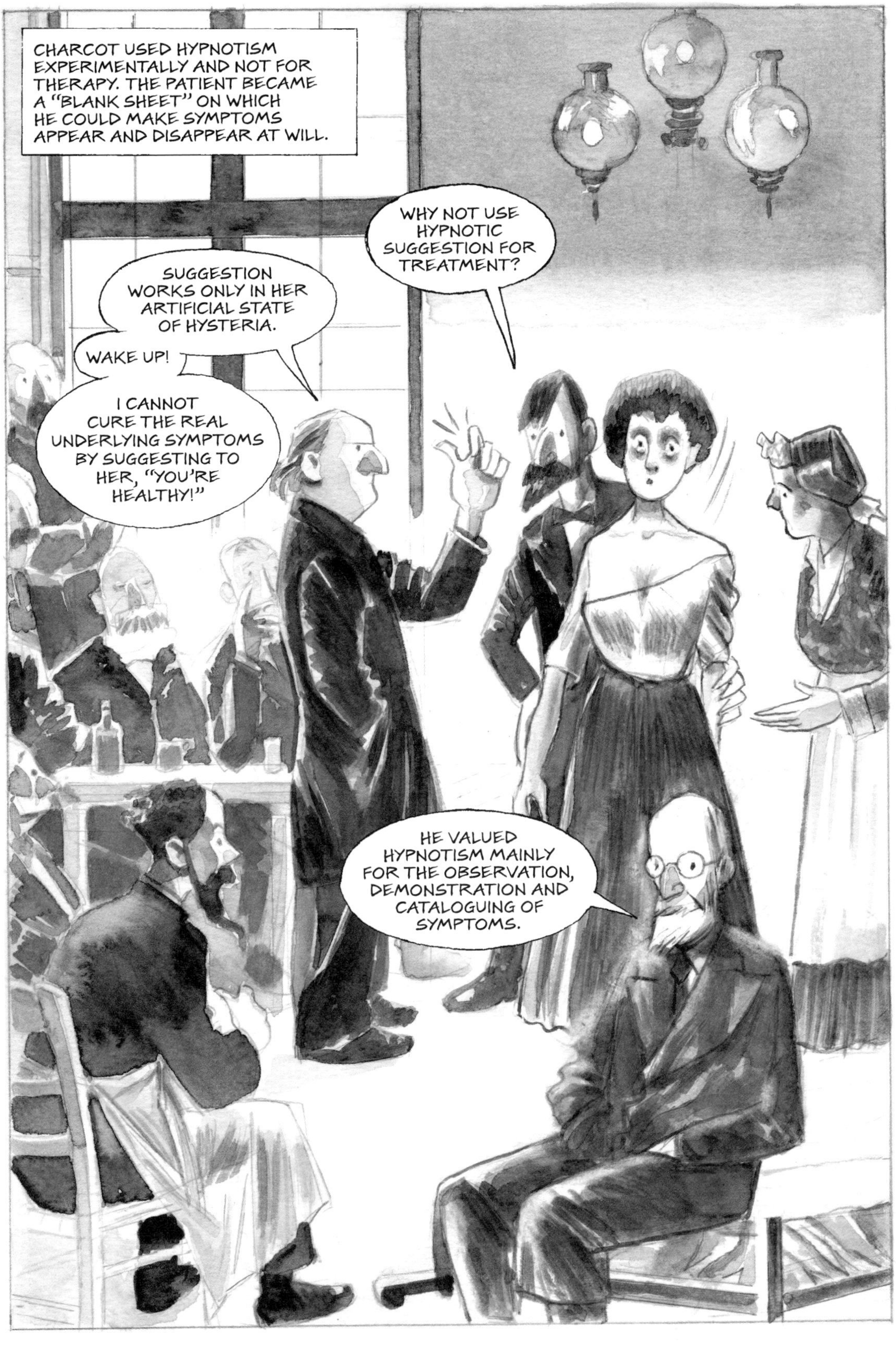

CHARCOT USED HYPNOTISM EXPERIMENTALLY AND NOT FOR THERAPY. THE PATIENT BECAME A "BLANK SHEET" ON WHICH HE COULD MAKE SYMPTOMS APPEAR AND DISAPPEAR AT WILL.
WHY NOT USE HYPNOTIC SUGGESTION FOR TREATMENT?
SUGGESTION WORKS ONLY IN HER ARTIFICIAL STATE OF HYSTERIA.
WAKE UP!
I CANNOT CURE THE REAL UNDERLYING SYMPTOMS BY SUGGESTING TO HER, "YOU'RE HEALTHY!"
HE VALUED HYPNOTISM MAINLY FOR THE OBSERVATION, DEMONSTRATION AND CATALOGUING OF SYMPTOMS.

THERE WAS A LOGIC IN THE DISORDER OF THESE EXTRAORDINARY WOMEN THAT CHARCOT AND HIS ASSISTANT, DÉSIRÉ-MAGLOIRE BOURNEVILLE, BEGAN TO UNRAVEL FOR ME.

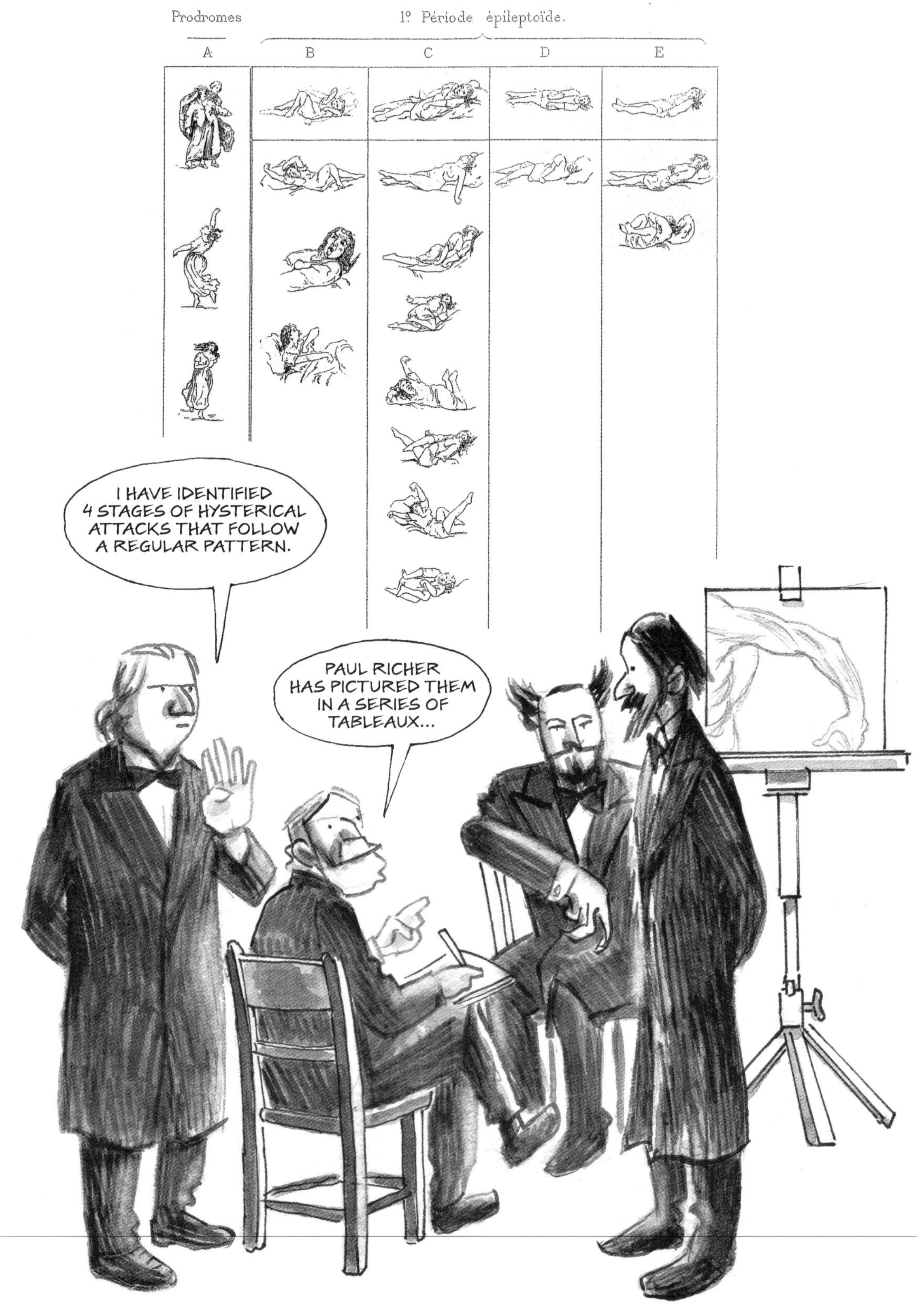
Prodromes
1º Période épileptoïde.
A
B
C
D
E
I HAVE IDENTIFIED 4 STAGES OF HYSTERICAL ATTACKS THAT FOLLOW A REGULAR PATTERN.
PAUL RICHER HAS PICTURED THEM IN A SERIES OF TABLEAUX...

PAUL RICHER, BEAUX-ARTS PROFESSOR OF ANATOMICAL ART, HAD ILLUSTRATED THE AUTOMATON-LIKE POSTURES OF HYSTERICS UNDERGOING EACH STAGE OF THEIR ATTACKS.

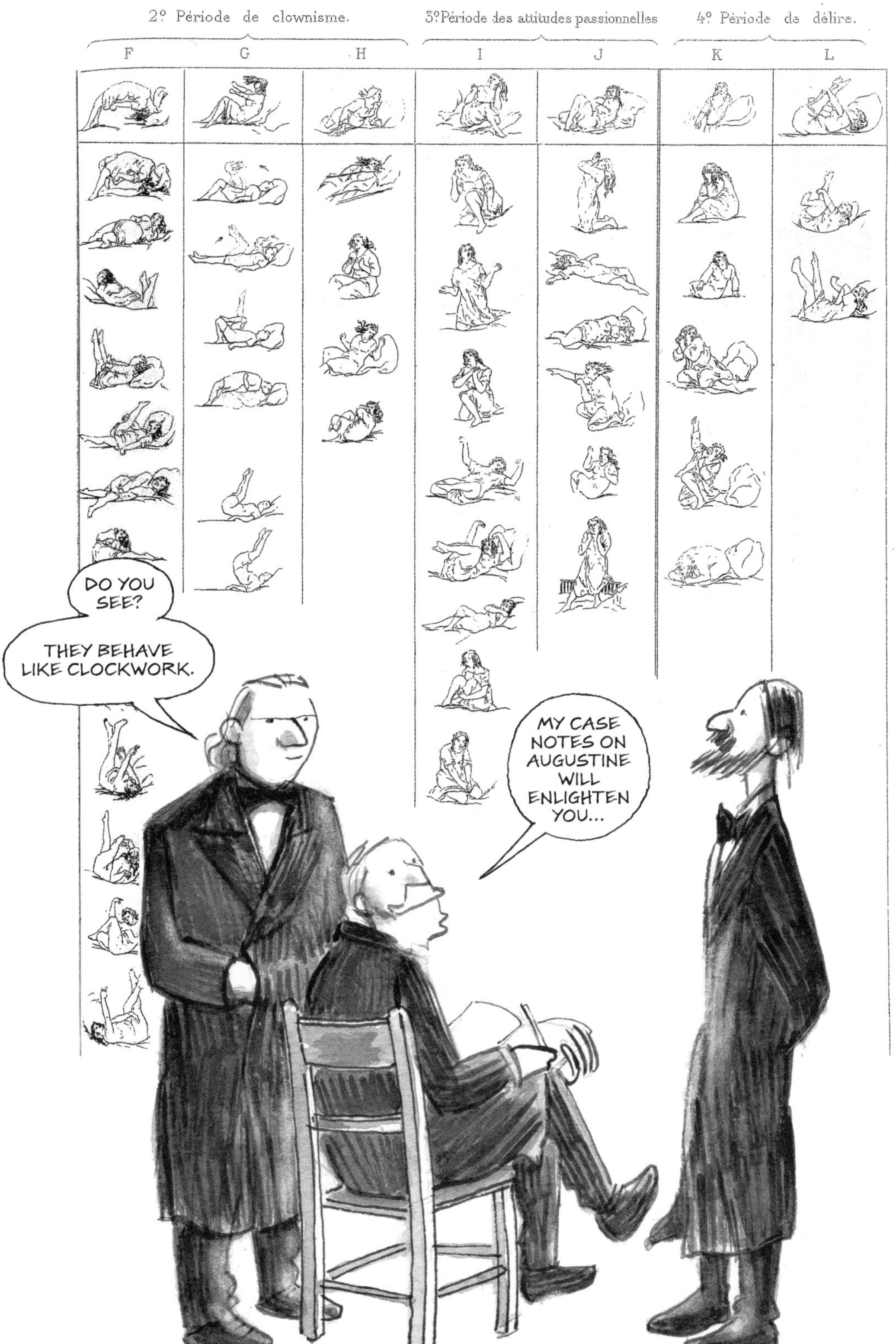

2º Période de clownisme.
3ºPériode des attitudes passionnelles
4º Période de délire.
F
G
H
I
J
K
L
DO YOU SEE?
THEY BEHAVE LIKE CLOCKWORK.
MY CASE NOTES ON AUGUSTINE WILL ENLIGHTEN YOU...

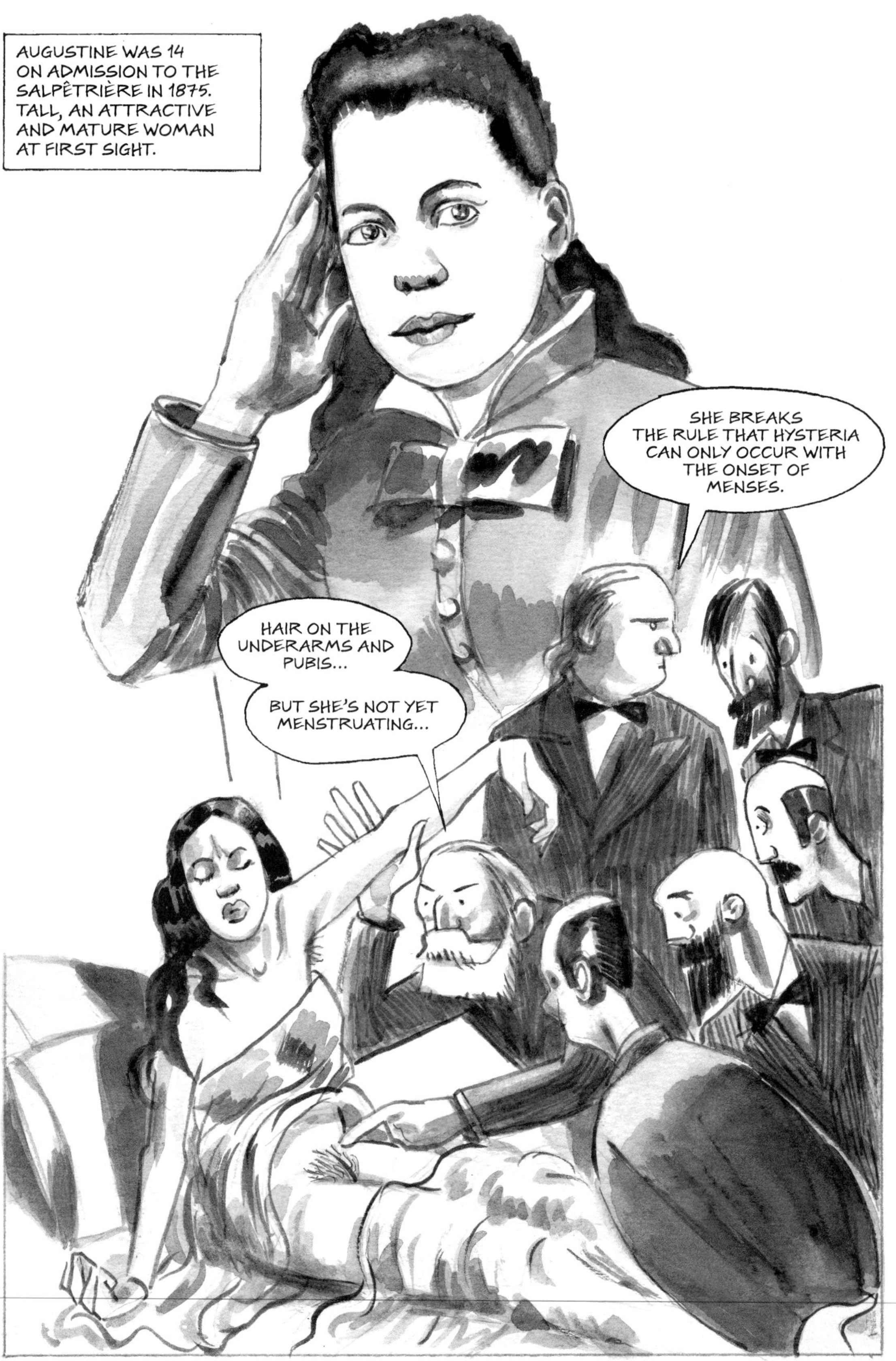
AUGUSTINE WAS 14 ON ADMISSION TO THE SALPÊTRIÈRE IN 1875. TALL, AN ATTRACTIVE AND MATURE WOMAN AT FIRST SIGHT.
HAIR ON THE UNDERARMS AND PUBIS...
BUT SHE'S NOT YET MENSTRUATING...
SHE BREAKS THE RULE THAT HYSTERIA CAN ONLY OCCUR WITH THE ONSET OF MENSES.

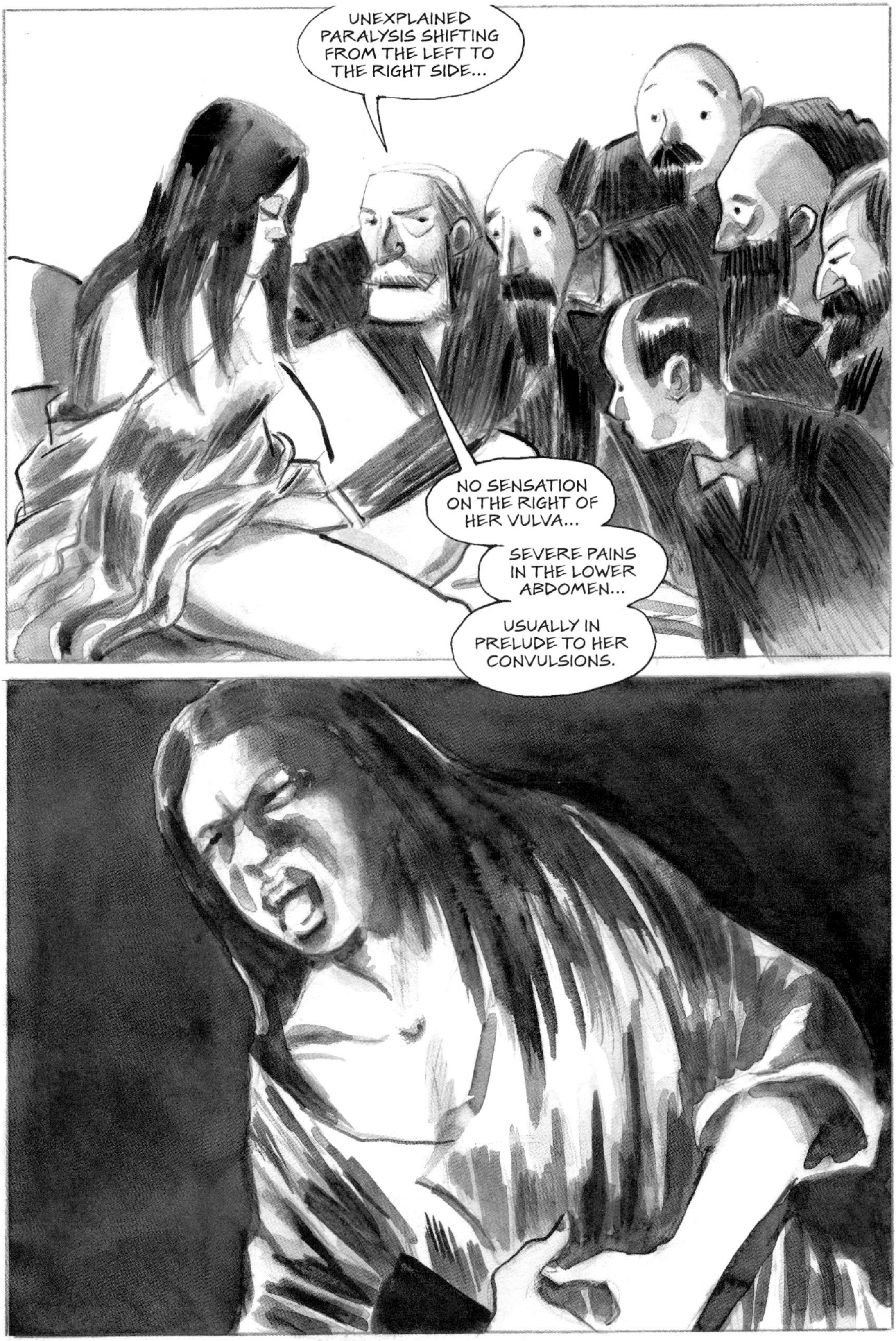
UNEXPLAINED PARALYSIS SHIFTING FROM THE LEFT TO THE RIGHT SIDE...
NO SENSATION ON THE RIGHT OF HER VULVA...
SEVERE PAINS IN THE LOWER ABDOMEN...
USUALLY IN PRELUDE TO HER CONVULSIONS.

AUGUSTINE TOLD THE STORY OF HER RAPE IN "DRAMATIC HYSTERO-MIMIC" POSES AND SCENES. CHARCOT'S ASSISTANT BOURNEVILLE, WHO RECORDED HER ACCOUNT, BECAME THE DEVOTED STENOGRAPHER OF ALL HER UTTERANCES.

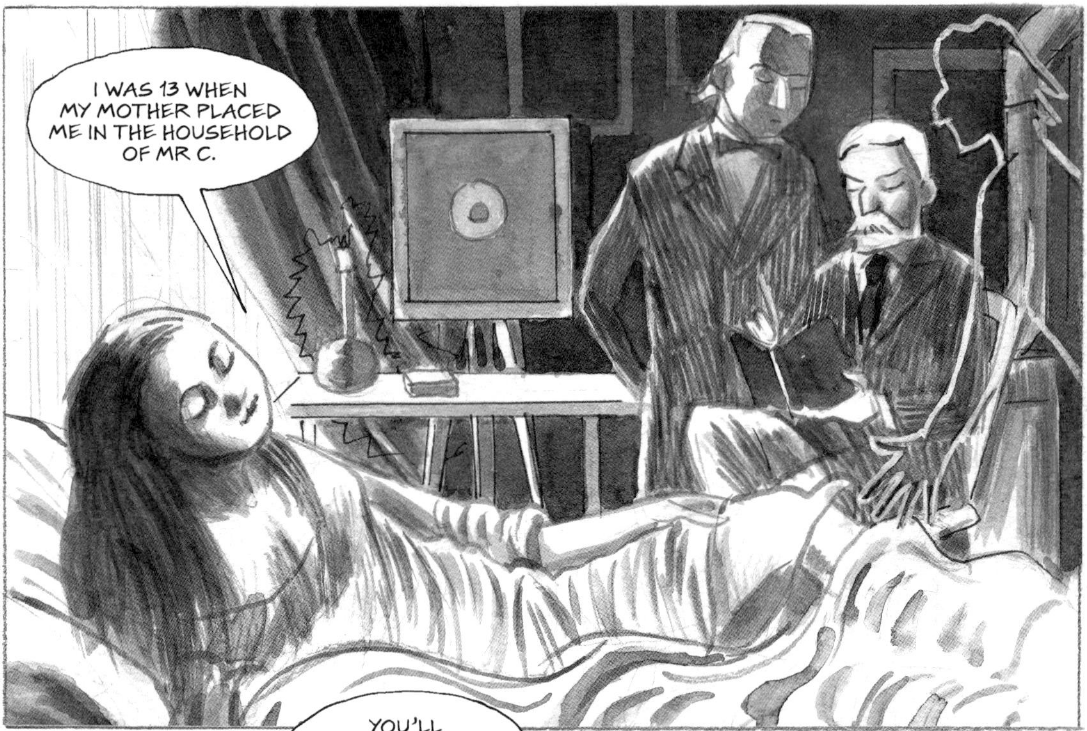
I WAS 13 WHEN MY MOTHER PLACED ME IN THE HOUSEHOLD OF MR C.

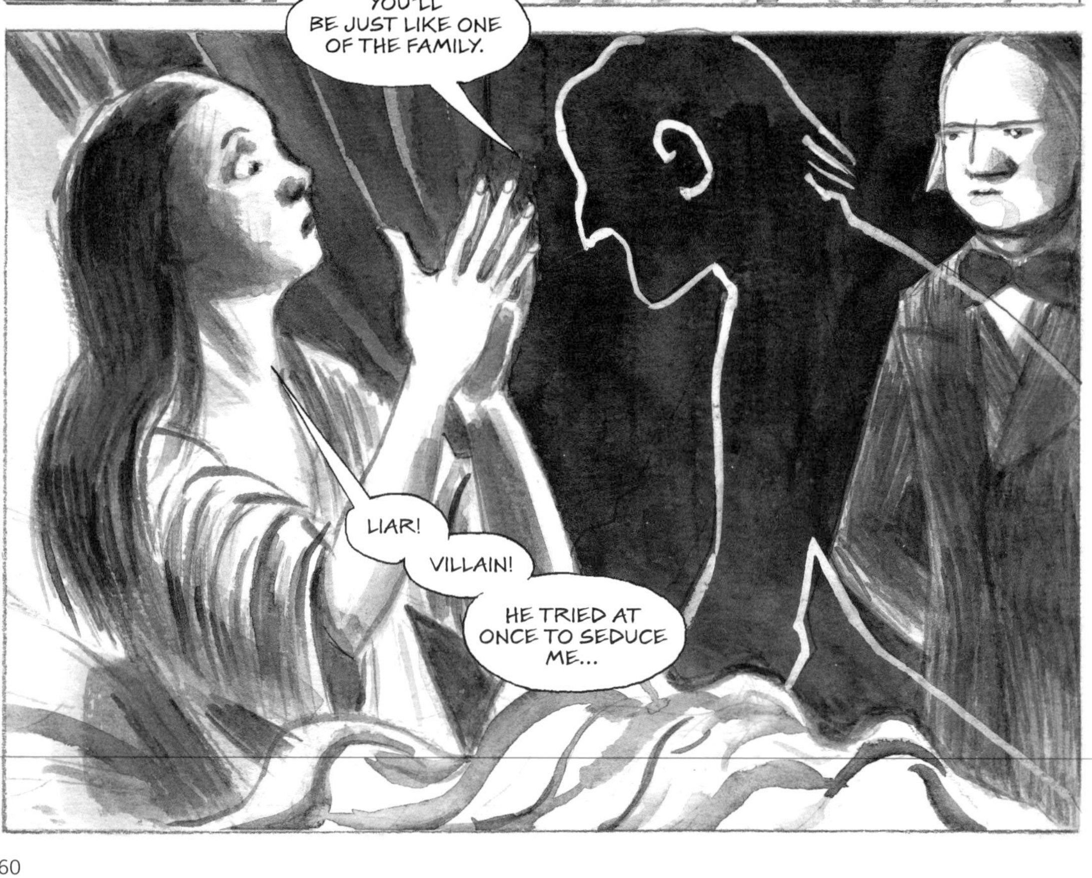
YOU'LL BE JUST LIKE ONE OF THE FAMILY.
LIAR!
VILLAIN!
HE TRIED AT ONCE TO SEDUCE ME...

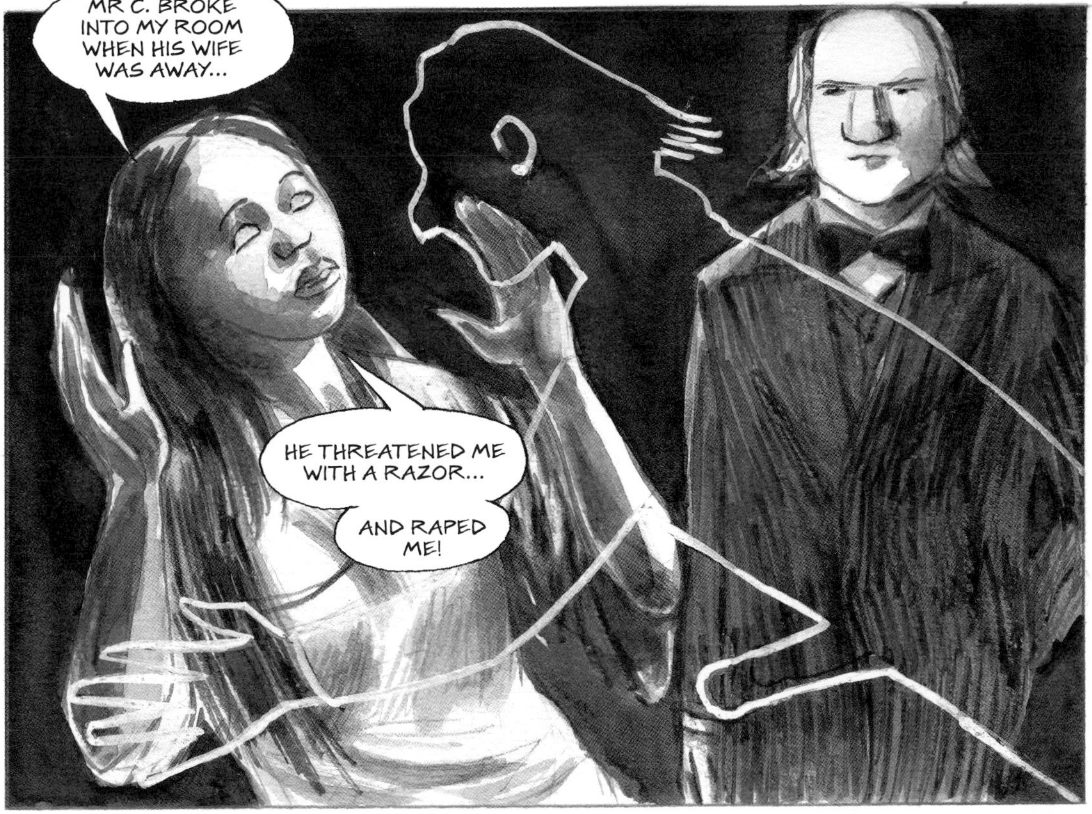
MR C. BROKE INTO MY ROOM WHEN HIS WIFE WAS AWAY...
HE THREATENED ME WITH A RAZOR...
AND RAPED ME!

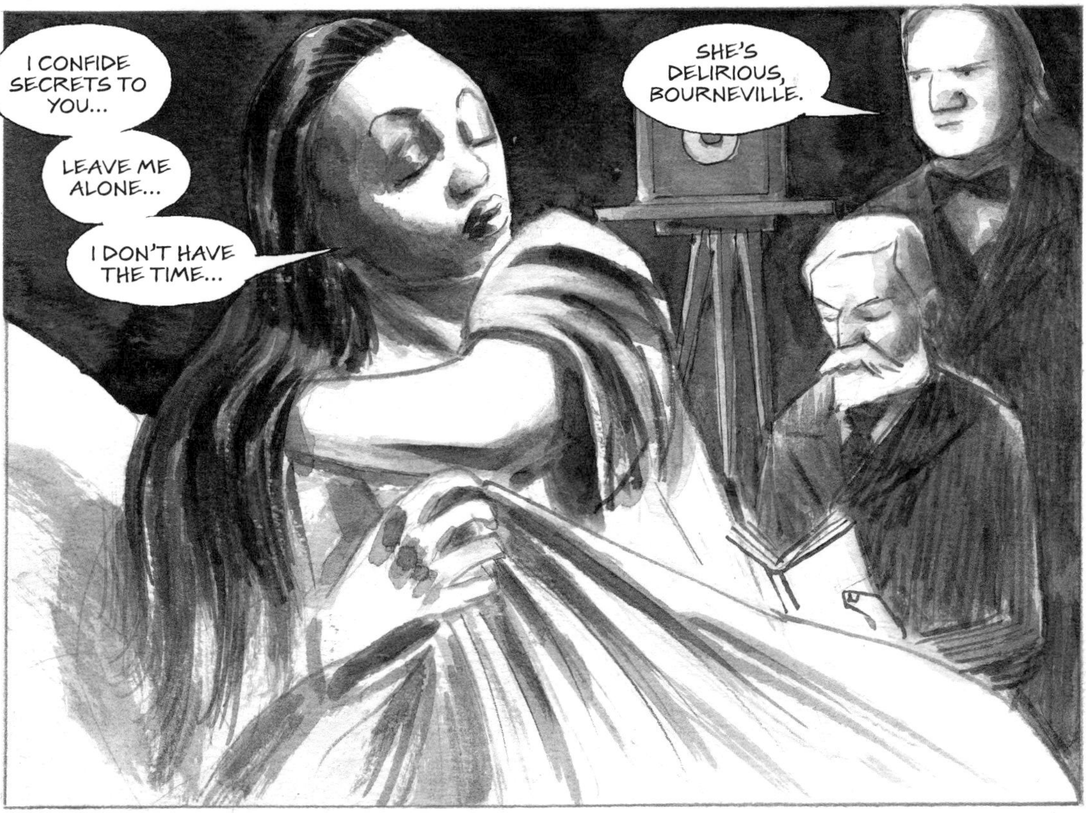
I CONFIDE SECRETS TO YOU...
LEAVE ME ALONE...
I DON'T HAVE THE TIME...
SHE'S DELIRIOUS, BOURNEVILLE.

AUGUSTINE CONFORMED WELL TO CHARCOT'S 4 STAGES, SIGNALLED BY THE PRELIMINARY "AURA" PHASE (FOREWARNING OF THE ATTACK).

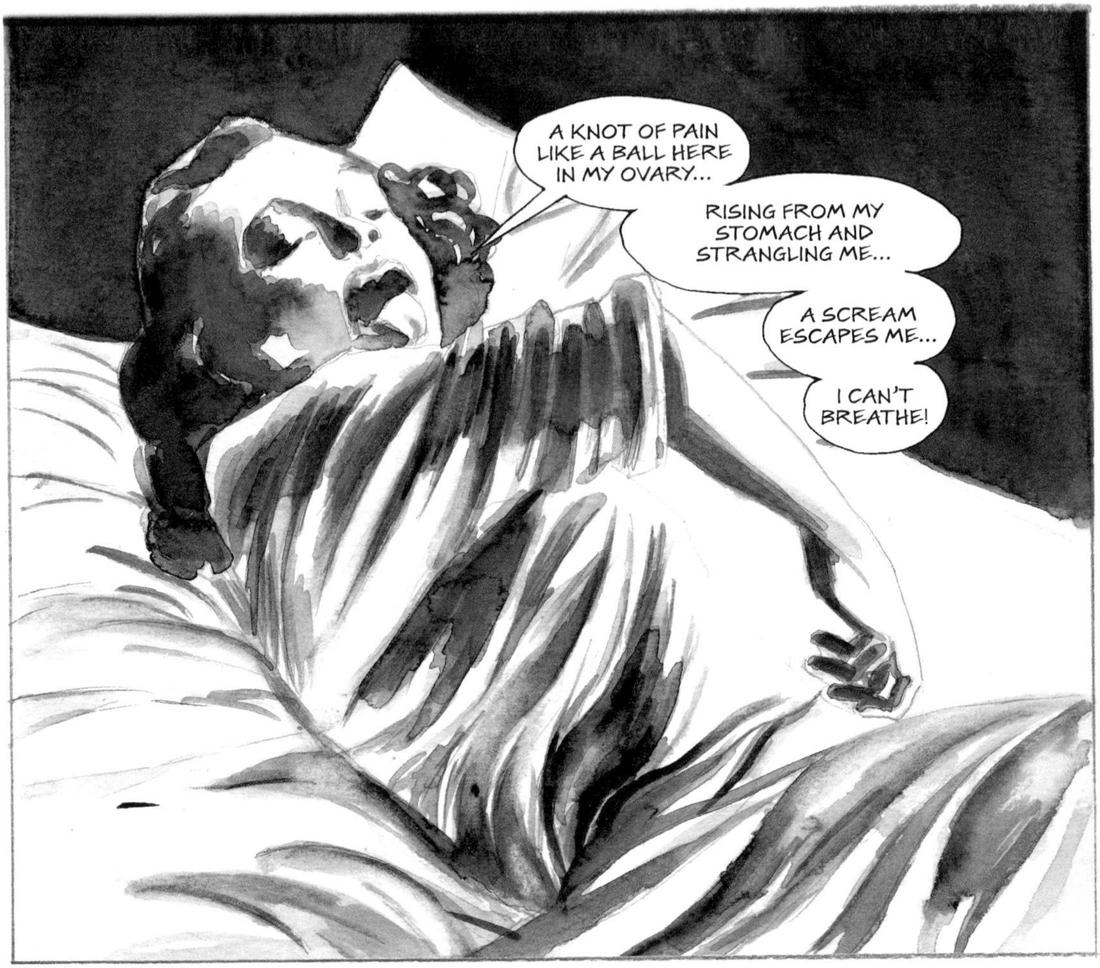
A KNOT OF PAIN LIKE A BALL HERE IN MY OVARY...
RISING FROM MY STOMACH AND STRANGLING ME...
A SCREAM ESCAPES ME...
I CAN'T BREATHE!

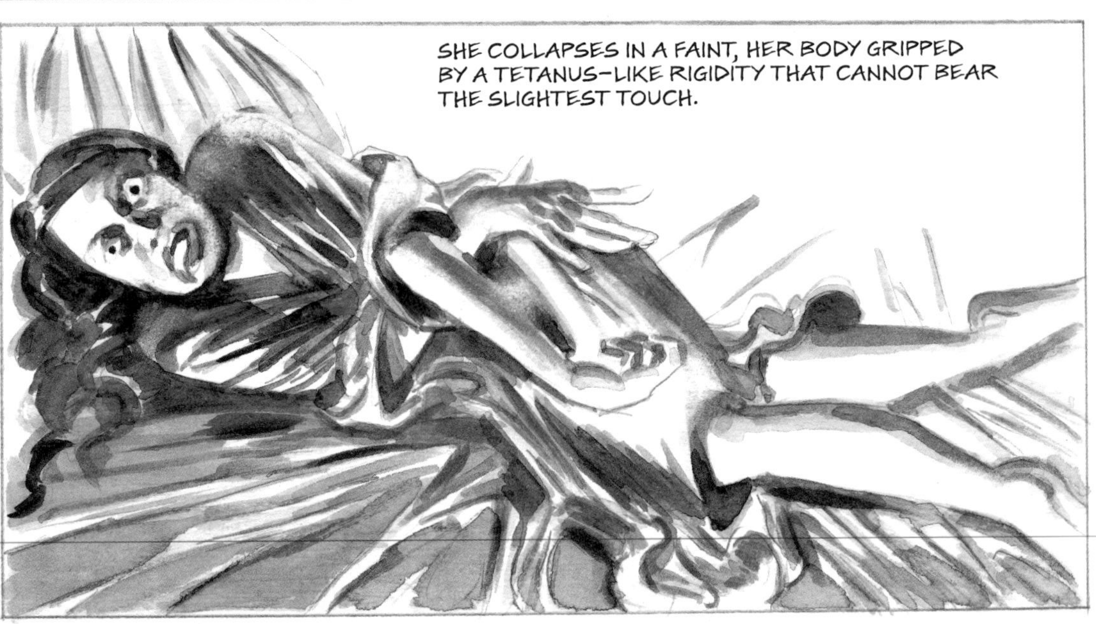
SHE COLLAPSES IN A FAINT, HER BODY GRIPPED BY A TETANUS-LIKE RIGIDITY THAT CANNOT BEAR THE SLIGHTEST TOUCH.

FIRST STAGE: EPILEPTOID CONVULSIONS

AUGUSTINE'S ATTACKS WERE RECORDED BY PAUL REGNARD IN THE SALPÊTRIÈRE'S PHOTO-STUDIO.

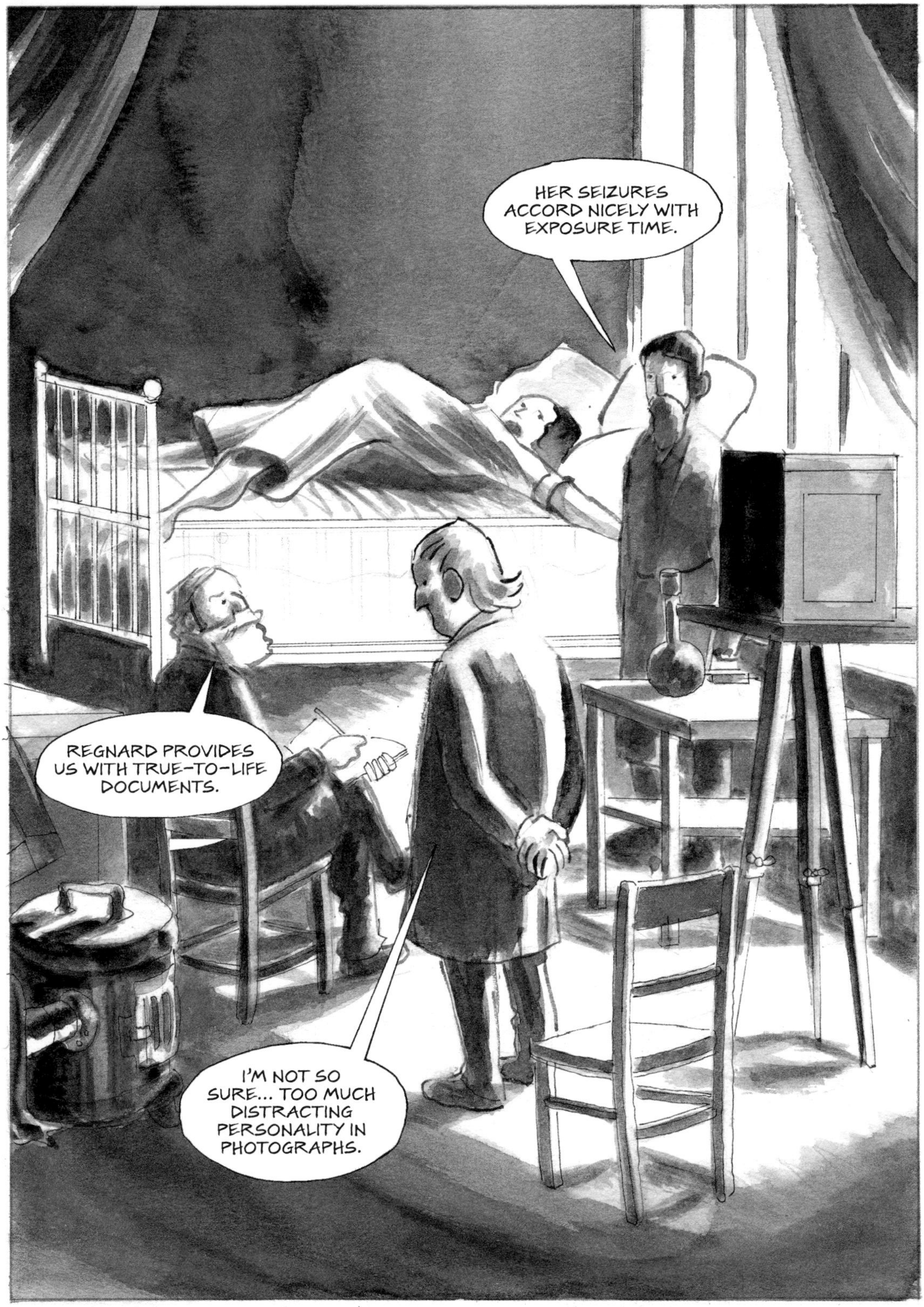
HER SEIZURES ACCORD NICELY WITH EXPOSURE TIME.
REGNARD PROVIDES US WITH TRUE-TO-LIFE DOCUMENTS.
I'M NOT SO SURE... TOO MUCH DISTRACTING PERSONALITY IN PHOTOGRAPHS.

SECOND STAGE: THE "CLOWNISM" SPASMS

HYSTERICS IN THIS STAGE PERFORM AMAZING ACROBATIC STUNTS THAT SEEM TO MOCK THE OBSERVERS.

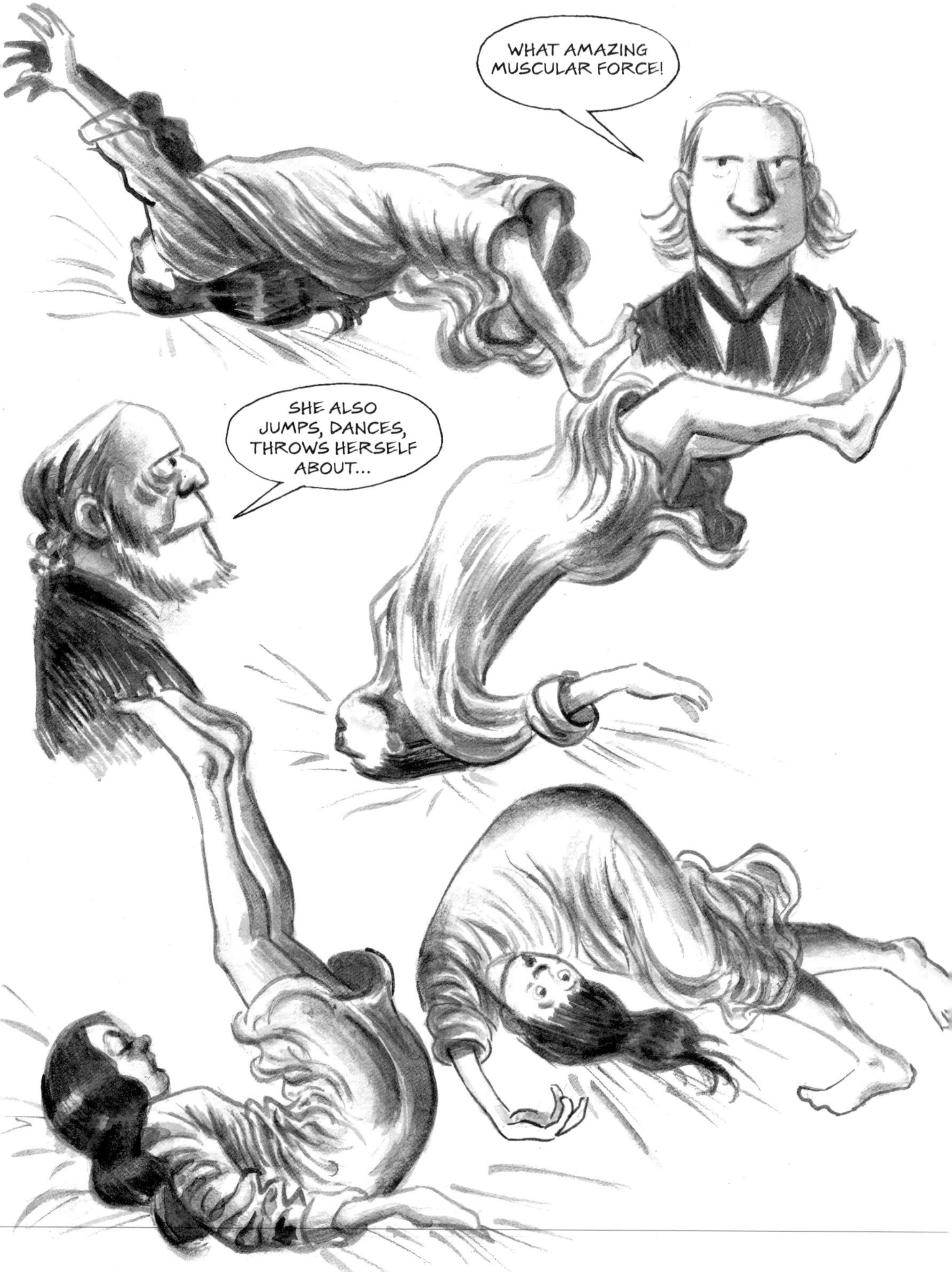
WHAT AMAZING MUSCULAR FORCE!
SHE ALSO JUMPS, DANCES, THROWS HERSELF ABOUT...

THIRD STAGE: THE PASSIONAL POSES

AUGUSTINE'S SERIES OF ECSTATIC POSTURES OFTEN BEGAN WITH THE "CRUCIFIXION" POSE. BOURNEVILLE REPORTED A STORY FROM HER CONVENT-SCHOOL CHILDHOOD.

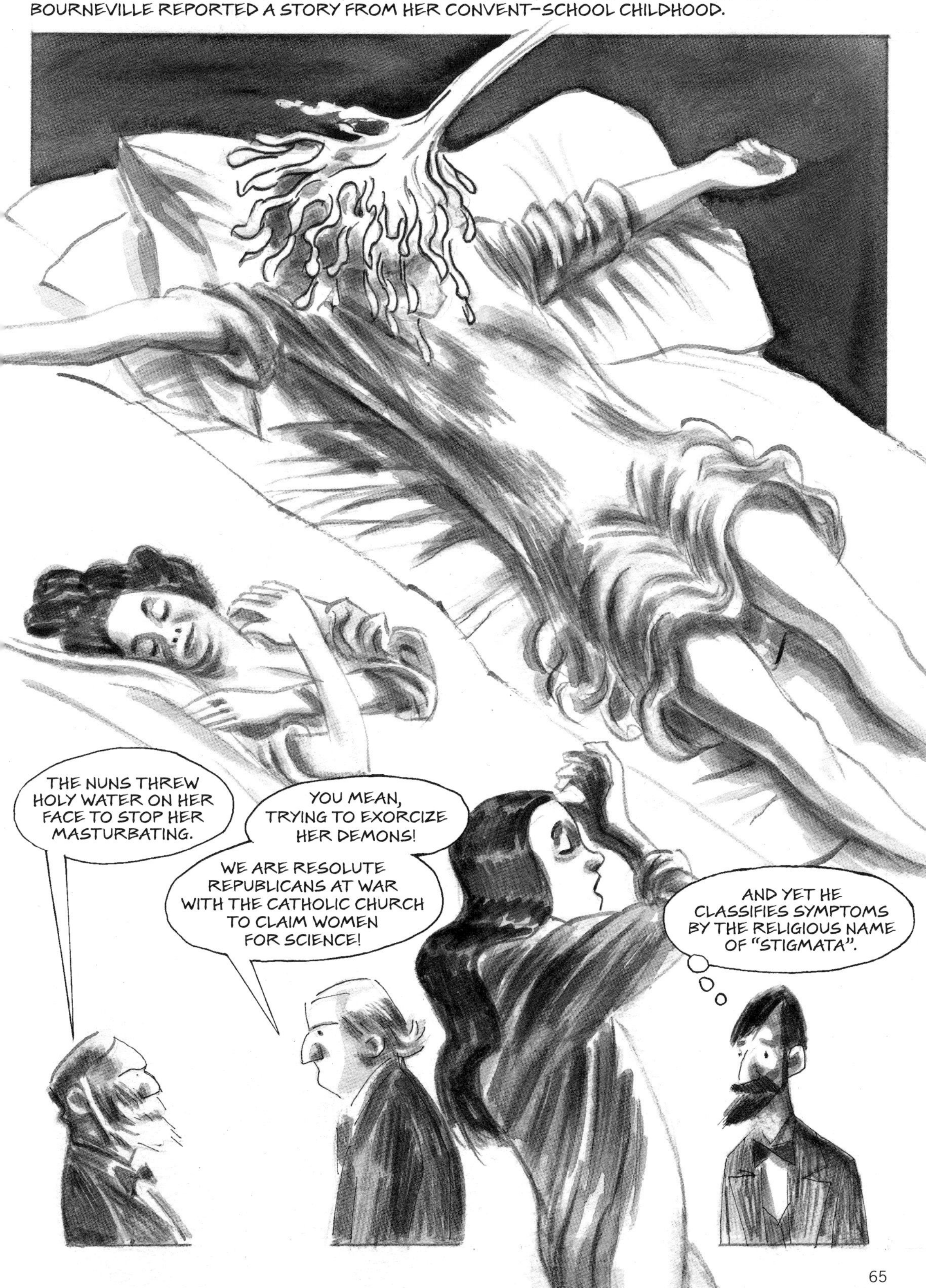

THE NUNS THREW HOLY WATER ON HER FACE TO STOP HER MASTURBATING.
YOU MEAN, TRYING TO EXORCIZE HER DEMONS!
WE ARE RESOLUTE REPUBLICANS AT WAR WITH THE CATHOLIC CHURCH TO CLAIM WOMEN FOR SCIENCE!
AND YET HE CLASSIFIES SYMPTOMS BY THE RELIGIOUS NAME OF "STIGMATA".

FOURTH STAGE: DELIRIUM

HALLUCINATIONS OF A TERRIFYING SOMATIC TYPE OVERCOME THE PATIENT IN THIS FINAL STAGE OF "HYSTERO-EPILEPTIC" ATTACKS.

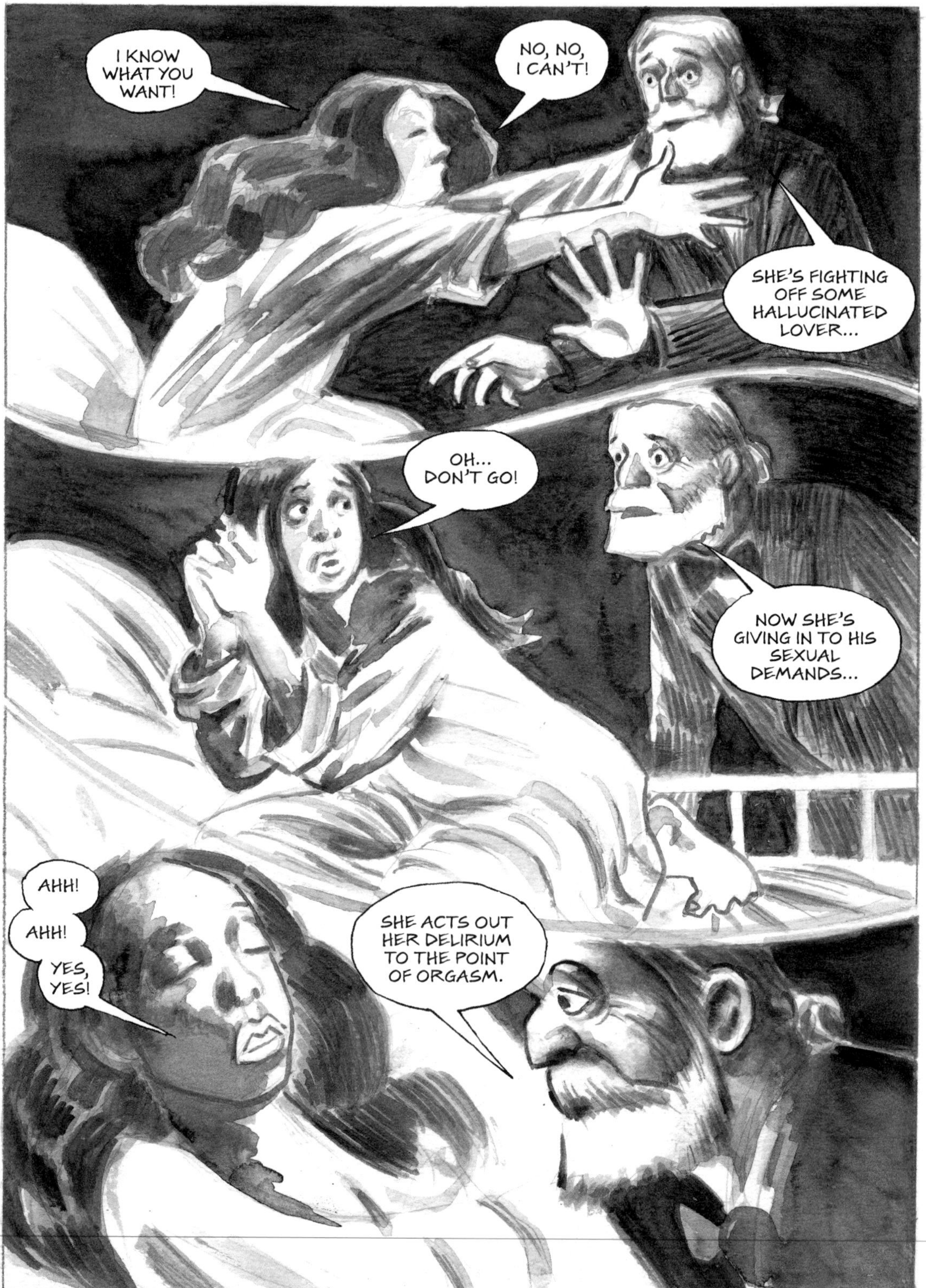

I KNOW WHAT YOU WANT!
NO, NO, I CAN'T!
SHE'S FIGHTING OFF SOME HALLUCINATED LOVER...
OH... DON'T GO!
NOW SHE'S GIVING IN TO HIS SEXUAL DEMANDS...
AHH!
AHH!
YES, YES!
SHE ACTS OUT HER DELIRIUM TO THE POINT OF ORGASM.

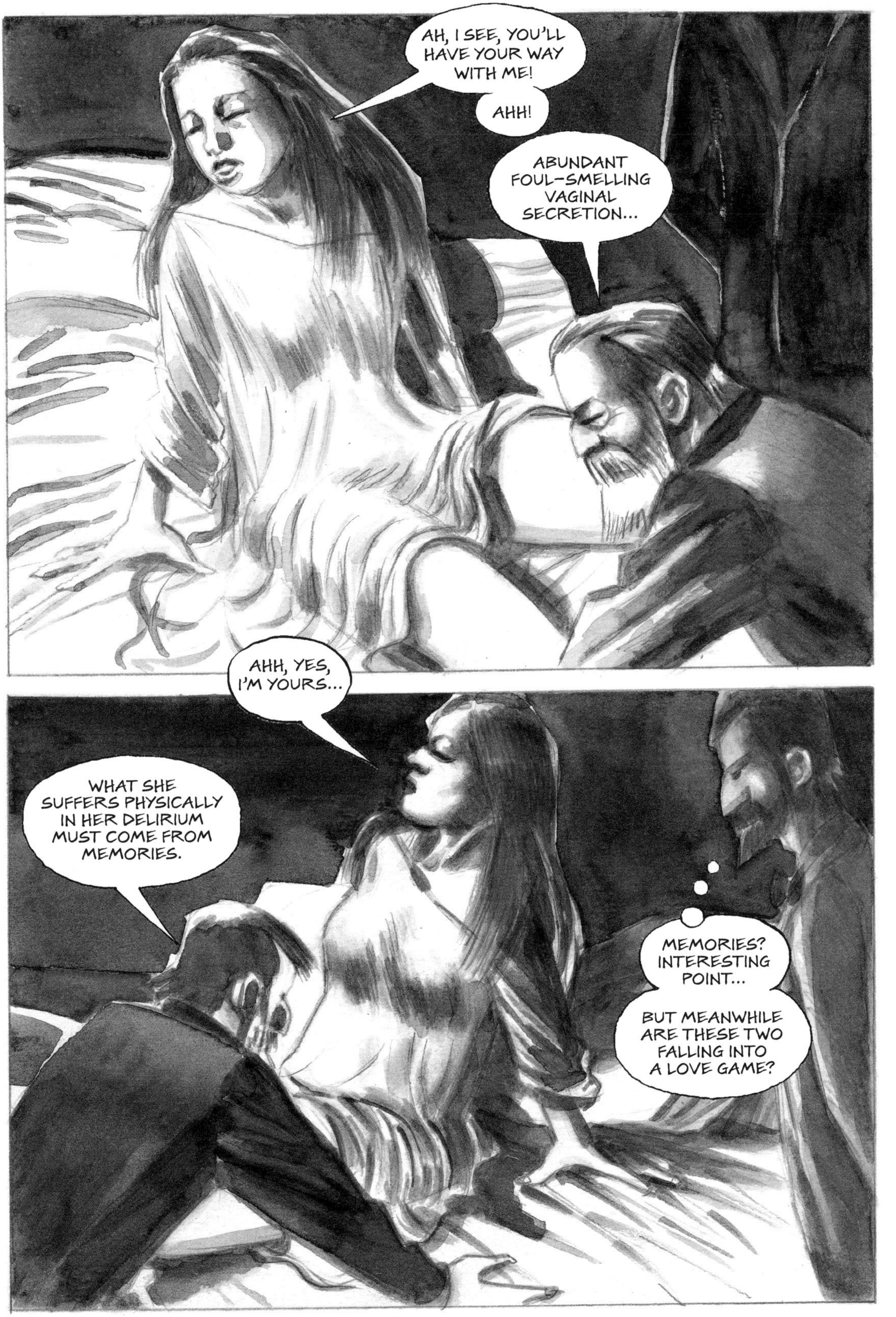
AH, I SEE, YOU'LL HAVE YOUR WAY WITH ME!
AHH!
ABUNDANT FOUL-SMELLING VAGINAL SECRETION...
AHH, YES, I'M YOURS...
WHAT SHE SUFFERS PHYSICALLY IN HER DELIRIUM MUST COME FROM MEMORIES.
MEMORIES? INTERESTING POINT...
BUT MEANWHILE ARE THESE TWO FALLING INTO A LOVE GAME?

CHARCOT BROKE WITH THE UTERINE MYTH OF HYSTERIA WHICH PERMITTED HYSTERECTOMIES AND CLITORAL EXCISIONS. BUT HE MAINTAINED THAT HYSTERO-EPILEPSY WAS OVARIAN IN ORIGIN.

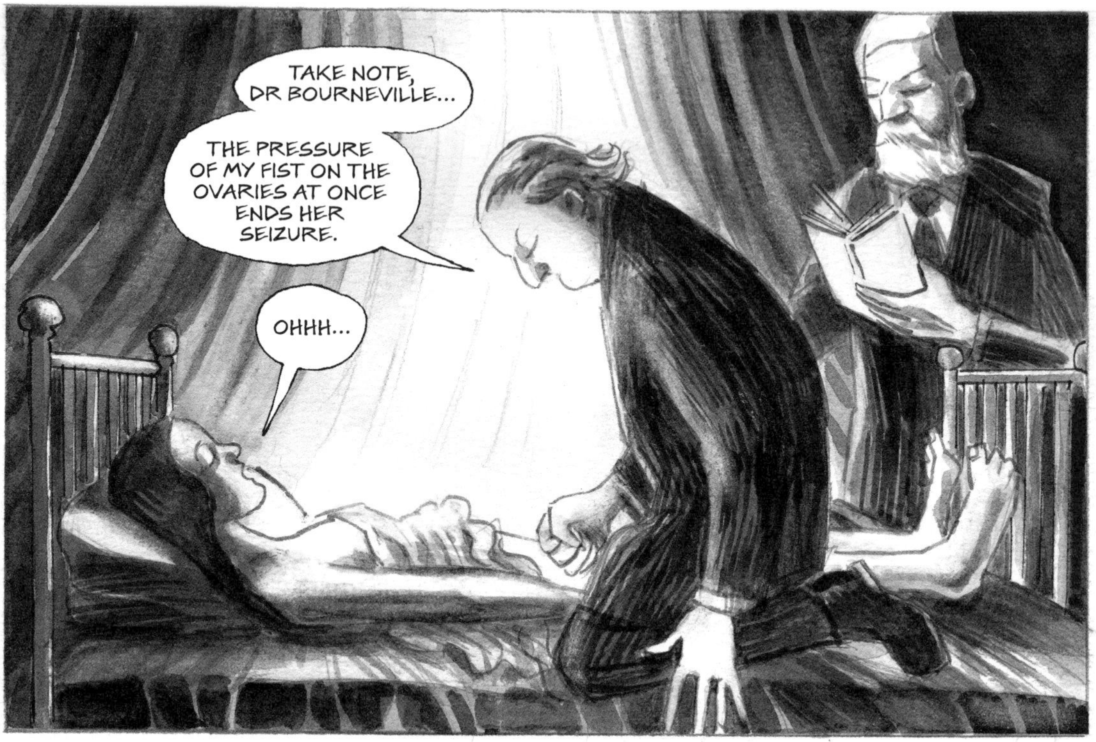
TAKE NOTE, DR BOURNEVILLE...
THE PRESSURE OF MY FIST ON THE OVARIES AT ONCE ENDS HER SEIZURE.
OHHH...

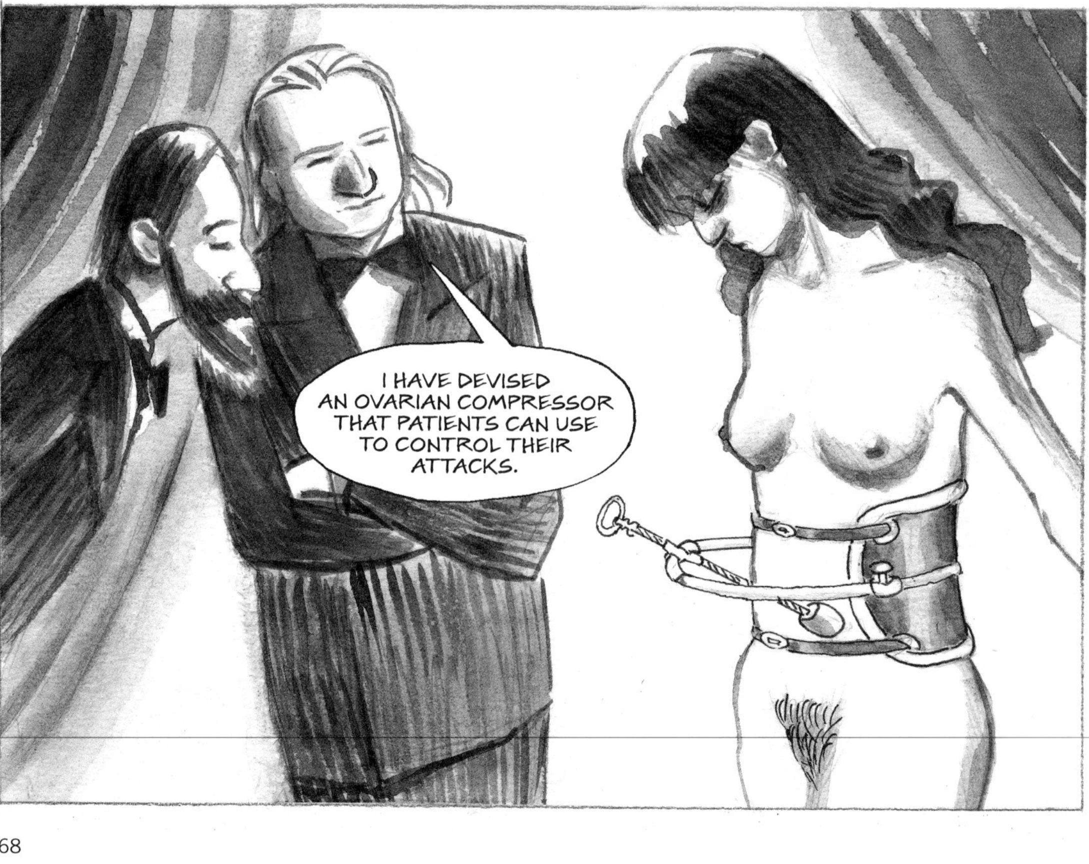
I HAVE DEVISED AN OVARIAN COMPRESSOR THAT PATIENTS CAN USE TO CONTROL THEIR ATTACKS.

BOURNEVILLE RECORDED AUGUSTINE'S DREAM OF A SLAUGHTERHOUSE FROM WHICH SHE AWOKE, MENSTRUATING FOR THE FIRST TIME. HE NOTED SOMETHING ELSE.

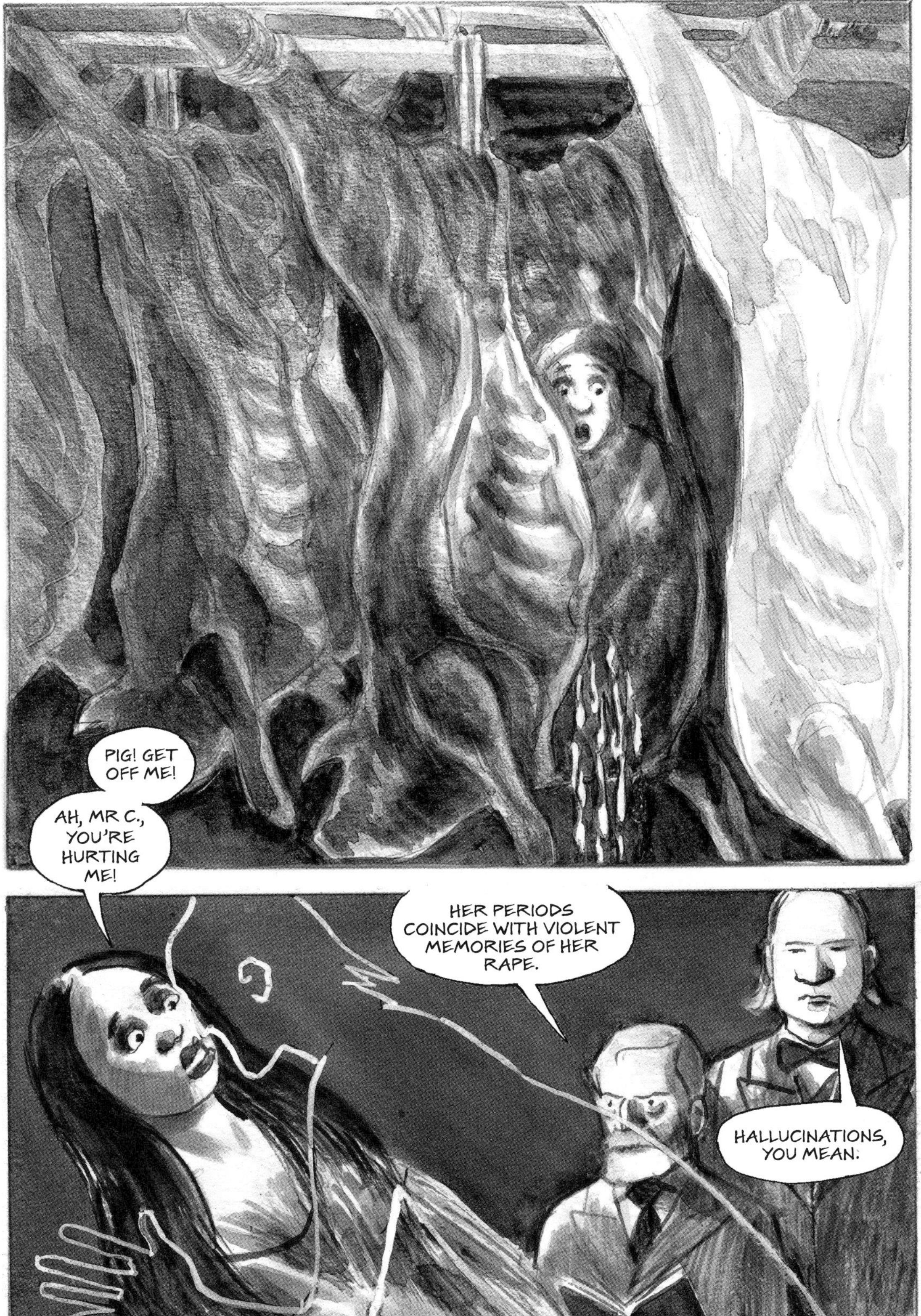
PIG! GET OFF ME!
AH, MR C., YOU'RE HURTING ME!
HER PERIODS COINCIDE WITH VIOLENT MEMORIES OF HER RAPE.
HALLUCINATIONS, YOU MEAN.

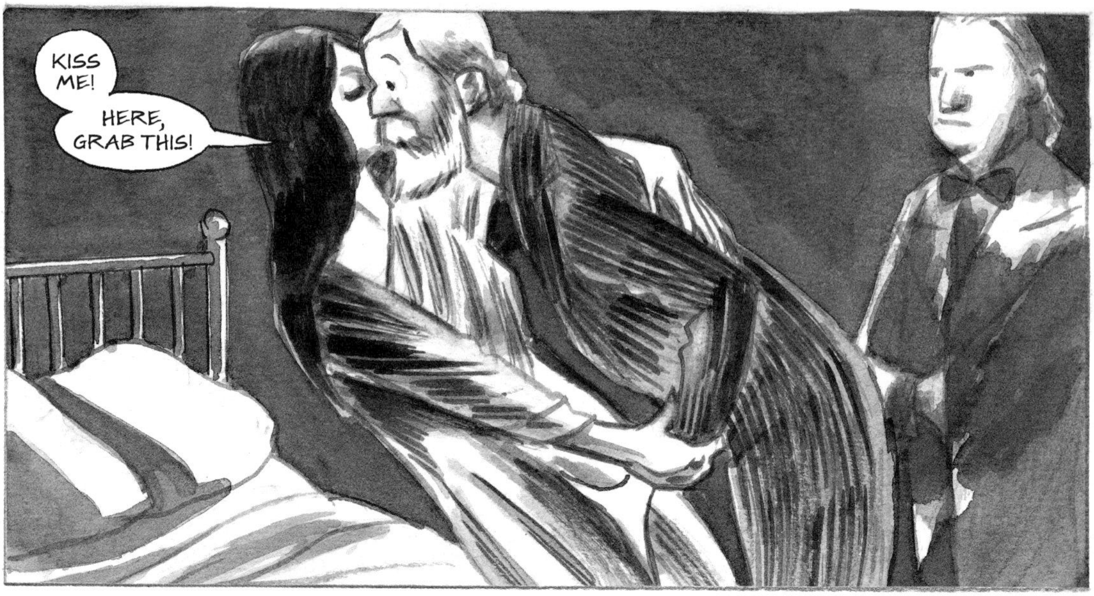
KISS ME!
HERE, GRAB THIS!

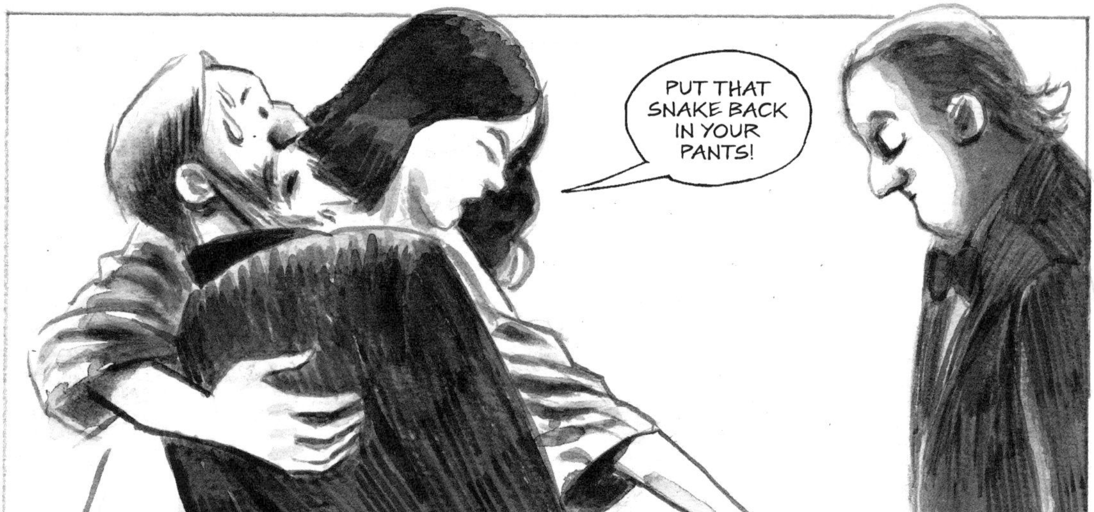
PUT THAT SNAKE BACK IN YOUR PANTS!

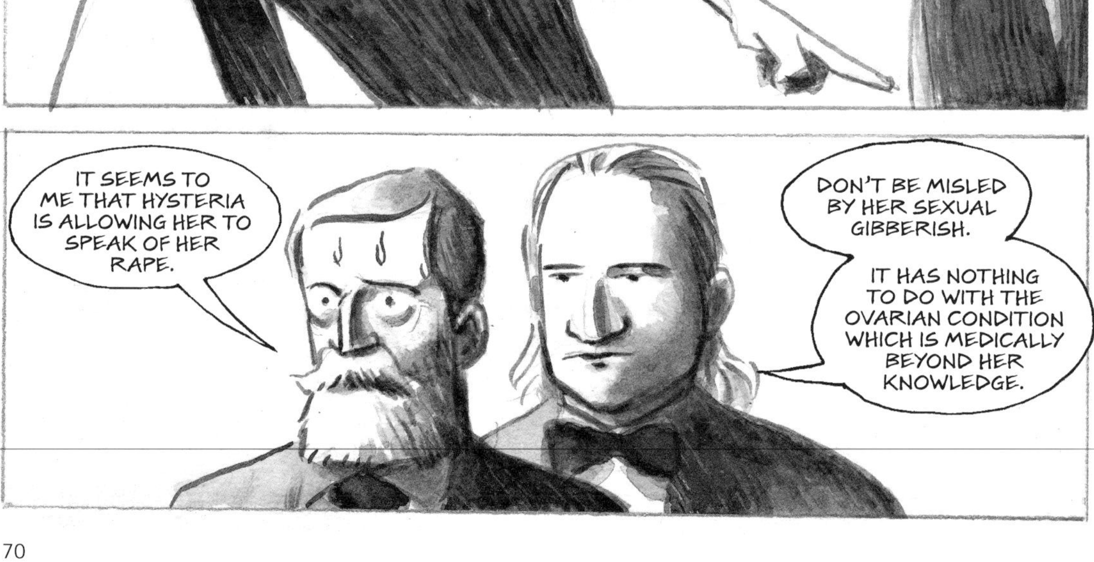
IT SEEMS TO ME THAT HYSTERIA IS ALLOWING HER TO SPEAK OF HER RAPE.
DON'T BE MISLED BY HER SEXUAL GIBBERISH.
IT HAS NOTHING TO DO WITH THE OVARIAN CONDITION WHICH IS MEDICALLY BEYOND HER KNOWLEDGE.

SEXUAL ASSAULT MUST SURELY BE A CAUSE OF HYSTERIA. AND CHARCOT MUST BE AWARE OF IT. I HEARD HIM ADMITTING IT TO A COLLEAGUE AT A SOIRÉE AS HE JUMPED UP AND DOWN IN EXCITEMENT AND HUGGED HIMSELF.

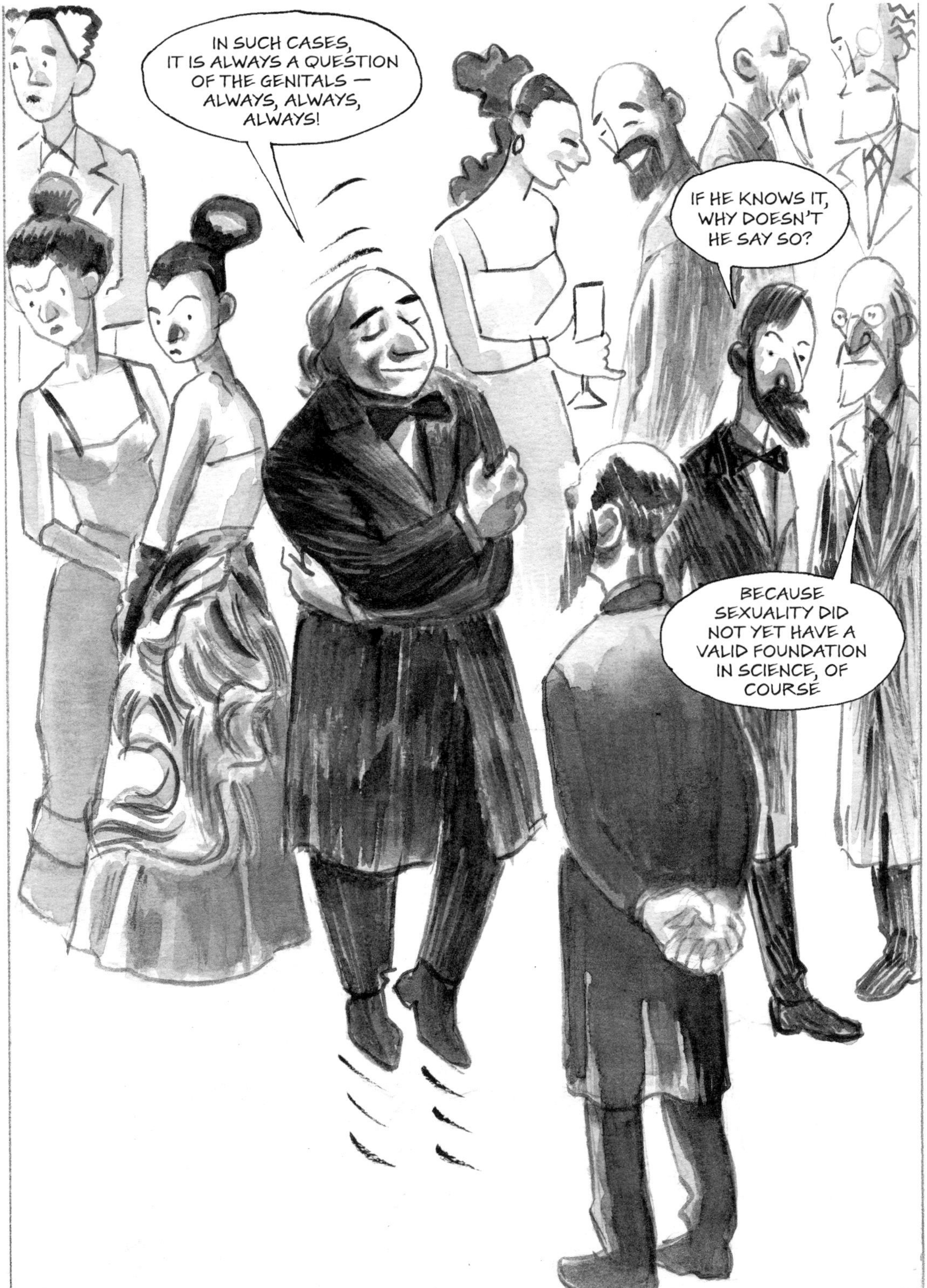
IN SUCH CASES, IT IS ALWAYS A QUESTION OF THE GENITALS — ALWAYS, ALWAYS, ALWAYS!
IF HE KNOWS IT, WHY DOESN'T HE SAY SO?
BECAUSE SEXUALITY DID NOT YET HAVE A VALID FOUNDATION IN SCIENCE, OF COURSE

AUGUSTINE WAS CHARCOT'S STAR ATTRACTION. HER MODEL BEHAVIOUR EARNED HER THE JOB OF ASSISTANT NURSE.

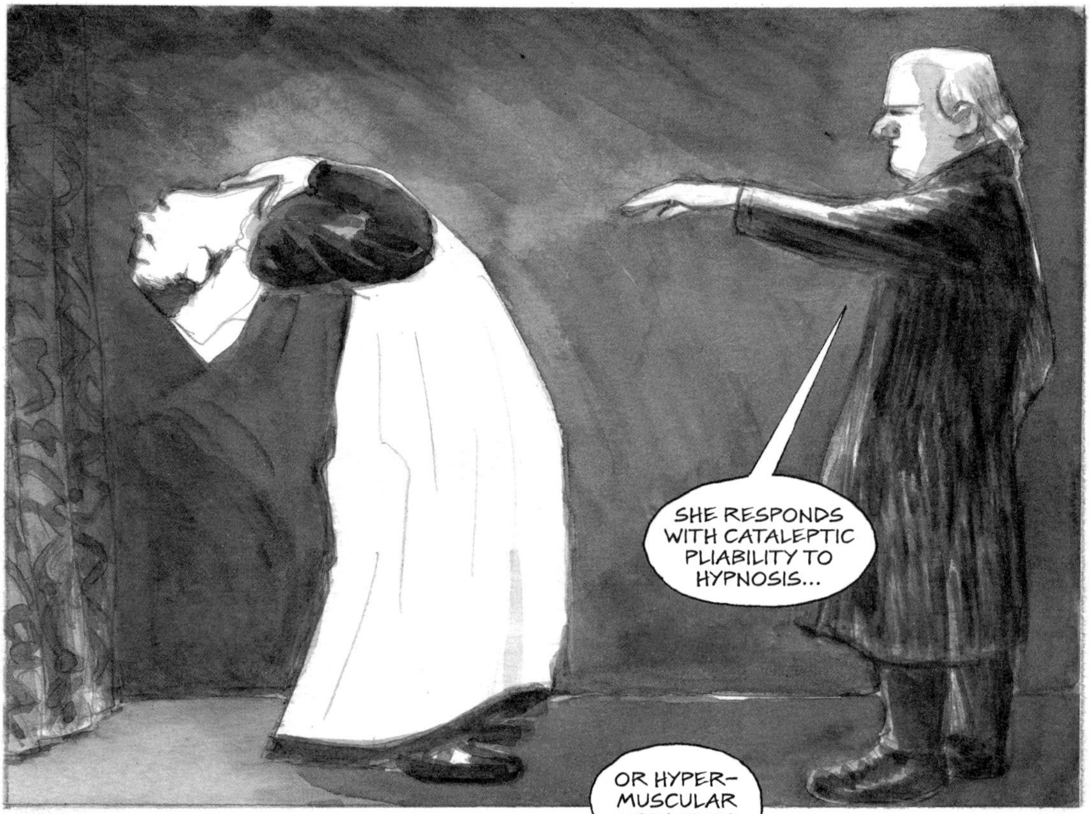
SHE RESPONDS WITH CATALEPTIC PLIABILITY TO HYPNOSIS...
OR HYPER-MUSCULAR LETHARGY.

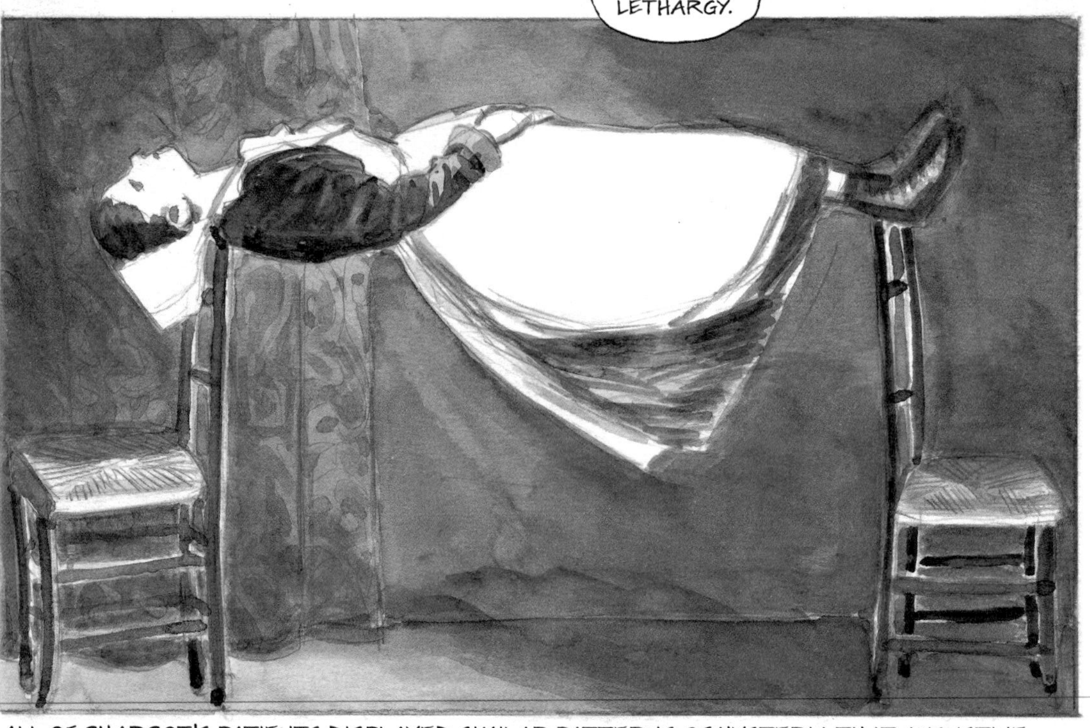

ALL OF CHARCOT'S PATIENTS DISPLAYED SIMILAR PATTERNS OF HYSTERIA THAT AUGUSTINE PERFORMED WITH GREATER TALENT.

HYPNOSIS COULD TRIGGER OR ARREST SYMPTOMS. OTHER CONTROLS INCLUDED ELECTRO-THERAPY, INHALATIONS OF AMYL NITRATE, CHLORAL AND ETHER. AUGUSTINE BECAME ADDICTED TO ETHER.

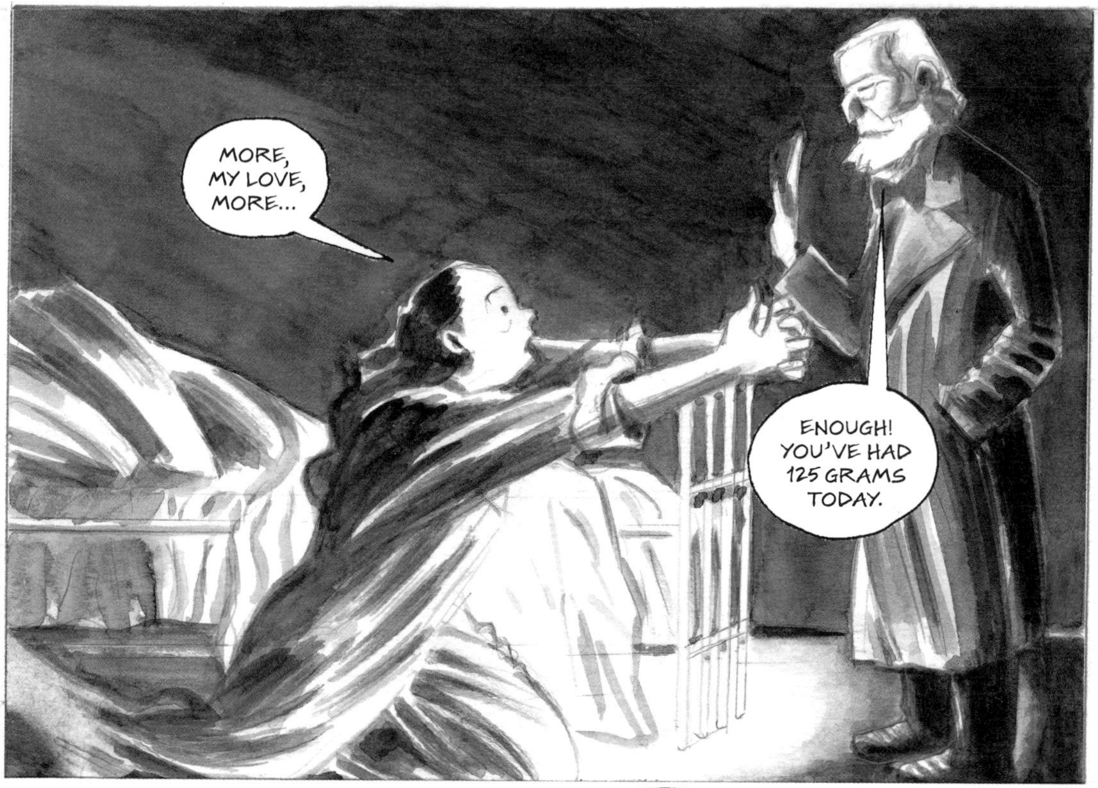
MORE, MY LOVE, MORE...
ENOUGH! YOU'VE HAD 125 GRAMS TODAY.

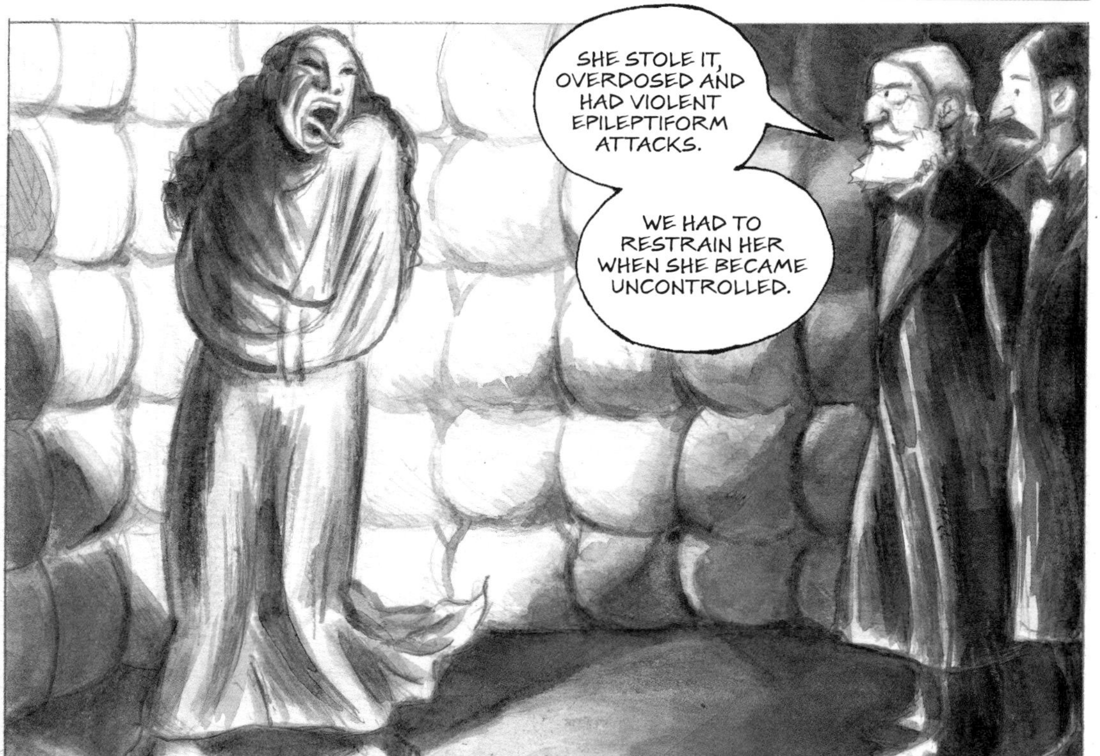
SHE STOLE IT, OVERDOSED AND HAD VIOLENT EPILEPTIFORM ATTACKS.
WE HAD TO RESTRAIN HER WHEN SHE BECAME UNCONTROLLED.

AUGUSTINE SAW — OR IMAGINED SEEING — HER RAPIST MR C. IN THE AUDIENCE AT ONE OF CHARCOT'S DEMONSTRATIONS. MR C., THE 'C' OF CHARCOT?
I COULD ONLY WONDER.

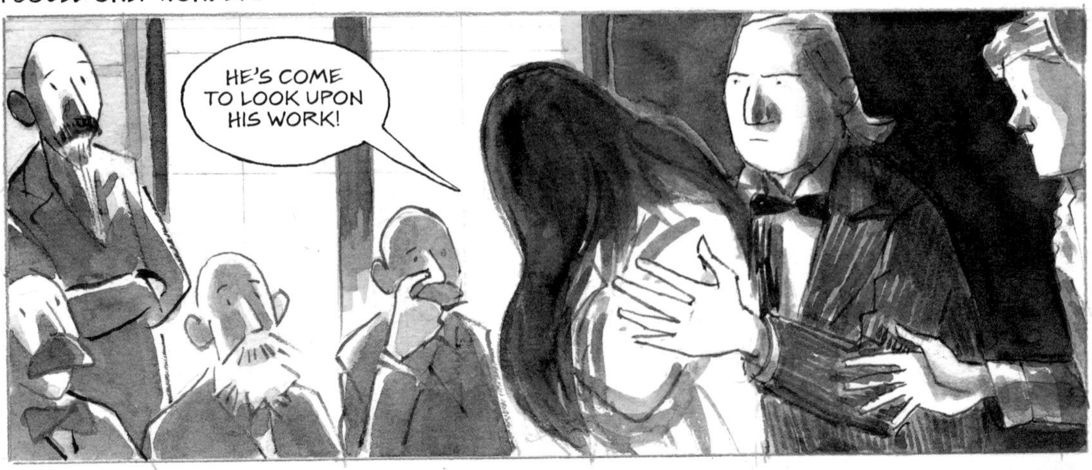
HE'S COME TO LOOK UPON HIS WORK!

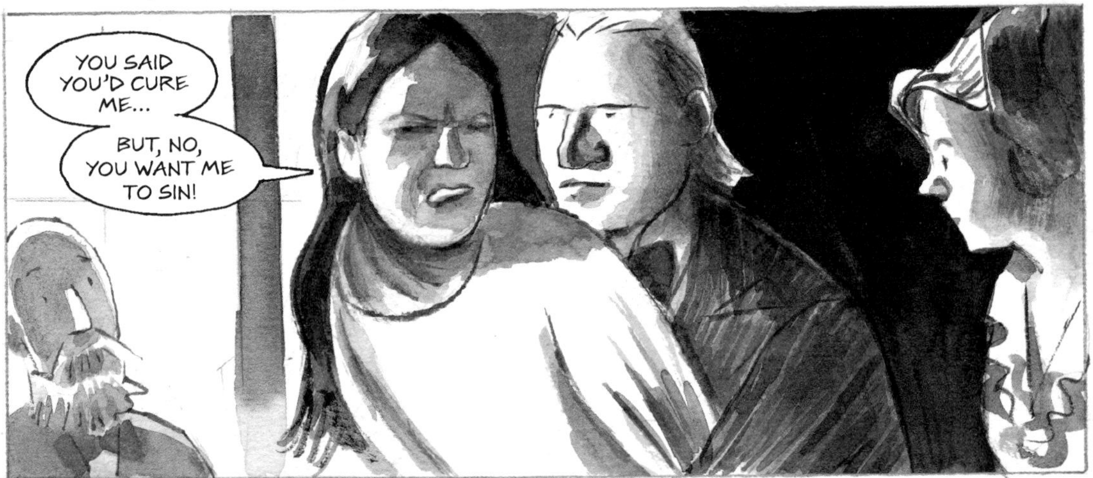
YOU SAID YOU'D CURE ME...
BUT, NO, YOU WANT ME TO SIN!

125 ATTACKS FOLLOWED THAT DAY. IN HER DELIRIUM SHE EXCLAIMED...

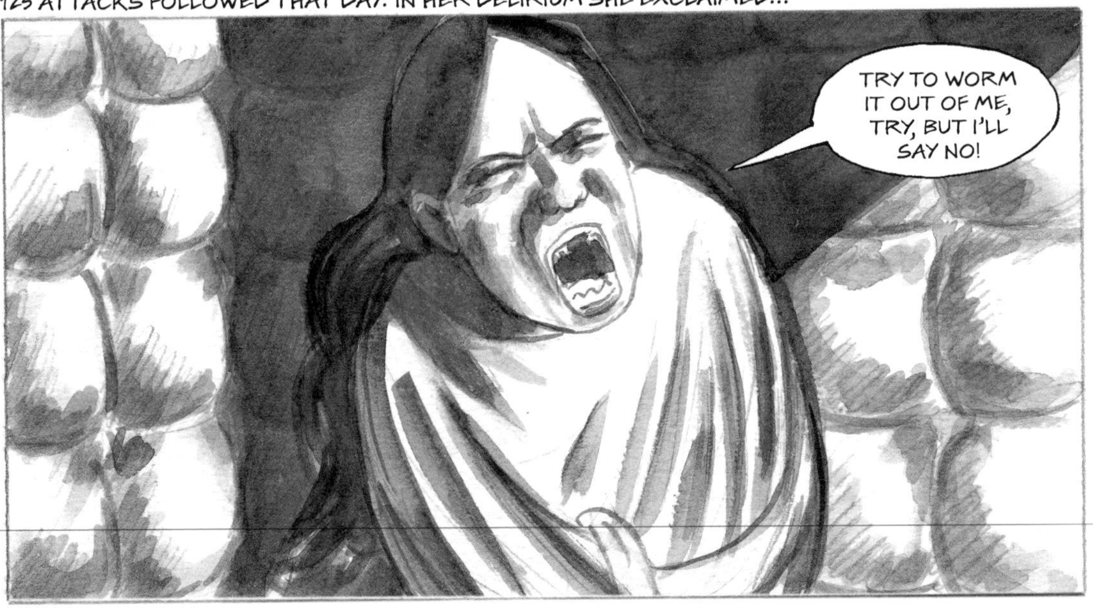
TRY TO WORM IT OUT OF ME, TRY, BUT I'LL SAY NO!

AUGUSTINE'S 16 MONTHS AS APPRENTICE NURSE ENDED WITH HER RELAPSE. SHE BECAME VIOLENT, TORE HER STRAITJACKET AND WAS PUT IN A CELL FOR TWO MONTHS.

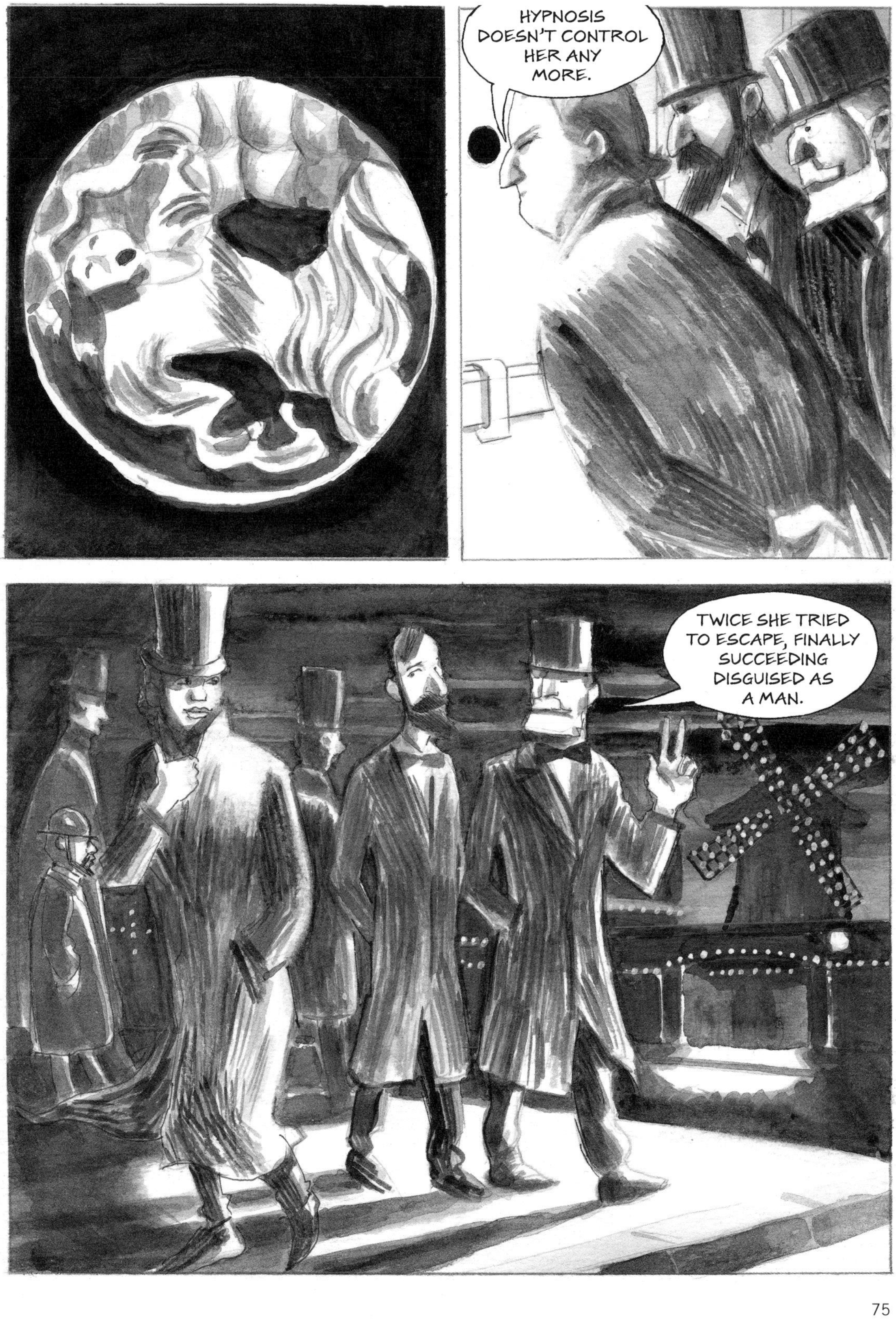
HYPNOSIS DOESN'T CONTROL HER ANY MORE.
TWICE SHE TRIED TO ESCAPE, FINALLY SUCCEEDING DISGUISED AS A MAN.

I VISITED A FORMER SALPÊTRIÈRE PATIENT, JANE AVRIL, NOW A FAMOUS CANCAN DANCER AT THE MOULIN ROUGE.

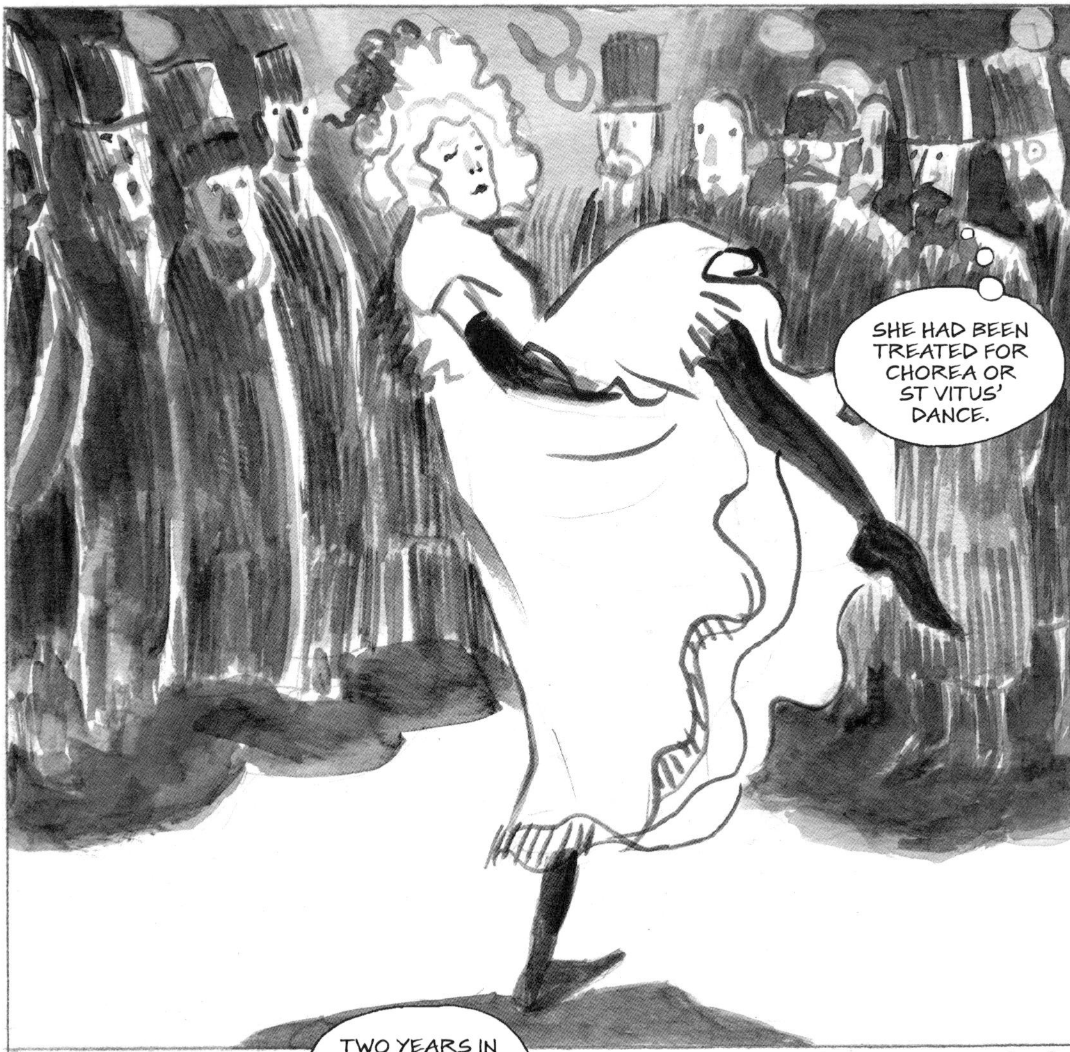
SHE HAD BEEN TREATED FOR CHOREA OR ST VITUS' DANCE.

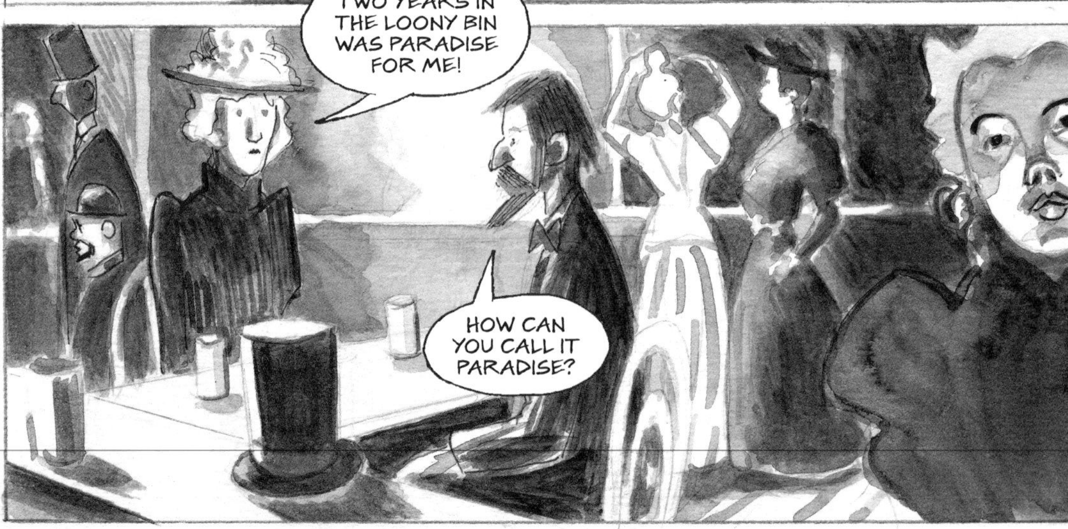
TWO YEARS IN THE LOONY BIN WAS PARADISE FOR ME!
HOW CAN YOU CALL IT PARADISE?

PARADISE FOR A GIRL OF 14, ILL-TREATED AT HOME, WHO FOUND PROTECTION WITH "THE FAT PARTRIDGE", "THE GNOME" AND OTHERS IN CHARCOT'S WARD OF HYSTERICS.

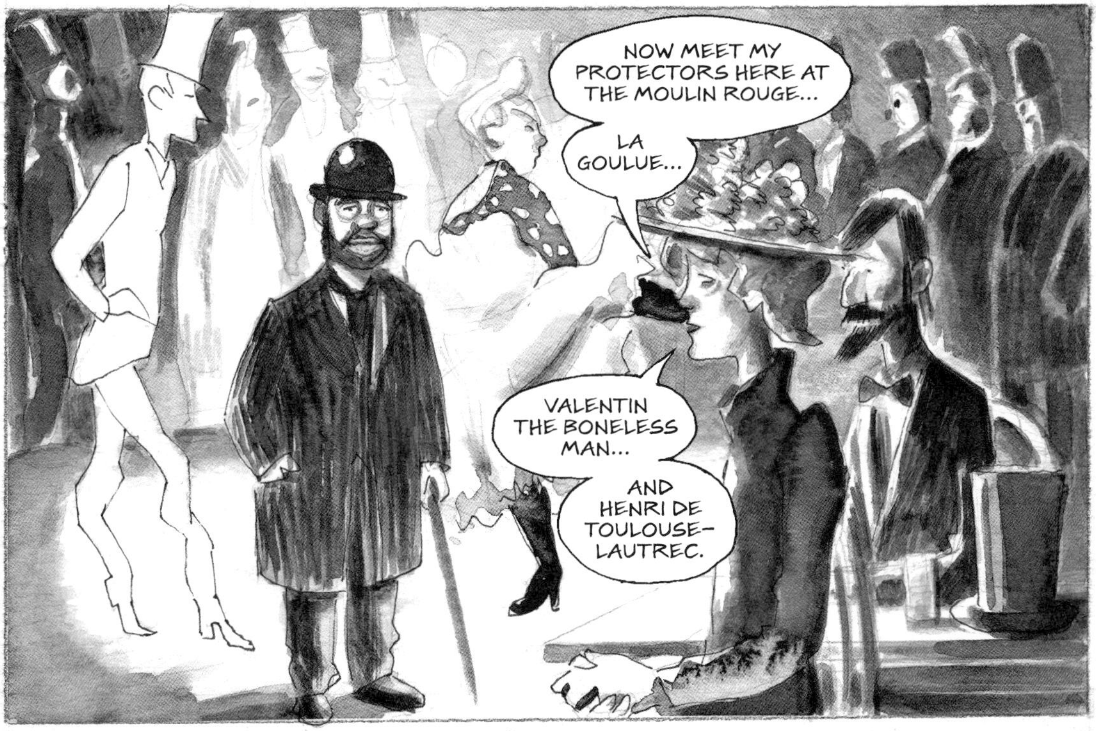

NOW MEET MY PROTECTORS HERE AT THE MOULIN ROUGE...
LA GOULUE...
VALENTIN THE BONELESS MAN...
AND HENRI DE TOULOUSE-LAUTREC.

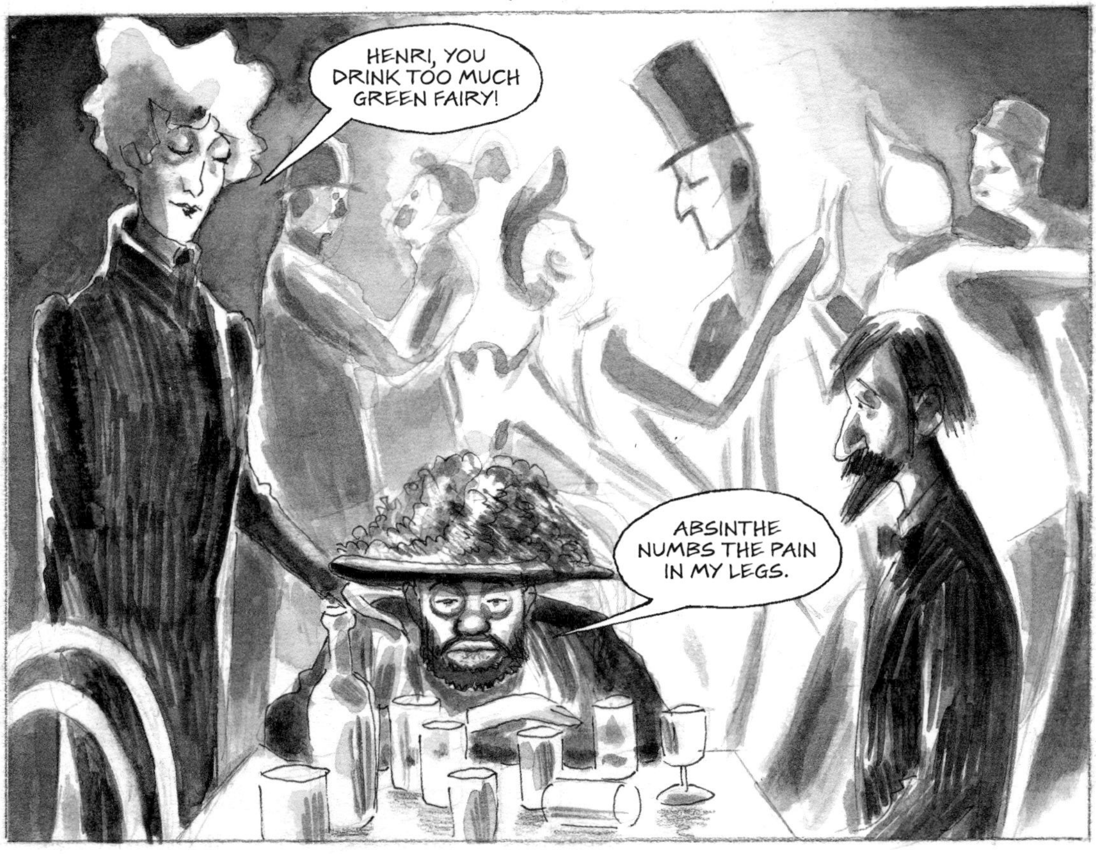

HENRI, YOU DRINK TOO MUCH GREEN FAIRY!
ABSINTHE NUMBS THE PAIN IN MY LEGS.

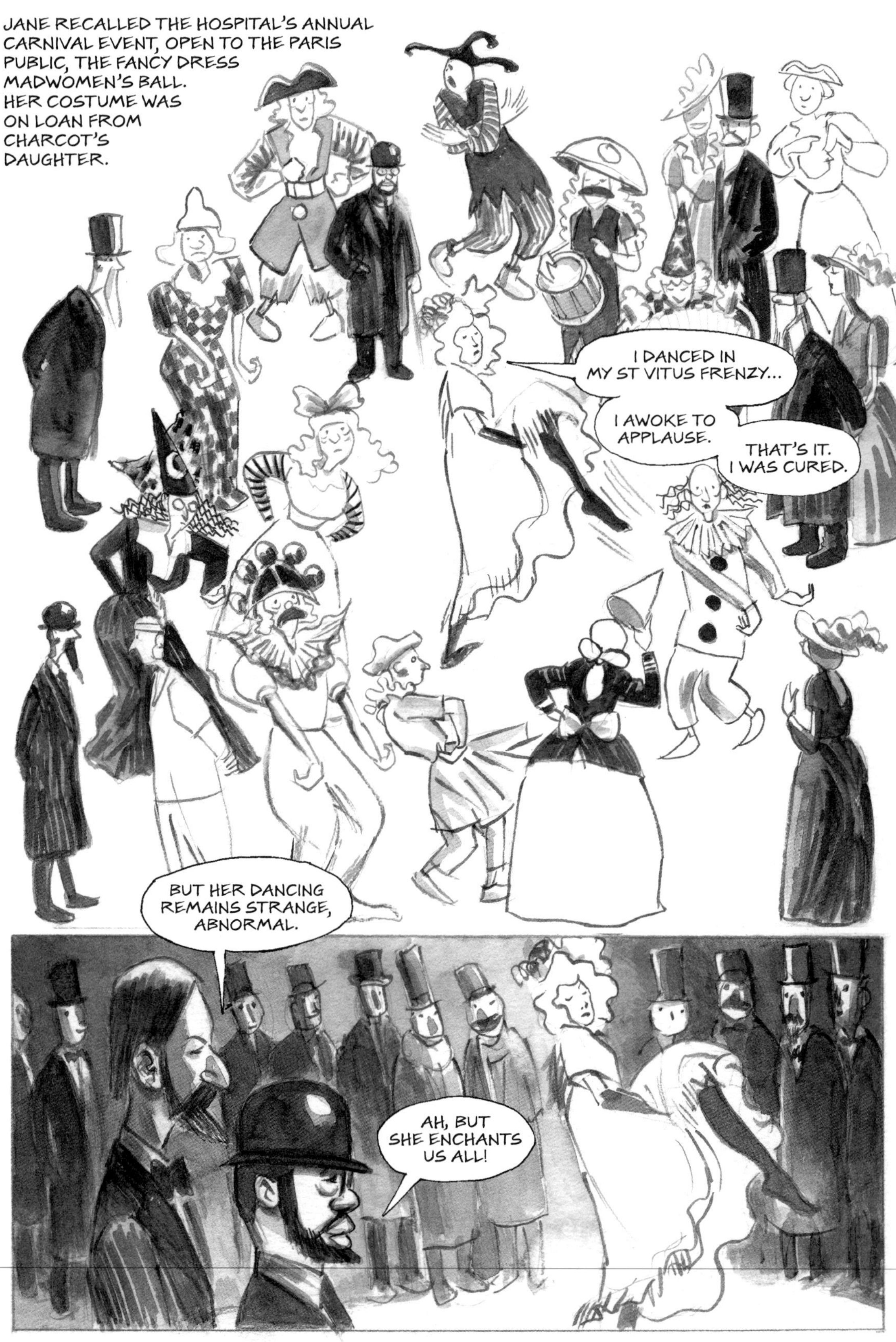
JANE RECALLED THE HOSPITAL'S ANNUAL CARNIVAL EVENT, OPEN TO THE PARIS PUBLIC, THE FANCY DRESS MADWOMEN'S BALL. HER COSTUME WAS ON LOAN FROM CHARCOT'S DAUGHTER.
I DANCED IN MY ST VITUS FRENZY...
I AWOKE TO APPLAUSE.
THAT'S IT. I WAS CURED.
BUT HER DANCING REMAINS STRANGE, ABNORMAL.
AH, BUT SHE ENCHANTS US ALL!

JANE HAD NO DOUBT. ALL HYSTERICS WERE ACTRESSES PLOTTING EVER NEW ANTICS TO SECURE THE INTEREST OF CHARCOT AND HIS INTERNS. SHE REMEMBERED TAKING PART AS A LOOK-OUT IN THOSE CONTRIVED "HYSTERIC" SPECTACLES.

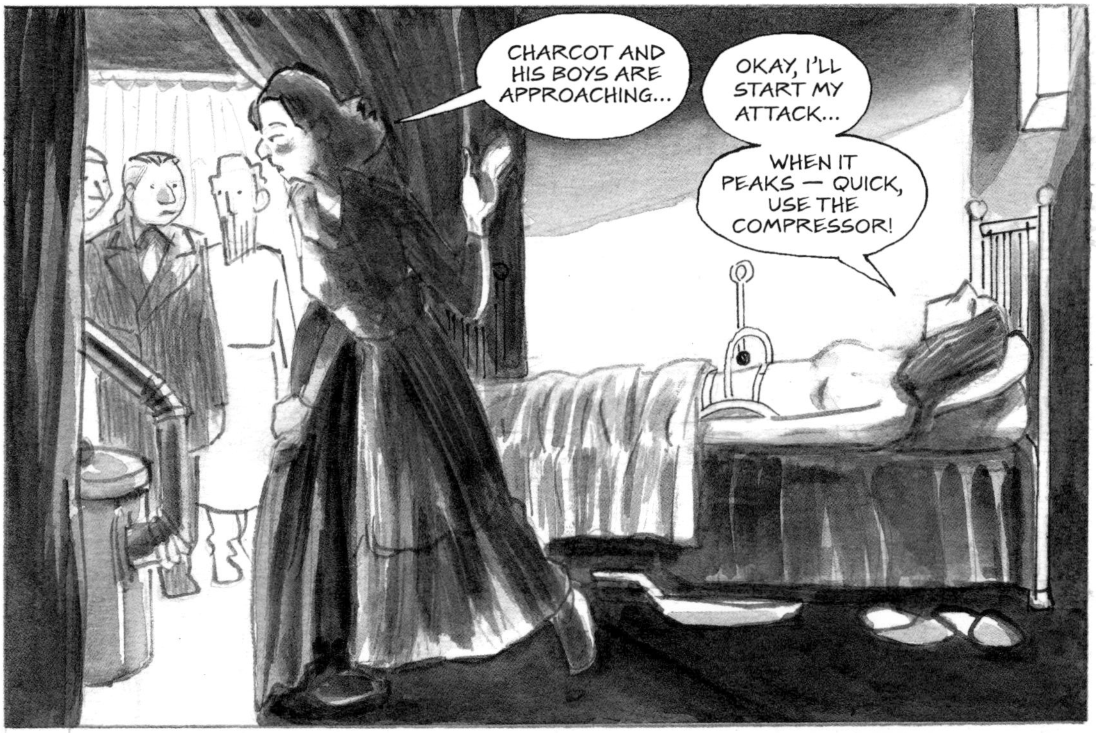
CHARCOT AND HIS BOYS ARE APPROACHING...
OKAY, I'LL START MY ATTACK...
WHEN IT PEAKS — QUICK, USE THE COMPRESSOR!

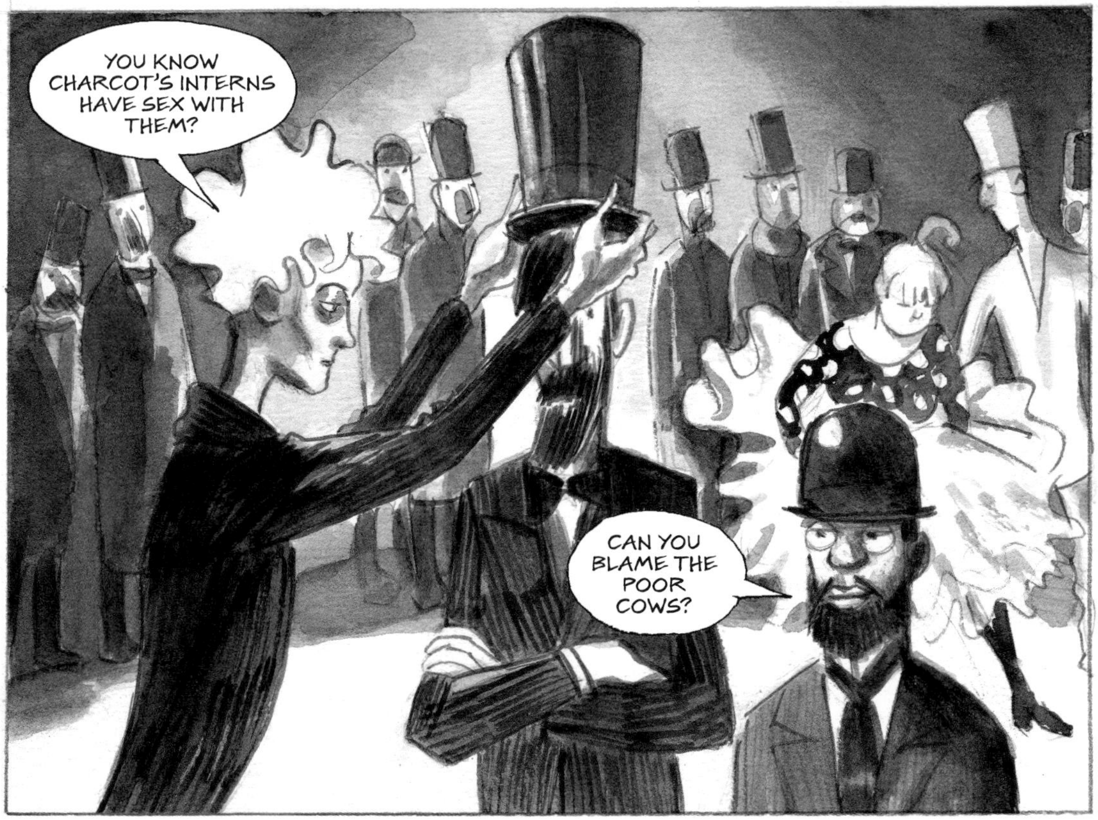
YOU KNOW CHARCOT'S INTERNS HAVE SEX WITH THEM?
CAN YOU BLAME THE POOR COWS?

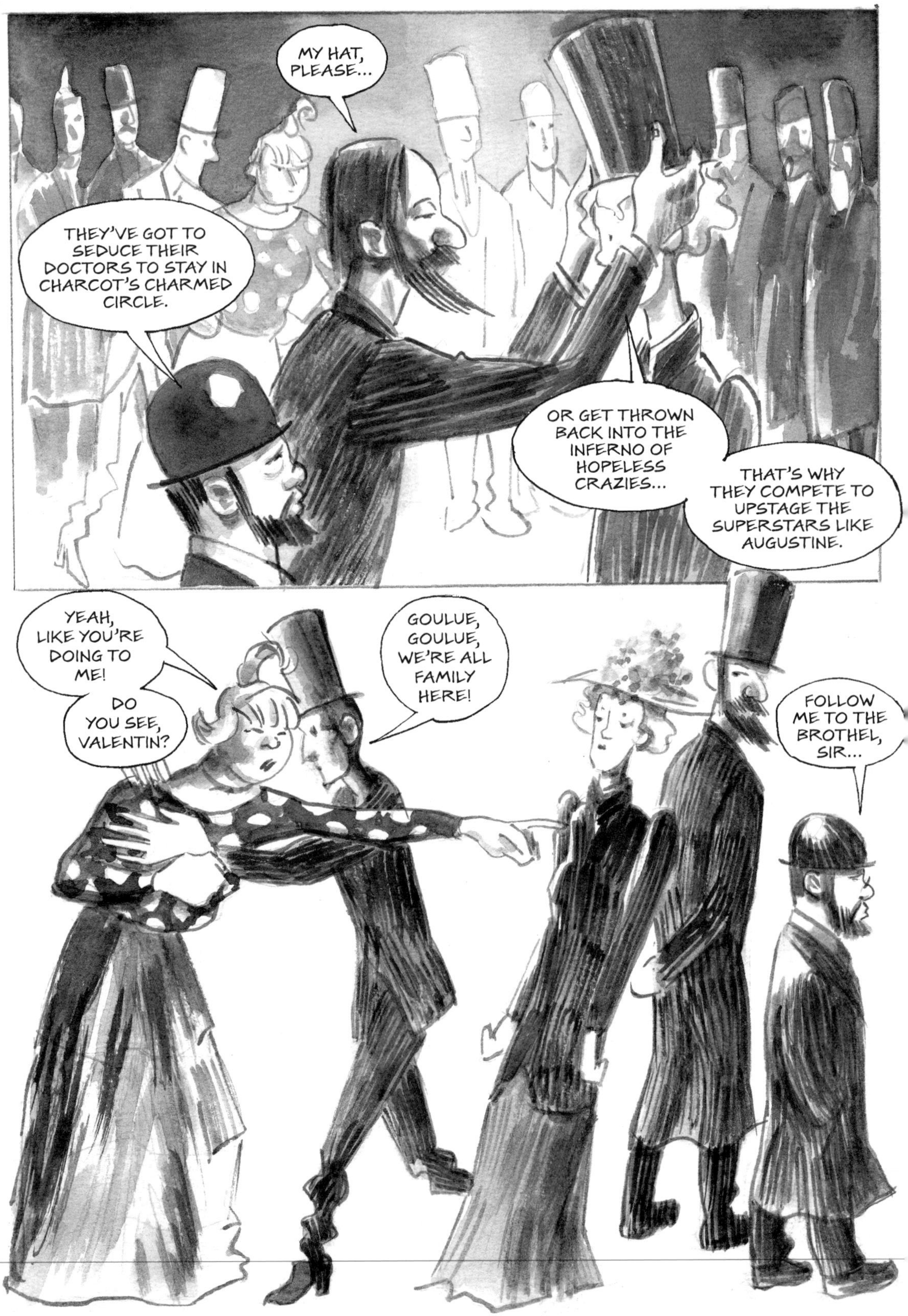
MY HAT, PLEASE...
THEY'VE GOT TO SEDUCE THEIR DOCTORS TO STAY IN CHARCOT'S CHARMED CIRCLE.
OR GET THROWN BACK INTO THE INFERNO OF HOPELESS CRAZIES...
THAT'S WHY THEY COMPETE TO UPSTAGE THE SUPERSTARS LIKE AUGUSTINE.
YEAH, LIKE YOU'RE DOING TO ME!
DO YOU SEE, VALENTIN?
GOULUE, GOULUE, WE'RE ALL FAMILY HERE!
FOLLOW ME TO THE BROTHEL, SIR...

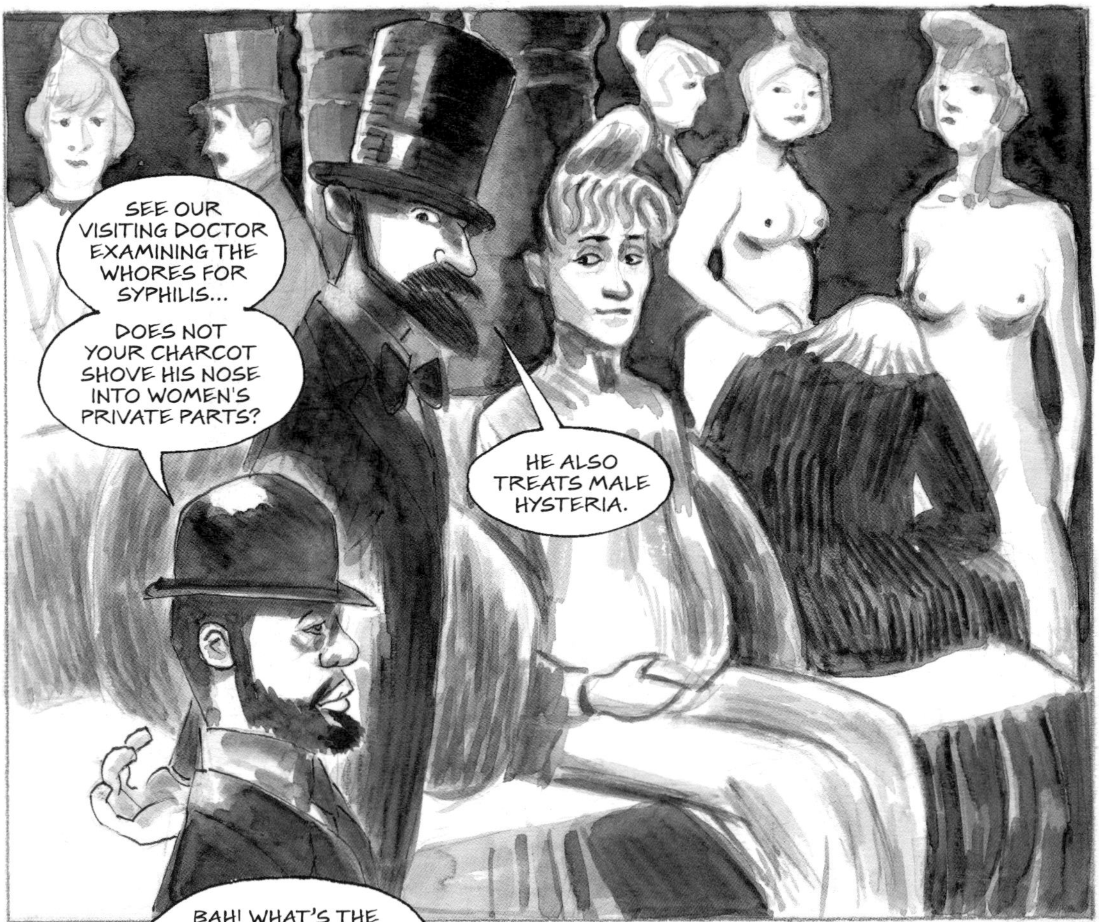
SEE OUR VISITING DOCTOR EXAMINING THE WHORES FOR SYPHILIS...
DOES NOT YOUR CHARCOT SHOVE HIS NOSE INTO WOMEN'S PRIVATE PARTS?
HE ALSO TREATS MALE HYSTERIA.

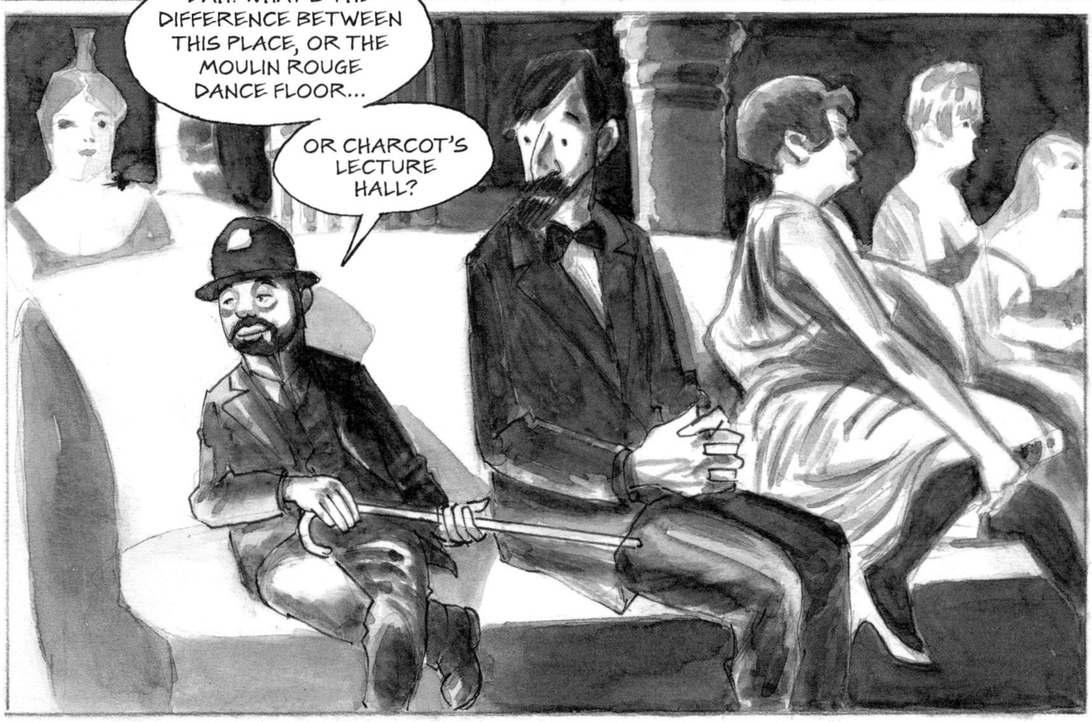
BAH! WHAT'S THE DIFFERENCE BETWEEN THIS PLACE, OR THE MOULIN ROUGE DANCE FLOOR...
OR CHARCOT'S LECTURE HALL?

CHARCOT ACKNOWLEDGED THE THEATRICALITY OF HYSTERIA. BUT ITS DEEP DISTRESS WAS REAL, NOT SIMULATED.

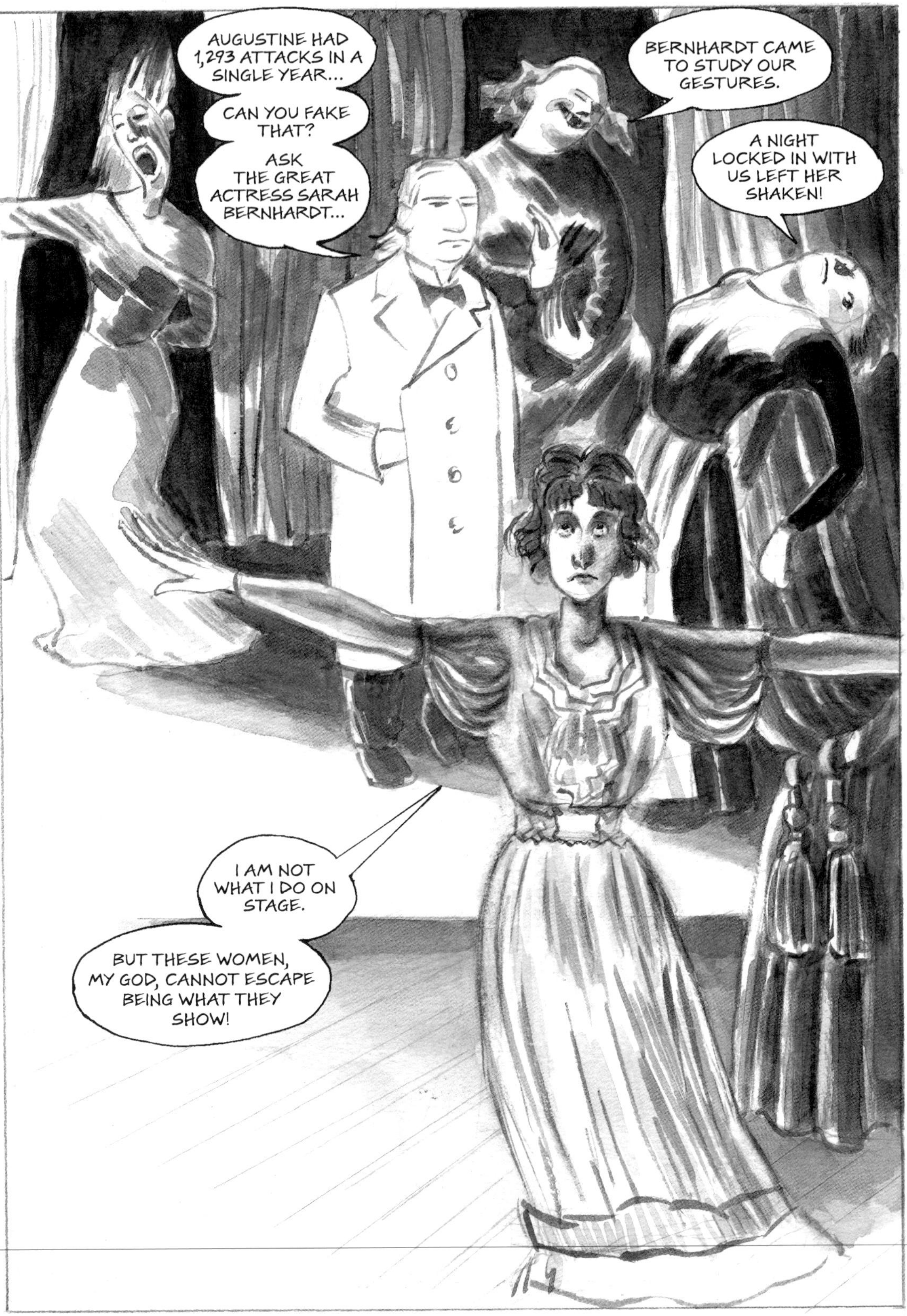
AUGUSTINE HAD 1,293 ATTACKS IN A SINGLE YEAR...
CAN YOU FAKE THAT?
ASK THE GREAT ACTRESS SARAH BERNHARDT...
BERNHARDT CAME TO STUDY OUR GESTURES.
A NIGHT LOCKED IN WITH US LEFT HER SHAKEN!
I AM NOT WHAT I DO ON STAGE.
BUT THESE WOMEN, MY GOD, CANNOT ESCAPE BEING WHAT THEY SHOW!

WAS HYSTERIA AFTER ALL AN IATROGENIC ILLNESS, ONE LITERALLY FORGED IN THE CLINIC BETWEEN PATIENT AND DOCTOR? HYSTERIA SEEMED TO DISAPPEAR AFTER CHARCOT'S DEATH IN 1893.

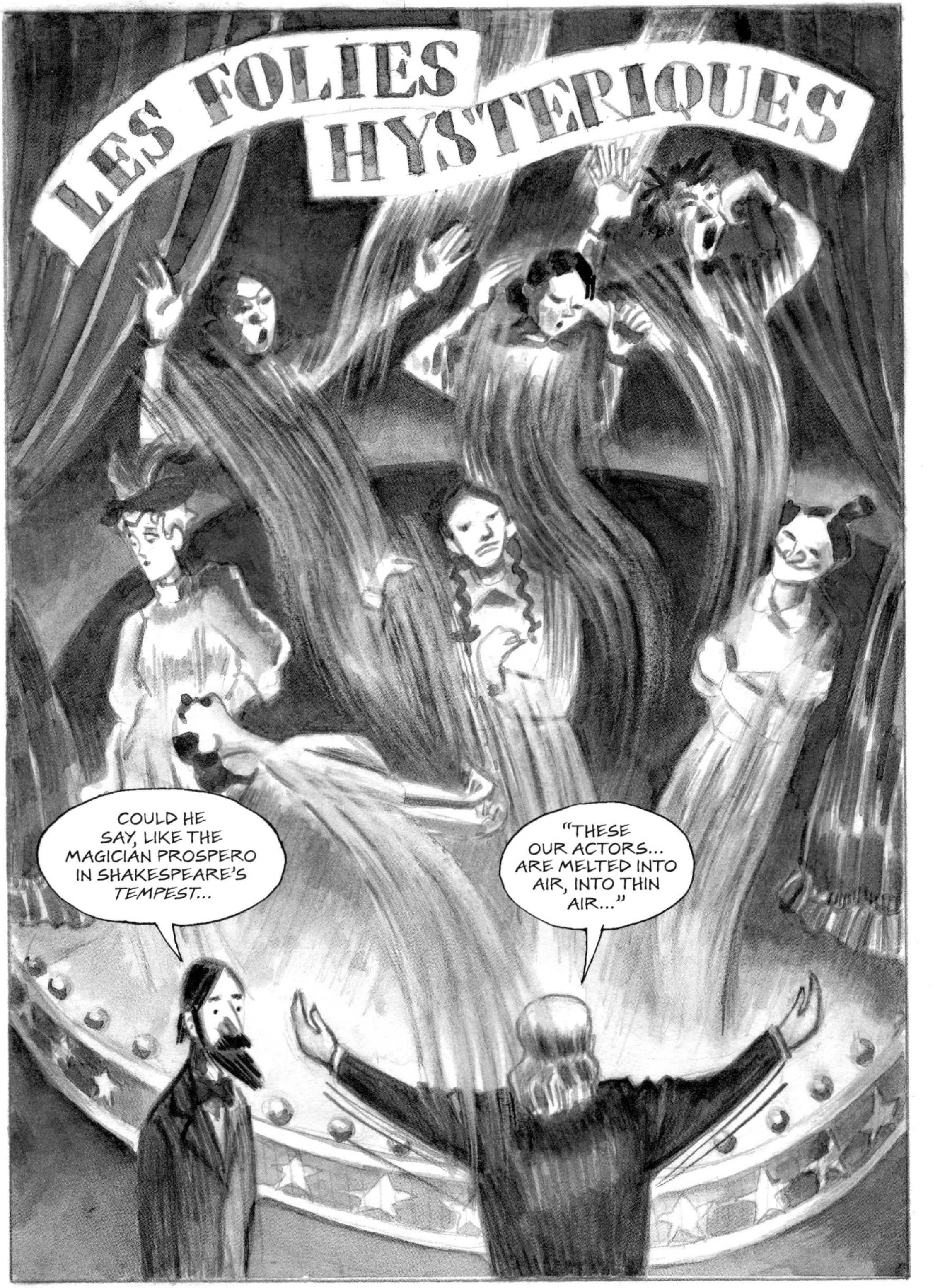
LES FOLIES HYSTERIQUES
COULD HE SAY, LIKE THE MAGICIAN PROSPERO IN SHAKESPEARE'S *TEMPEST*...
"THESE OUR ACTORS... ARE MELTED INTO AIR, INTO THIN AIR..."

FIVE MONTHS WITH CHARCOT TURNED MY WORLD UPSIDE DOWN. BACK IN VIENNA I ANNOUNCED THE START OF MY PRIVATE PRACTICE IN NEWSPAPER ADS: 25 APRIL 1886, EASTER SUNDAY. EVERYONE WOULD BE ON HOLIDAY, MARTHA REMINDED ME.

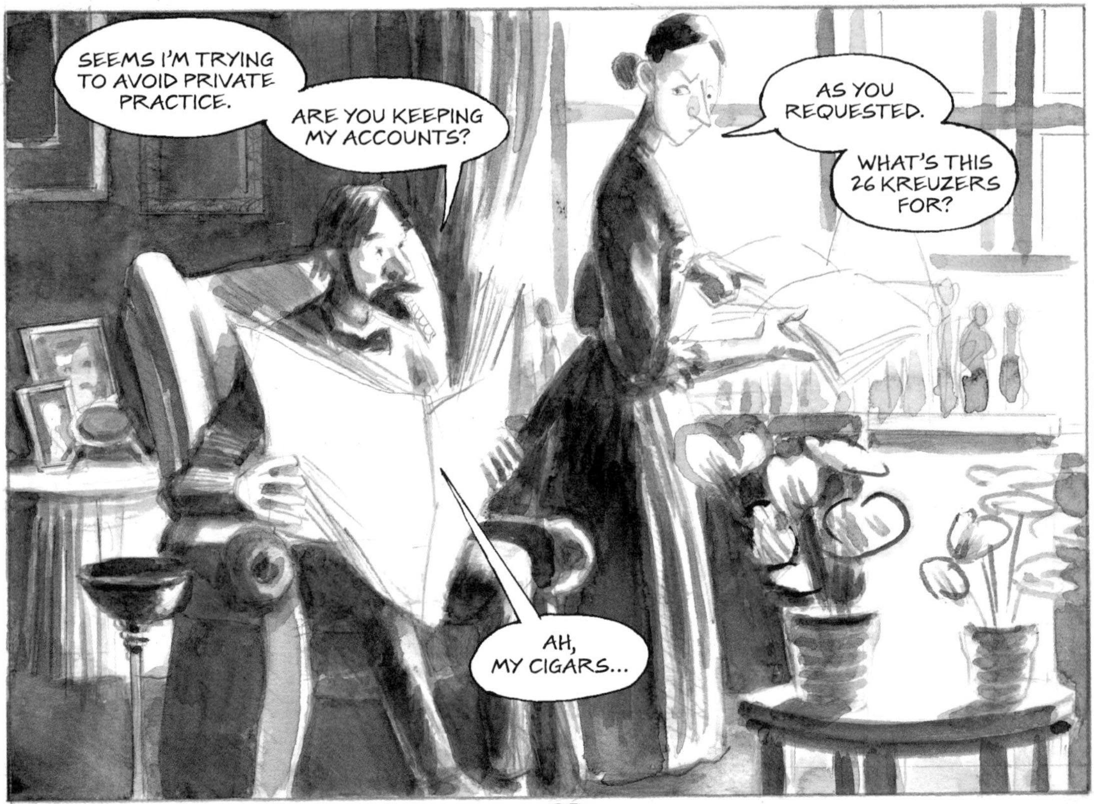
SEEMS I'M TRYING TO AVOID PRIVATE PRACTICE.
ARE YOU KEEPING MY ACCOUNTS?
AS YOU REQUESTED.
WHAT'S THIS 26 KREUZERS FOR?
AH, MY CIGARS...

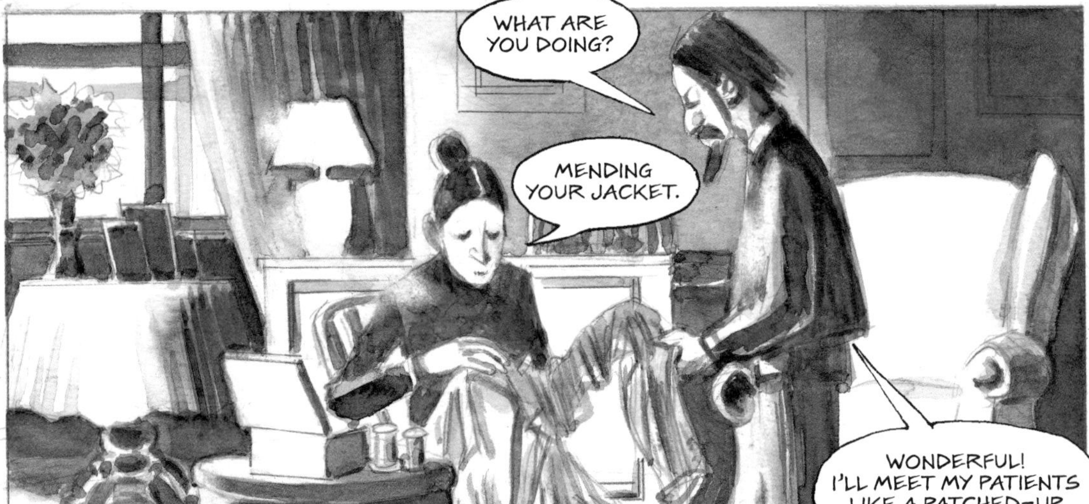
WHAT ARE YOU DOING?
MENDING YOUR JACKET.
WONDERFUL! I'LL MEET MY PATIENTS LIKE A PATCHED-UP CLOWN.

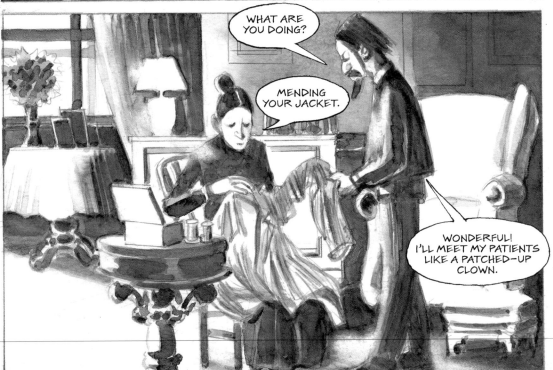

POVERTY, WRETCHED POVERTY! I OWED MONEY TO MY FRIENDS, ESPECIALLY MY CLOSEST ONE, THE SUCCESSFUL PHYSICIAN AND SCIENTIST JOSEF BREUER.

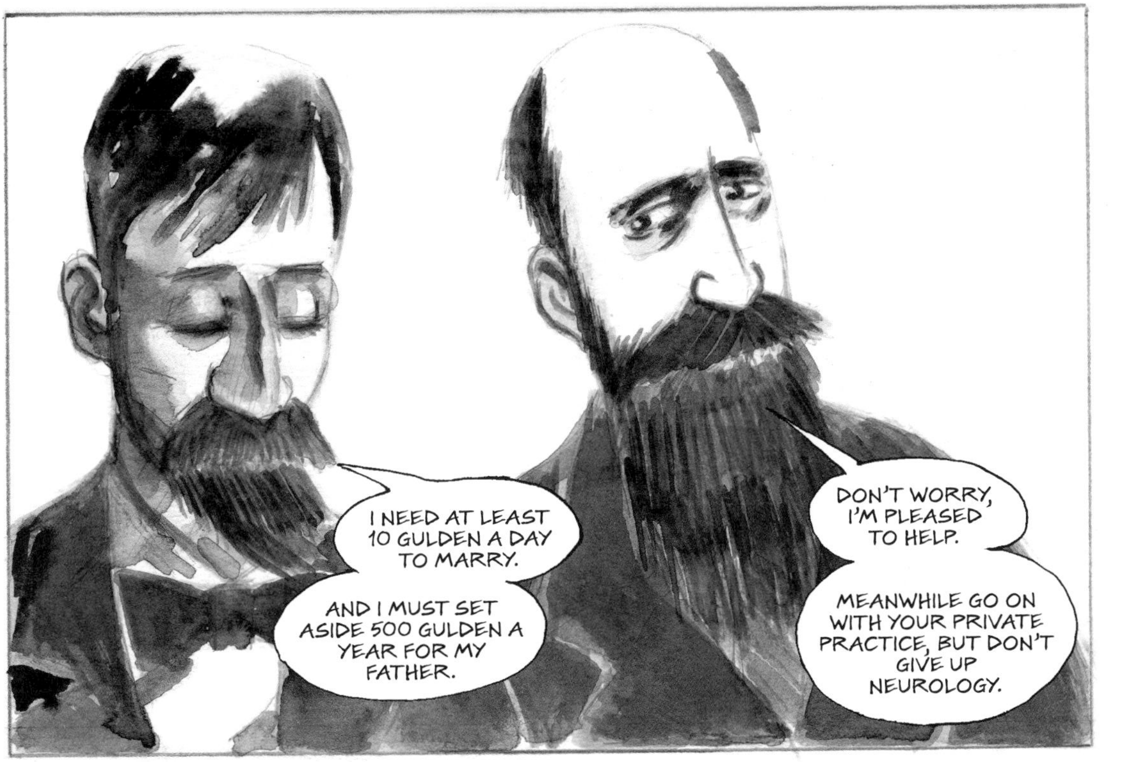
I NEED AT LEAST 10 GULDEN A DAY TO MARRY.
AND I MUST SET ASIDE 500 GULDEN A YEAR FOR MY FATHER.
DON'T WORRY, I'M PLEASED TO HELP.
MEANWHILE GO ON WITH YOUR PRIVATE PRACTICE, BUT DON'T GIVE UP NEUROLOGY.

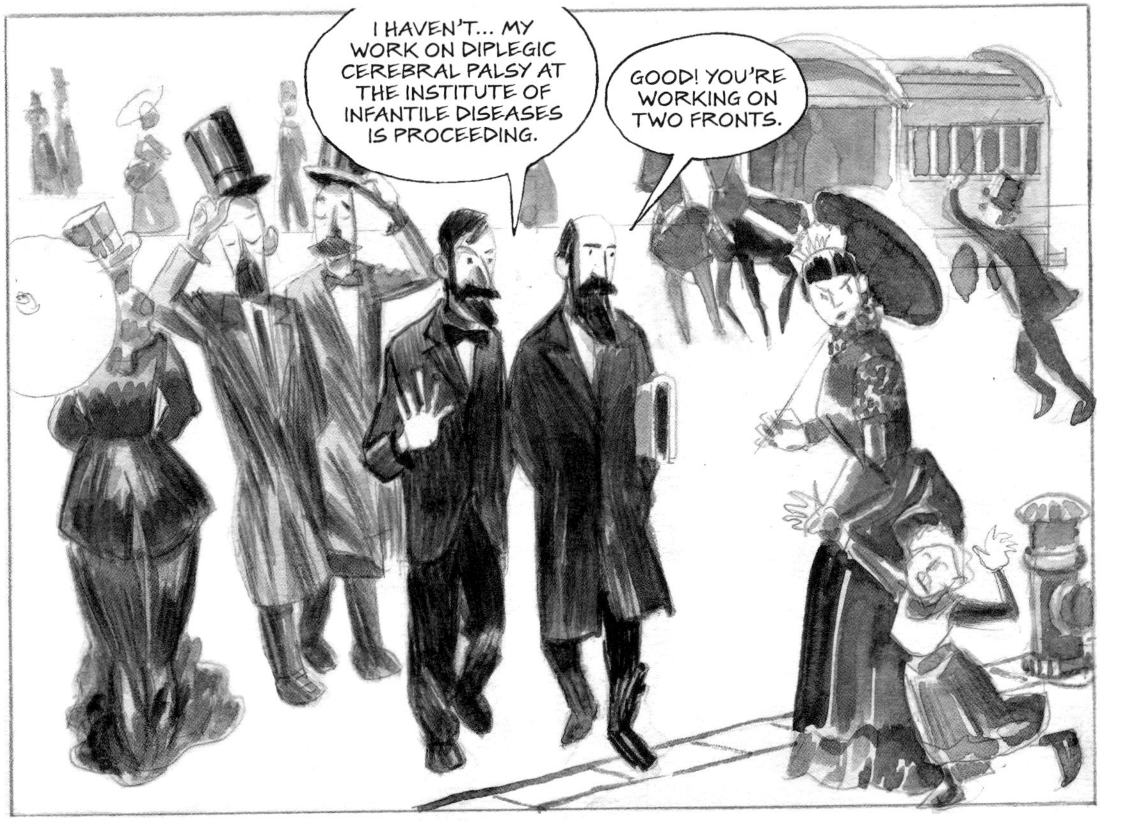
I HAVEN'T... MY WORK ON DIPLEGIC CEREBRAL PALSY AT THE INSTITUTE OF INFANTILE DISEASES IS PROCEEDING.
GOOD! YOU'RE WORKING ON TWO FRONTS.

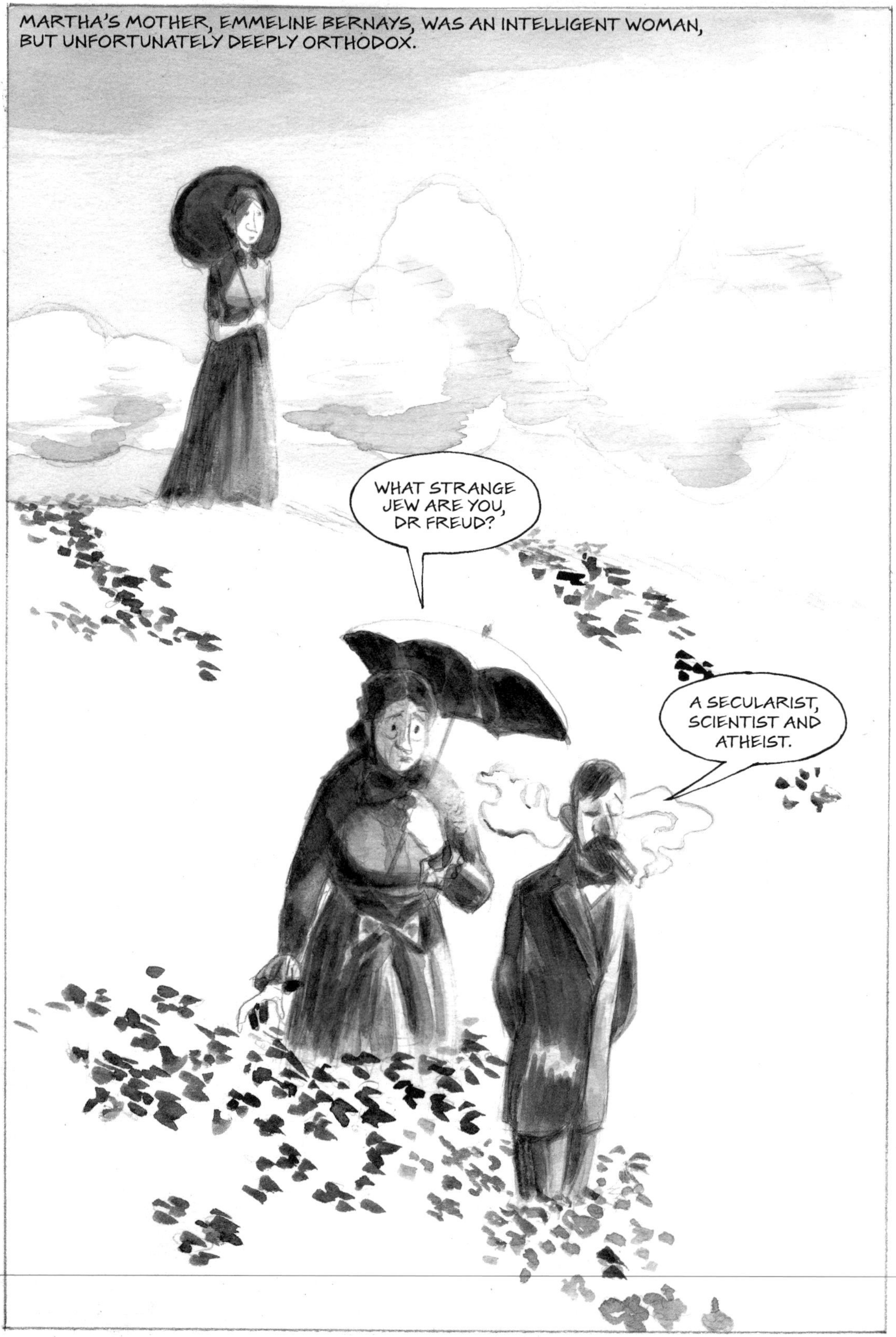
MARTHA'S MOTHER, EMMELINE BERNAYS, WAS AN INTELLIGENT WOMAN, BUT UNFORTUNATELY DEEPLY ORTHODOX.
WHAT STRANGE JEW ARE YOU, DR FREUD?
A SECULARIST, SCIENTIST AND ATHEIST.

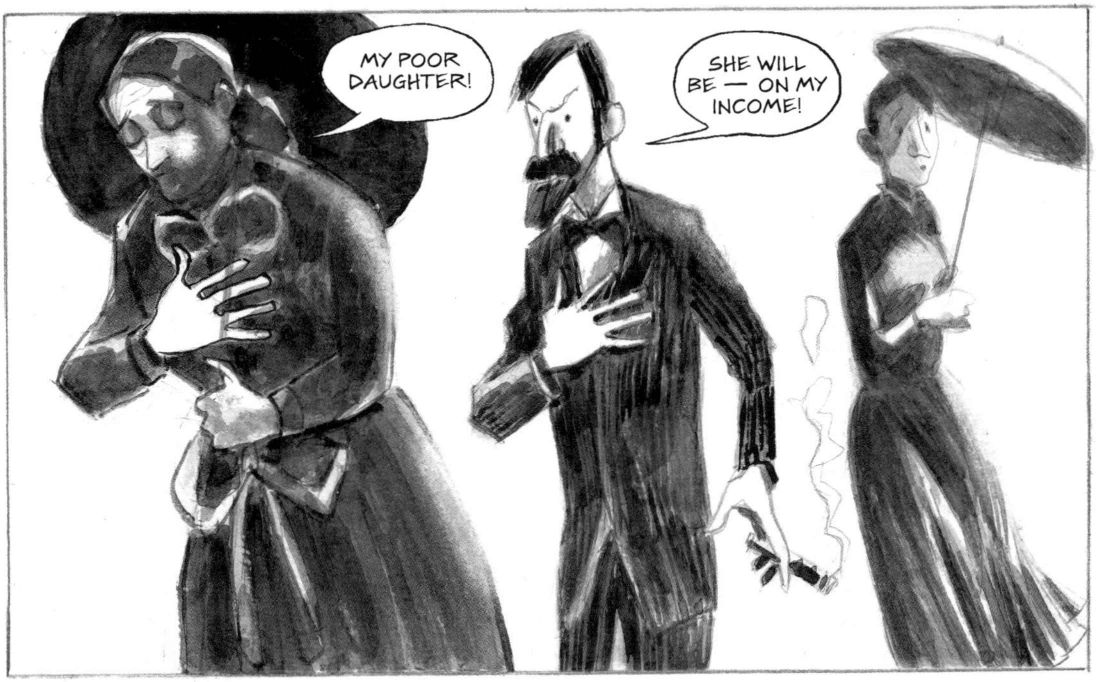
MY POOR DAUGHTER!
SHE WILL BE — ON MY INCOME!

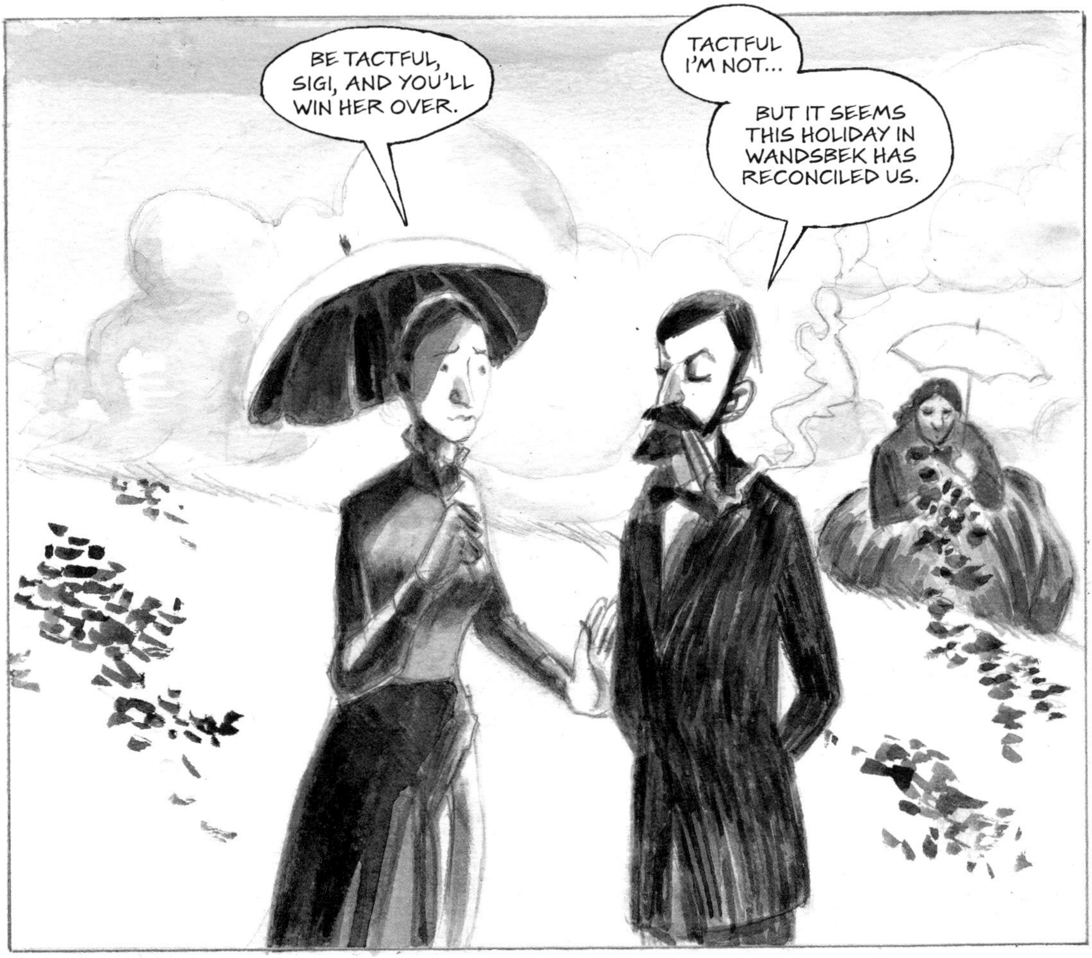
BE TACTFUL, SIGI, AND YOU'LL WIN HER OVER.
TACTFUL I'M NOT...
BUT IT SEEMS THIS HOLIDAY IN WANDSBEK HAS RECONCILED US.

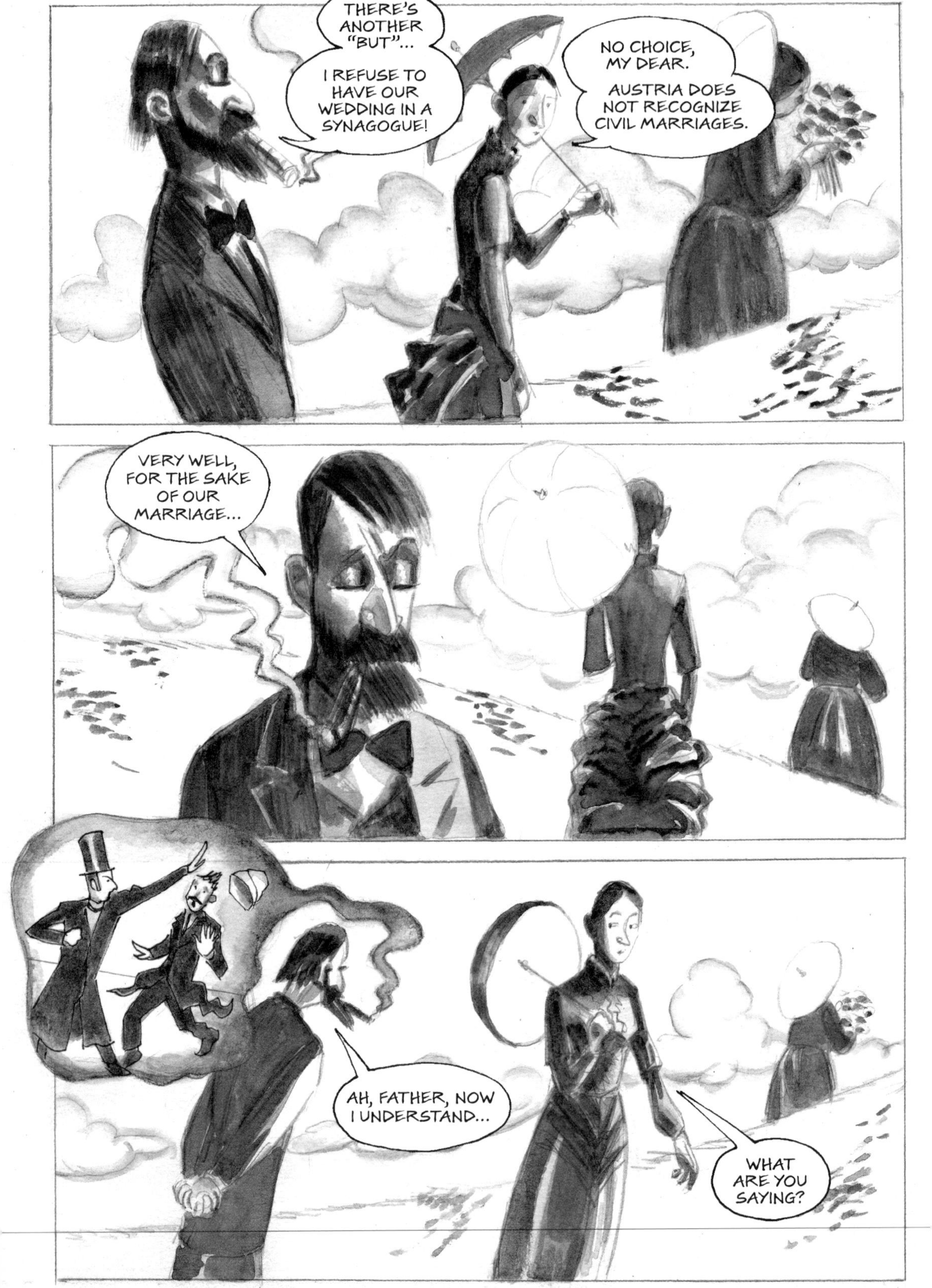
THERE'S ANOTHER "BUT"...
I REFUSE TO HAVE OUR WEDDING IN A SYNAGOGUE!
NO CHOICE, MY DEAR.
AUSTRIA DOES NOT RECOGNIZE CIVIL MARRIAGES.
VERY WELL, FOR THE SAKE OF OUR MARRIAGE...
AH, FATHER, NOW I UNDERSTAND...
WHAT ARE YOU SAYING?

I BEGAN TO COUNT FREQUENT CASES OF HYSTERIA AS MY PRIVATE PRACTICE EVOLVED AFTER 1886. CHARCOT LINGERED WITH ME, IN SPIRIT, IF NOT IN THE FLESH.

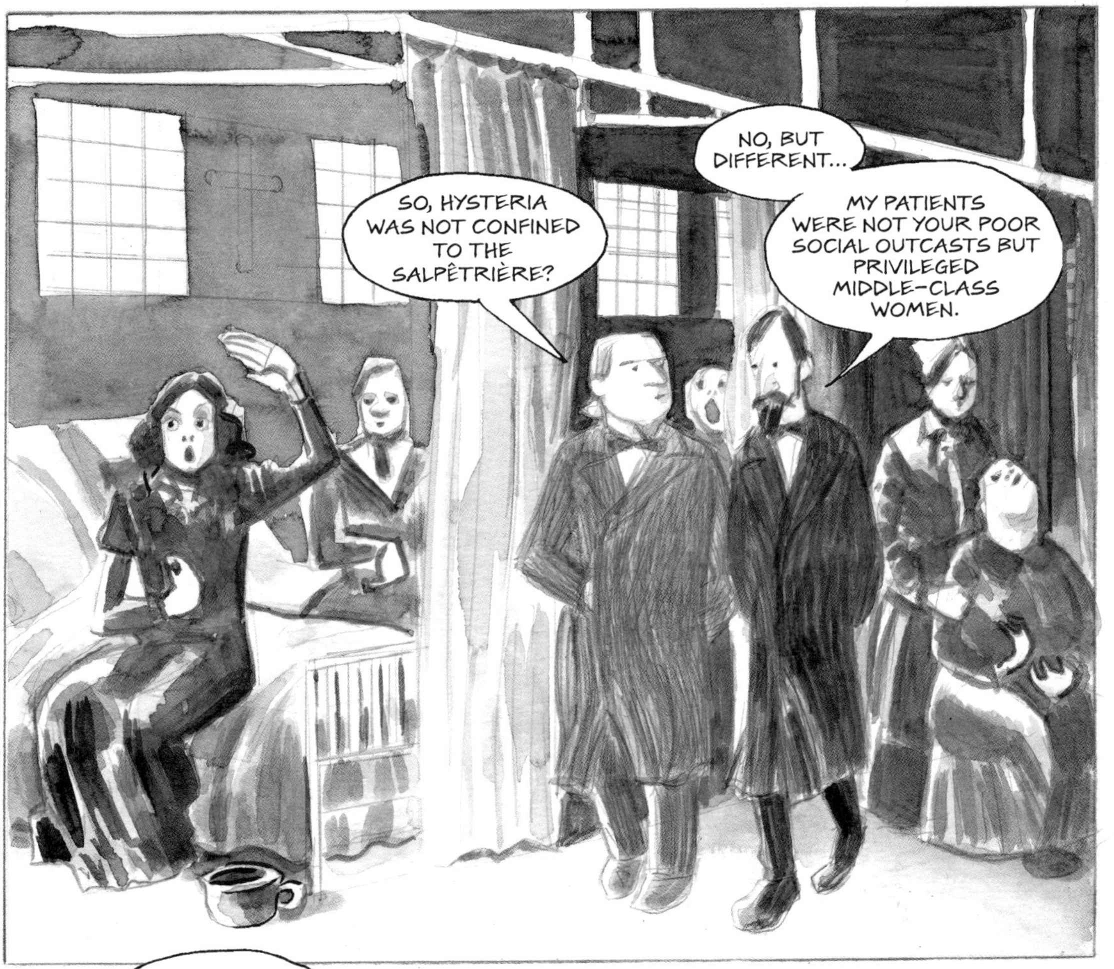
SO, HYSTERIA WAS NOT CONFINED TO THE SALPÊTRIÈRE?
NO, BUT DIFFERENT...
MY PATIENTS WERE NOT YOUR POOR SOCIAL OUTCASTS BUT PRIVILEGED MIDDLE-CLASS WOMEN.

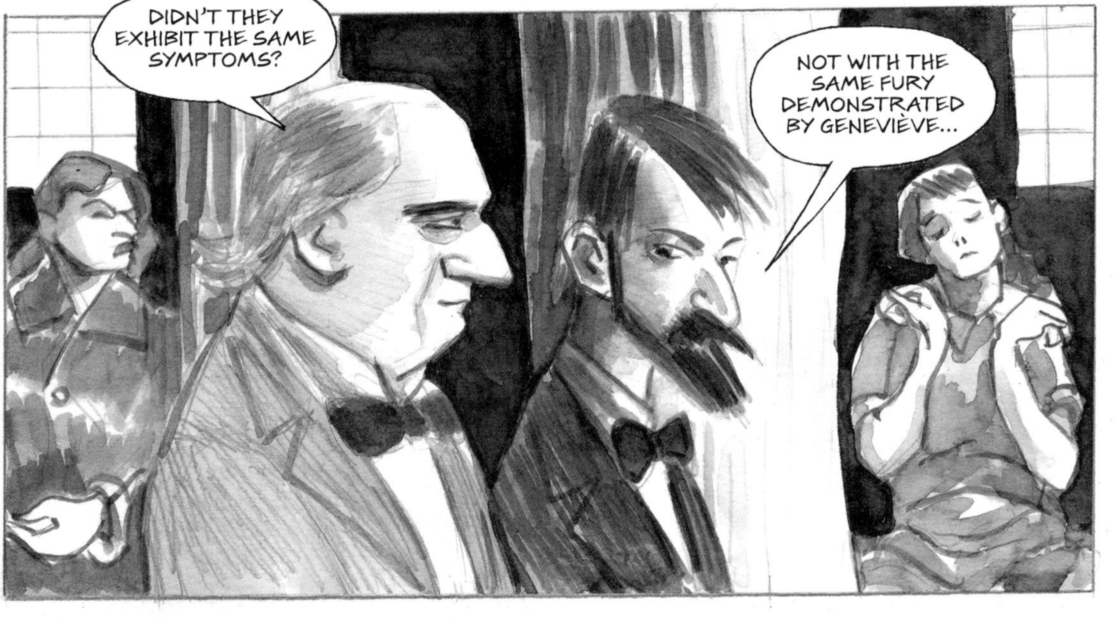
DIDN'T THEY EXHIBIT THE SAME SYMPTOMS?
NOT WITH THE SAME FURY DEMONSTRATED BY GENEVIÈVE...

MY PATIENTS' HYSTERIA DEVELOPED IN THE PRIVACY OF BOURGEOIS VIENNESE HOUSEHOLDS, A WORLD REMOTE FROM THE SALPÊTRIÈRE'S PUBLIC THEATRE. I RECALLED THE CASE NOTES OF CHARCOT'S OTHER STAR PERFORMER, GENEVIÈVE.

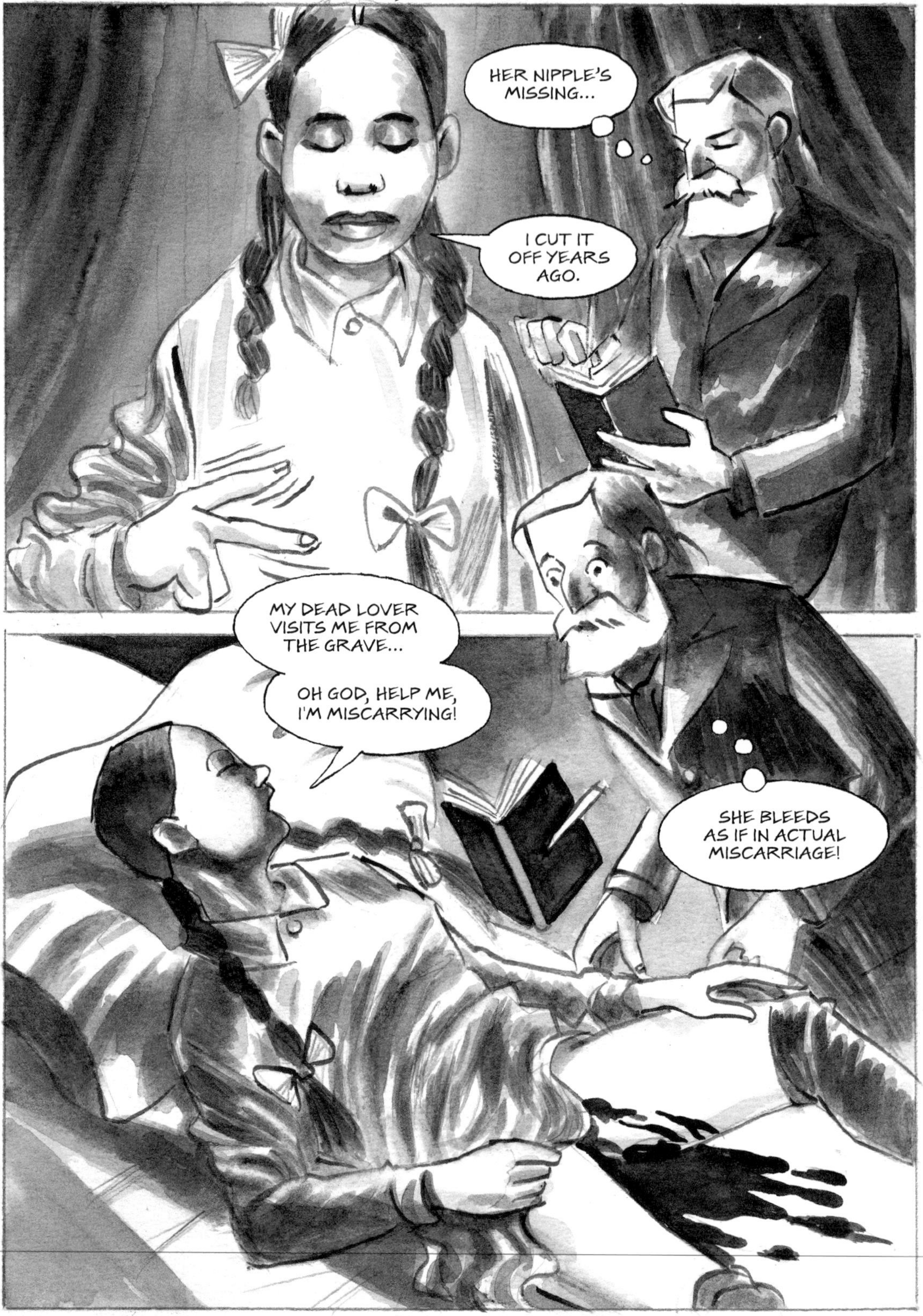
HER NIPPLE'S MISSING...
I CUT IT OFF YEARS AGO.
MY DEAD LOVER VISITS ME FROM THE GRAVE...
OH GOD, HELP ME, I'M MISCARRYING!
SHE BLEEDS AS IF IN ACTUAL MISCARRIAGE!

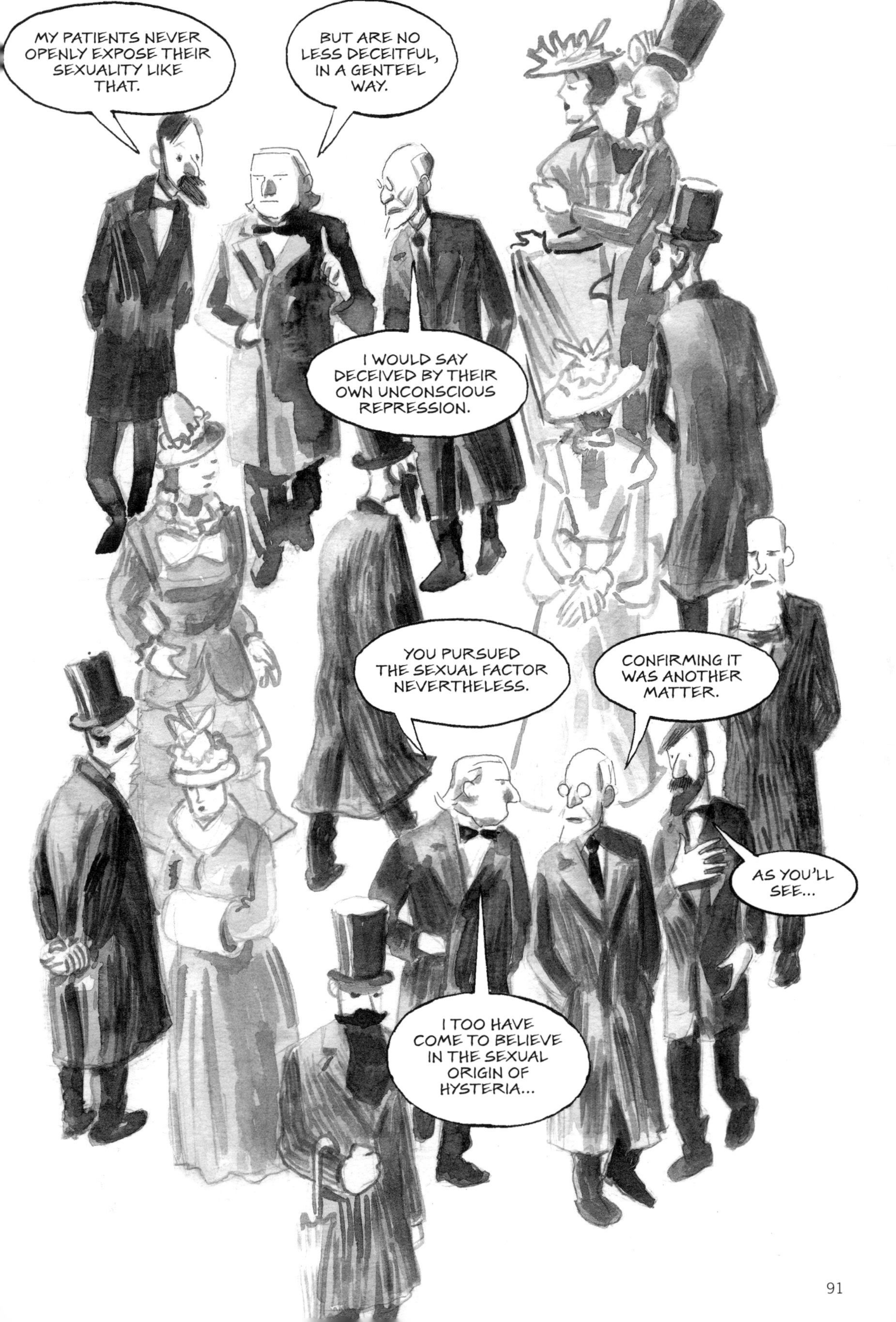
MY PATIENTS NEVER OPENLY EXPOSE THEIR SEXUALITY LIKE THAT.
BUT ARE NO LESS DECEITFUL, IN A GENTEEL WAY.
I WOULD SAY DECEIVED BY THEIR OWN UNCONSCIOUS REPRESSION.
YOU PURSUED THE SEXUAL FACTOR NEVERTHELESS.
CONFIRMING IT WAS ANOTHER MATTER.
AS YOU'LL SEE...
I TOO HAVE COME TO BELIEVE IN THE SEXUAL ORIGIN OF HYSTERIA...

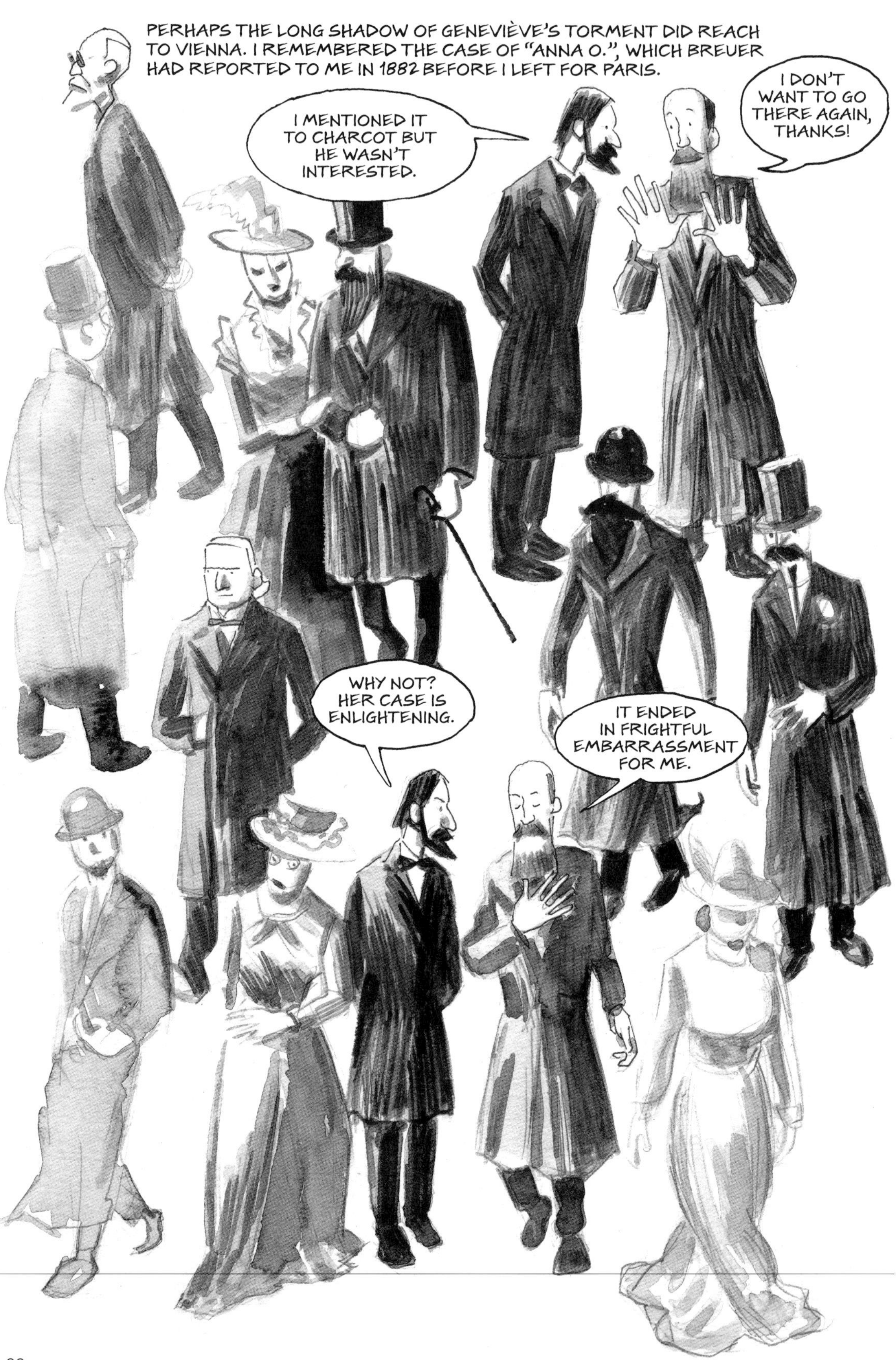
PERHAPS THE LONG SHADOW OF GENEVIÈVE'S TORMENT DID REACH TO VIENNA. I REMEMBERED THE CASE OF "ANNA O.", WHICH BREUER HAD REPORTED TO ME IN 1882 BEFORE I LEFT FOR PARIS.
I MENTIONED IT TO CHARCOT BUT HE WASN'T INTERESTED.
I DON'T WANT TO GO THERE AGAIN, THANKS!
WHY NOT? HER CASE IS ENLIGHTENING.
IT ENDED IN FRIGHTFUL EMBARRASSMENT FOR ME.

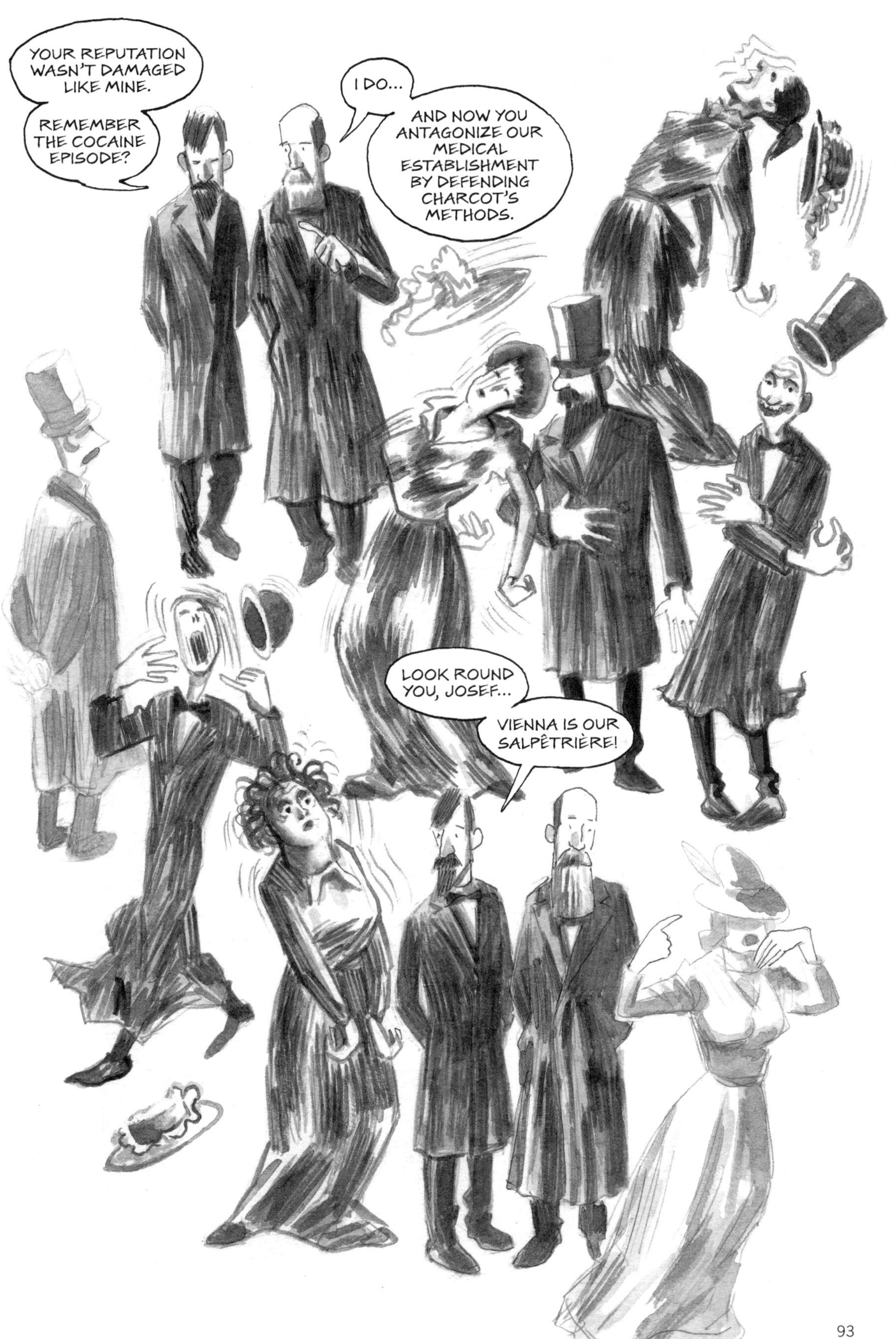

YOUR REPUTATION WASN'T DAMAGED LIKE MINE.
REMEMBER THE COCAINE EPISODE?
I DO...
AND NOW YOU ANTAGONIZE OUR MEDICAL ESTABLISHMENT BY DEFENDING CHARCOT'S METHODS.
LOOK ROUND YOU, JOSEF...
VIENNA IS OUR SALPÊTRIÈRE!

THE CASE OF ANNA O.

BREUER AGREED TO DISCUSS THE CASE WITH ME. *"I WAS SUMMONED IN 1880 TO TREAT ANNA'S PERSISTENT NERVOUS COUGH — THE LEAST OF HER WORRIES..."*

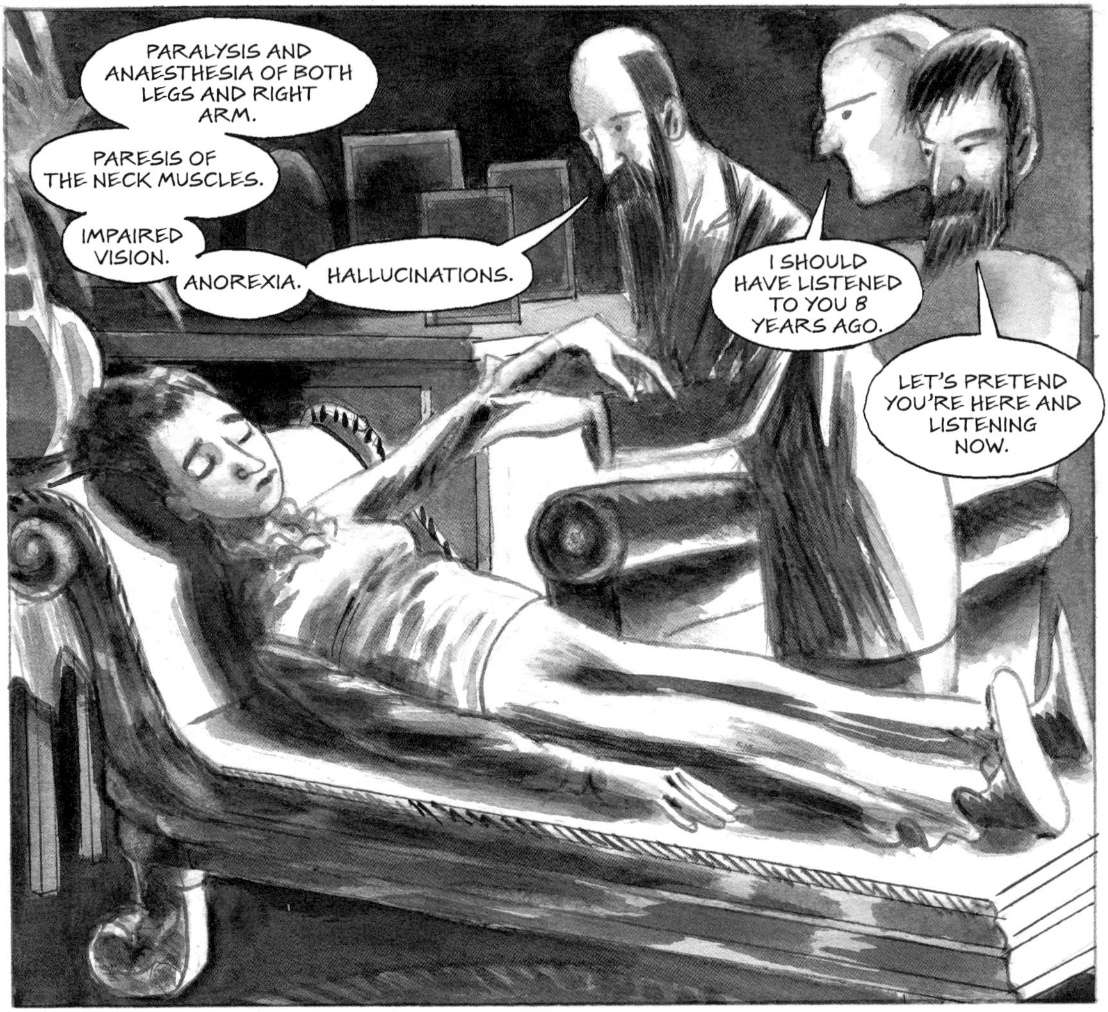
PARALYSIS AND ANAESTHESIA OF BOTH LEGS AND RIGHT ARM.
PARESIS OF THE NECK MUSCLES.
IMPAIRED VISION.
ANOREXIA.
HALLUCINATIONS.
I SHOULD HAVE LISTENED TO YOU 8 YEARS AGO.
LET'S PRETEND YOU'RE HERE AND LISTENING NOW.

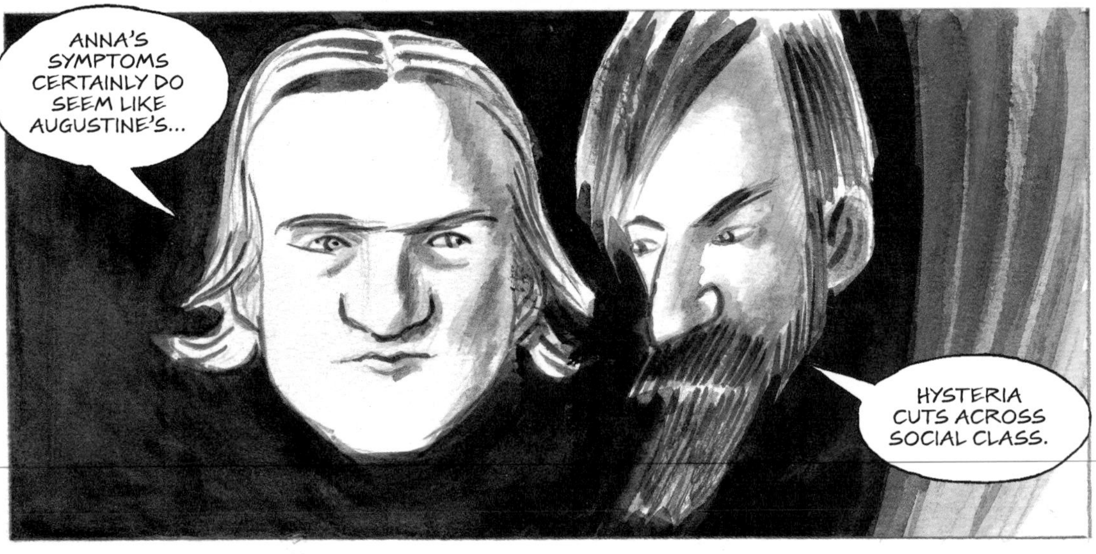
ANNA'S SYMPTOMS CERTAINLY DO SEEM LIKE AUGUSTINE'S...
HYSTERIA CUTS ACROSS SOCIAL CLASS.

"ANNA WAS A GIFTED, ATTRACTIVE WOMAN OF 21, REDUCED TO MONOTONY BY HER WEALTHY, OVER-PROTECTIVE FAMILY. NO INTEREST AT ALL IN SEX. SHE TOOK REFUGE IN DAYDREAMING 'ABSENCES'."

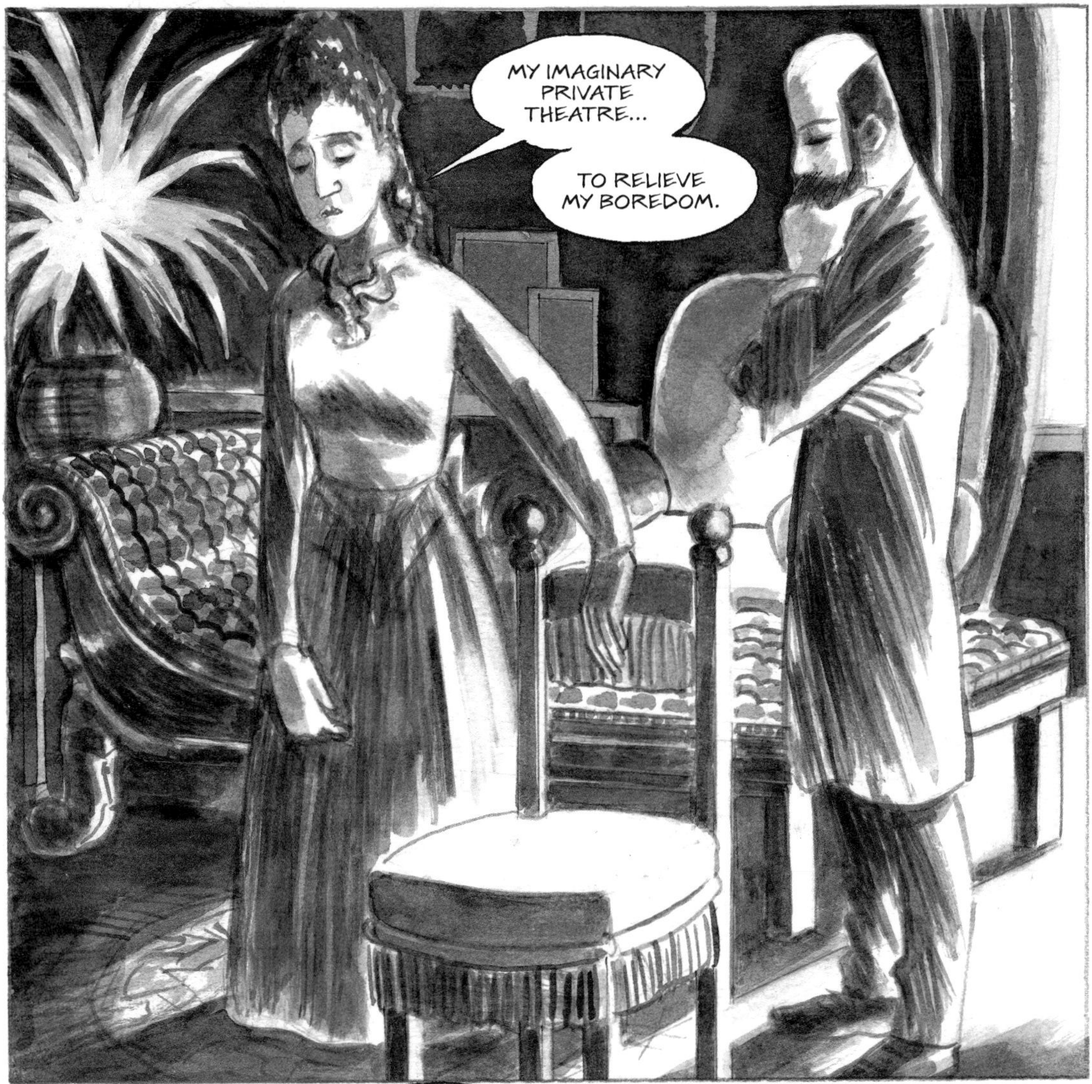

MY IMAGINARY PRIVATE THEATRE...
TO RELIEVE MY BOREDOM.

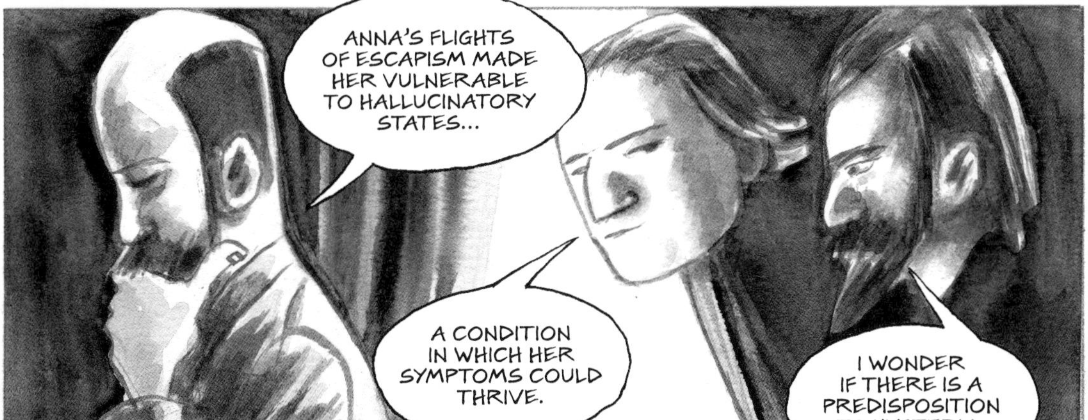

ANNA'S FLIGHTS OF ESCAPISM MADE HER VULNERABLE TO HALLUCINATORY STATES...
A CONDITION IN WHICH HER SYMPTOMS COULD THRIVE.
I WONDER IF THERE IS A PREDISPOSITION TO HYSTERIA.

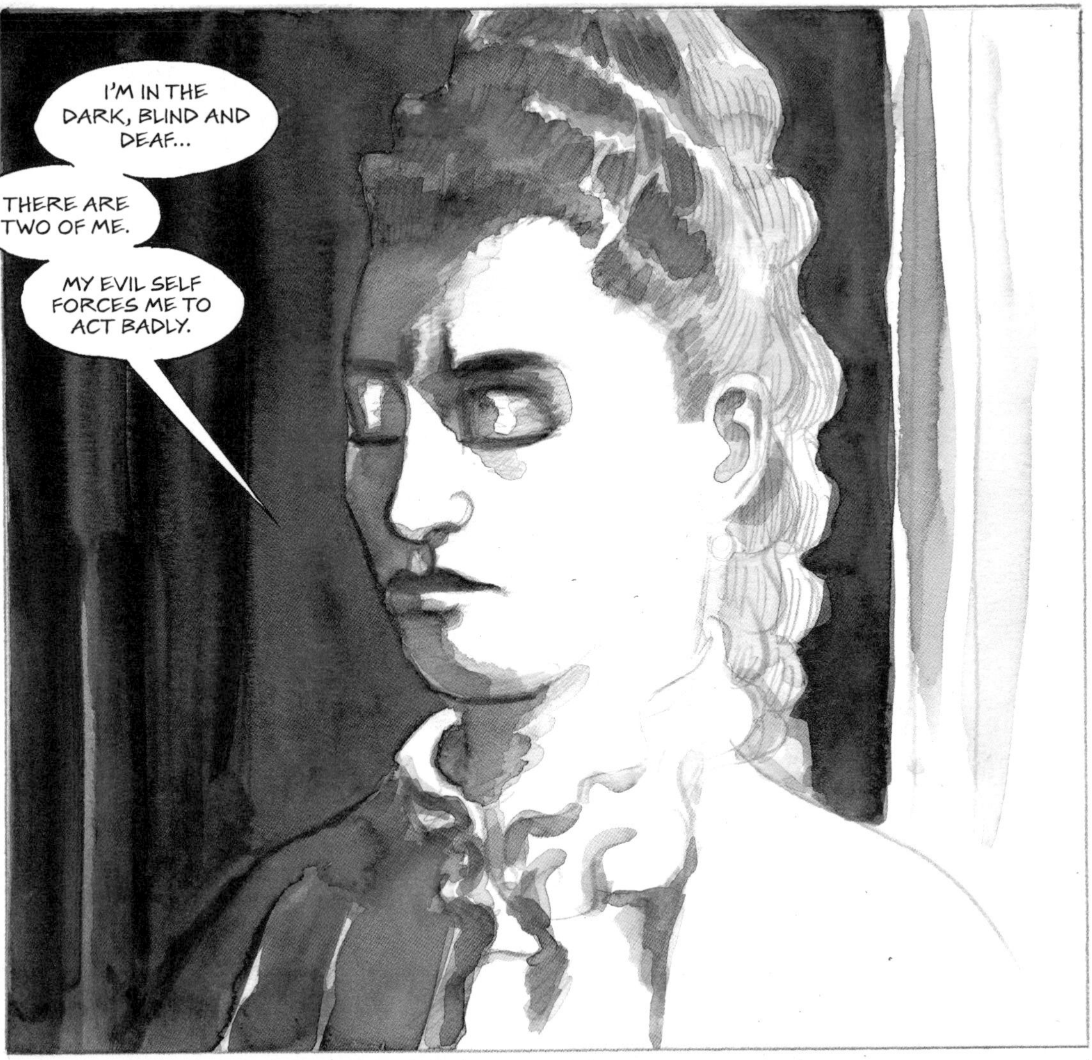
I'M IN THE DARK, BLIND AND DEAF...
THERE ARE TWO OF ME.
MY EVIL SELF FORCES ME TO ACT BADLY.

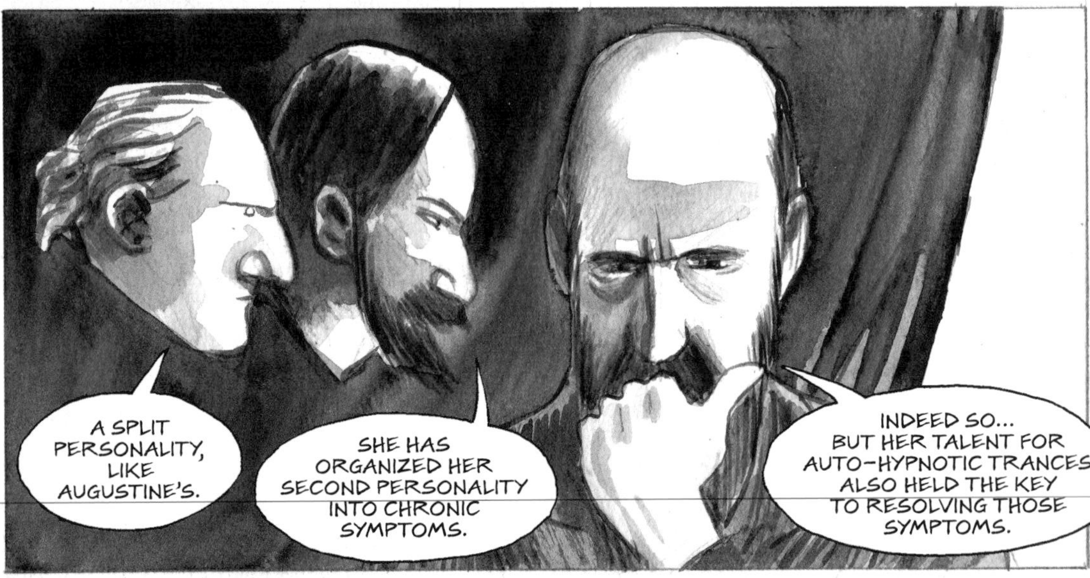
A SPLIT PERSONALITY, LIKE AUGUSTINE'S.
SHE HAS ORGANIZED HER SECOND PERSONALITY INTO CHRONIC SYMPTOMS.
INDEED SO... BUT HER TALENT FOR AUTO-HYPNOTIC TRANCES ALSO HELD THE KEY TO RESOLVING THOSE SYMPTOMS.

"SHE SPOKE OF A VISIT TO SOME RELATIVES, BEFORE HER ILLNESS, WHERE SHE FAINTED ON ENTERING THE ROOM."

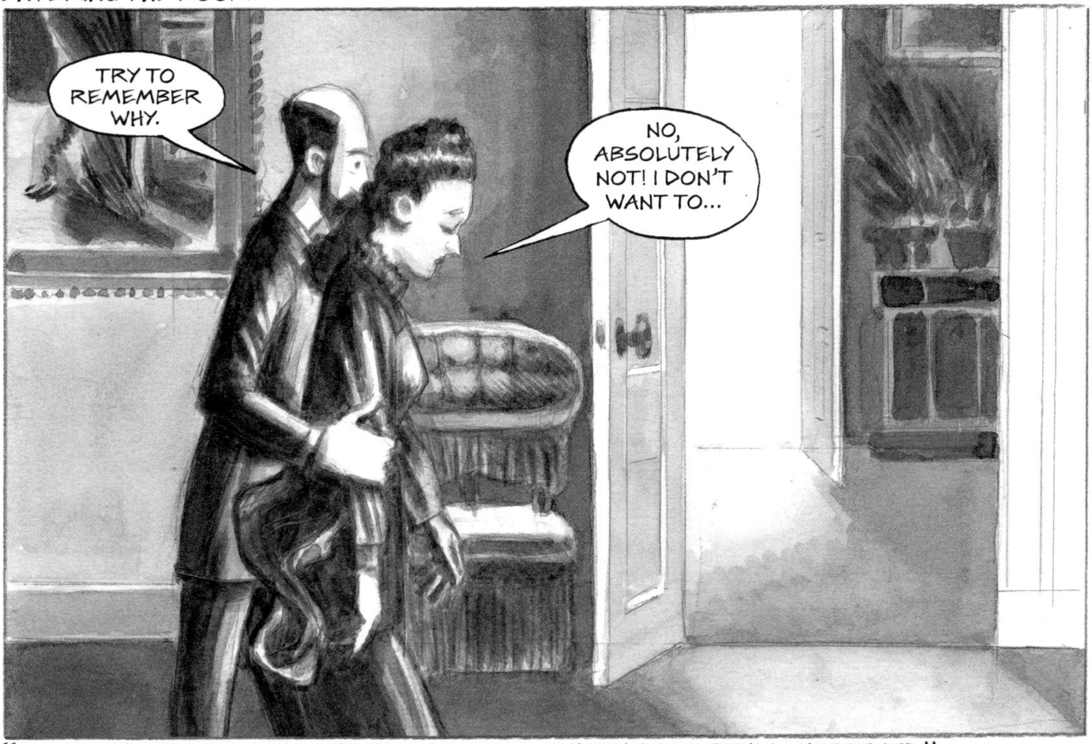
TRY TO REMEMBER WHY.
NO, ABSOLUTELY NOT! I DON'T WANT TO...

"I BROUGHT HER BACK TO THE SAME ROOM... AND THE SAME THING HAPPENED."

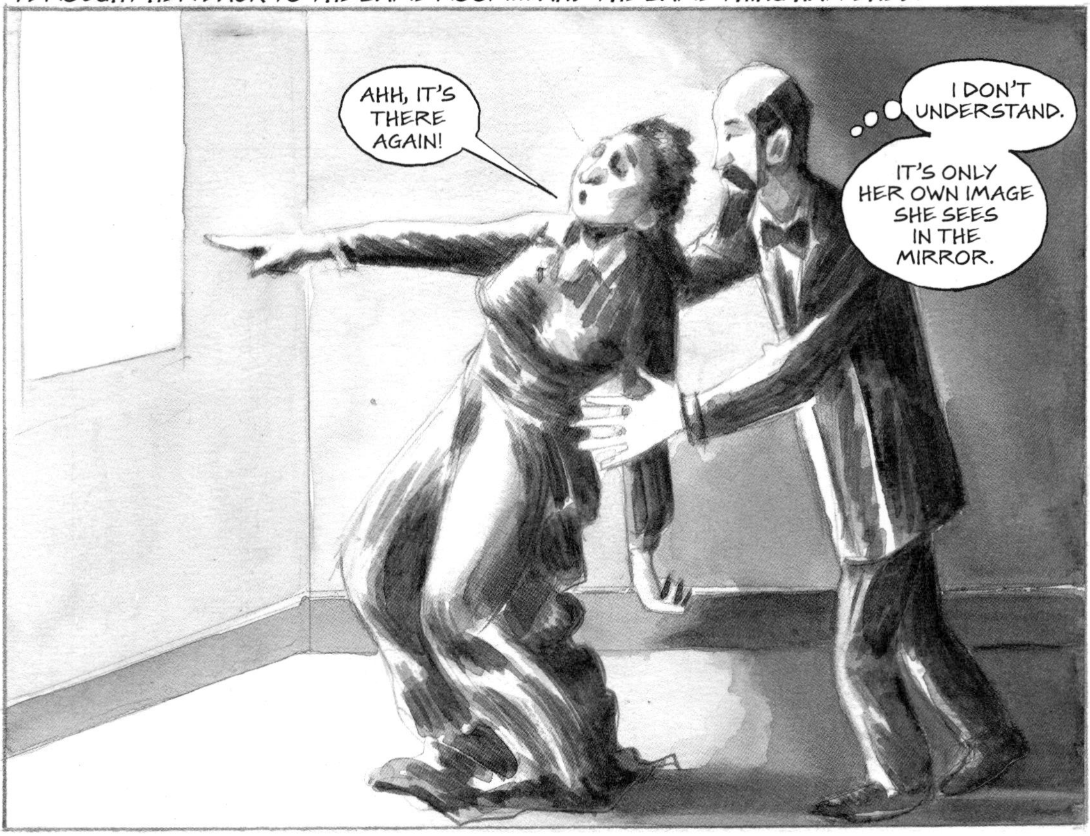
AHH, IT'S THERE AGAIN!
I DON'T UNDERSTAND.
IT'S ONLY HER OWN IMAGE SHE SEES IN THE MIRROR.

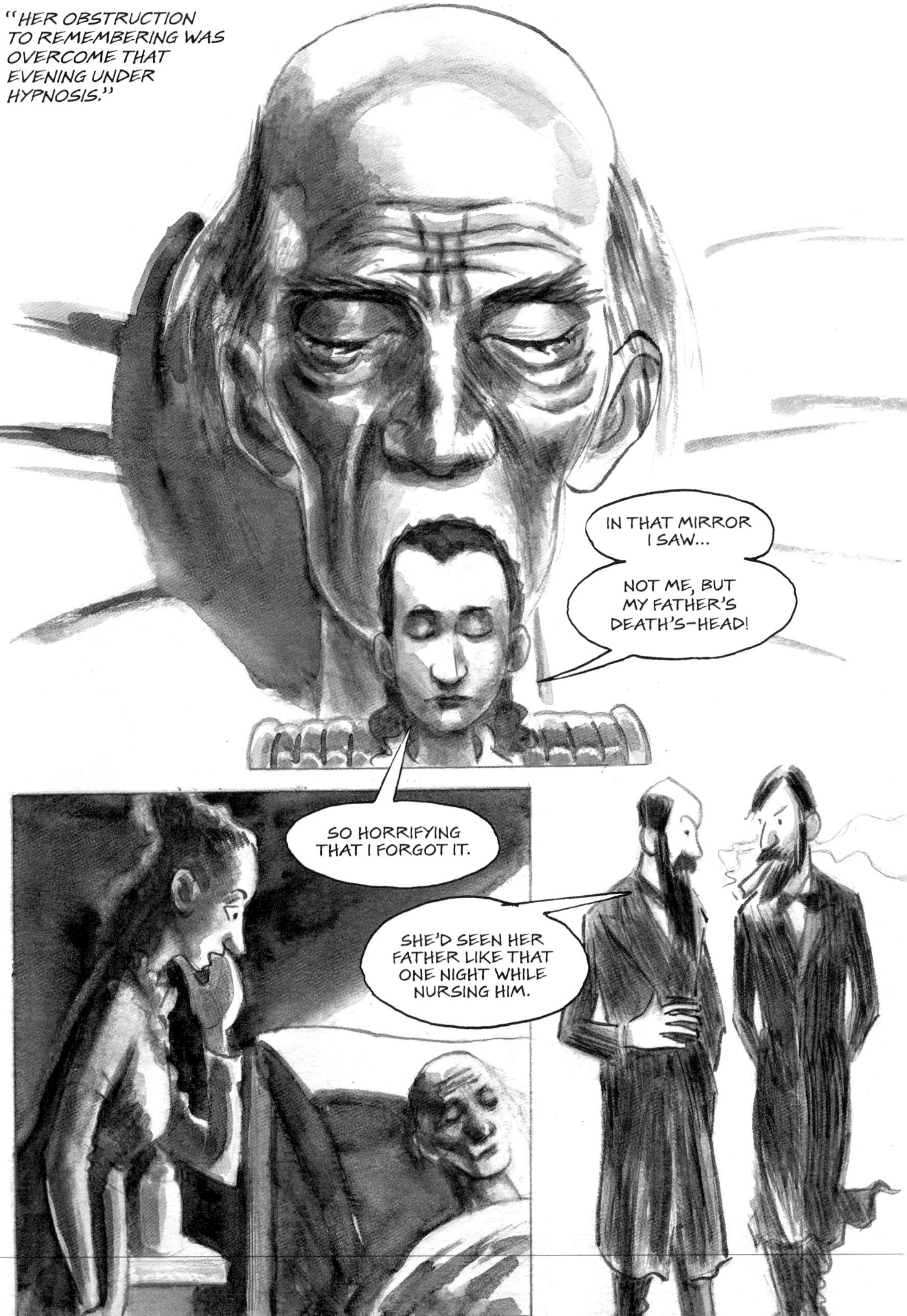
"HER OBSTRUCTION TO REMEMBERING WAS OVERCOME THAT EVENING UNDER HYPNOSIS."
IN THAT MIRROR I SAW...
NOT ME, BUT MY FATHER'S DEATH'S-HEAD!
SO HORRIFYING THAT I FORGOT IT.
SHE'D SEEN HER FATHER LIKE THAT ONE NIGHT WHILE NURSING HIM.

"EVERYTHING POINTED BACK TO THE MONTHS OF CONSTANT NURSING FROM JULY 1880, WHEN HE BECAME ILL WITH A SUB-PLEURAL ABSCESS, UNTIL HER CRIPPLING SYMPTOMS BEGAN IN DECEMBER."

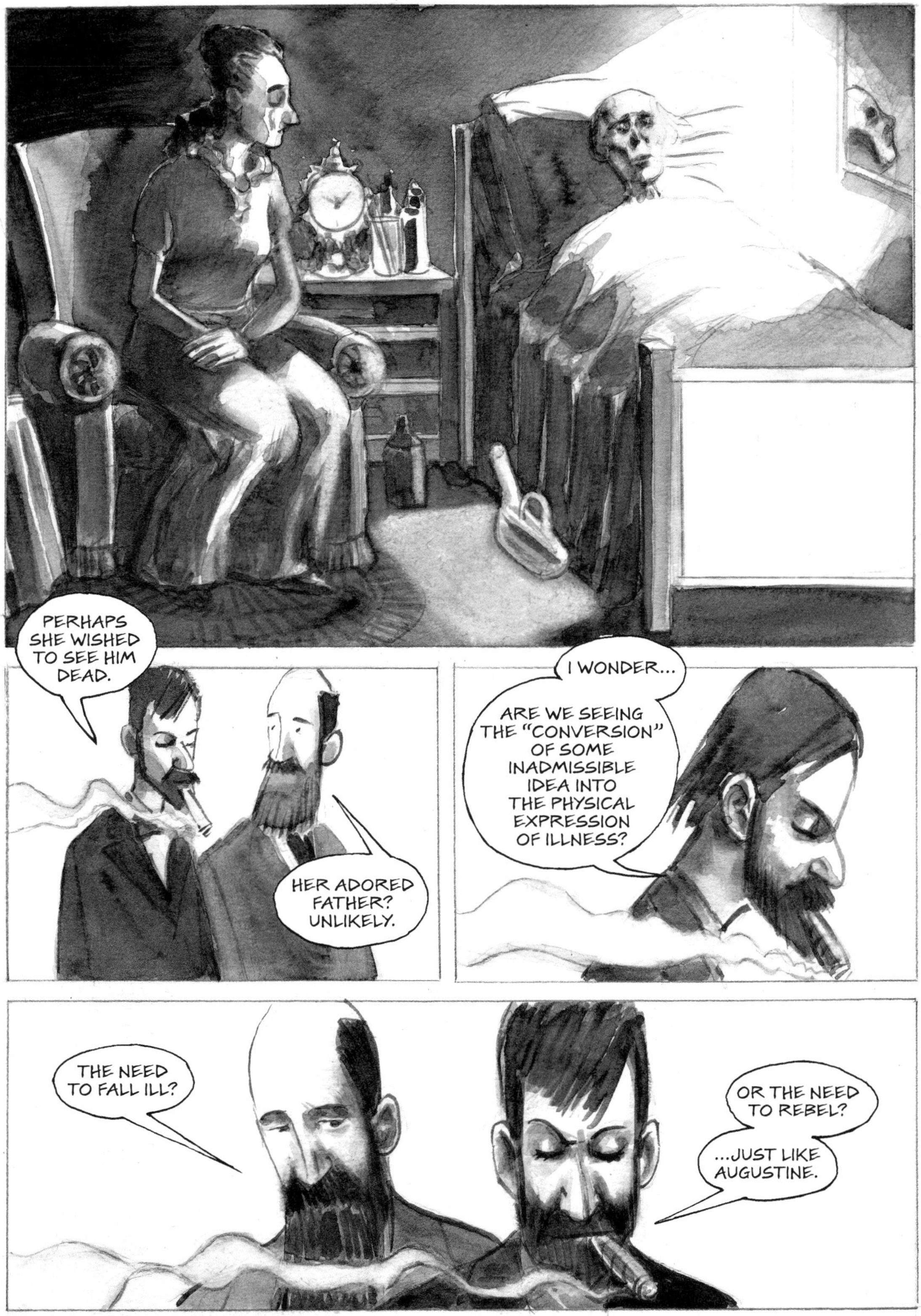
PERHAPS SHE WISHED TO SEE HIM DEAD.
HER ADORED FATHER? UNLIKELY.
I WONDER...
ARE WE SEEING THE "CONVERSION" OF SOME INADMISSIBLE IDEA INTO THE PHYSICAL EXPRESSION OF ILLNESS?
THE NEED TO FALL ILL?
OR THE NEED TO REBEL?
...JUST LIKE AUGUSTINE.

"HER TREATMENT INCHED ALONG INTO 1882, WHEN A PECULIAR PATTERN OF BEHAVIOUR EMERGED. IN HER NIGHT-TIME TRANCES SHE EXISTED ENTIRELY IN THE WINTER OF 1881, PREVIOUS TO HER FATHER'S DEATH IN APRIL, WHILE DAY-TIMES RETURNED HER TO 1882."

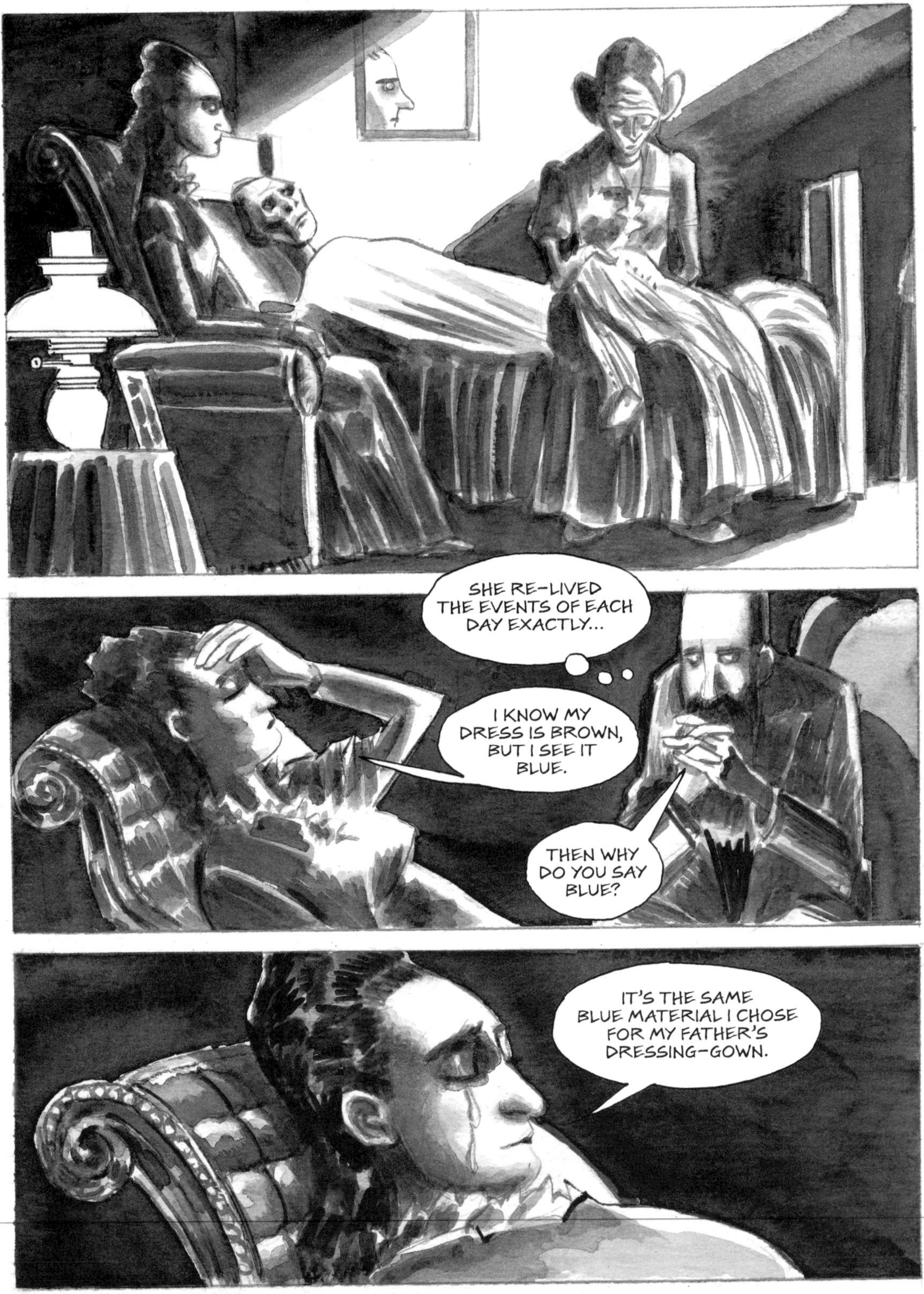

SHE RE-LIVED THE EVENTS OF EACH DAY EXACTLY...
I KNOW MY DRESS IS BROWN, BUT I SEE IT BLUE.
THEN WHY DO YOU SAY BLUE?
IT'S THE SAME BLUE MATERIAL I CHOSE FOR MY FATHER'S DRESSING-GOWN.

"HER MOTHER'S DIARY OF 1881 CONFIRMED THE ACCURACY OF ANNA'S TRANCE IMMERSIONS IN THE PAST. I NOTICED THAT A SYMPTOM WOULD DISAPPEAR IF SHE RE-LIVED A PAST PAINFUL EVENT TO ITS CONCLUSION."

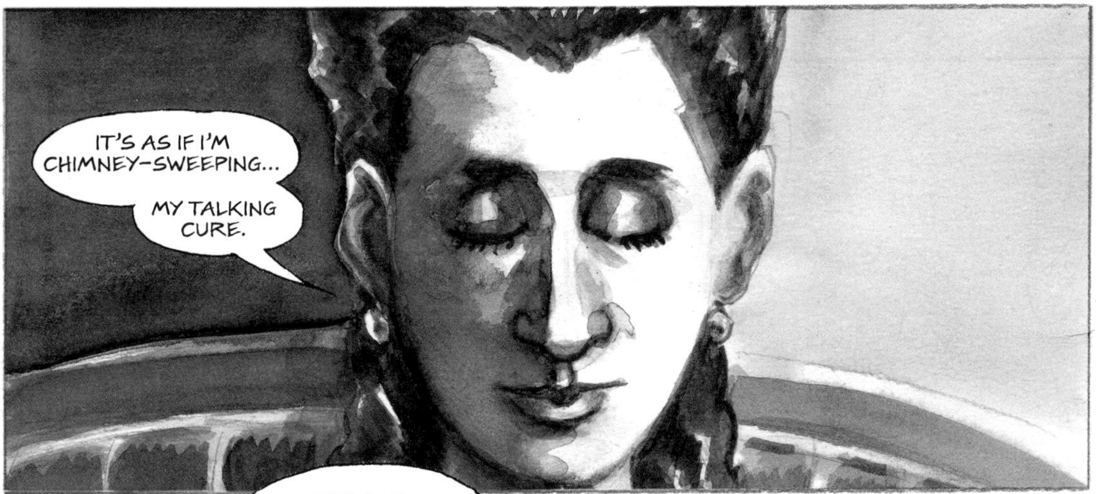

IT'S AS IF I'M CHIMNEY-SWEEPING...
MY TALKING CURE.

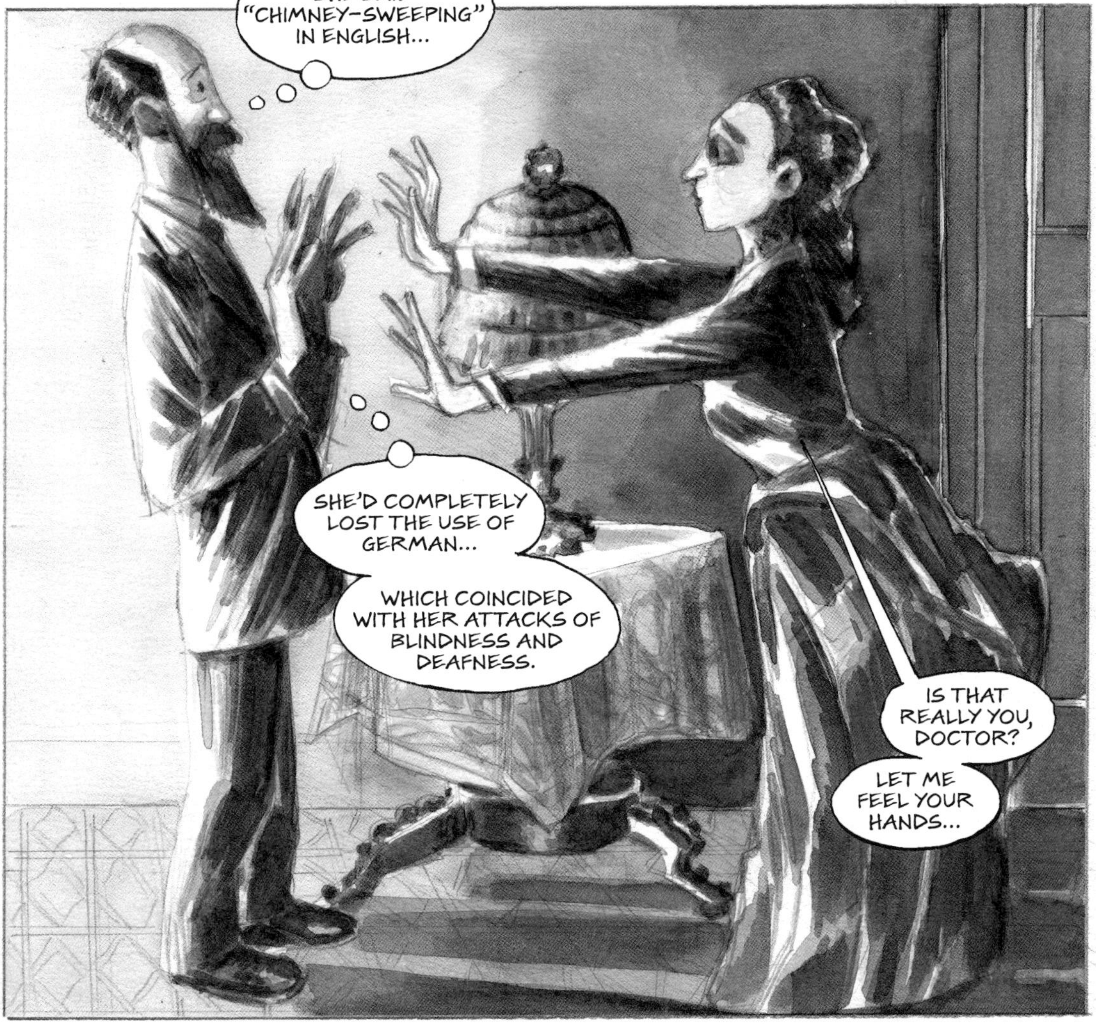

SHE SAID "CHIMNEY-SWEEPING" IN ENGLISH...
SHE'D COMPLETELY LOST THE USE OF GERMAN...
WHICH COINCIDED WITH HER ATTACKS OF BLINDNESS AND DEAFNESS.
IS THAT REALLY YOU, DOCTOR?
LET ME FEEL YOUR HANDS...

"ANNA OPENED MY EYES TO THE 'CATHARTIC METHOD' — TALKING SYMPTOMS AWAY BY RECALLING THEIR SCENE OF ORIGIN. PROGRESS IN HER TREATMENT NEVERTHELESS STUMBLED ON RELAPSES."

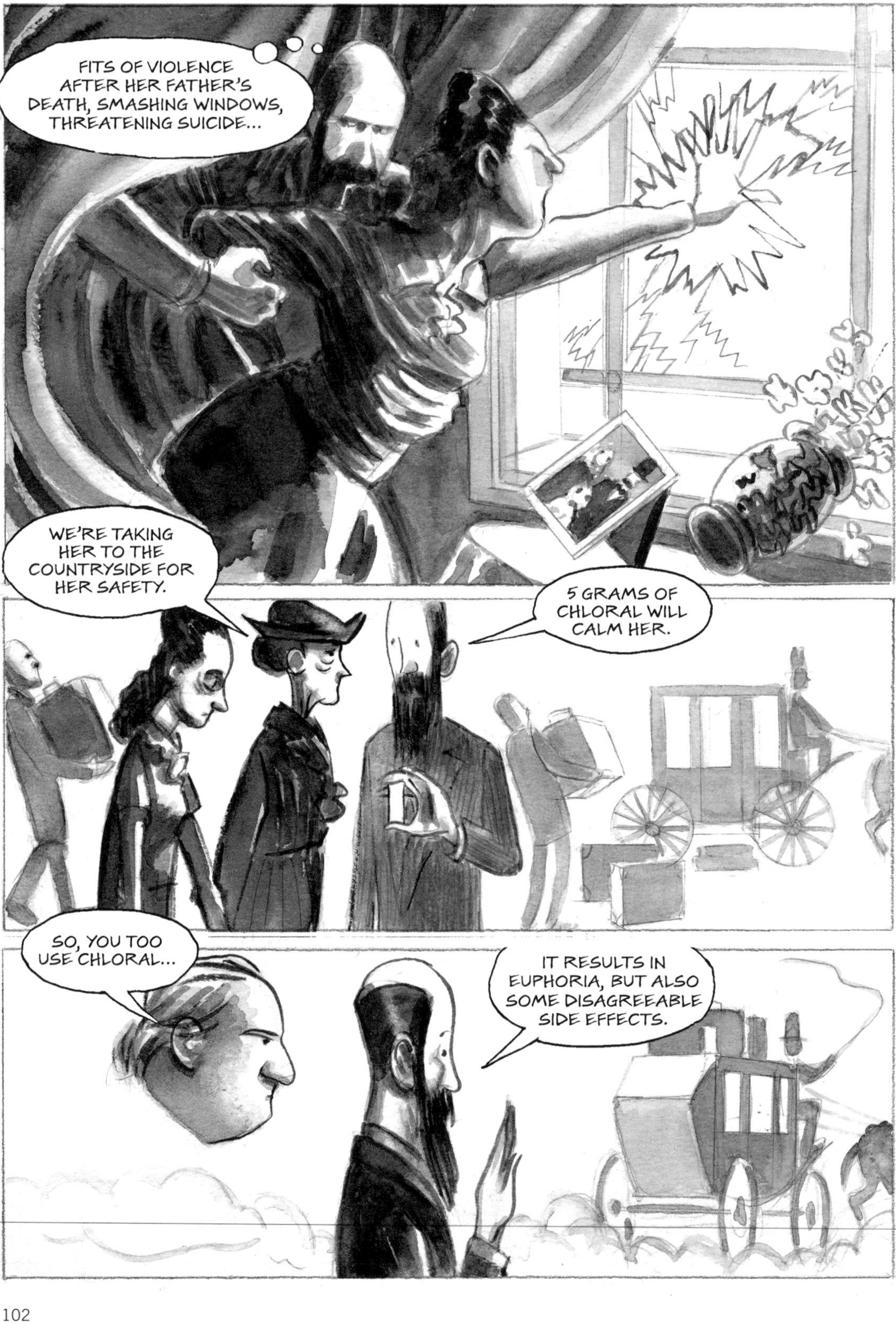
FITS OF VIOLENCE AFTER HER FATHER'S DEATH, SMASHING WINDOWS, THREATENING SUICIDE...
WE'RE TAKING HER TO THE COUNTRYSIDE FOR HER SAFETY.
5 GRAMS OF CHLORAL WILL CALM HER.
SO, YOU TOO USE CHLORAL...
IT RESULTS IN EUPHORIA, BUT ALSO SOME DISAGREEABLE SIDE EFFECTS.

"IN THE INTERVALS BETWEEN MY FEWER VISITS TO HER IN THE COUNTRY, SHE WORSENED, AND REFUSED TO TALK, EVEN UNDER HYPNOSIS."

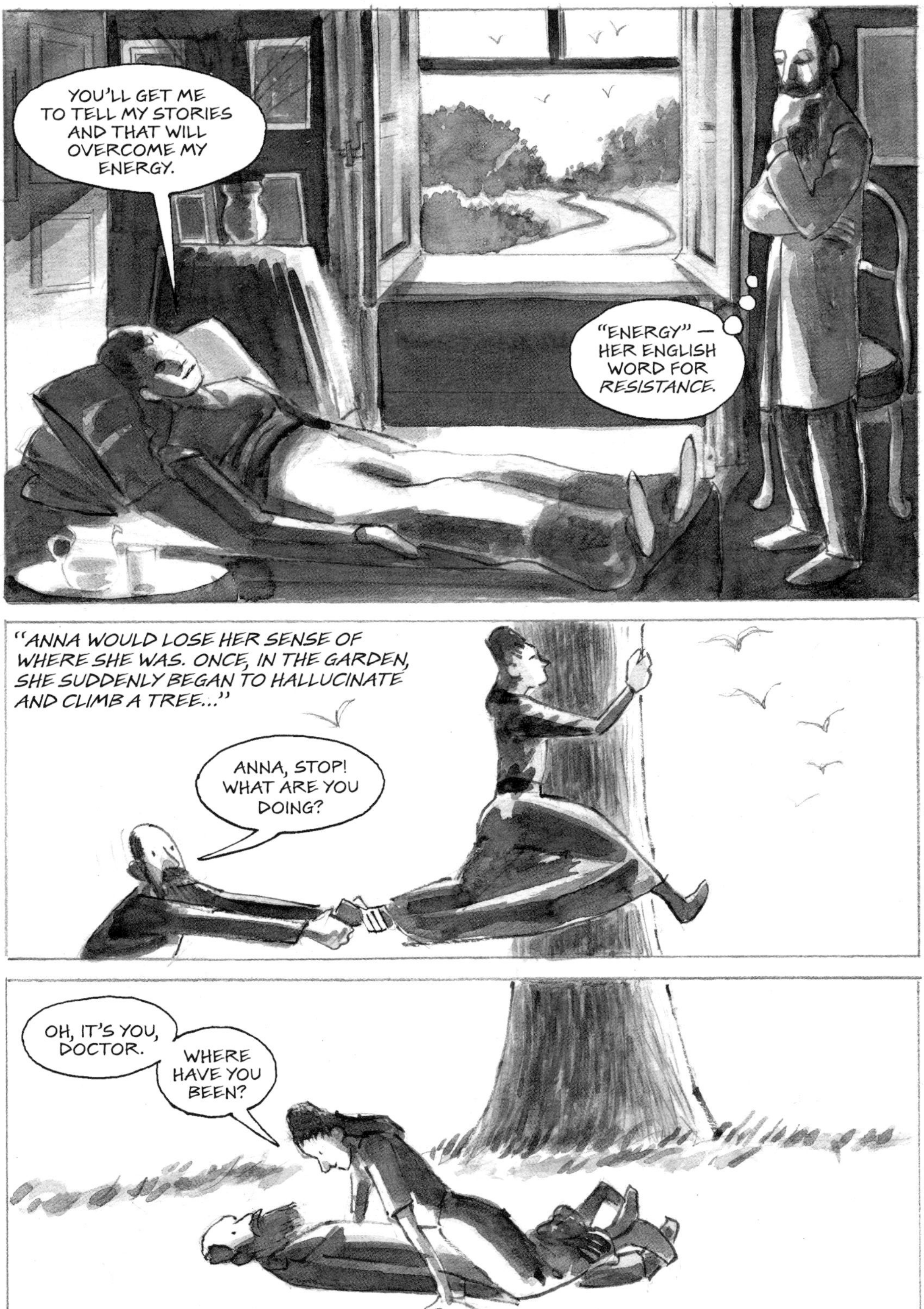
YOU'LL GET ME TO TELL MY STORIES AND THAT WILL OVERCOME MY ENERGY.
"ENERGY" — HER ENGLISH WORD FOR RESISTANCE.
"ANNA WOULD LOSE HER SENSE OF WHERE SHE WAS. ONCE, IN THE GARDEN, SHE SUDDENLY BEGAN TO HALLUCINATE AND CLIMB A TREE..."
ANNA, STOP! WHAT ARE YOU DOING?
OH, IT'S YOU, DOCTOR.
WHERE HAVE YOU BEEN?

"HER BOUTS OF ANOREXIA PERSISTED. I COAXED HER TO EAT A LITTLE, BUT THEN, DESPITE THAT SUMMER'S GREAT HEAT, SHE WOULD NOT DRINK ANY WATER."

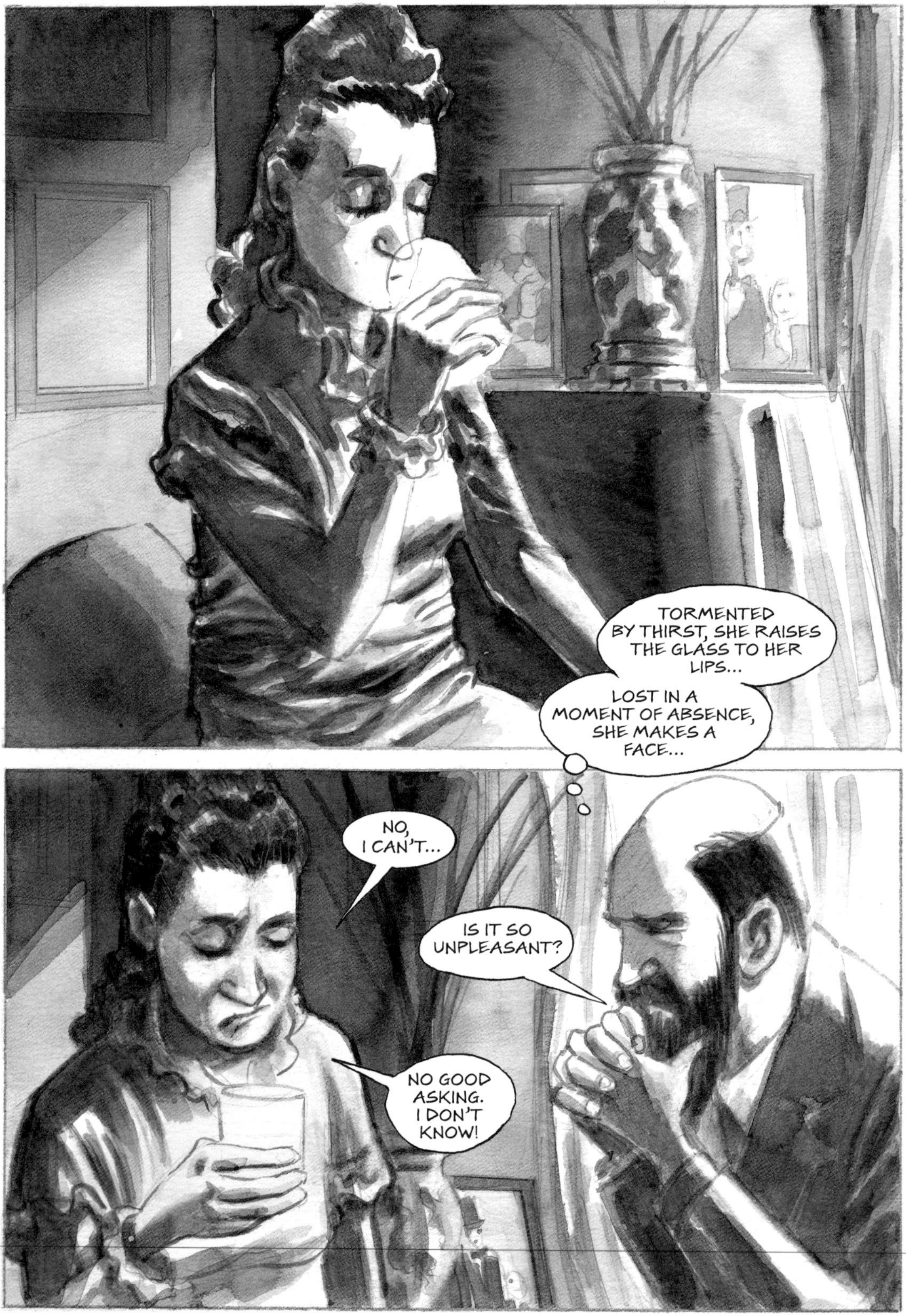
TORMENTED BY THIRST, SHE RAISES THE GLASS TO HER LIPS...
LOST IN A MOMENT OF ABSENCE, SHE MAKES A FACE...
NO, I CAN'T...
IS IT SO UNPLEASANT?
NO GOOD ASKING. I DON'T KNOW!

"SHE SURVIVED HER HYDROPHOBIA BY EATING FRUIT FOR SIX WEEKS. ONE DAY, UNDER HYPNOSIS, SHE BEGAN GRUMBLING ABOUT AN ENGLISH LADY COMPANION IN THE PAST."

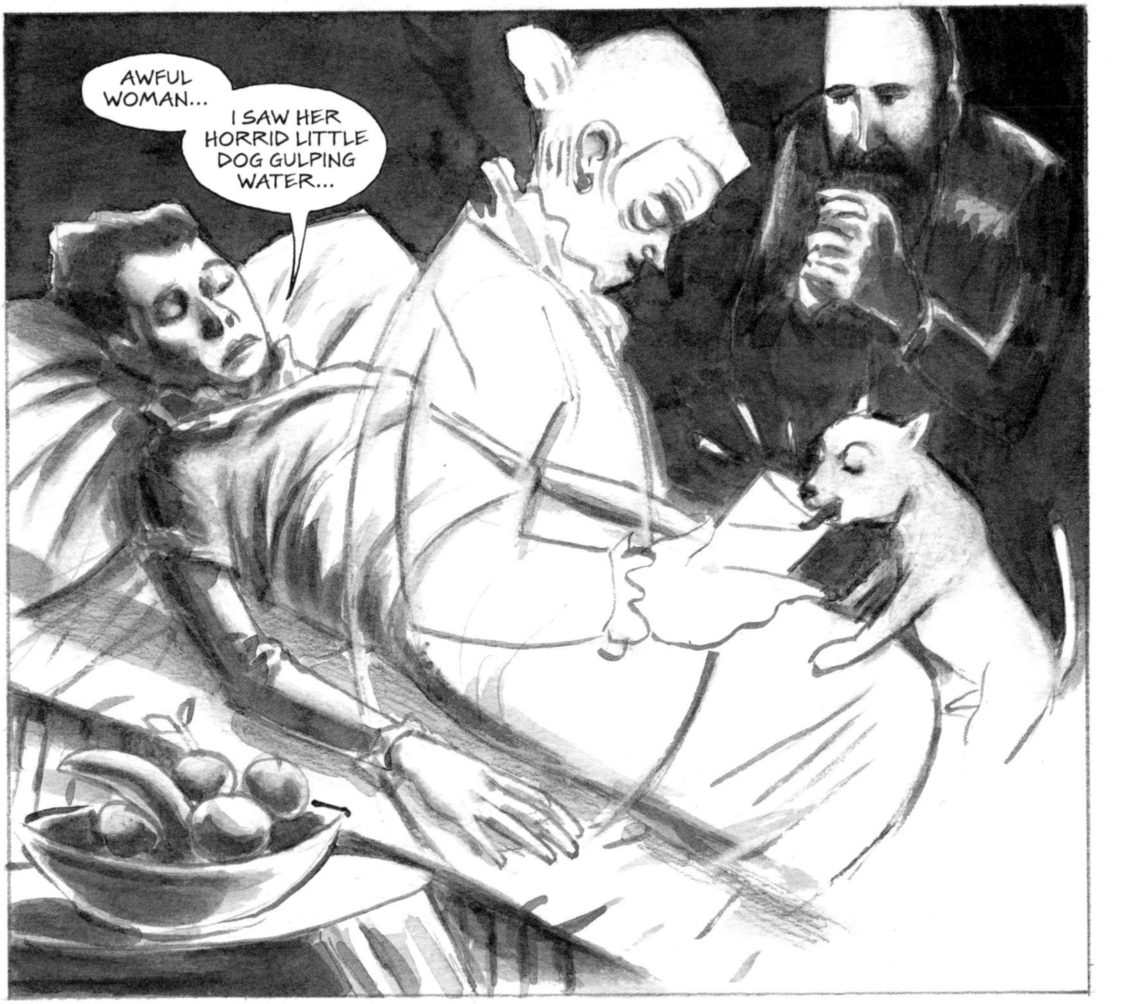
AWFUL WOMAN...
I SAW HER HORRID LITTLE DOG GULPING WATER...

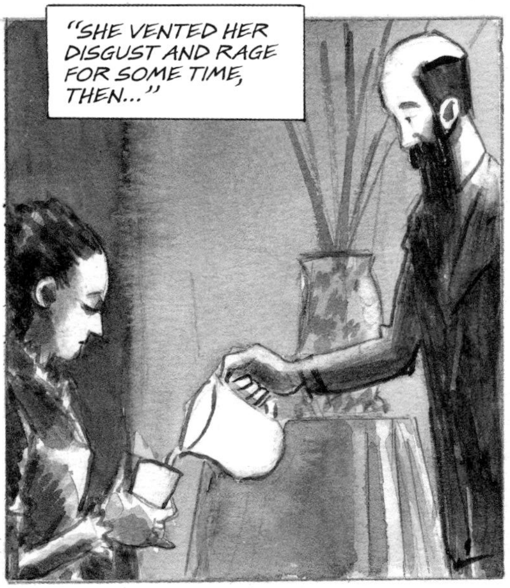
"SHE VENTED HER DISGUST AND RAGE FOR SOME TIME, THEN..."

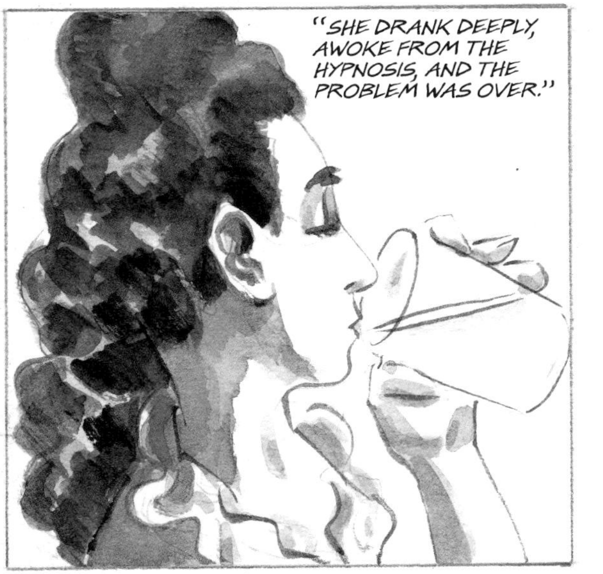
"SHE DRANK DEEPLY, AWOKE FROM THE HYPNOSIS, AND THE PROBLEM WAS OVER."

"HER ABILITY TO BRIDGE THE HYPNOTIC AND CONSCIOUS STATES MUST BE THE ANSWER! WE NOW HAD A WAY TO EXPEDITE HER TREATMENT."

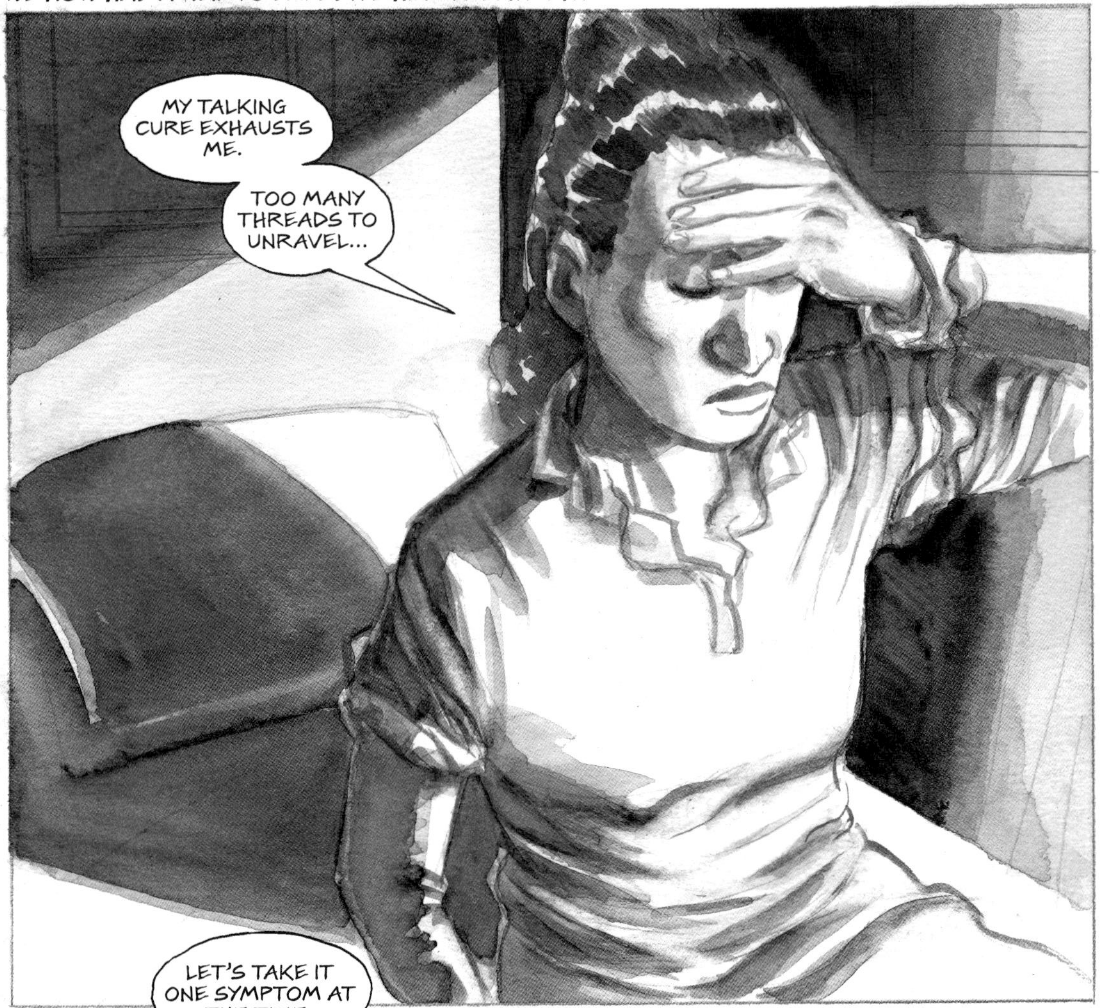
MY TALKING CURE EXHAUSTS ME.
TOO MANY THREADS TO UNRAVEL...

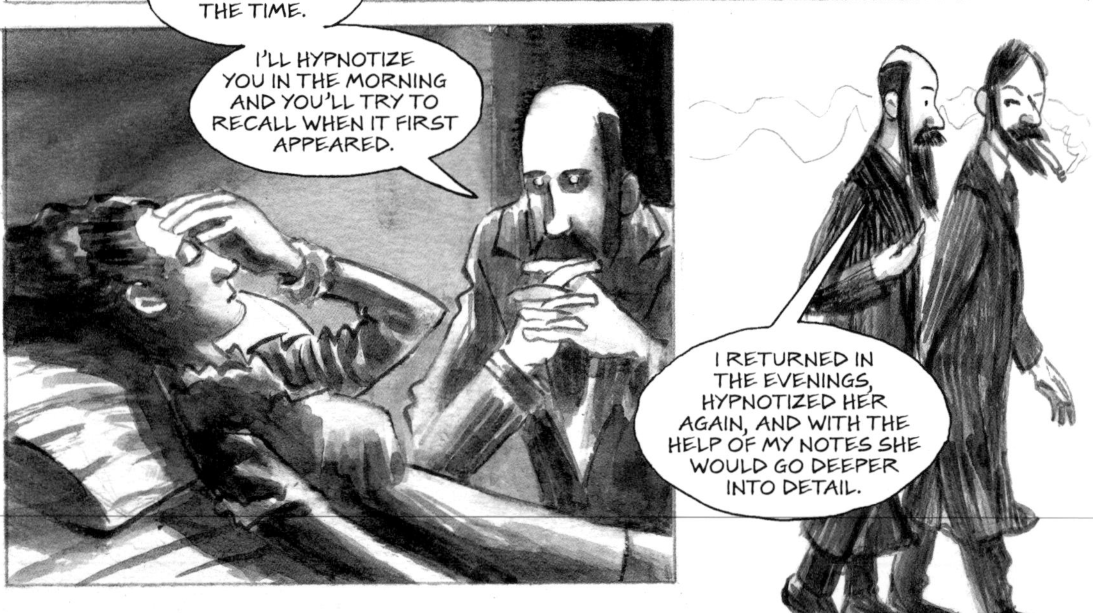
LET'S TAKE IT ONE SYMPTOM AT THE TIME.
I'LL HYPNOTIZE YOU IN THE MORNING AND YOU'LL TRY TO RECALL WHEN IT FIRST APPEARED.
I RETURNED IN THE EVENINGS, HYPNOTIZED HER AGAIN, AND WITH THE HELP OF MY NOTES SHE WOULD GO DEEPER INTO DETAIL.

"WE WERE LED BACK TO THE INCUBATION PERIOD OF HER ILLNESS, THE NURSING OF HER FATHER, AND A REPRESSED MEMORY WOULD THEN EMERGE TO UNDERGO ABREACTION."

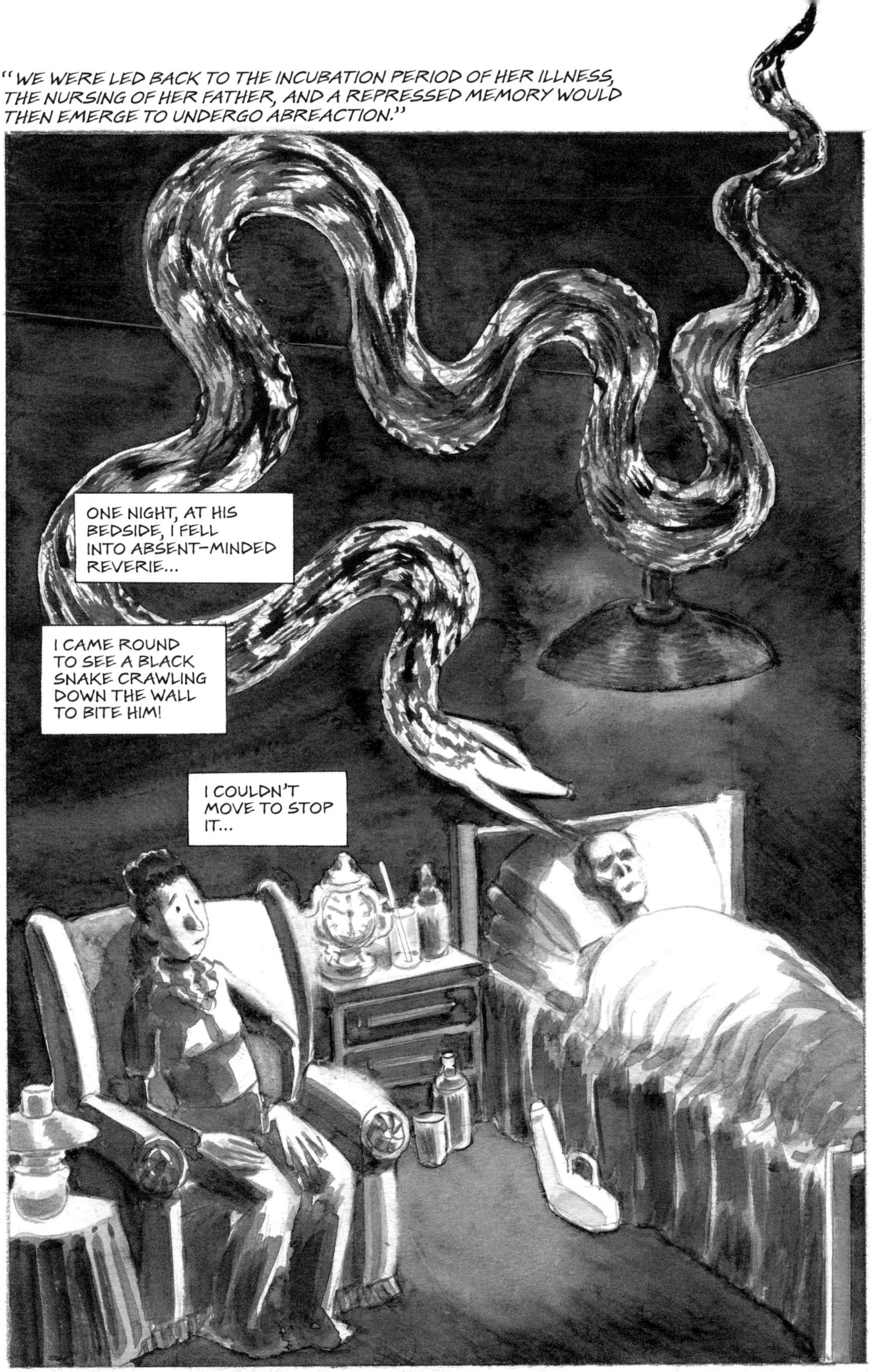
ONE NIGHT, AT HIS BEDSIDE, I FELL INTO ABSENT-MINDED REVERIE...
I CAME ROUND TO SEE A BLACK SNAKE CRAWLING DOWN THE WALL TO BITE HIM!
I COULDN'T MOVE TO STOP IT...

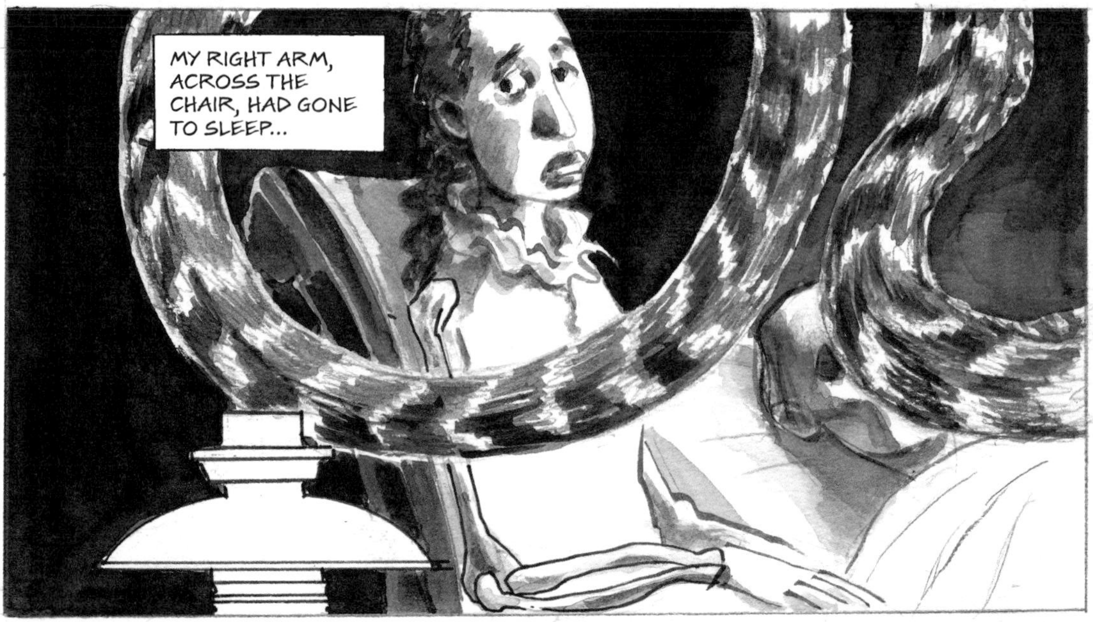
MY RIGHT ARM, ACROSS THE CHAIR, HAD GONE TO SLEEP...

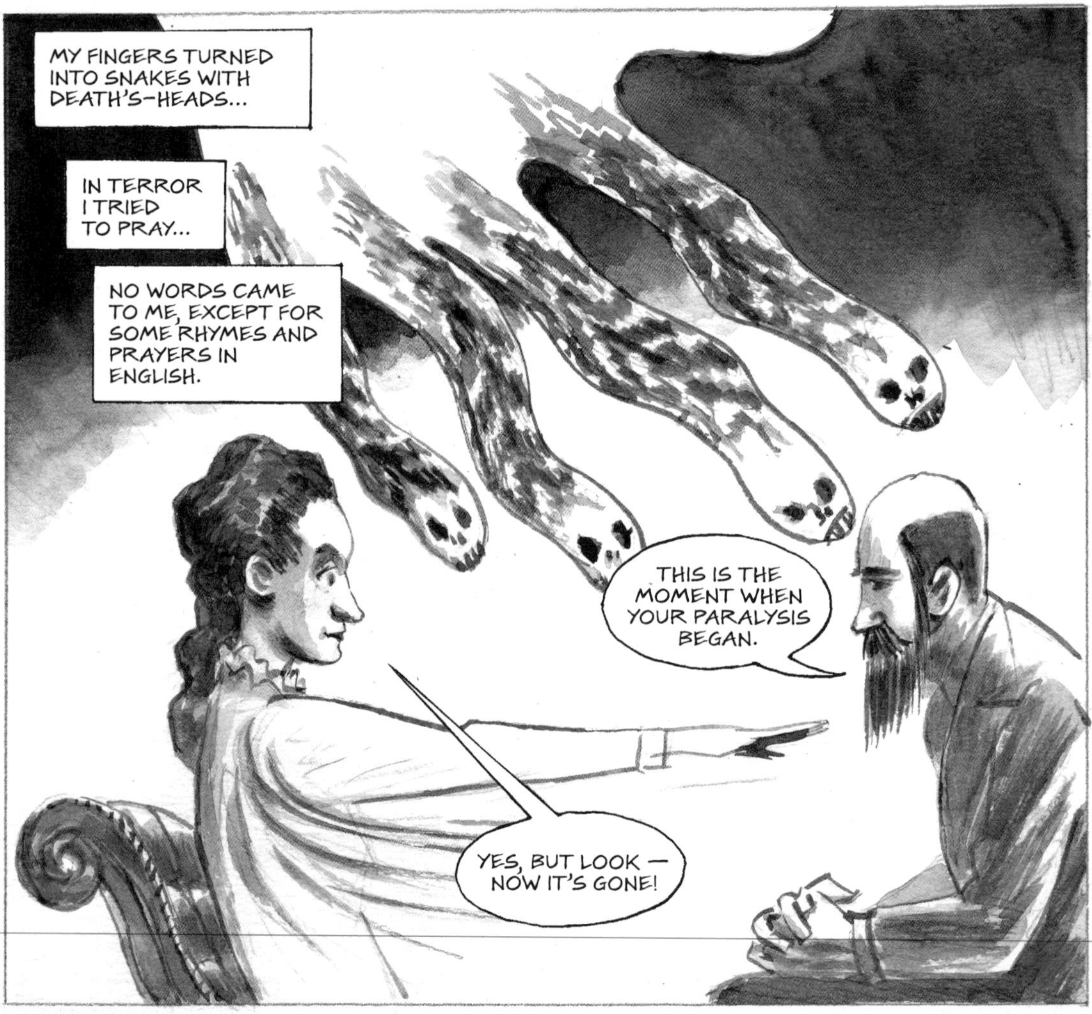
MY FINGERS TURNED INTO SNAKES WITH DEATH'S-HEADS...
IN TERROR I TRIED TO PRAY...
NO WORDS CAME TO ME, EXCEPT FOR SOME RHYMES AND PRAYERS IN ENGLISH.
THIS IS THE MOMENT WHEN YOUR PARALYSIS BEGAN.
YES, BUT LOOK — NOW IT'S GONE!

"WE ALSO TRACED BACK HER SYMPTOM OF IMPAIRED EYESIGHT TO ITS FIRST OCCURRENCE."

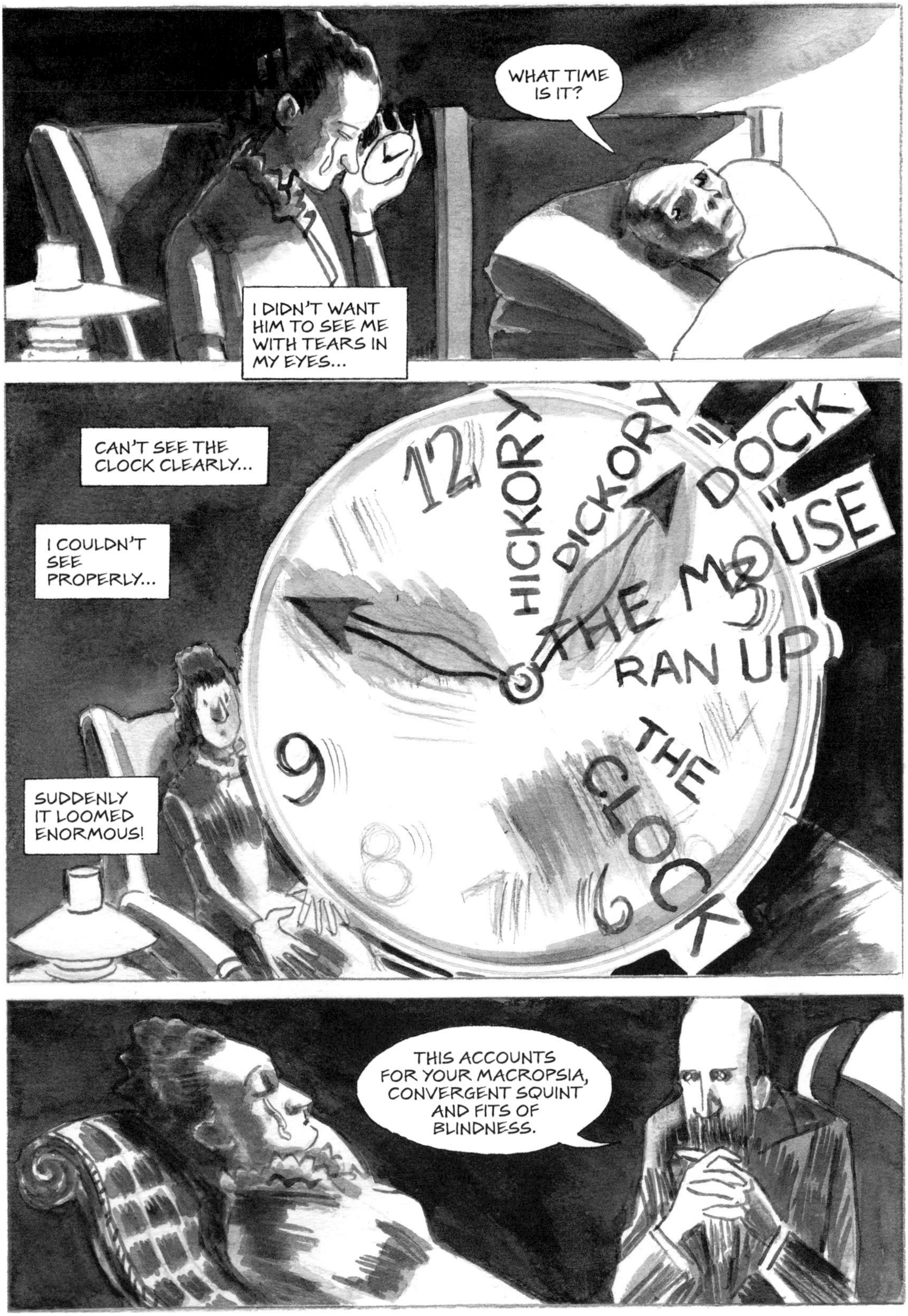
WHAT TIME IS IT?
I DIDN'T WANT HIM TO SEE ME WITH TEARS IN MY EYES...
CAN'T SEE THE CLOCK CLEARLY...
I COULDN'T SEE PROPERLY...
SUDDENLY IT LOOMED ENORMOUS!
HICKORY DICKORY DOCK
THE MOUSE RAN UP THE CLOCK
THIS ACCOUNTS FOR YOUR MACROPSIA, CONVERGENT SQUINT AND FITS OF BLINDNESS.

"ONE BY ONE, WITH ANNA'S COOPERATION, ALL HER SYMPTOMS WERE ELIMINATED BY JUNE 1882. SUCCESS, AFTER 18 MONTHS OF HARD WORK." I WAS TOO ENGROSSED IN ANNA'S CASE TO NOTICE MY WIFE'S REACTION.

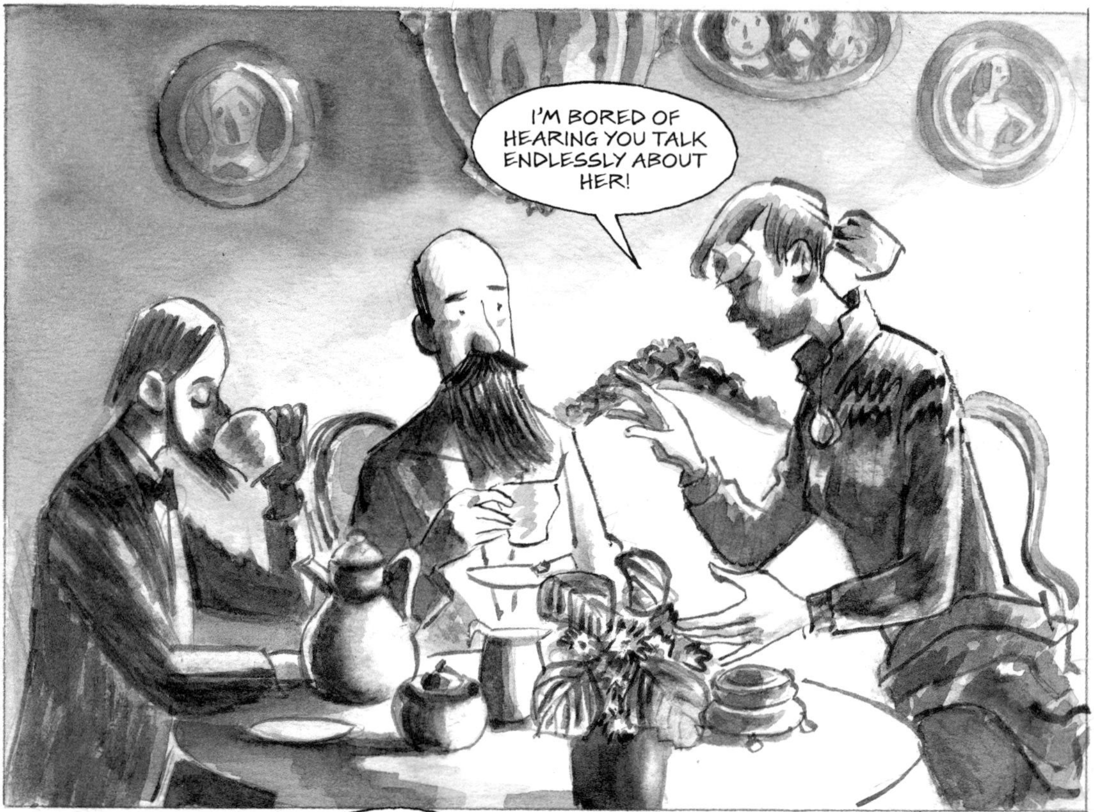
I'M BORED OF HEARING YOU TALK ENDLESSLY ABOUT HER!

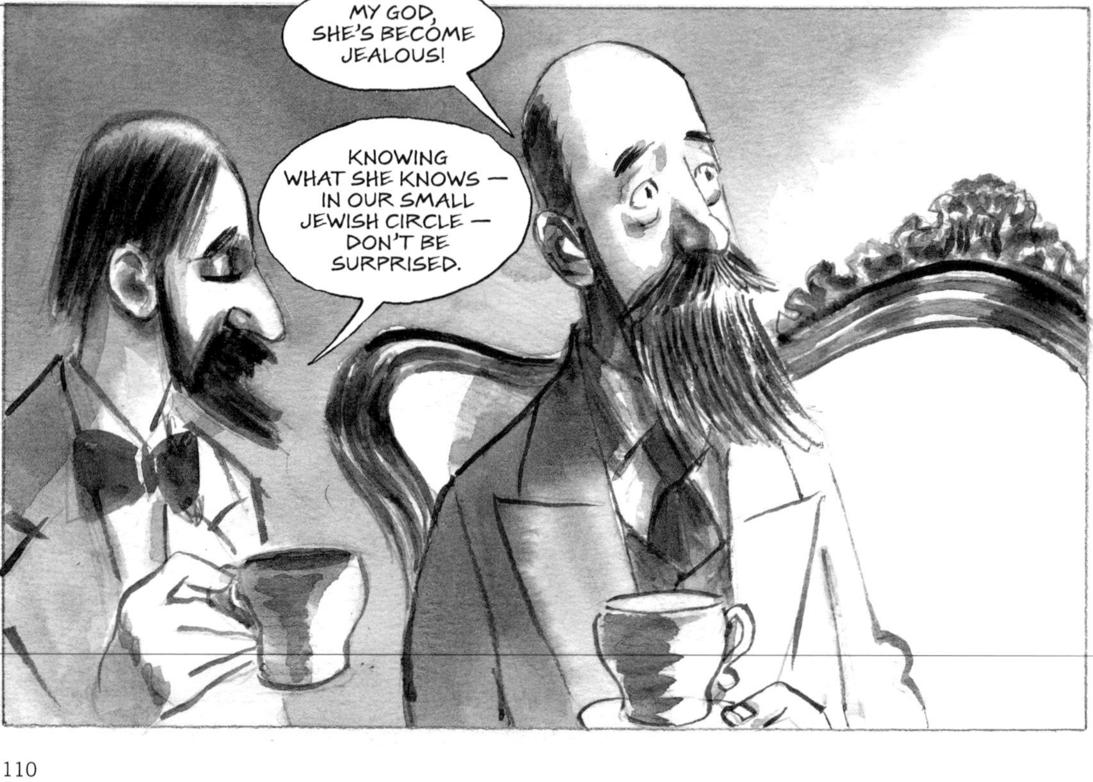
MY GOD, SHE'S BECOME JEALOUS!
KNOWING WHAT SHE KNOWS — IN OUR SMALL JEWISH CIRCLE — DON'T BE SURPRISED.

BREUER'S WIFE KNEW "ANNA O." AS BERTHA PAPPENHEIM, A SEDUCTIVELY ATTRACTIVE YOUNG WOMAN. HE AT ONCE TOLD ANNA THAT HER TREATMENT WAS OVER.

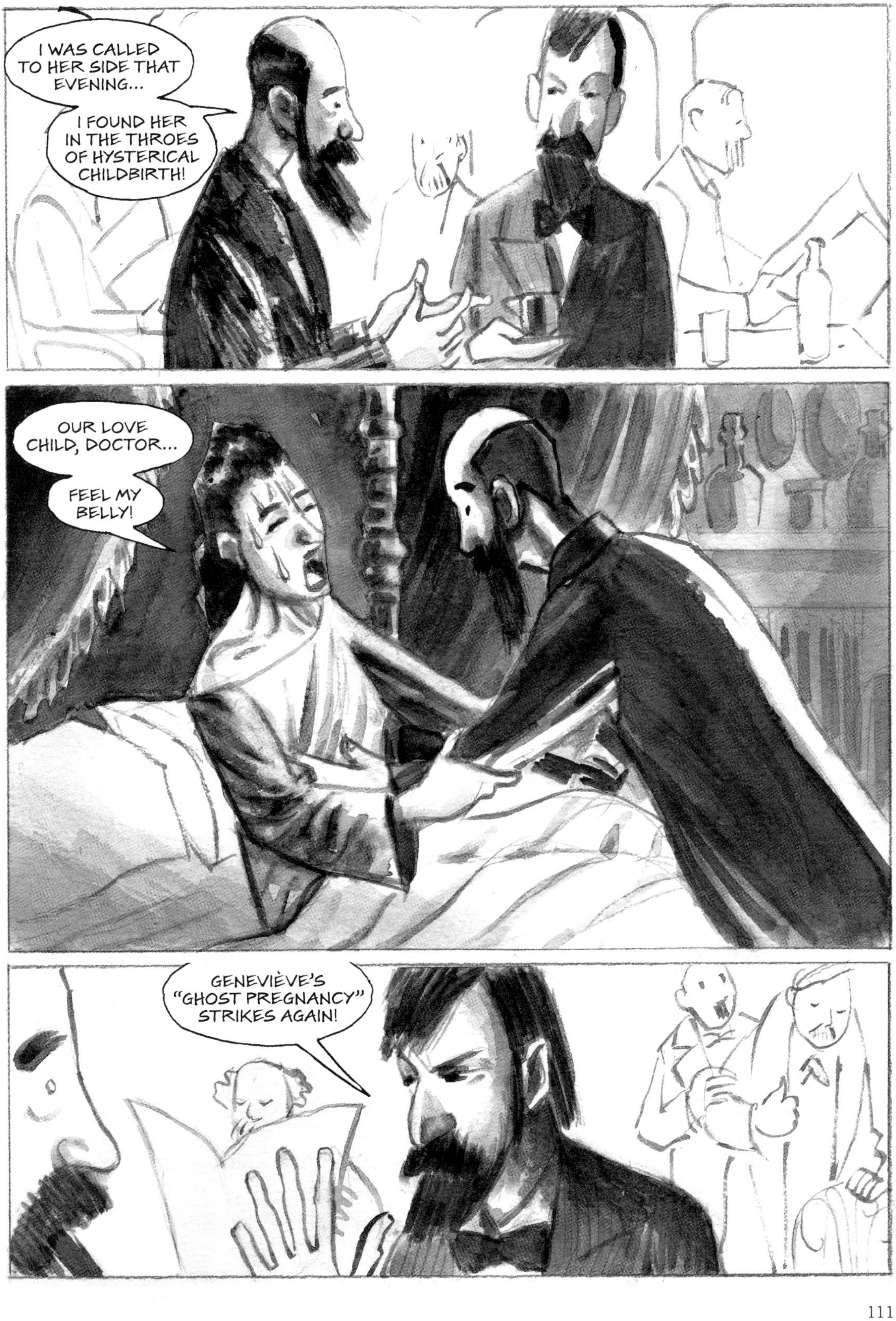
I WAS CALLED TO HER SIDE THAT EVENING...
I FOUND HER IN THE THROES OF HYSTERICAL CHILDBIRTH!
OUR LOVE CHILD, DOCTOR...
FEEL MY BELLY!
GENEVIÈVE'S "GHOST PREGNANCY" STRIKES AGAIN!

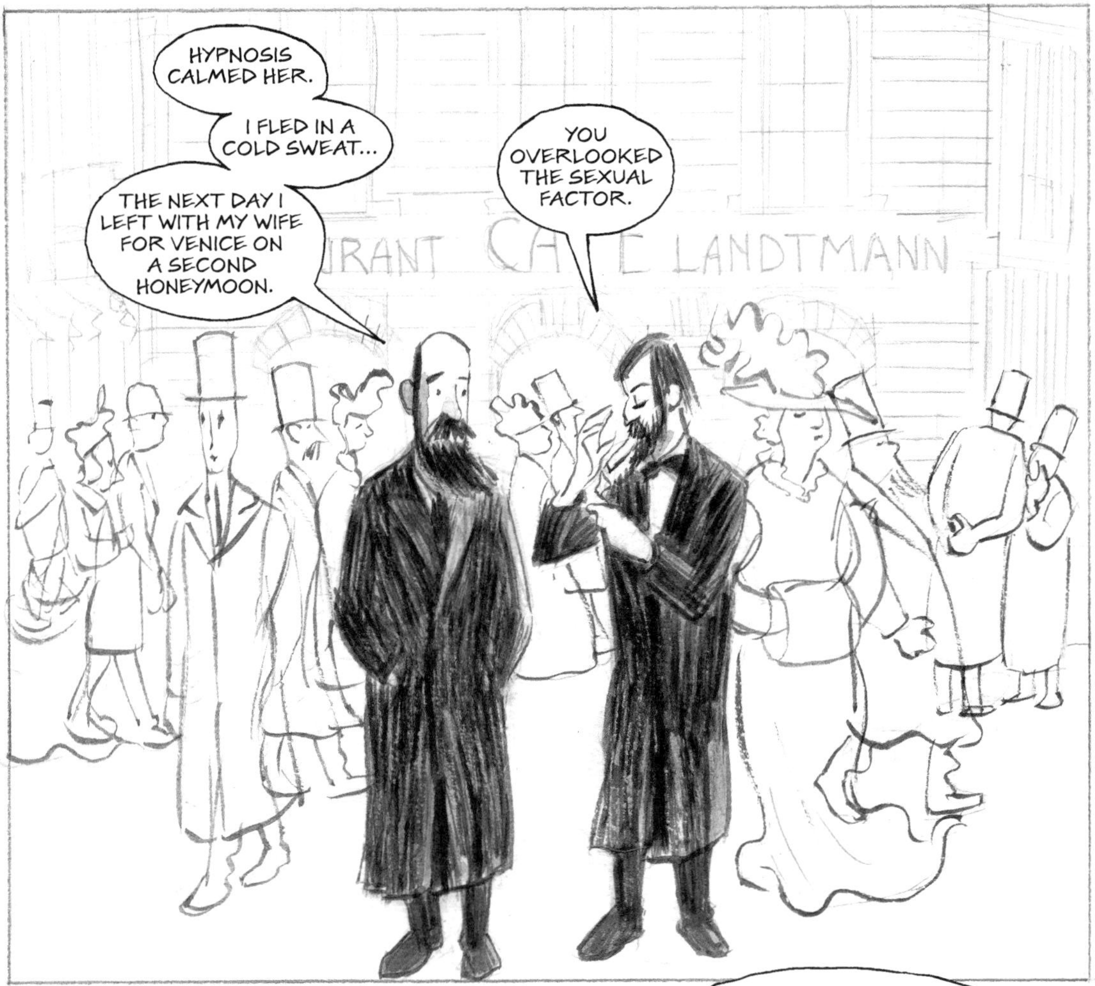
HYPNOSIS CALMED HER.
I FLED IN A COLD SWEAT...
THE NEXT DAY I LEFT WITH MY WIFE FOR VENICE ON A SECOND HONEYMOON.
YOU OVERLOOKED THE SEXUAL FACTOR.
URANT CA E LANDTMANN

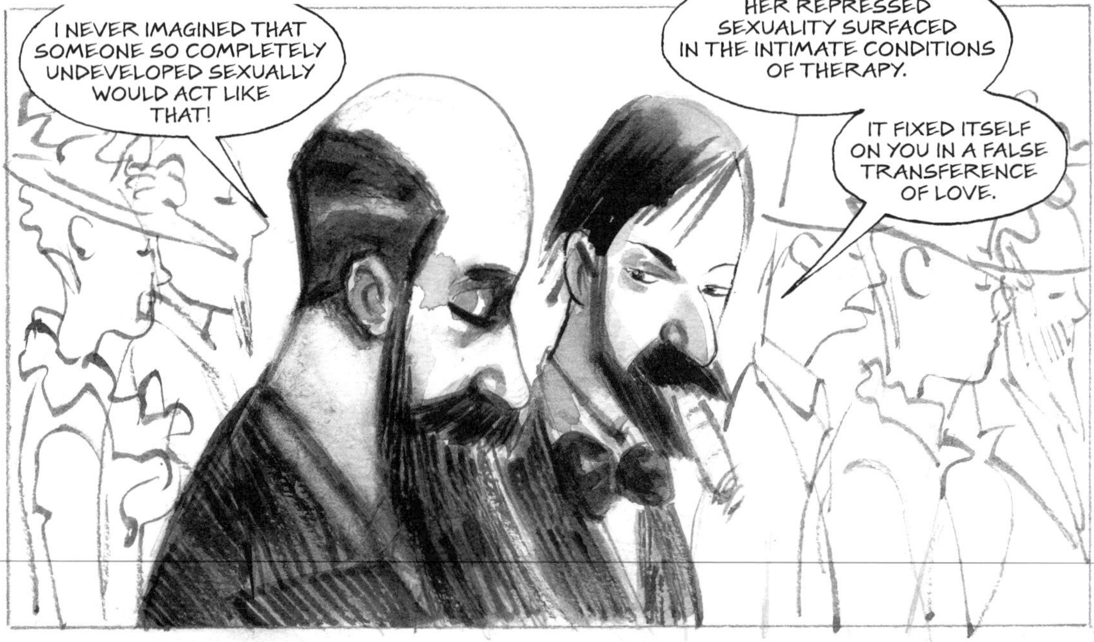
I NEVER IMAGINED THAT SOMEONE SO COMPLETELY UNDEVELOPED SEXUALLY WOULD ACT LIKE THAT!
HER REPRESSED SEXUALITY SURFACED IN THE INTIMATE CONDITIONS OF THERAPY.
IT FIXED ITSELF ON YOU IN A FALSE TRANSFERENCE OF LOVE.

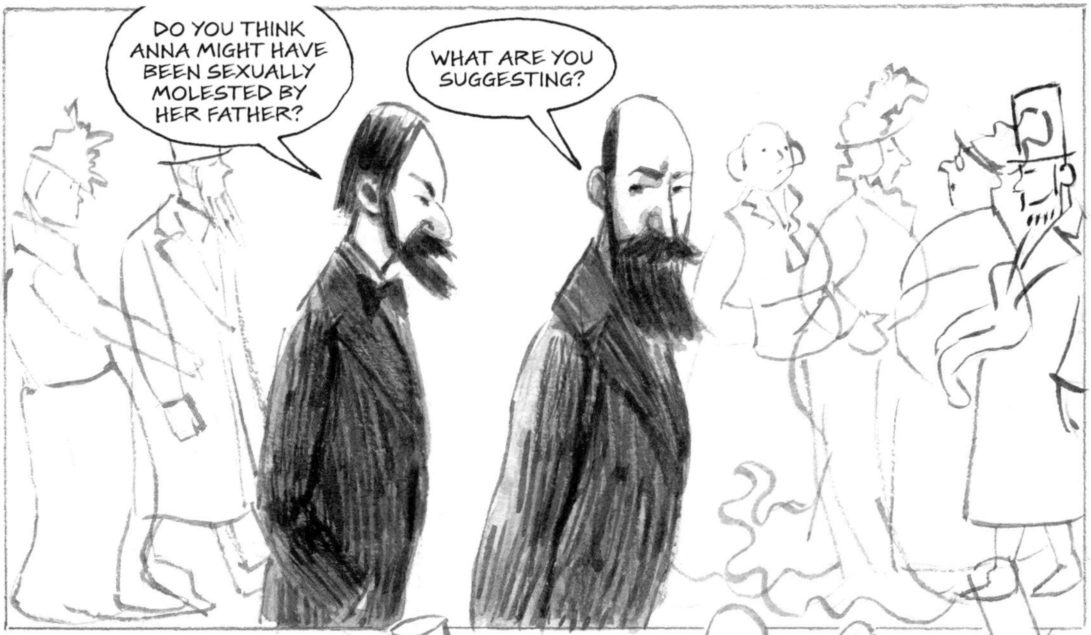
DO YOU THINK ANNA MIGHT HAVE BEEN SEXUALLY MOLESTED BY HER FATHER?
WHAT ARE YOU SUGGESTING?

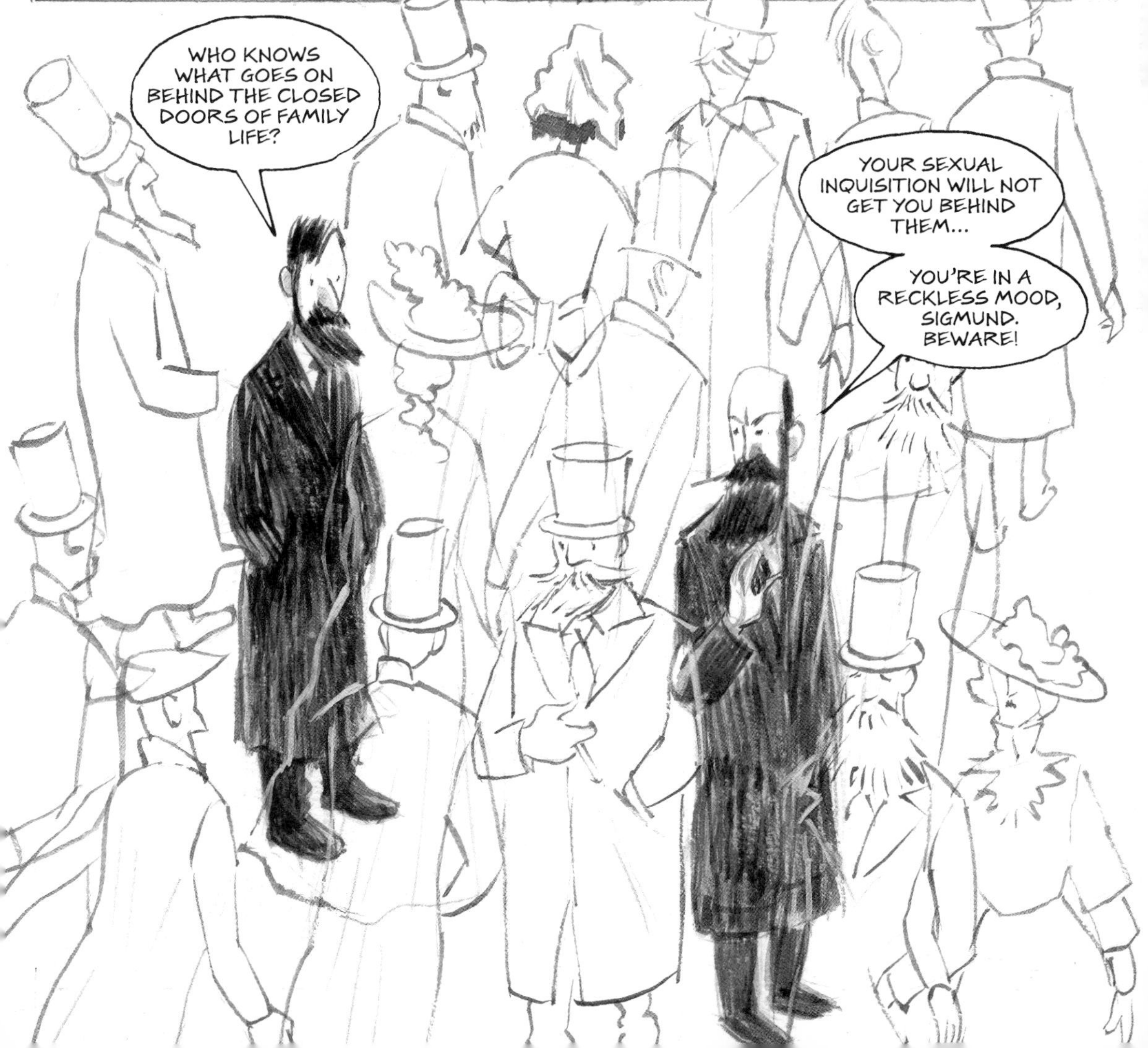
WHO KNOWS WHAT GOES ON BEHIND THE CLOSED DOORS OF FAMILY LIFE?
YOUR SEXUAL INQUISITION WILL NOT GET YOU BEHIND THEM...
YOU'RE IN A RECKLESS MOOD, SIGMUND. BEWARE!

BREUER'S WRITTEN ACCOUNT ALLEGES "ANNA O.'S COMPLETE CURE". BERTHA PAPPENHEIM WAS A CLOSE FRIEND OF MY WIFE MARTHA.

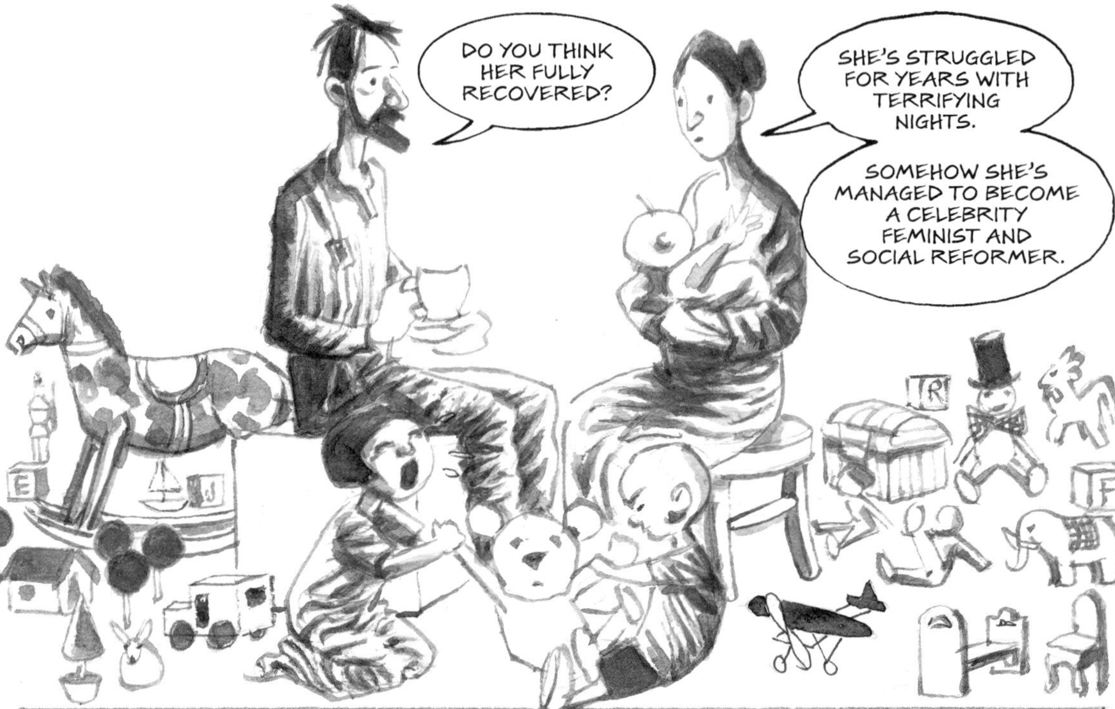
DO YOU THINK HER FULLY RECOVERED?
SHE'S STRUGGLED FOR YEARS WITH TERRIFYING NIGHTS.
SOMEHOW SHE'S MANAGED TO BECOME A CELEBRITY FEMINIST AND SOCIAL REFORMER.

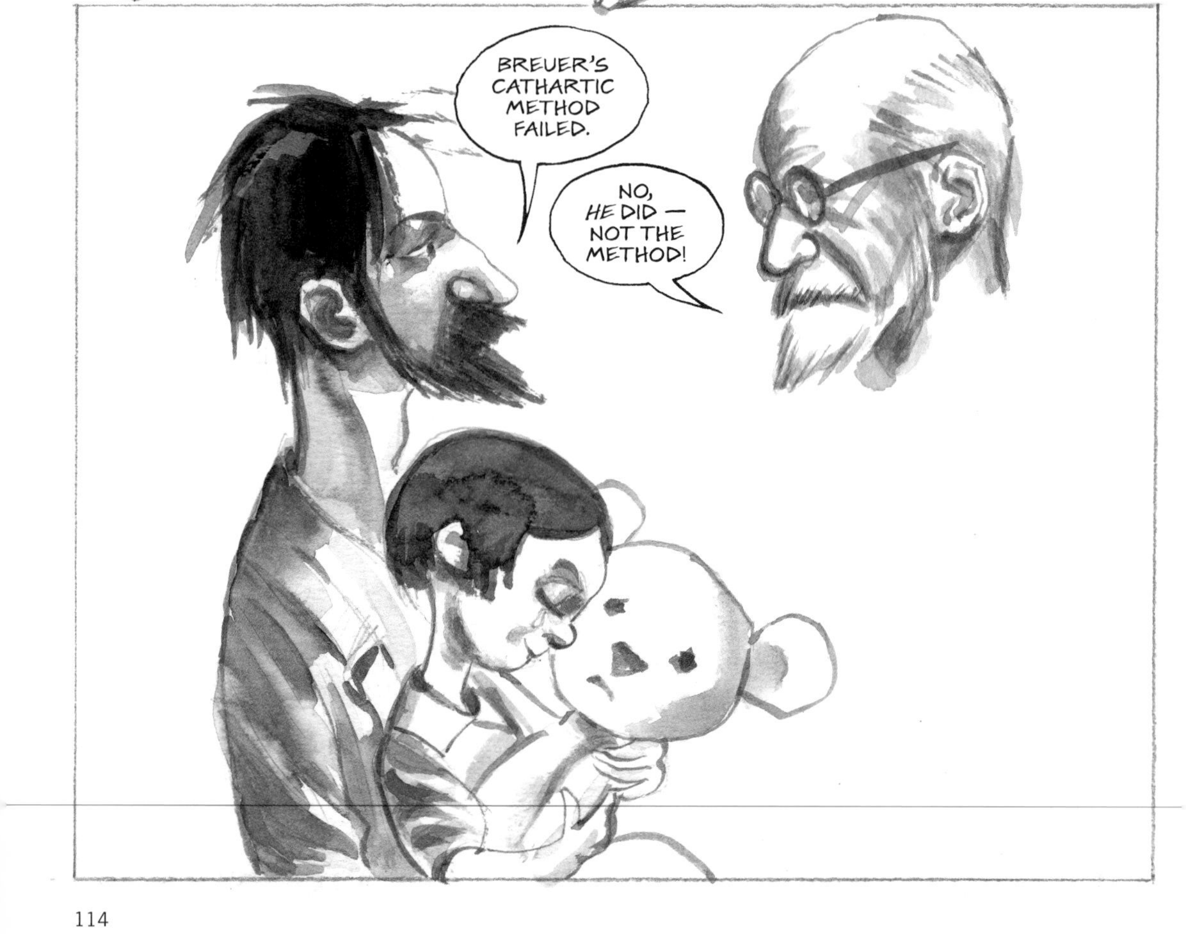
BREUER'S CATHARTIC METHOD FAILED.
NO, *HE* DID — NOT THE METHOD!

THE CASE OF FRÄULEIN ELISABETH VON R.

A MYSTERIOUS CASE OF HYSTERIA WAS REFERRED TO ME IN 1892. FRÄULEIN ELISABETH VON R., A BRIGHT, SELF-POSSESSED LADY OF 24.

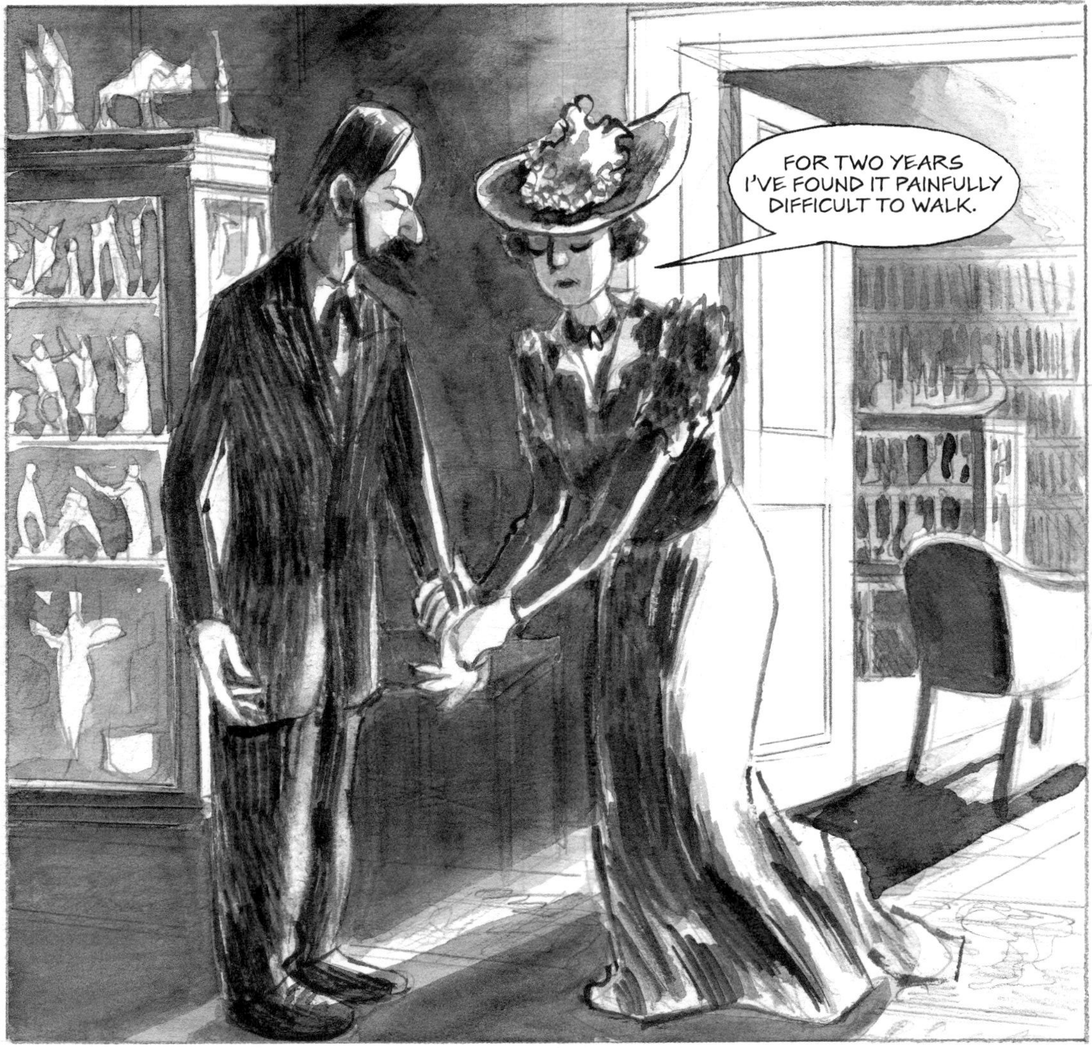
FOR TWO YEARS I'VE FOUND IT PAINFULLY DIFFICULT TO WALK.

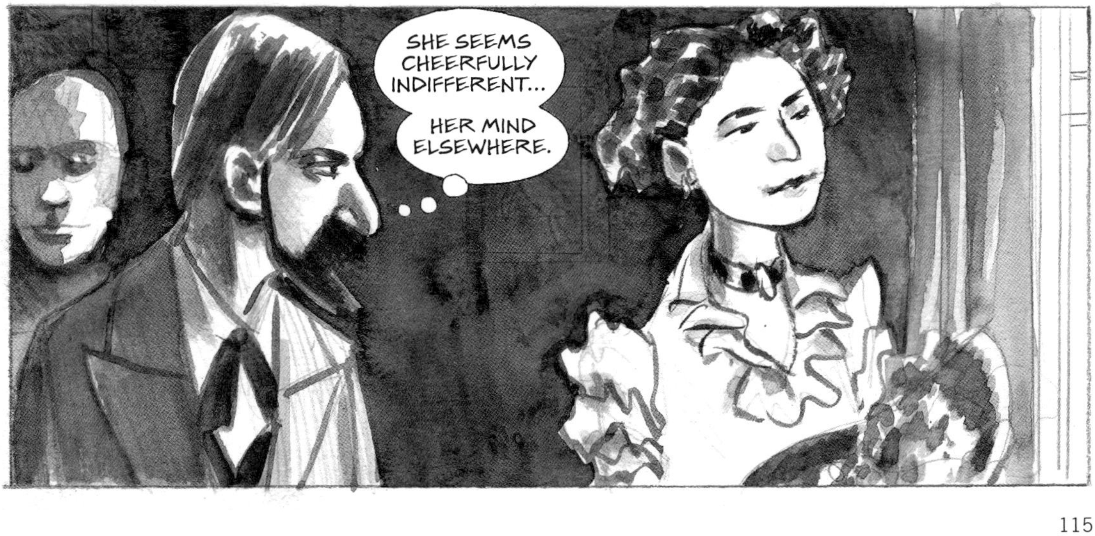
SHE SEEMS CHEERFULLY INDIFFERENT...
HER MIND ELSEWHERE.

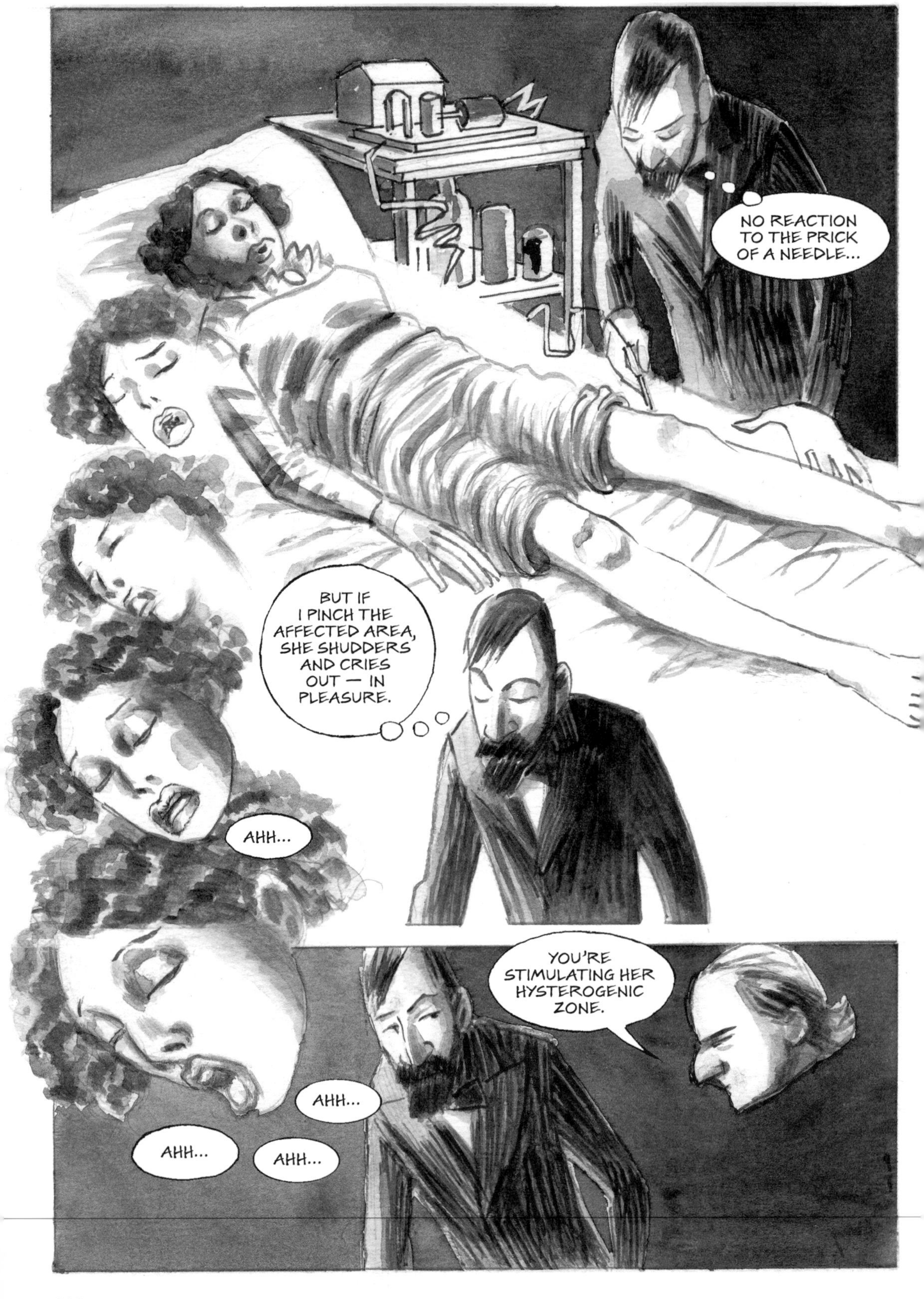
NO REACTION TO THE PRICK OF A NEEDLE...
BUT IF I PINCH THE AFFECTED AREA, SHE SHUDDERS AND CRIES OUT — IN PLEASURE.
AHH...
YOU'RE STIMULATING HER HYSTEROGENIC ZONE.
AHH...
AHH...
AHH...

HER EXPRESSION OF PLEASURE MUST IDENTIFY SOME THOUGHT CONCEALED BEHIND THE PAINS SHE UNDOUBTEDLY FELT. A SIGN OF HYSTERIA — PROBABLY LINKED TO A DEGREE OF MUSCULAR RHEUMATISM.

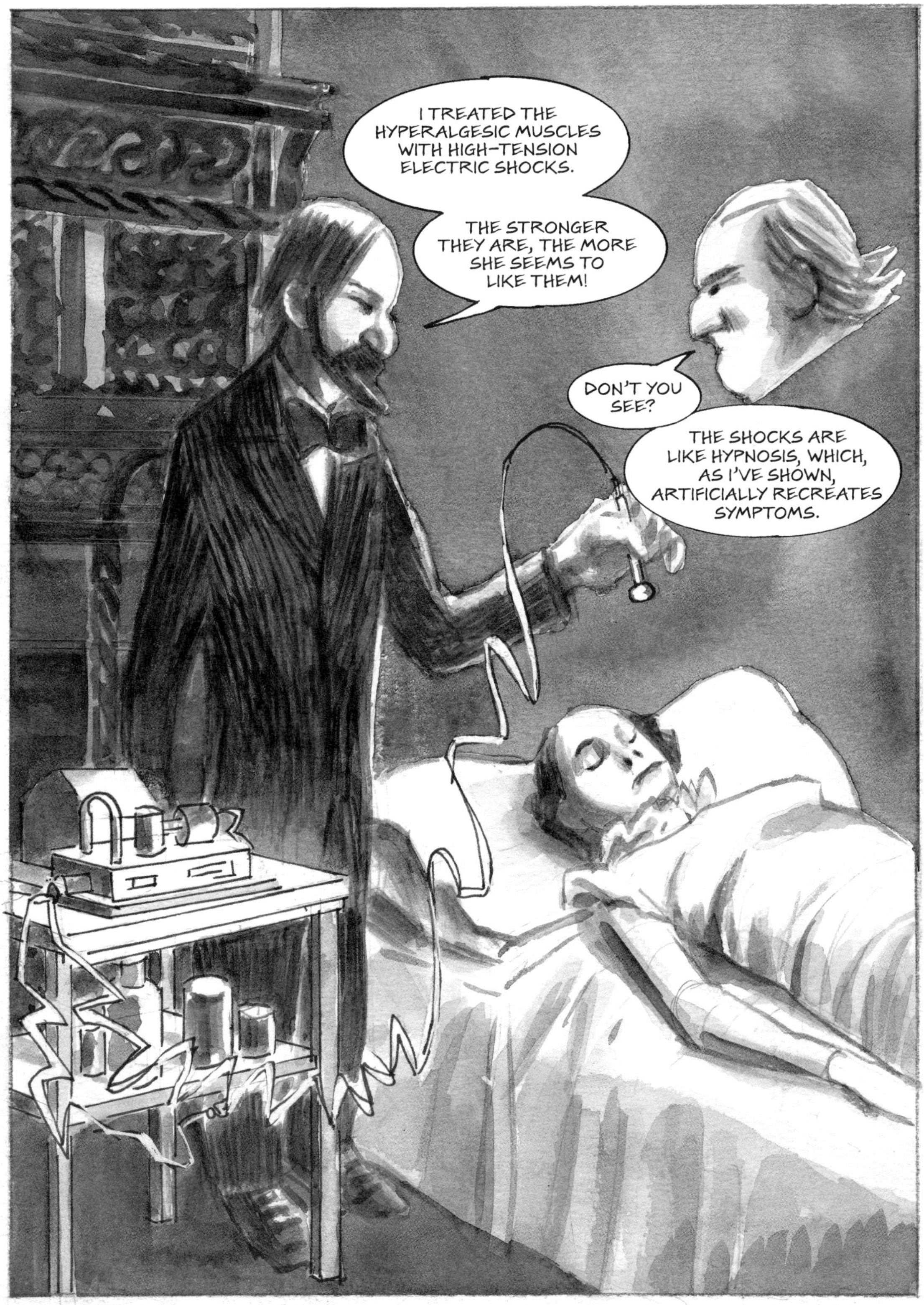
I TREATED THE HYPERALGESIC MUSCLES WITH HIGH-TENSION ELECTRIC SHOCKS.
THE STRONGER THEY ARE, THE MORE SHE SEEMS TO LIKE THEM!
DON'T YOU SEE?
THE SHOCKS ARE LIKE HYPNOSIS, WHICH, AS I'VE SHOWN, ARTIFICIALLY RECREATES SYMPTOMS.

I SUSPECTED THAT HER DISABILITY HAD NO ORGANIC BASIS. SHE MIGHT BENEFIT FROM THE CATHARTIC METHOD, AS I EXPLAINED, AND SHE READILY AGREED TO TRY IT.

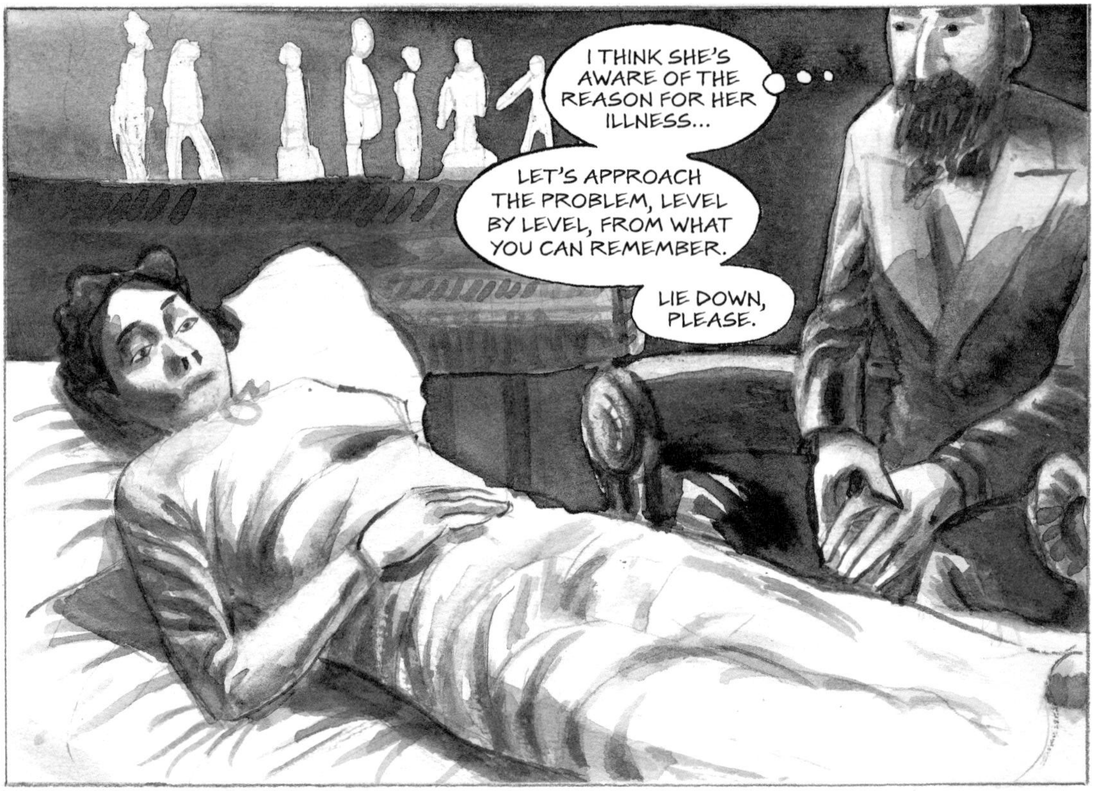
I THINK SHE'S AWARE OF THE REASON FOR HER ILLNESS...
LET'S APPROACH THE PROBLEM, LEVEL BY LEVEL, FROM WHAT YOU CAN REMEMBER.
LIE DOWN, PLEASE.

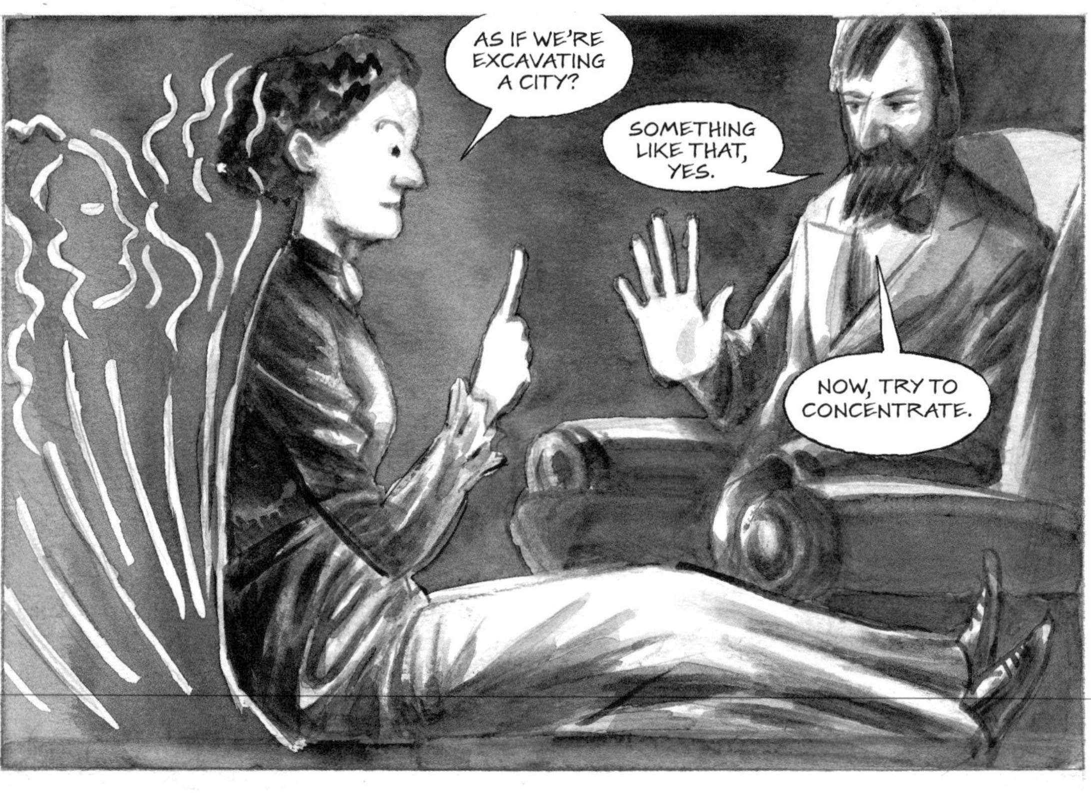
AS IF WE'RE EXCAVATING A CITY?
SOMETHING LIKE THAT, YES.
NOW, TRY TO CONCENTRATE.

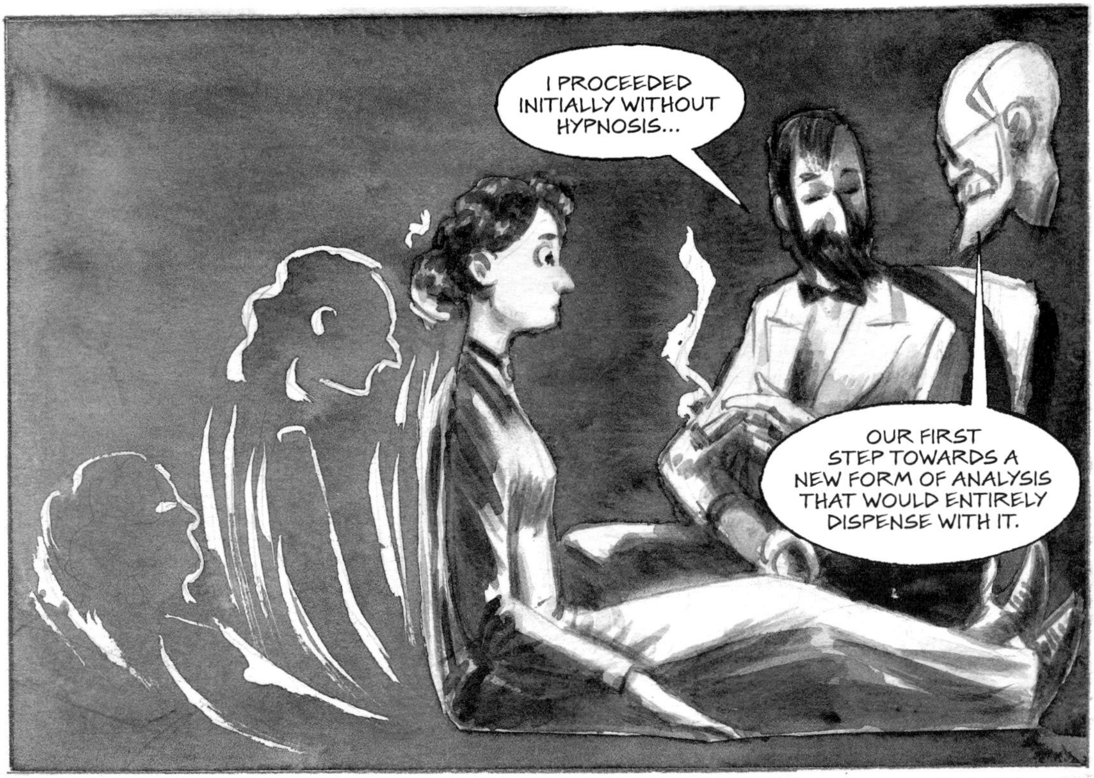
I PROCEEDED INITIALLY WITHOUT HYPNOSIS...
OUR FIRST STEP TOWARDS A NEW FORM OF ANALYSIS THAT WOULD ENTIRELY DISPENSE WITH IT.

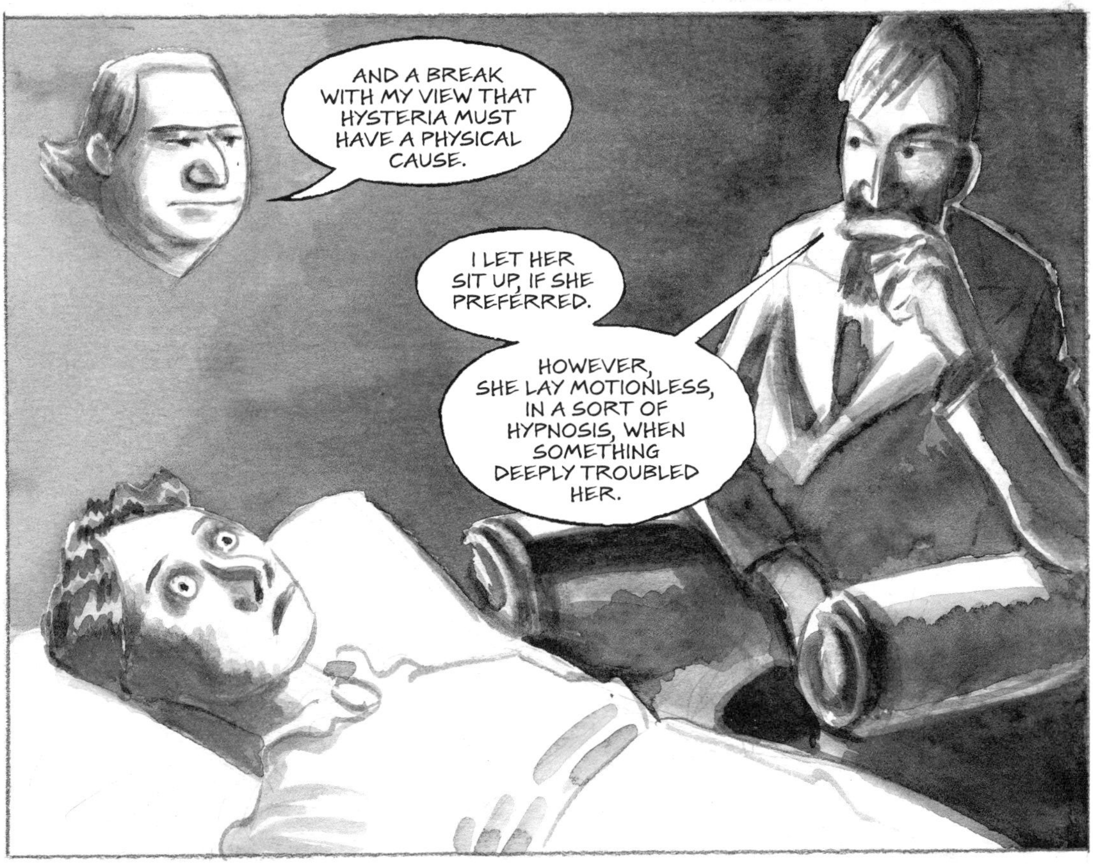
AND A BREAK WITH MY VIEW THAT HYSTERIA MUST HAVE A PHYSICAL CAUSE.
I LET HER SIT UP, IF SHE PREFERRED.
HOWEVER, SHE LAY MOTIONLESS, IN A SORT OF HYPNOSIS, WHEN SOMETHING DEEPLY TROUBLED HER.

ELISABETH REPORTED THAT SHE WAS THE YOUNGEST OF THREE SISTERS AND HAD GROWN UP ON THE FAMILY ESTATE IN HUNGARY. HER MOTHER'S HEALTH WAS POOR. SHE FELT CLOSE TO HER FATHER, A GALLANT MAN OF THE WORLD.

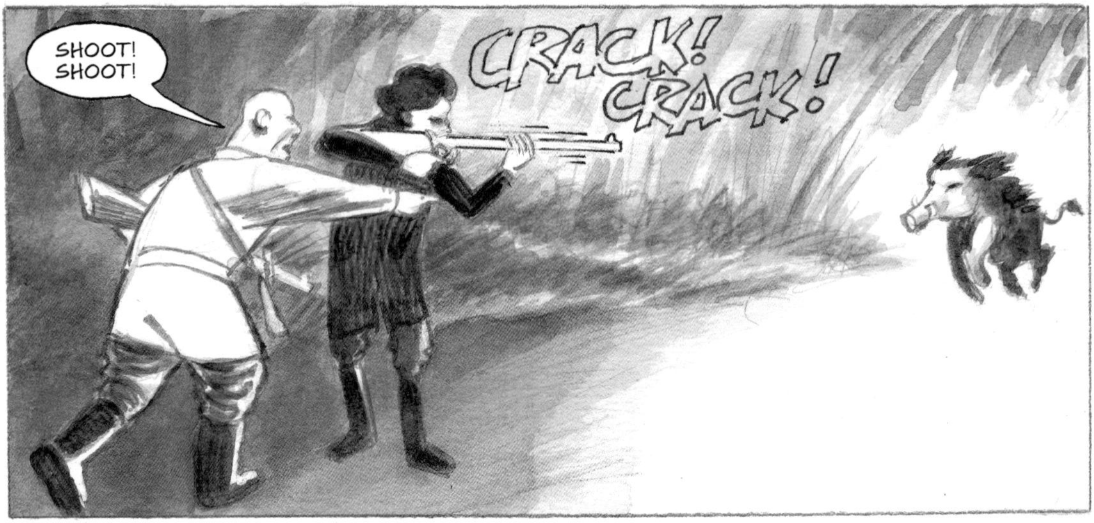
SHOOT! SHOOT!
CRACK! CRACK!

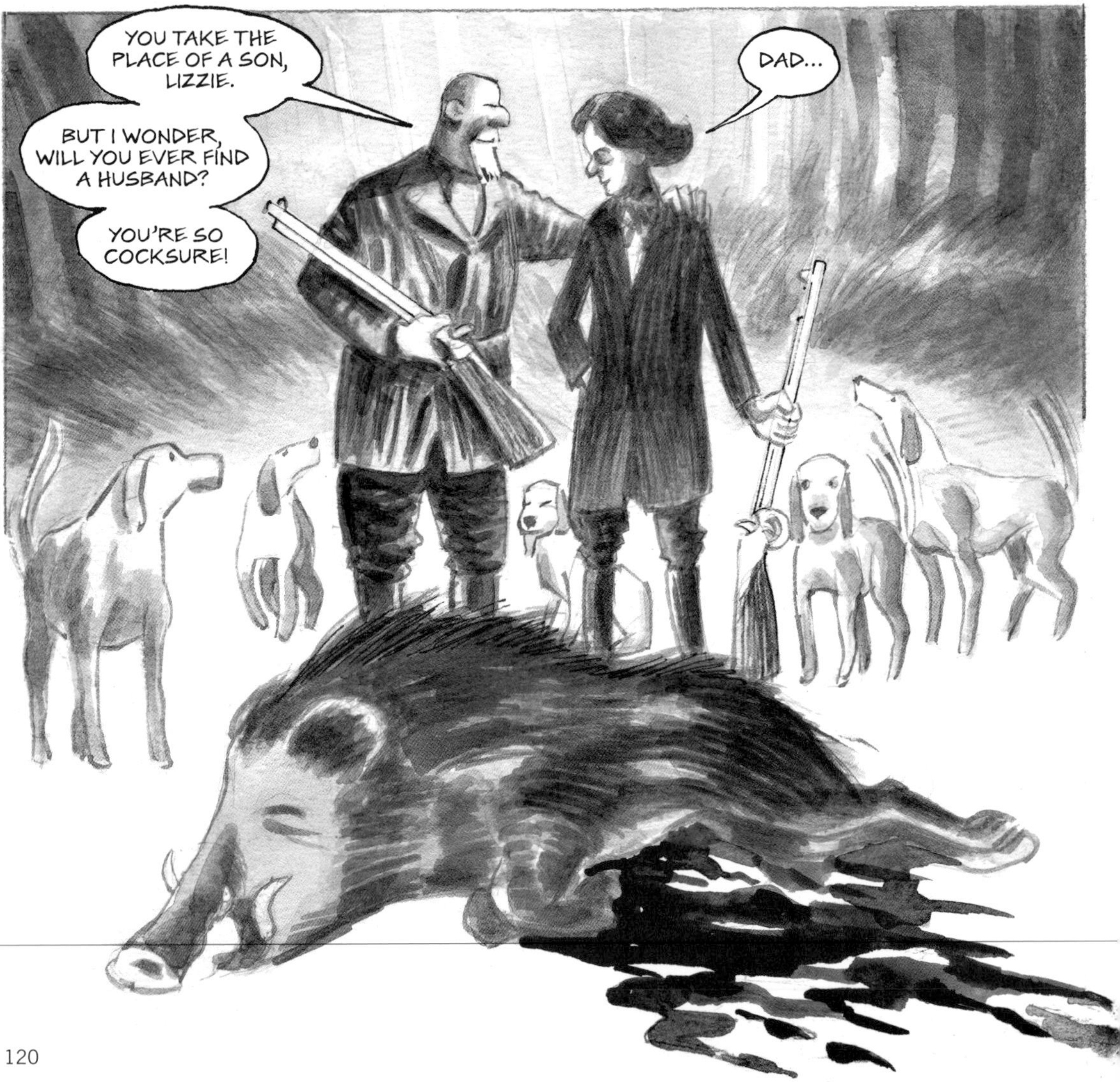
YOU TAKE THE PLACE OF A SON, LIZZIE.
BUT I WONDER, WILL YOU EVER FIND A HUSBAND?
YOU'RE SO COCKSURE!
DAD...

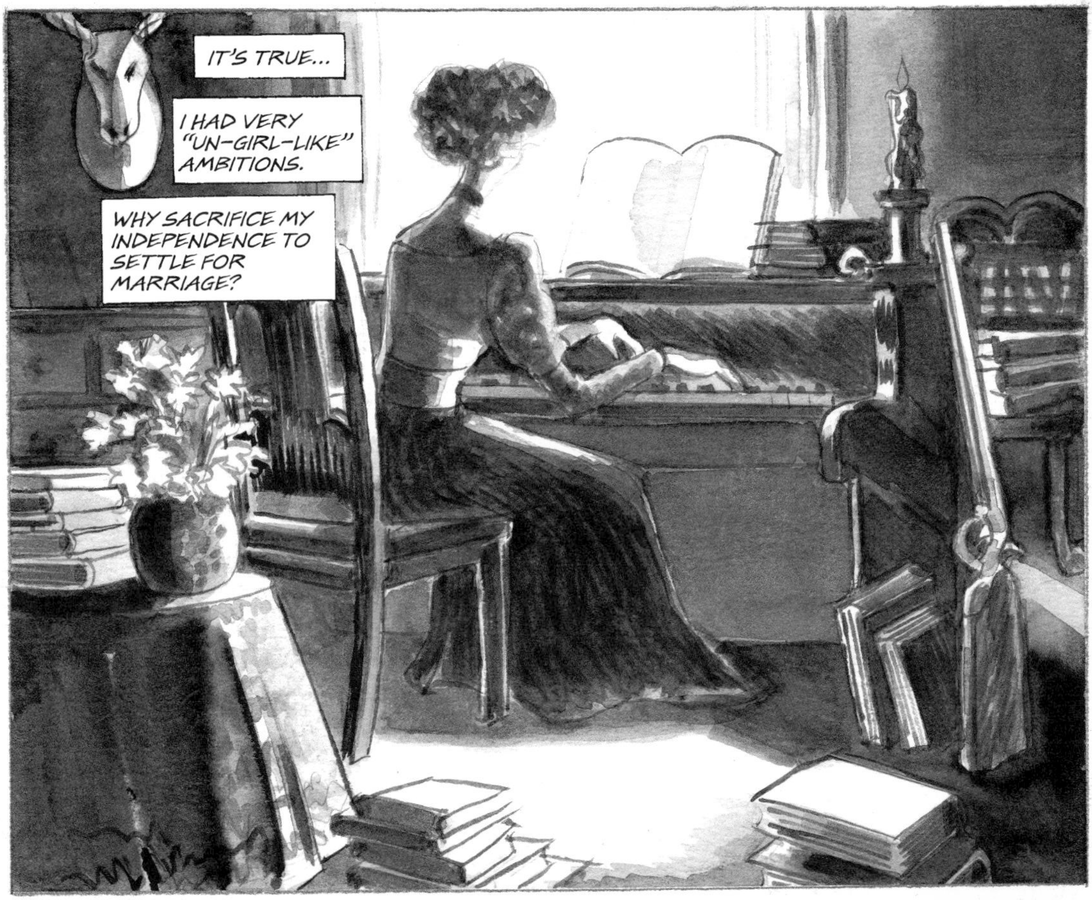
IT'S TRUE...
I HAD VERY "UN-GIRL-LIKE" AMBITIONS.
WHY SACRIFICE MY INDEPENDENCE TO SETTLE FOR MARRIAGE?

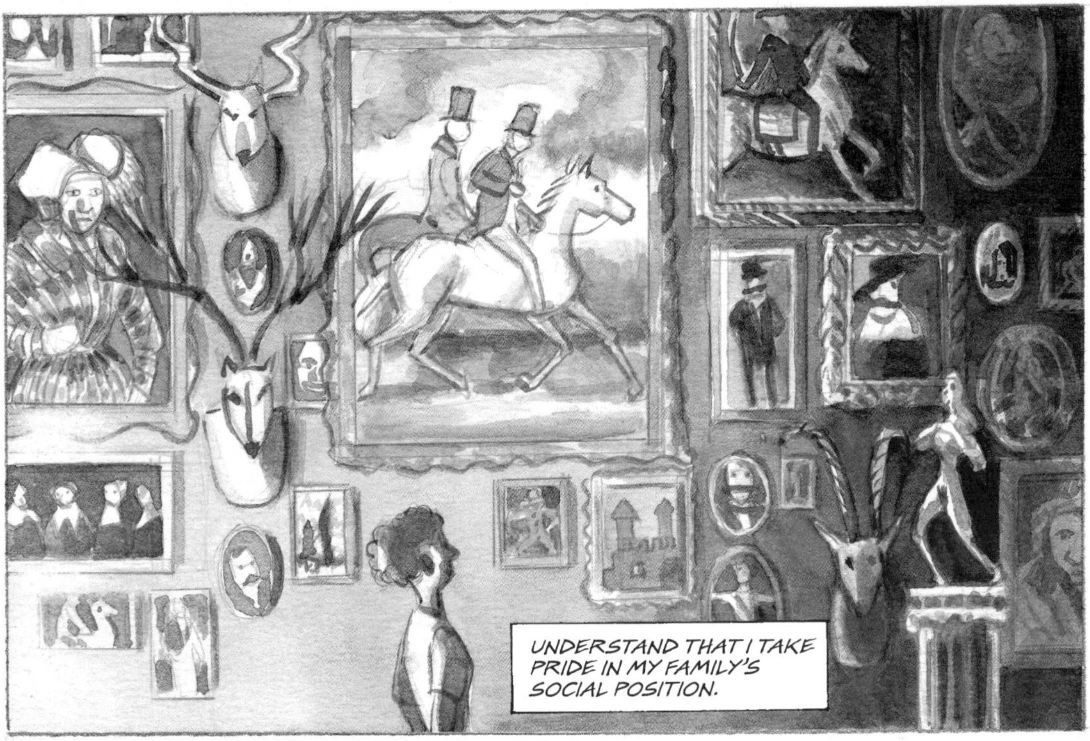
UNDERSTAND THAT I TAKE PRIDE IN MY FAMILY'S SOCIAL POSITION.

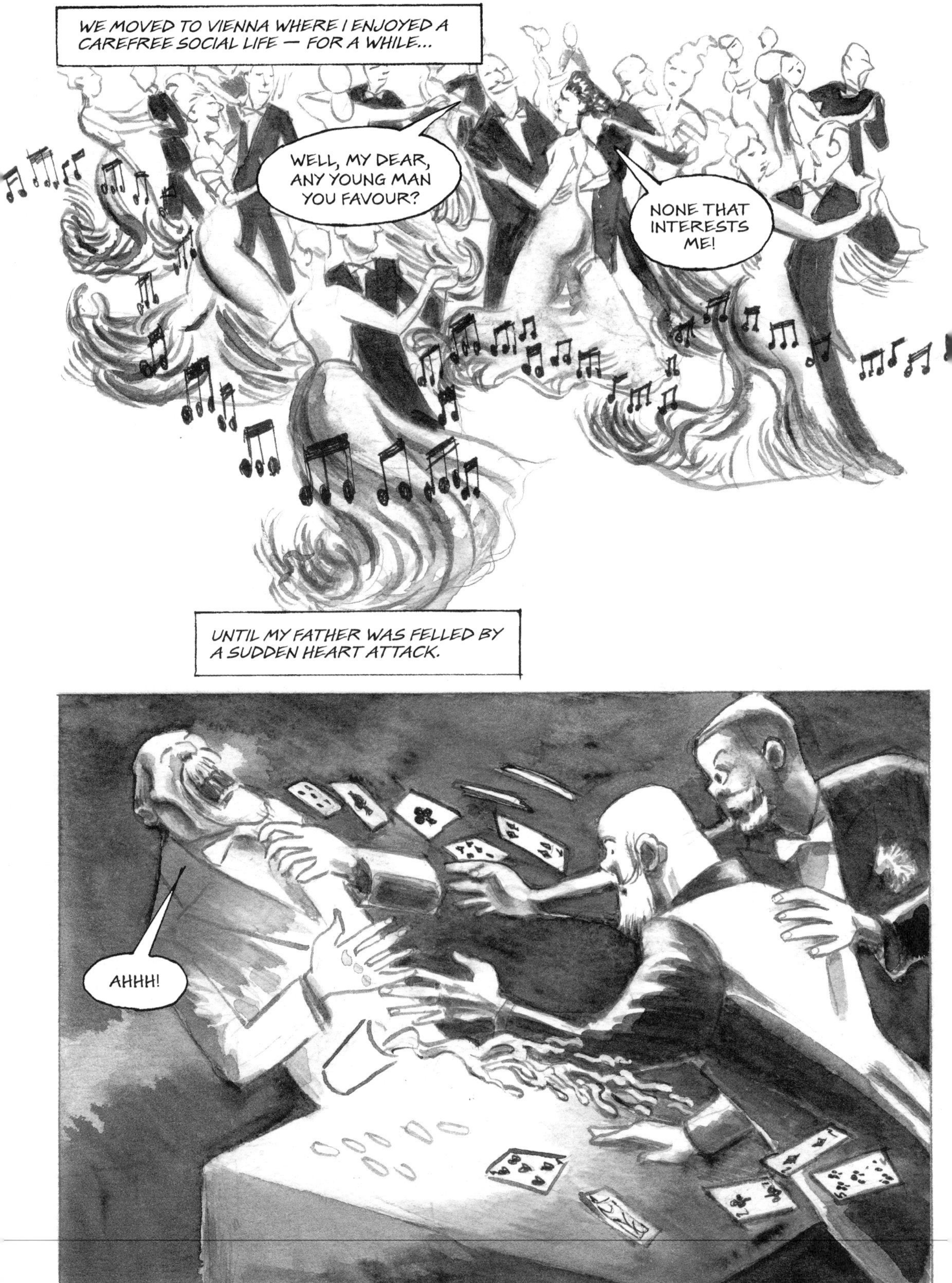
WE MOVED TO VIENNA WHERE I ENJOYED A CAREFREE SOCIAL LIFE — FOR A WHILE...
WELL, MY DEAR, ANY YOUNG MAN YOU FAVOUR?
NONE THAT INTERESTS ME!
UNTIL MY FATHER WAS FELLED BY A SUDDEN HEART ATTACK.
AHHH!

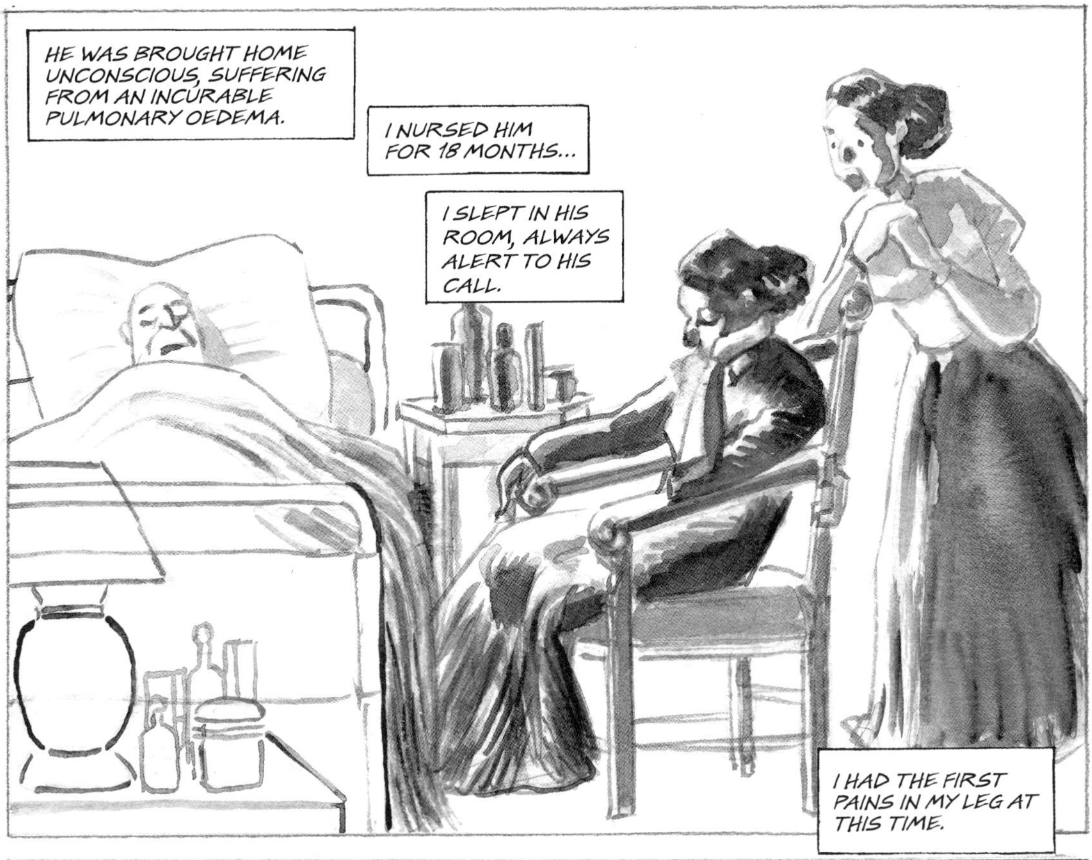
HE WAS BROUGHT HOME UNCONSCIOUS, SUFFERING FROM AN INCURABLE PULMONARY OEDEMA.
I NURSED HIM FOR 18 MONTHS...
I SLEPT IN HIS ROOM, ALWAYS ALERT TO HIS CALL.
I HAD THE FIRST PAINS IN MY LEG AT THIS TIME.

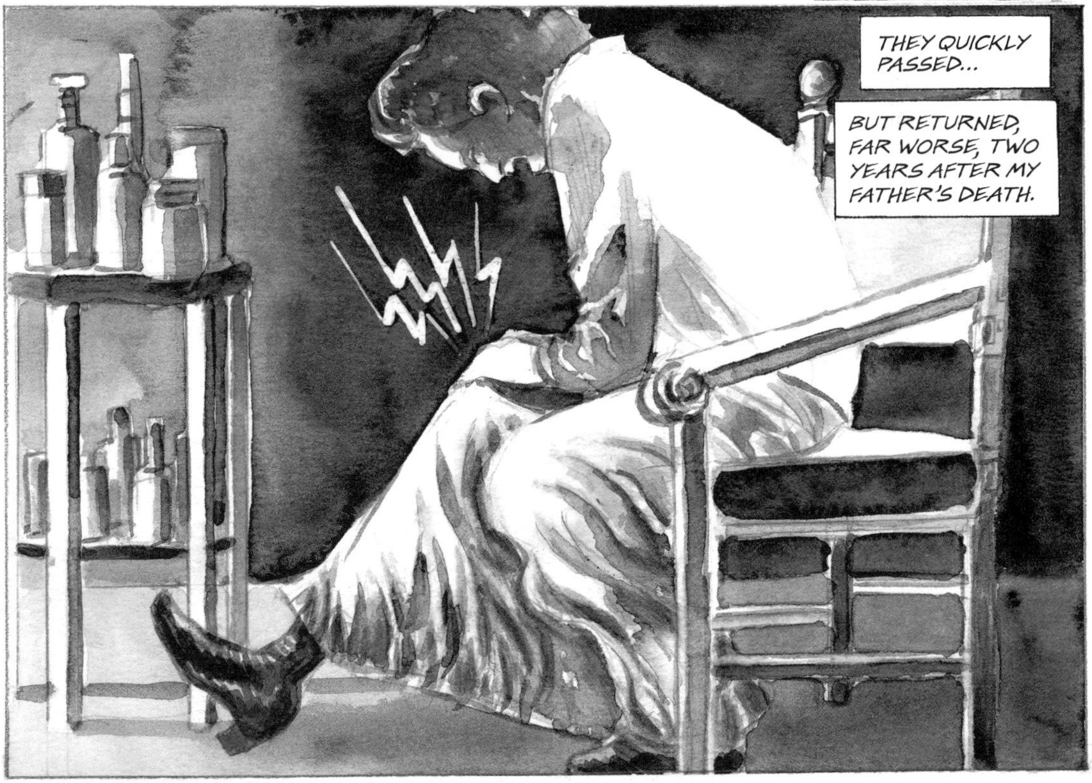
THEY QUICKLY PASSED...
BUT RETURNED, FAR WORSE, TWO YEARS AFTER MY FATHER'S DEATH.

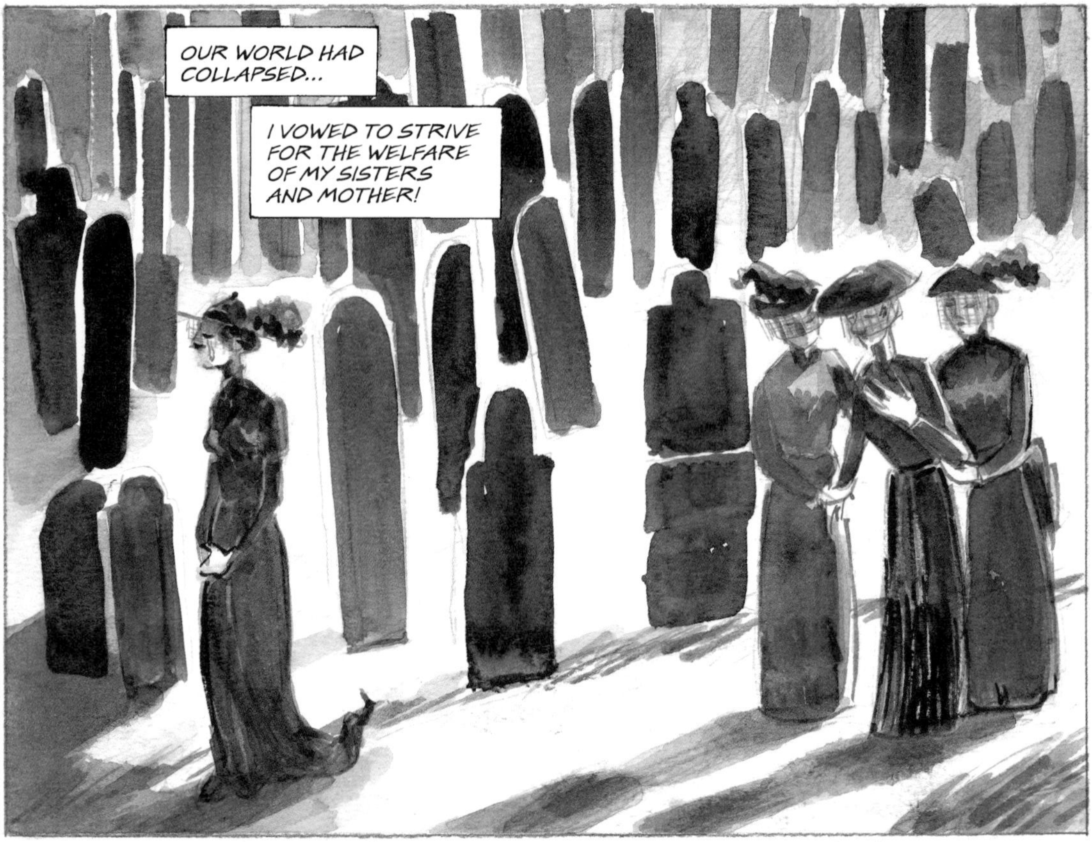
OUR WORLD HAD COLLAPSED...
I VOWED TO STRIVE FOR THE WELFARE OF MY SISTERS AND MOTHER!

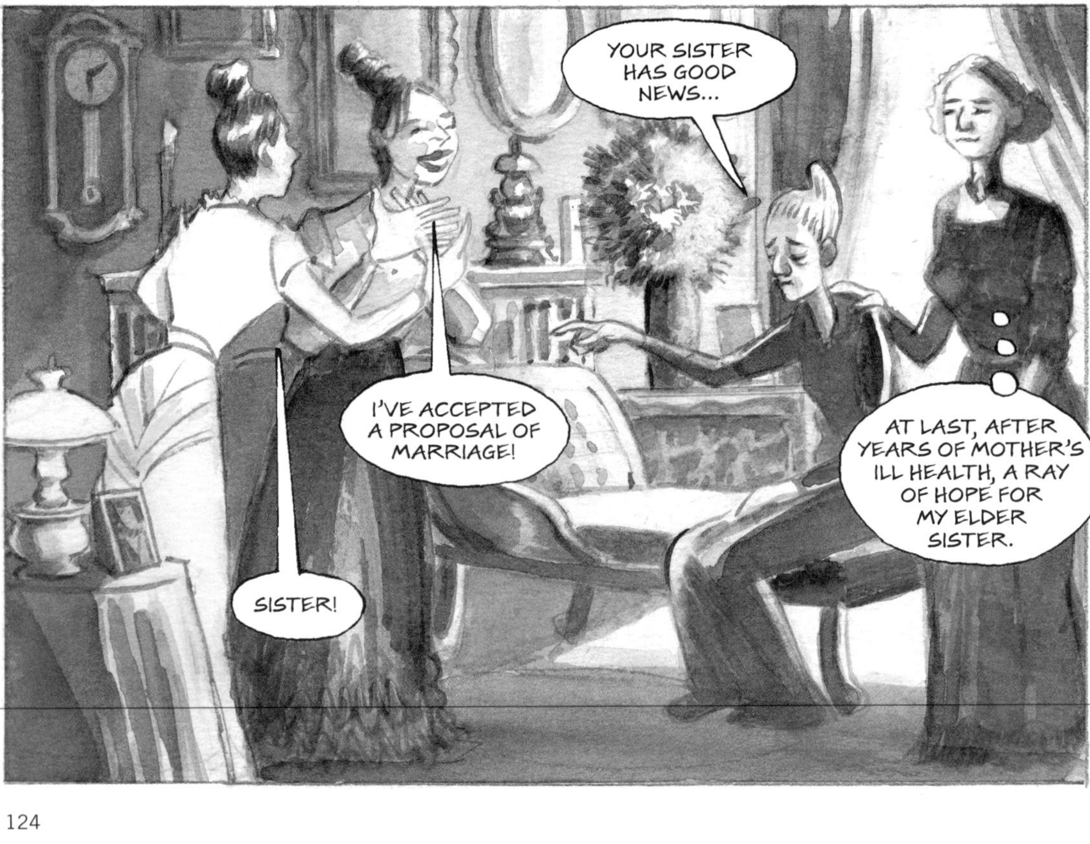
YOUR SISTER HAS GOOD NEWS...
I'VE ACCEPTED A PROPOSAL OF MARRIAGE!
SISTER!
AT LAST, AFTER YEARS OF MOTHER'S ILL HEALTH, A RAY OF HOPE FOR MY ELDER SISTER.

HER HUSBAND'S TALENTS PROMISED A GREAT FUTURE. UNFORTUNATELY, HE PROVED IN TIME TO BE IMPOSSIBLY SELF-CENTRED, WITH NO REGARD FOR OUR FAMILY.

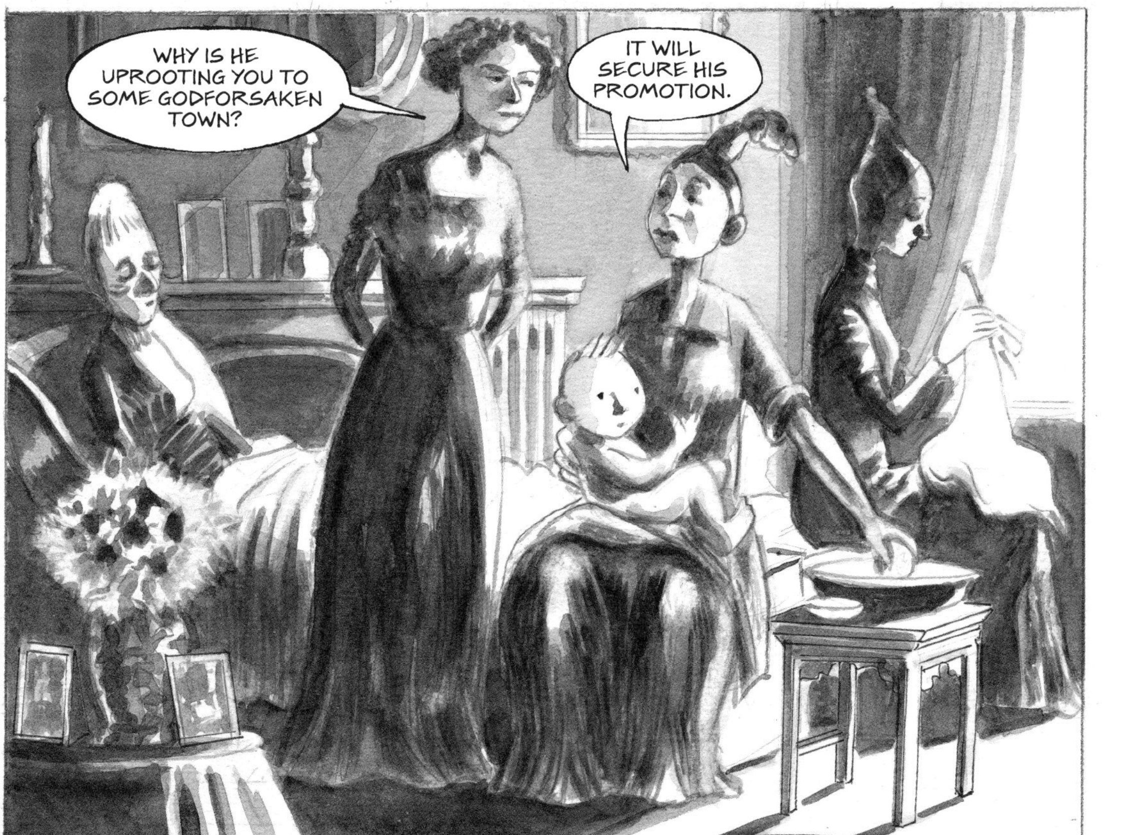
WHY IS HE UPROOTING YOU TO SOME GODFORSAKEN TOWN?
IT WILL SECURE HIS PROMOTION.

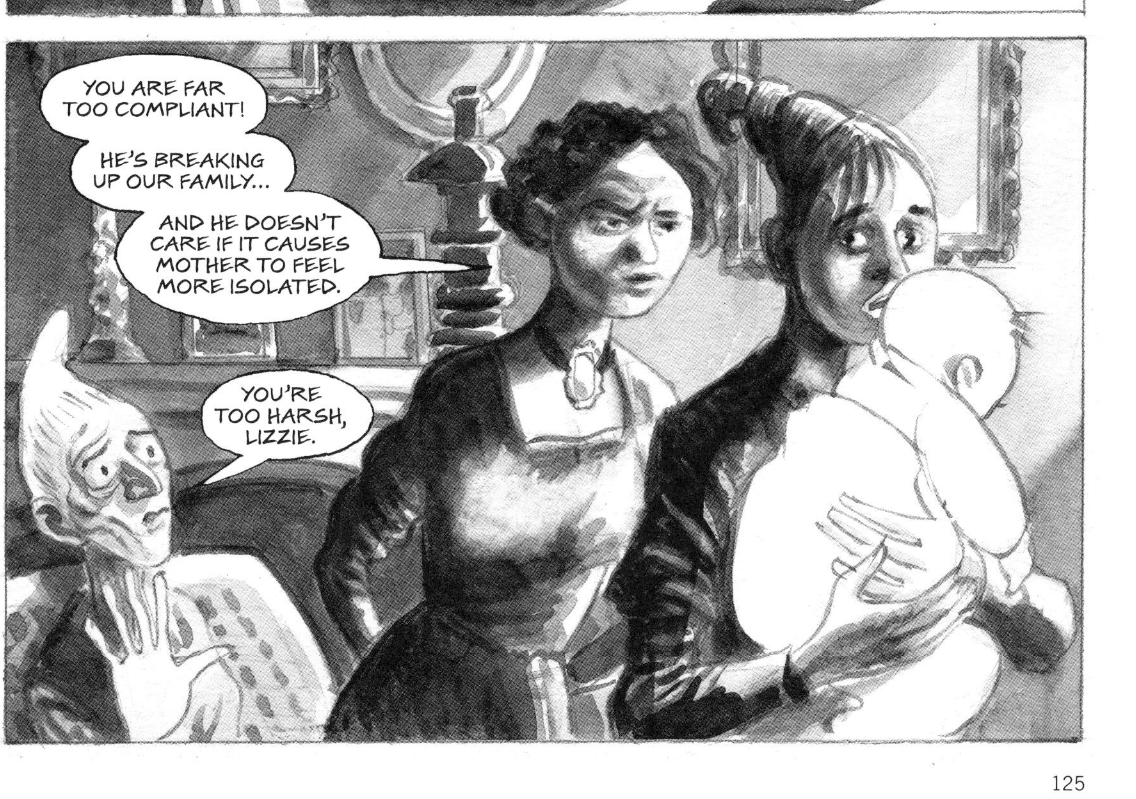
YOU ARE FAR TOO COMPLIANT!
HE'S BREAKING UP OUR FAMILY...
AND HE DOESN'T CARE IF IT CAUSES MOTHER TO FEEL MORE ISOLATED.
YOU'RE TOO HARSH, LIZZIE.

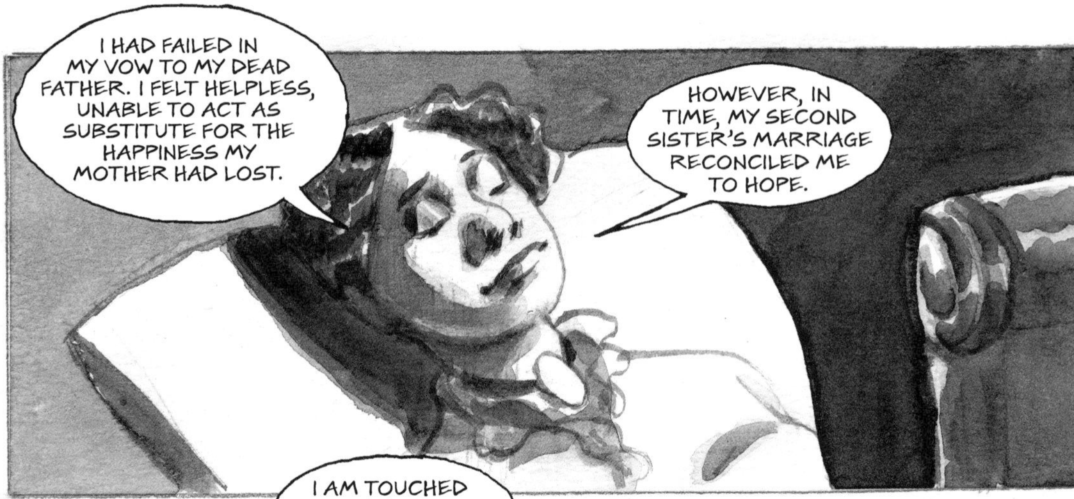
I HAD FAILED IN MY VOW TO MY DEAD FATHER. I FELT HELPLESS, UNABLE TO ACT AS SUBSTITUTE FOR THE HAPPINESS MY MOTHER HAD LOST.
HOWEVER, IN TIME, MY SECOND SISTER'S MARRIAGE RECONCILED ME TO HOPE.

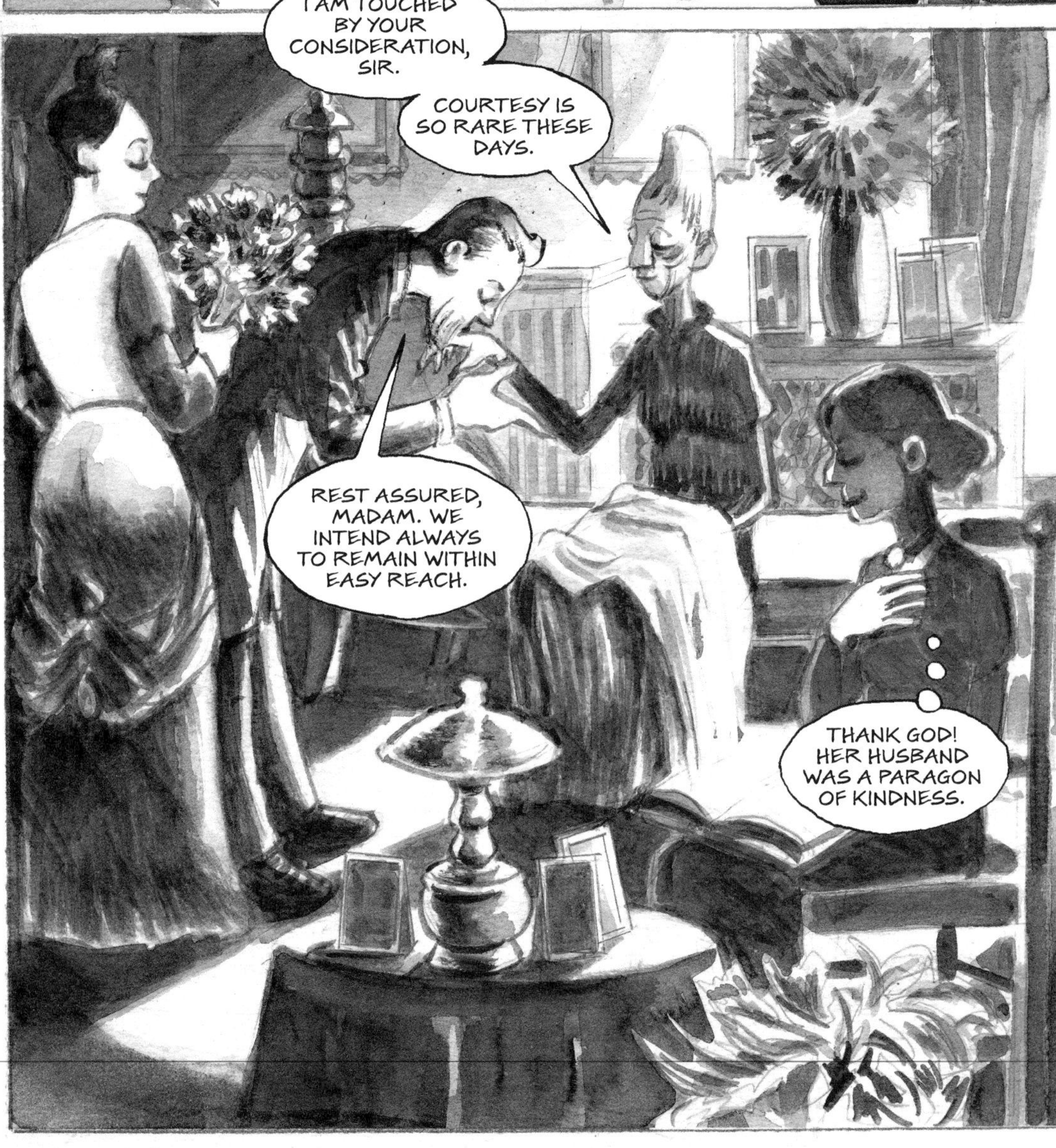
I AM TOUCHED BY YOUR CONSIDERATION, SIR.
COURTESY IS SO RARE THESE DAYS.
REST ASSURED, MADAM. WE INTEND ALWAYS TO REMAIN WITHIN EASY REACH.
THANK GOD! HER HUSBAND WAS A PARAGON OF KINDNESS.

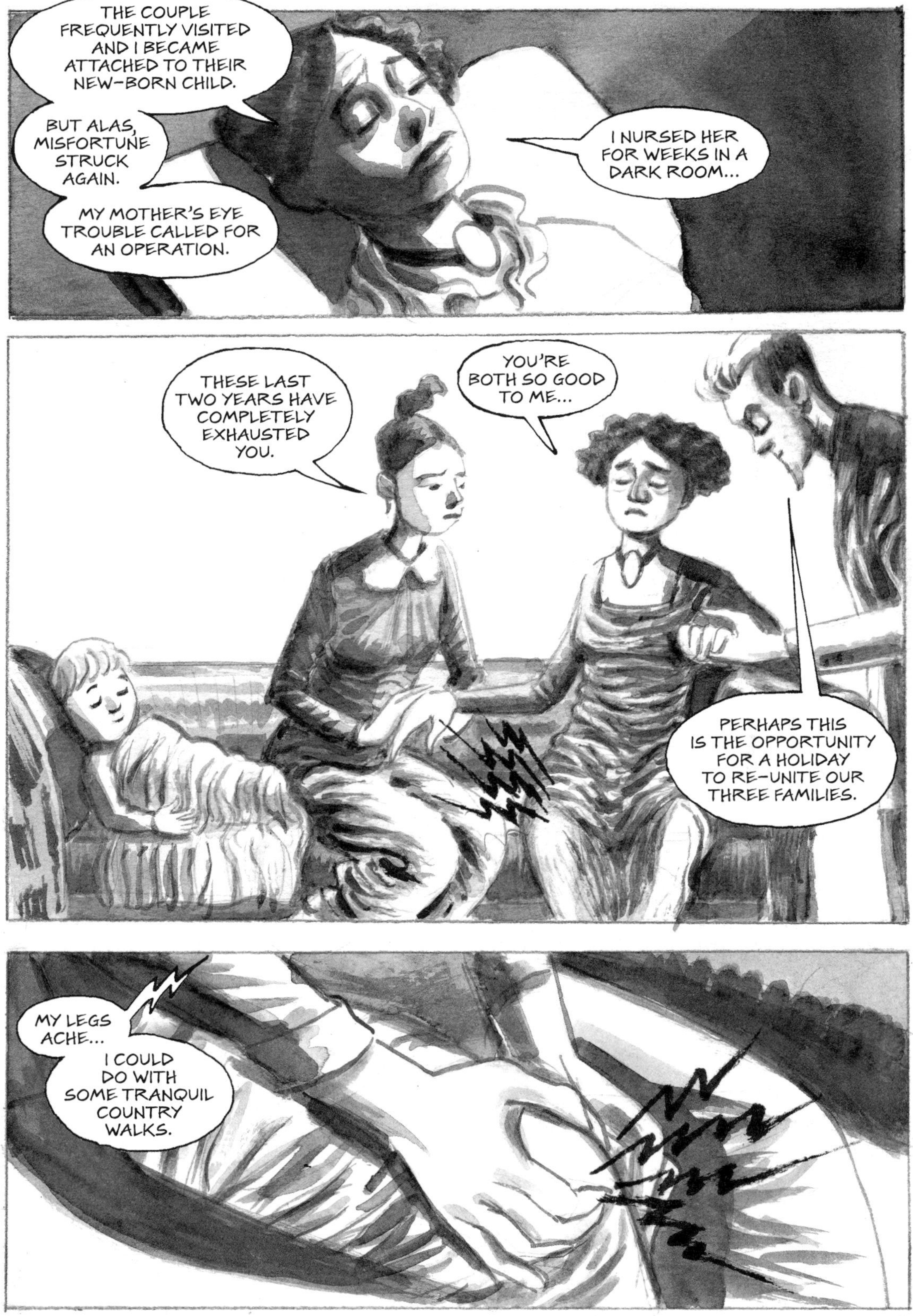
THE COUPLE FREQUENTLY VISITED AND I BECAME ATTACHED TO THEIR NEW-BORN CHILD.
BUT ALAS, MISFORTUNE STRUCK AGAIN.
MY MOTHER'S EYE TROUBLE CALLED FOR AN OPERATION.
I NURSED HER FOR WEEKS IN A DARK ROOM...
THESE LAST TWO YEARS HAVE COMPLETELY EXHAUSTED YOU.
YOU'RE BOTH SO GOOD TO ME...
PERHAPS THIS IS THE OPPORTUNITY FOR A HOLIDAY TO RE-UNITE OUR THREE FAMILIES.
MY LEGS ACHE...
I COULD DO WITH SOME TRANQUIL COUNTRY WALKS.

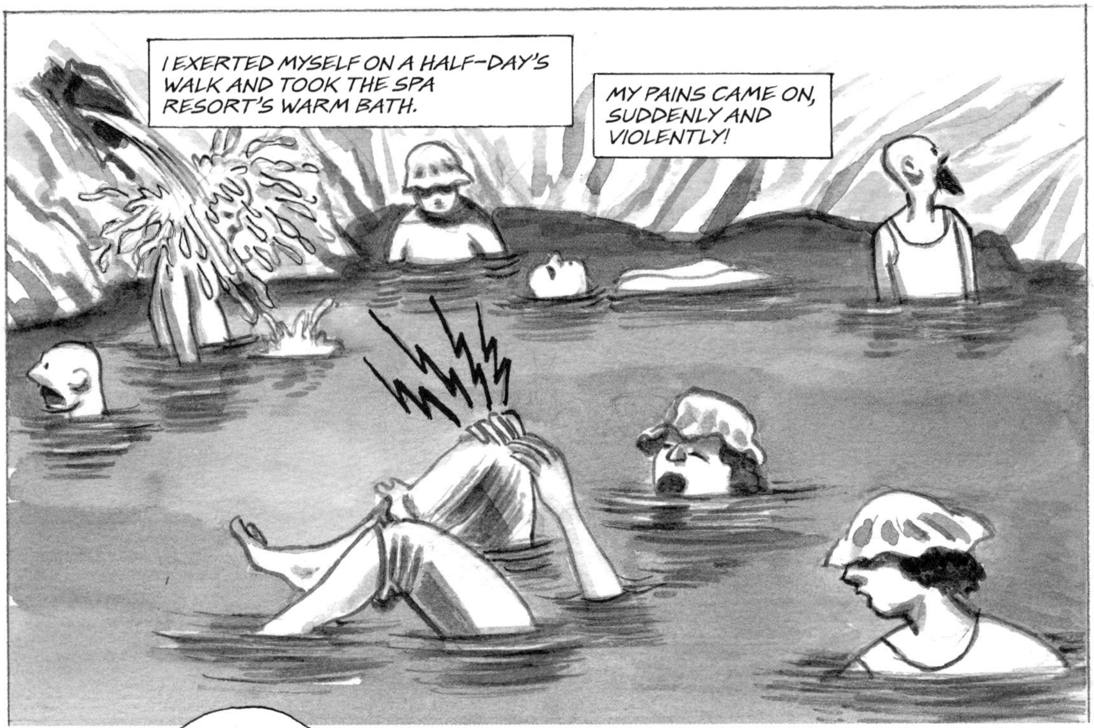
I EXERTED MYSELF ON A HALF-DAY'S WALK AND TOOK THE SPA RESORT'S WARM BATH.
MY PAINS CAME ON, SUDDENLY AND VIOLENTLY!

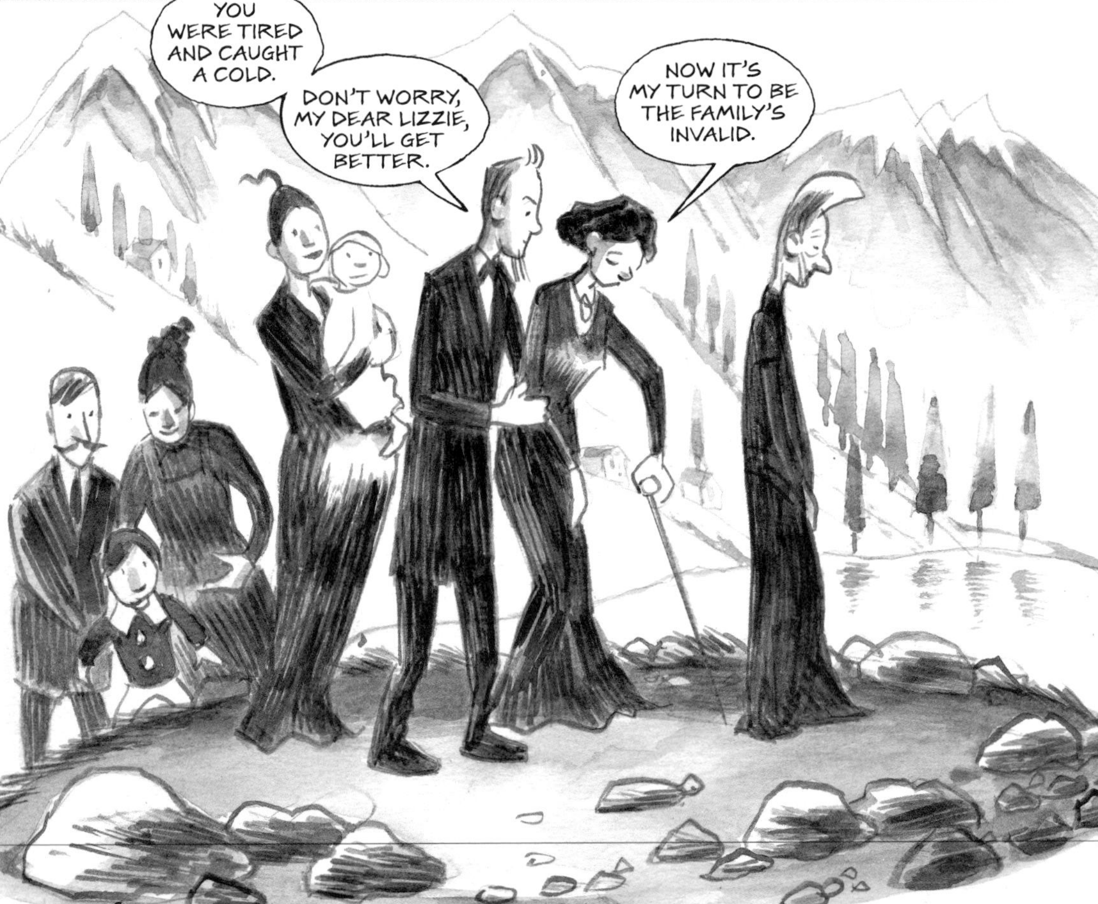
YOU WERE TIRED AND CAUGHT A COLD.
DON'T WORRY, MY DEAR LIZZIE, YOU'LL GET BETTER.
NOW IT'S MY TURN TO BE THE FAMILY'S INVALID.

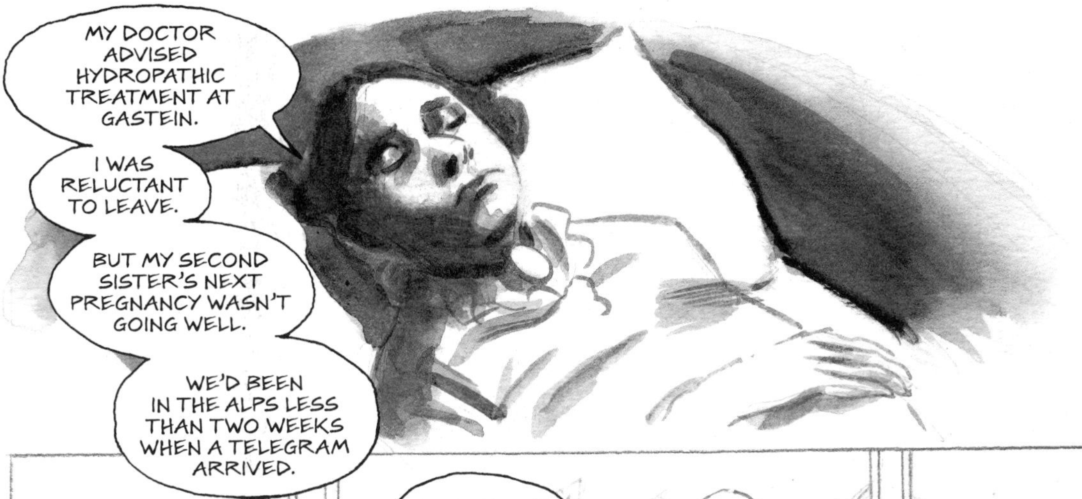
MY DOCTOR ADVISED HYDROPATHIC TREATMENT AT GASTEIN.
I WAS RELUCTANT TO LEAVE.
BUT MY SECOND SISTER'S NEXT PREGNANCY WASN'T GOING WELL.
WE'D BEEN IN THE ALPS LESS THAN TWO WEEKS WHEN A TELEGRAM ARRIVED.

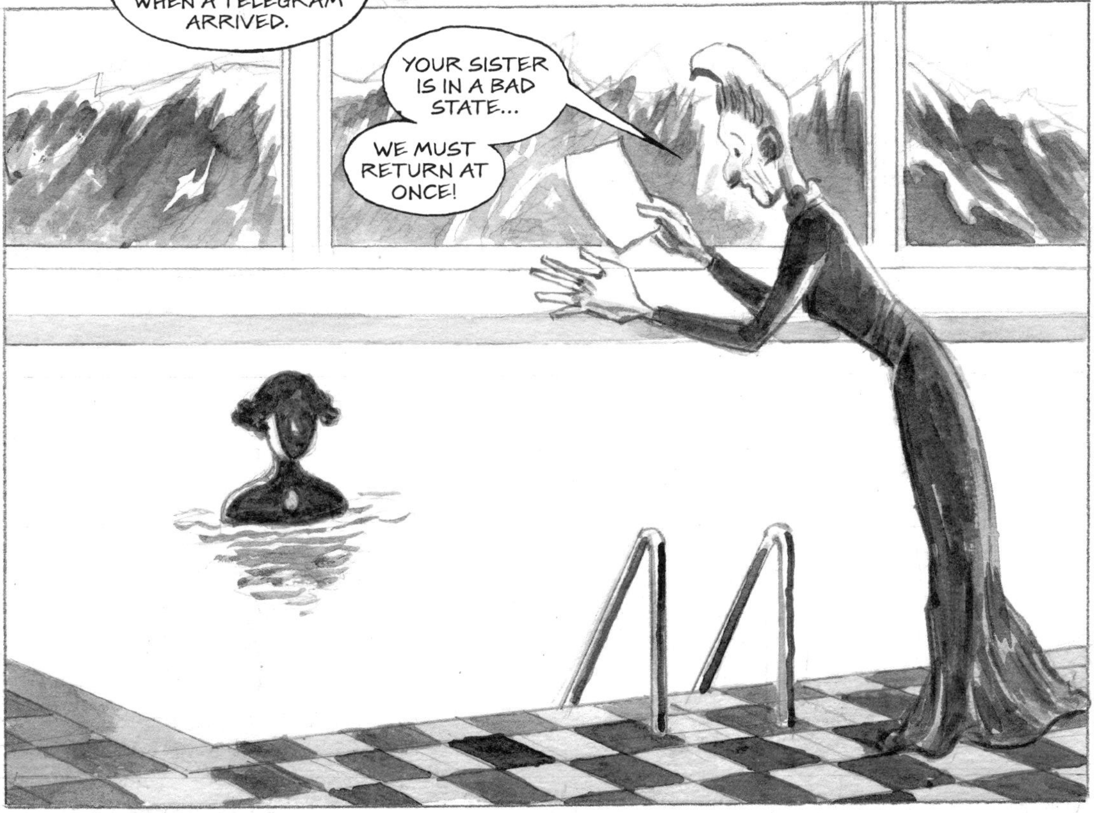
YOUR SISTER IS IN A BAD STATE...
WE MUST RETURN AT ONCE!

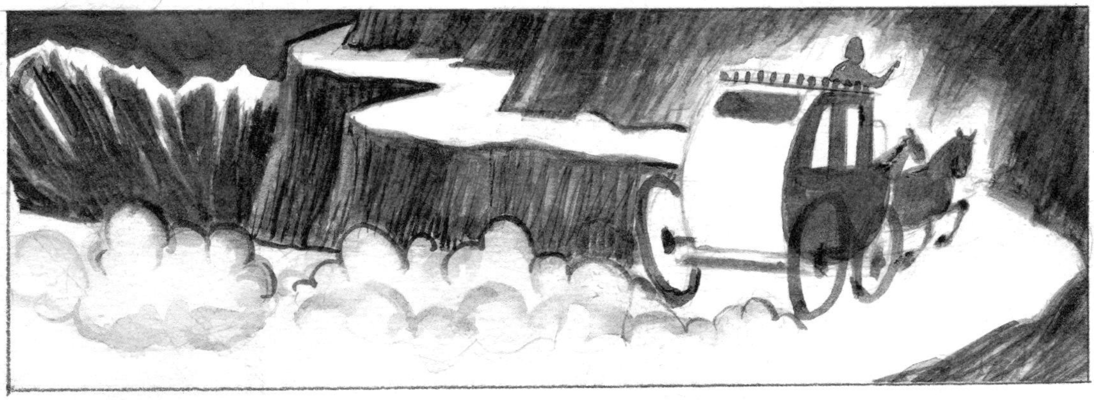

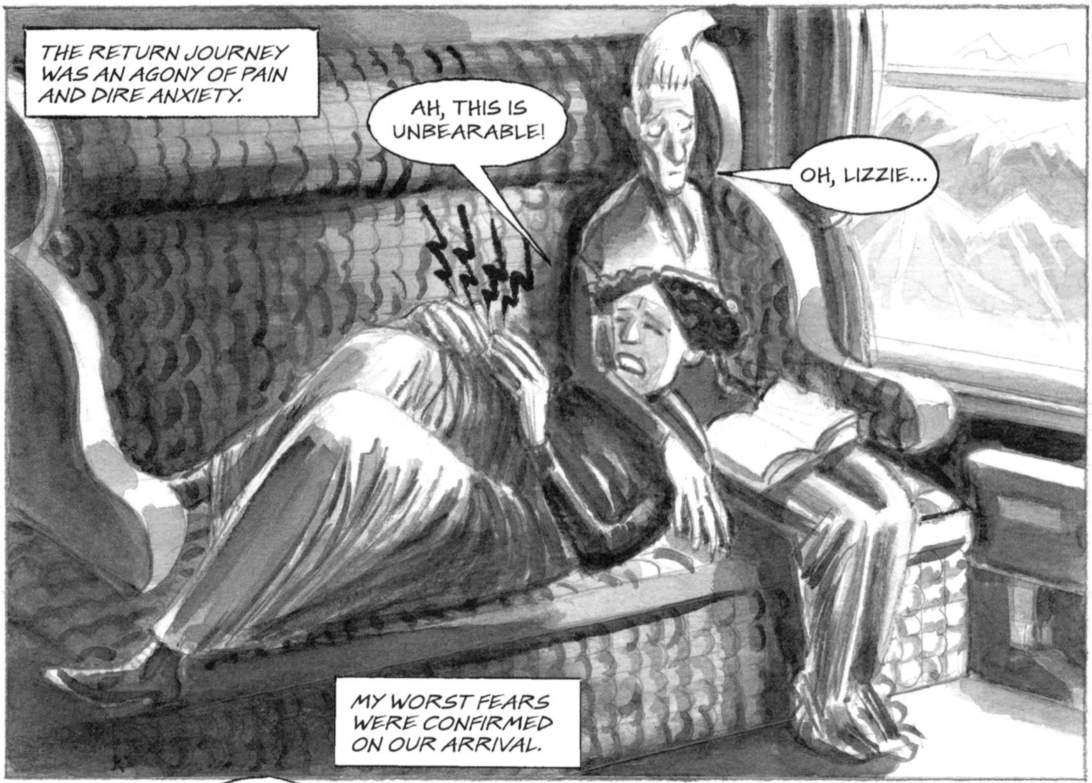
THE RETURN JOURNEY WAS AN AGONY OF PAIN AND DIRE ANXIETY.
AH, THIS IS UNBEARABLE!
OH, LIZZIE...
MY WORST FEARS WERE CONFIRMED ON OUR ARRIVAL.

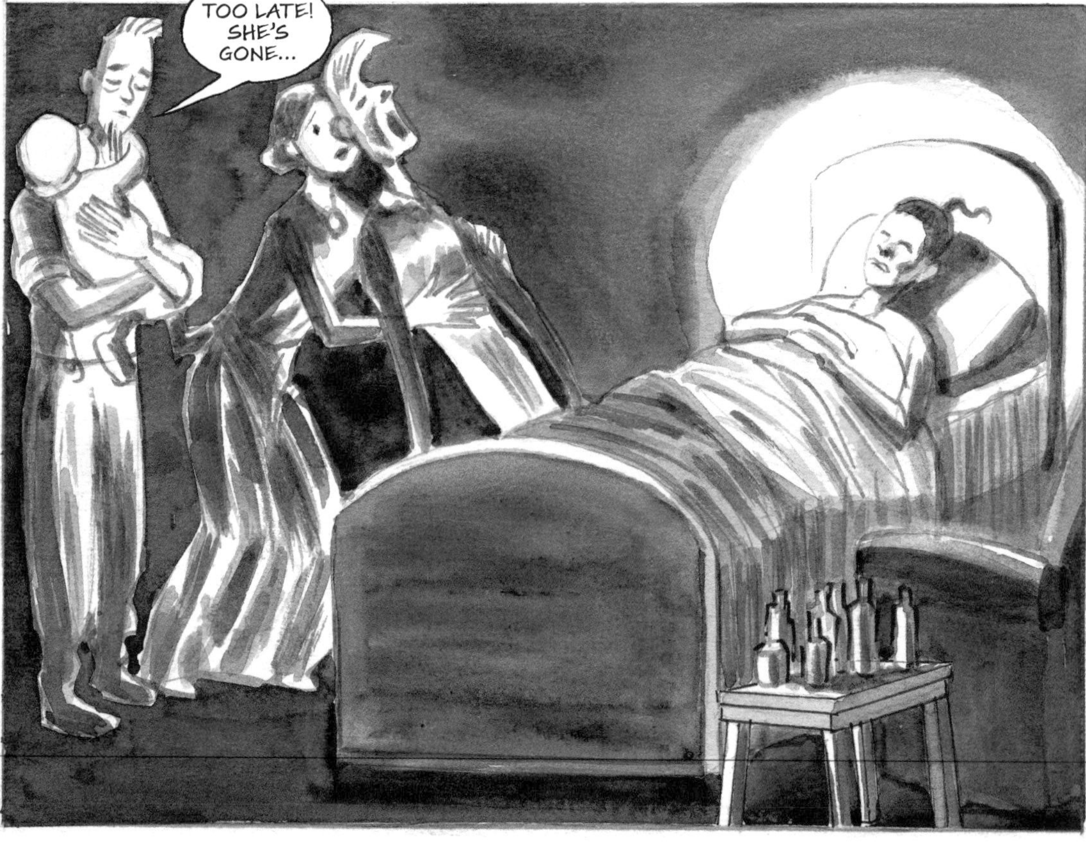
TOO LATE! SHE'S GONE...

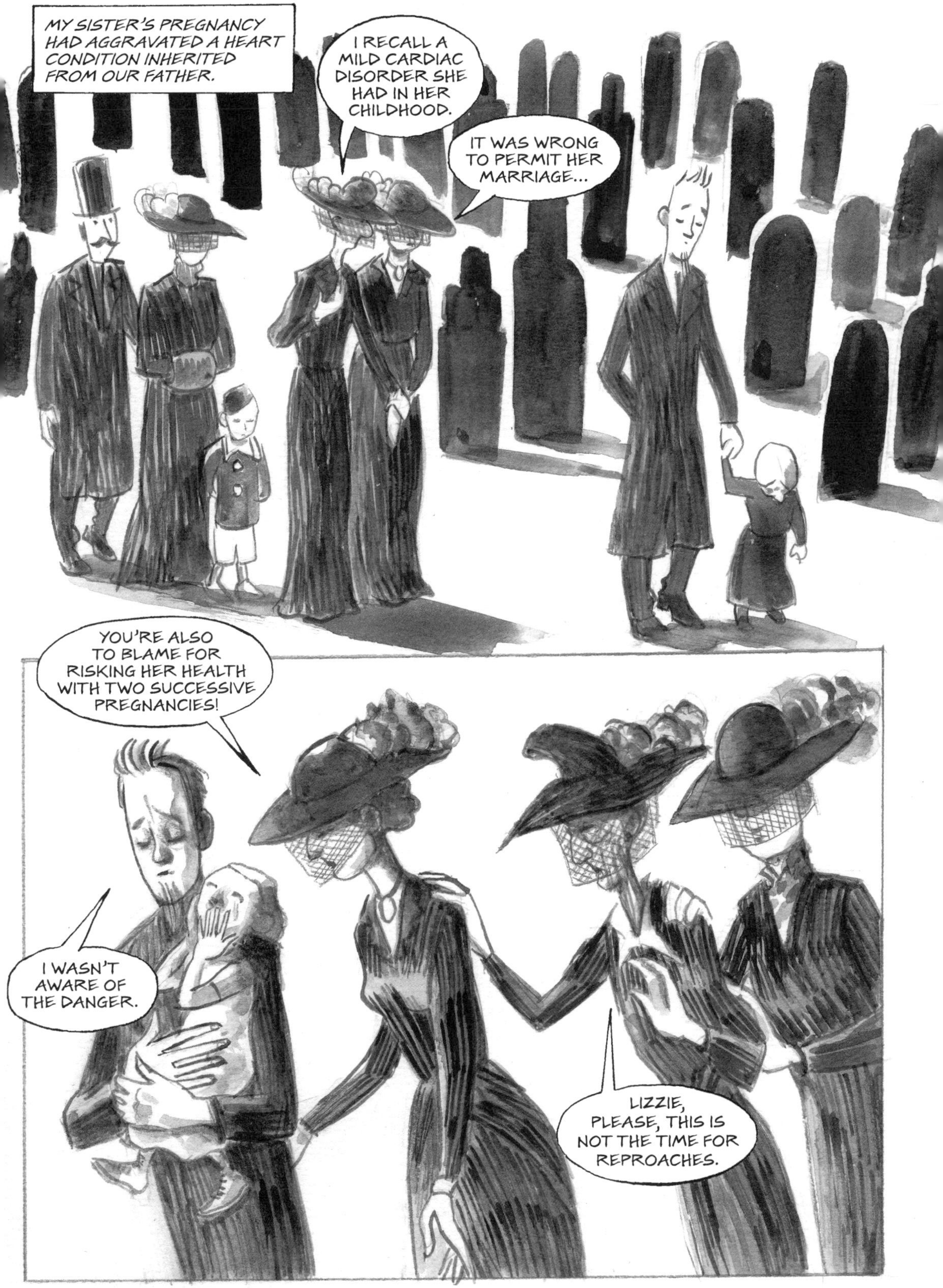
MY SISTER'S PREGNANCY HAD AGGRAVATED A HEART CONDITION INHERITED FROM OUR FATHER.
I RECALL A MILD CARDIAC DISORDER SHE HAD IN HER CHILDHOOD.
IT WAS WRONG TO PERMIT HER MARRIAGE...
YOU'RE ALSO TO BLAME FOR RISKING HER HEALTH WITH TWO SUCCESSIVE PREGNANCIES!
I WASN'T AWARE OF THE DANGER.
LIZZIE, PLEASE, THIS IS NOT THE TIME FOR REPROACHES.

PERHAPS MY CRUEL REPRIMAND DECIDED HIM TO RETURN TO HIS OWN FAMILY AND TAKE THE CHILD WITH HIM, MY SISTER'S "ONLY LEGACY", AS HE PUT IT.

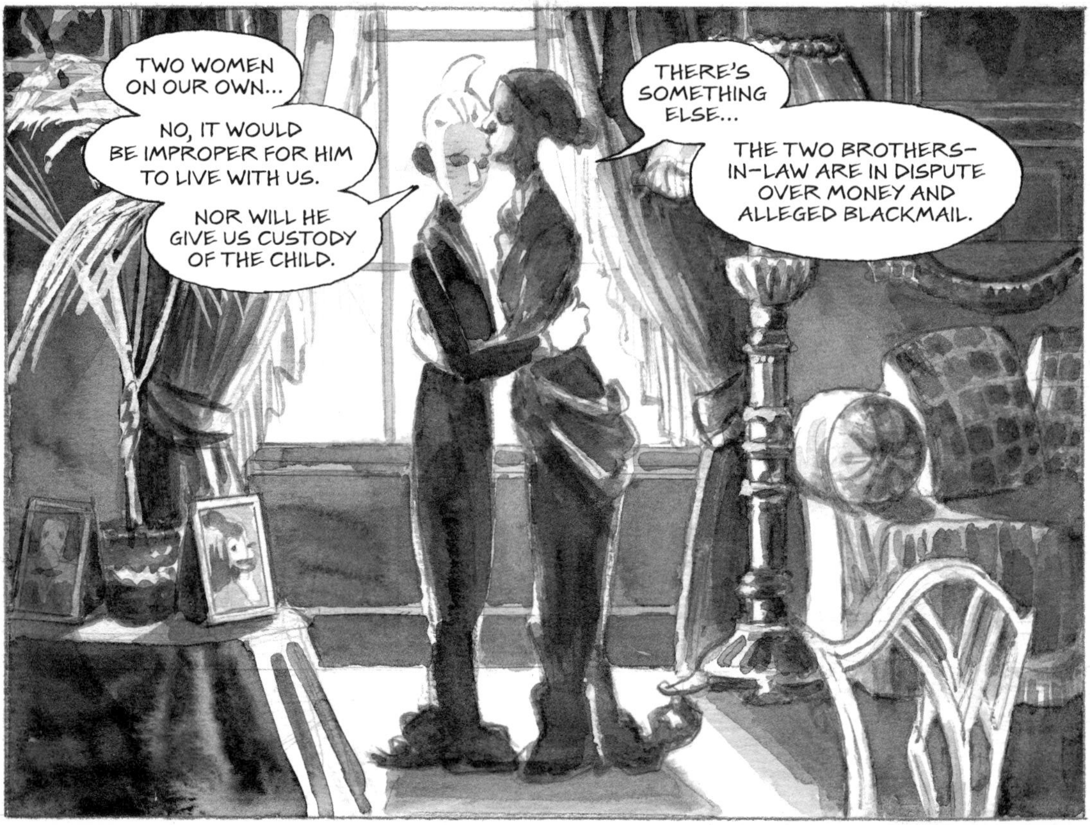
TWO WOMEN ON OUR OWN...
NO, IT WOULD BE IMPROPER FOR HIM TO LIVE WITH US.
NOR WILL HE GIVE US CUSTODY OF THE CHILD.
THERE'S SOMETHING ELSE...
THE TWO BROTHERS-IN-LAW ARE IN DISPUTE OVER MONEY AND ALLEGED BLACKMAIL.

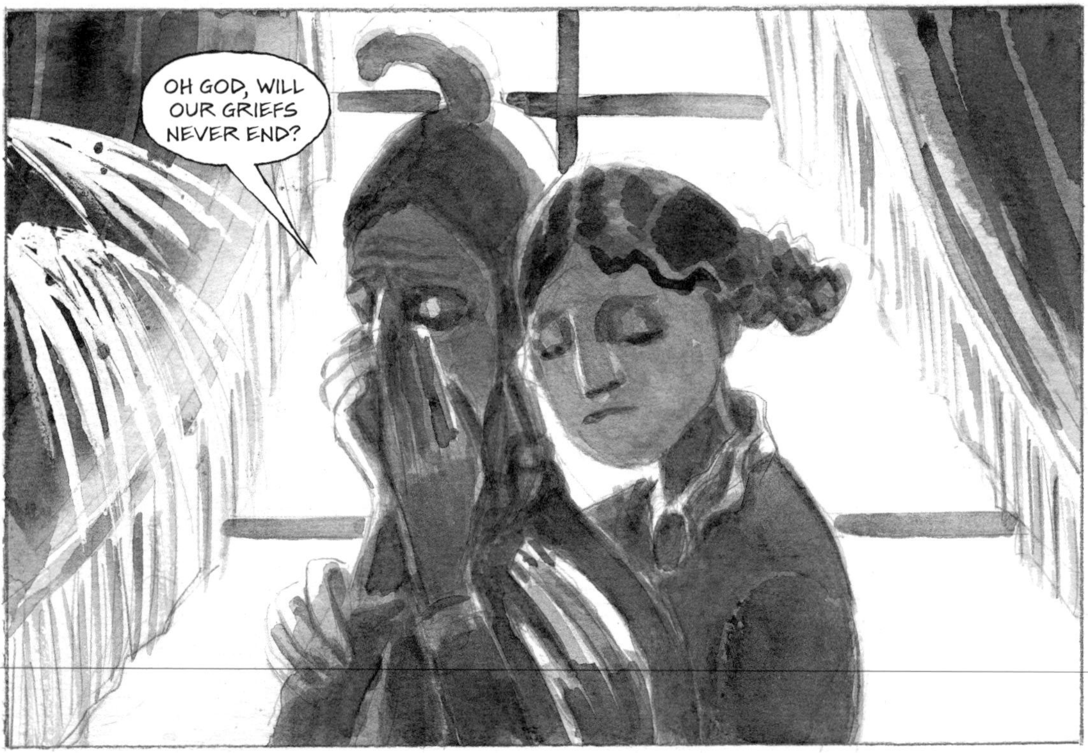
OH GOD, WILL OUR GRIEFS NEVER END?

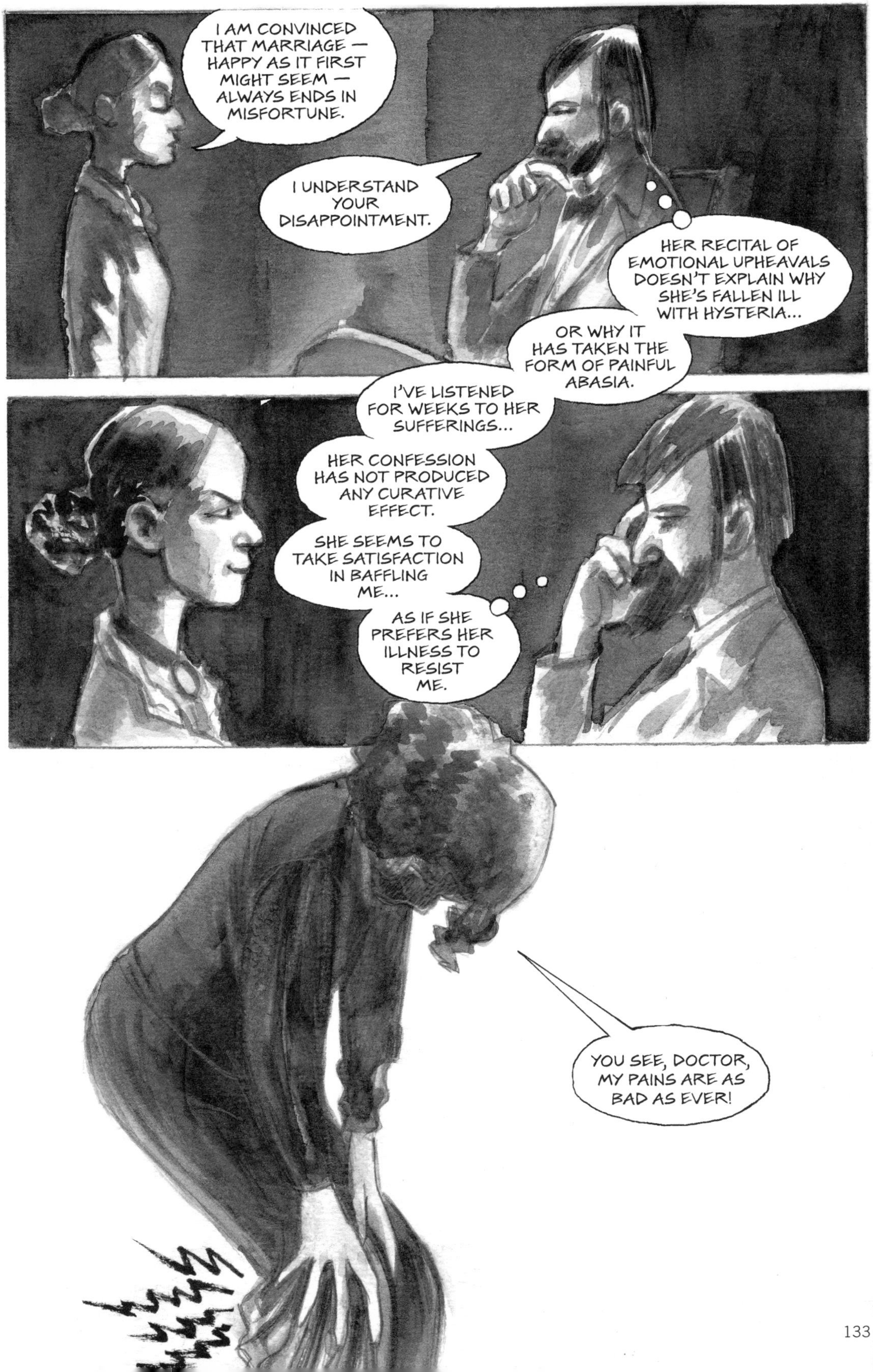
I AM CONVINCED THAT MARRIAGE — HAPPY AS IT FIRST MIGHT SEEM — ALWAYS ENDS IN MISFORTUNE.
I UNDERSTAND YOUR DISAPPOINTMENT.
HER RECITAL OF EMOTIONAL UPHEAVALS DOESN'T EXPLAIN WHY SHE'S FALLEN ILL WITH HYSTERIA...
OR WHY IT HAS TAKEN THE FORM OF PAINFUL ABASIA.
I'VE LISTENED FOR WEEKS TO HER SUFFERINGS...
HER CONFESSION HAS NOT PRODUCED ANY CURATIVE EFFECT.
SHE SEEMS TO TAKE SATISFACTION IN BAFFLING ME...
AS IF SHE PREFERS HER ILLNESS TO RESIST ME.
YOU SEE, DOCTOR, MY PAINS ARE AS BAD AS EVER!

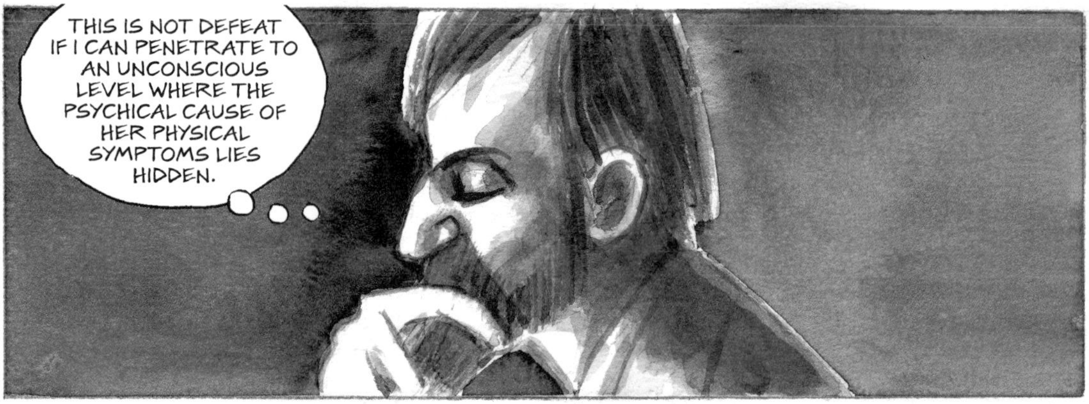
THIS IS NOT DEFEAT IF I CAN PENETRATE TO AN UNCONSCIOUS LEVEL WHERE THE PSYCHICAL CAUSE OF HER PHYSICAL SYMPTOMS LIES HIDDEN.

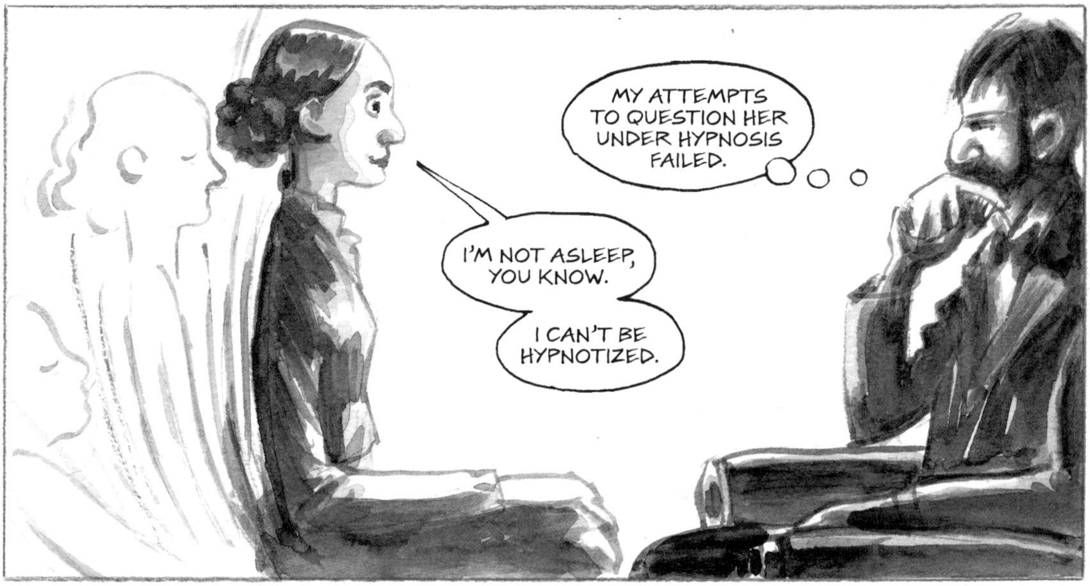
MY ATTEMPTS TO QUESTION HER UNDER HYPNOSIS FAILED.
I'M NOT ASLEEP, YOU KNOW.
I CAN'T BE HYPNOTIZED.

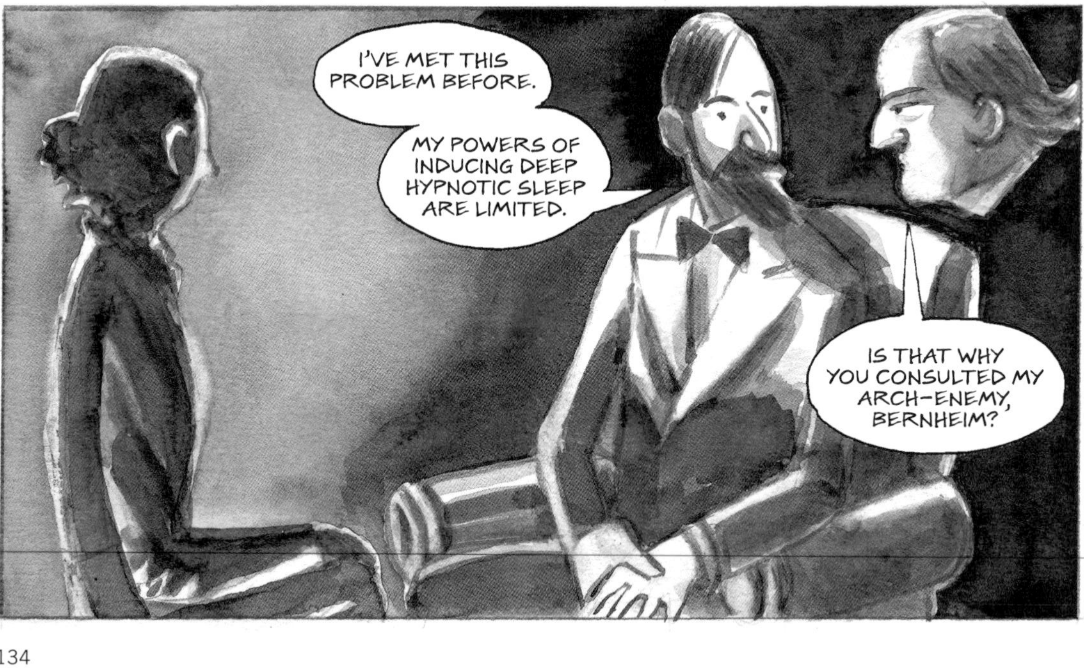
I'VE MET THIS PROBLEM BEFORE.
MY POWERS OF INDUCING DEEP HYPNOTIC SLEEP ARE LIMITED.
IS THAT WHY YOU CONSULTED MY ARCH-ENEMY, BERNHEIM?

HIPPOLYTE BERNHEIM OPPOSED CHARCOT'S NOTION THAT ONLY HYSTERICS ARE LIABLE TO HYPNOSIS. BERNHEIM ASSERTED THAT HYPNOSIS IS A PSYCHOLOGICAL PHENOMENON, WORKABLE ON NORMAL PERSONS.

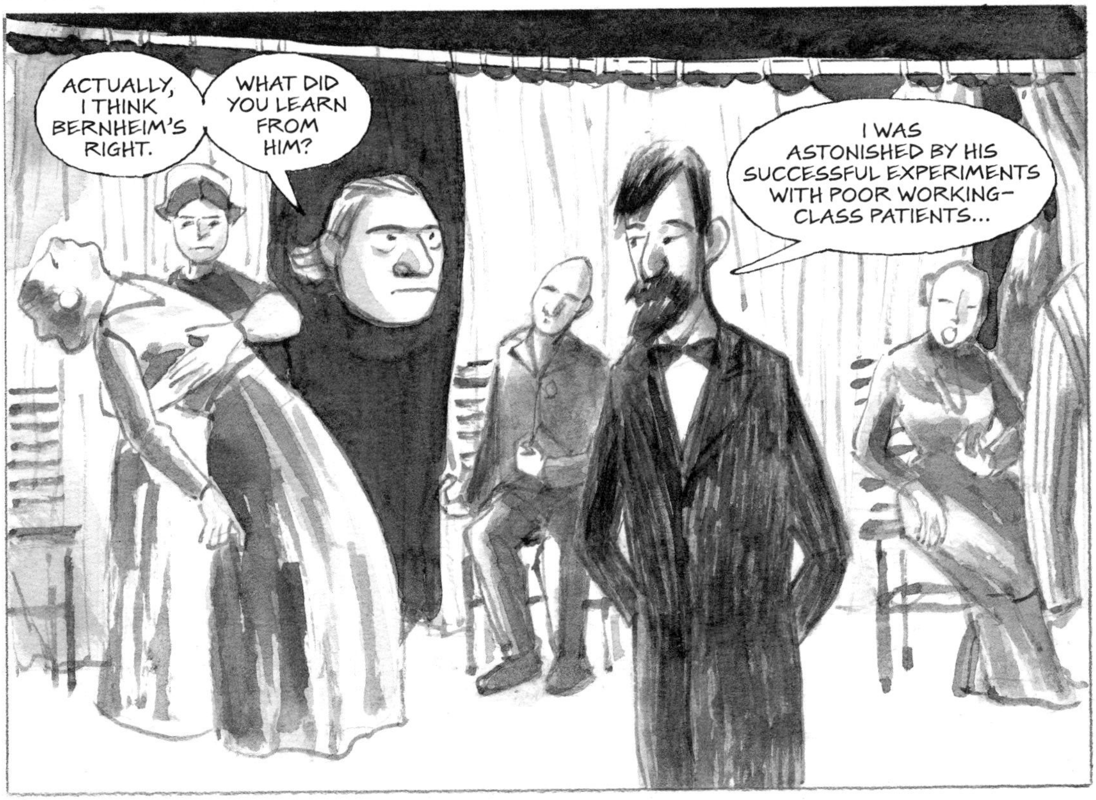
ACTUALLY, I THINK BERNHEIM'S RIGHT.
WHAT DID YOU LEARN FROM HIM?
I WAS ASTONISHED BY HIS SUCCESSFUL EXPERIMENTS WITH POOR WORKING-CLASS PATIENTS...

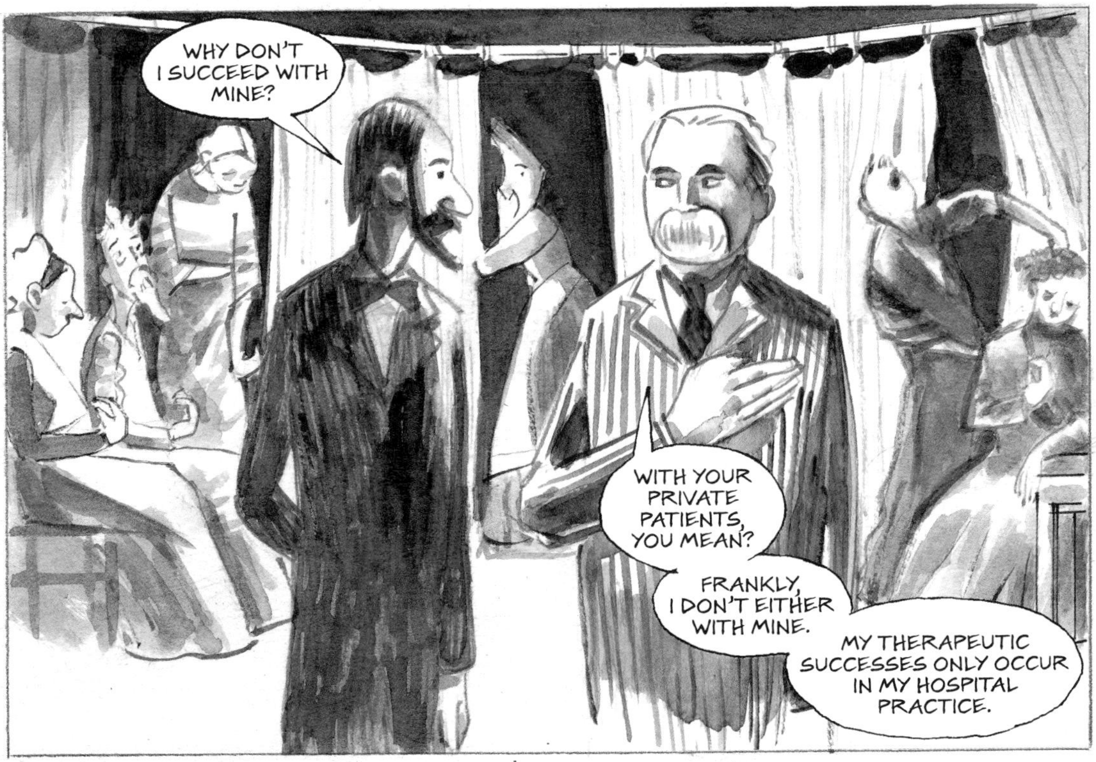
WHY DON'T I SUCCEED WITH MINE?
WITH YOUR PRIVATE PATIENTS, YOU MEAN?
FRANKLY, I DON'T EITHER WITH MINE.
MY THERAPEUTIC SUCCESSES ONLY OCCUR IN MY HOSPITAL PRACTICE.

I SPENT SEVERAL WEEKS IN 1889 AT BERNHEIM'S HOSPITAL CLINIC IN NANCY. ONE OF HIS REMARKS NOW CAME TO MY AID IN FRÄULEIN ELISABETH'S CASE.

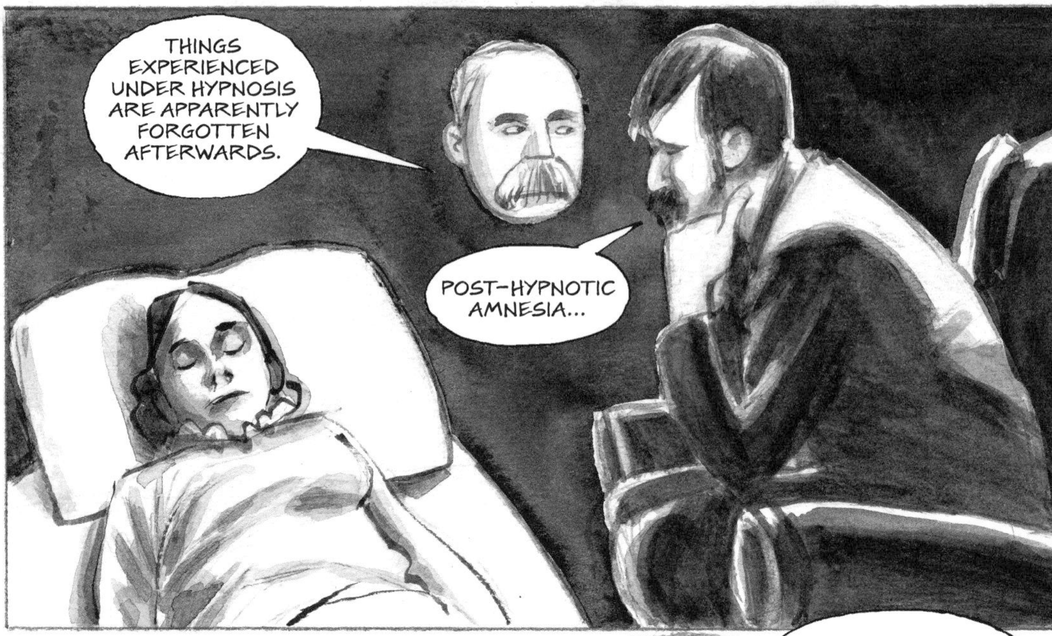
THINGS EXPERIENCED UNDER HYPNOSIS ARE APPARENTLY FORGOTTEN AFTERWARDS.
POST-HYPNOTIC AMNESIA...

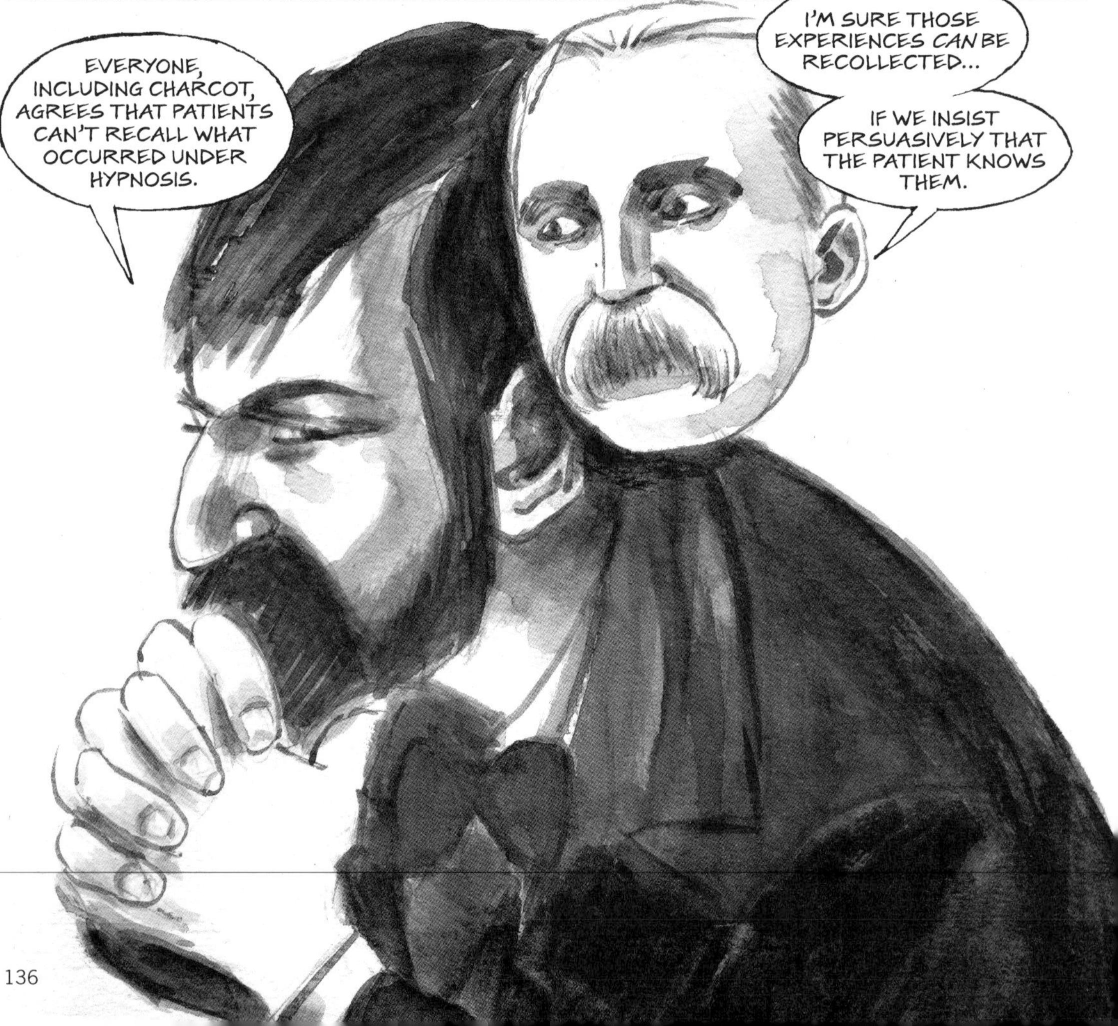
EVERYONE, INCLUDING CHARCOT, AGREES THAT PATIENTS CAN'T RECALL WHAT OCCURRED UNDER HYPNOSIS.
I'M SURE THOSE EXPERIENCES *CAN* BE RECOLLECTED...
IF WE INSIST PERSUASIVELY THAT THE PATIENT KNOWS THEM.

SURELY THIS MUST ALSO BE TRUE FOR THE "FORGOTTEN MEMORIES" OF HYSTERIA. SO I ATTEMPTED TO SUMMON THEM BY A SIMPLE METHOD OF CONCENTRATION, WITHOUT USING HYPNOSIS.

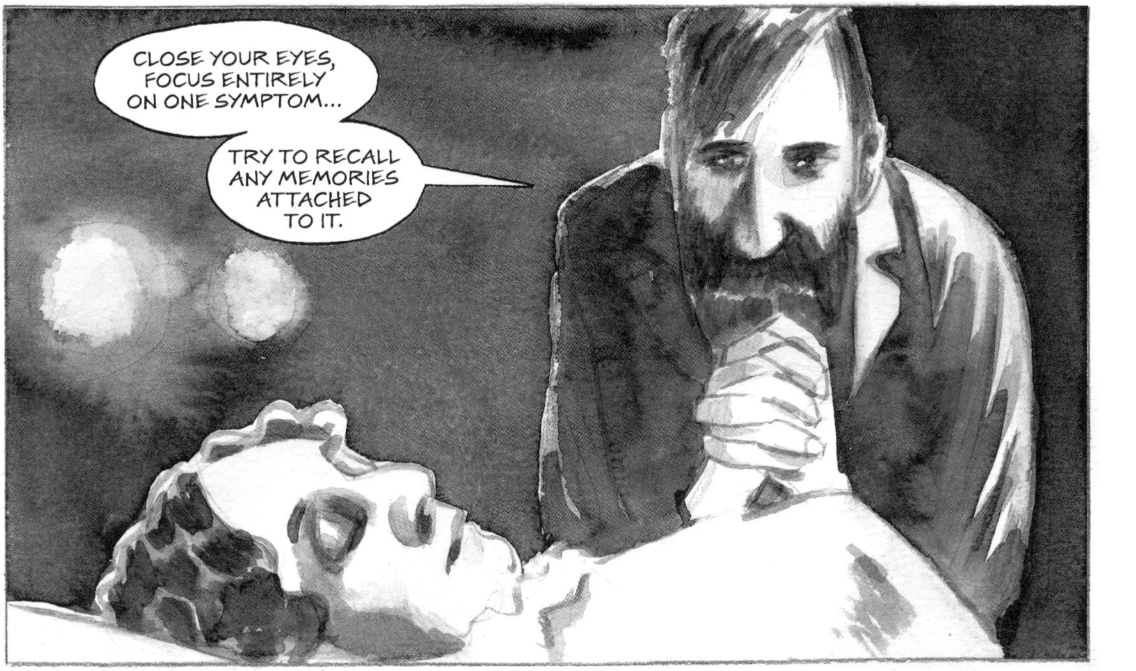
CLOSE YOUR EYES, FOCUS ENTIRELY ON ONE SYMPTOM...
TRY TO RECALL ANY MEMORIES ATTACHED TO IT.

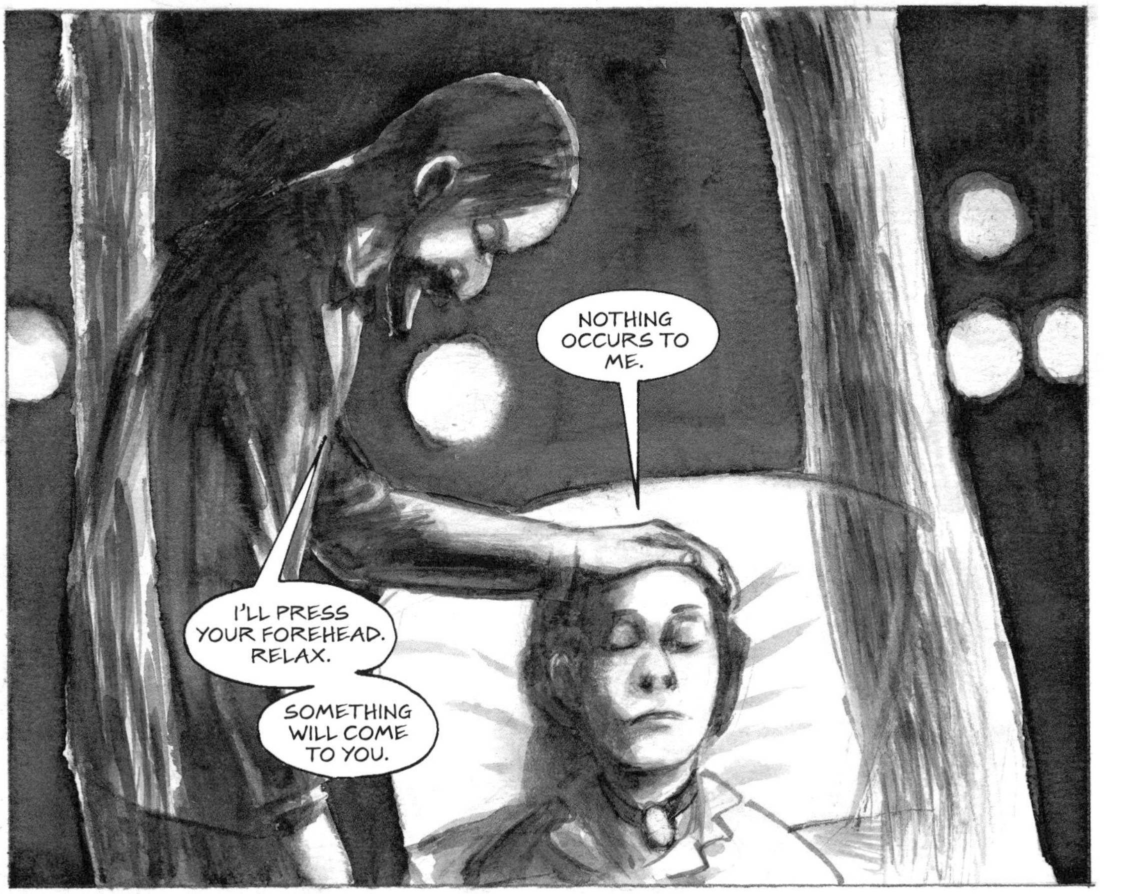
NOTHING OCCURS TO ME.
I'LL PRESS YOUR FOREHEAD. RELAX.
SOMETHING WILL COME TO YOU.

SHE REMAINED SILENT A LONG WHILE, BEFORE YIELDING A MEMORY...

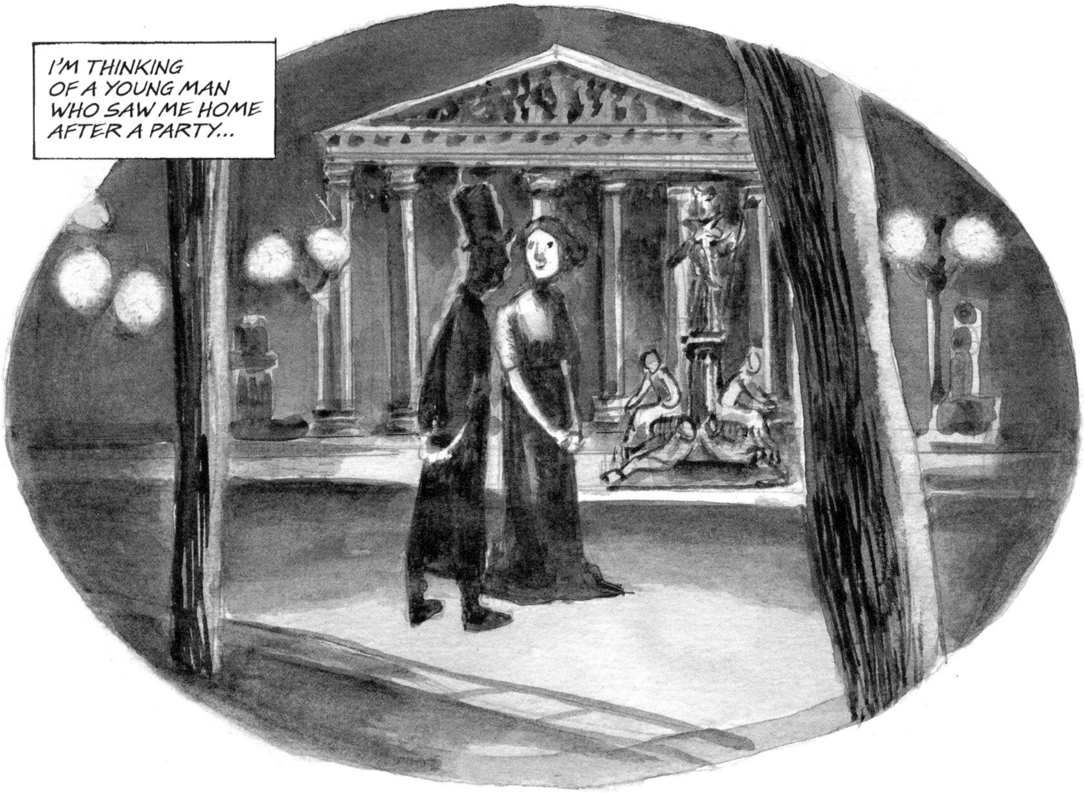
I'M THINKING OF A YOUNG MAN WHO SAW ME HOME AFTER A PARTY...

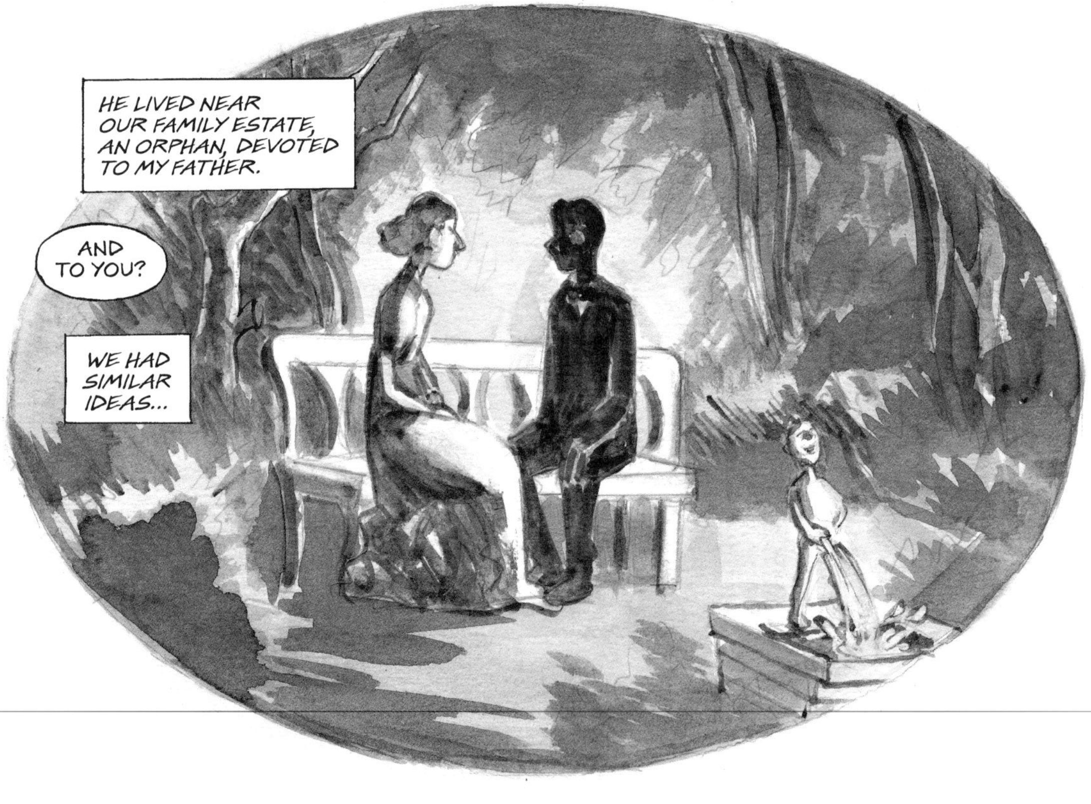
HE LIVED NEAR OUR FAMILY ESTATE, AN ORPHAN, DEVOTED TO MY FATHER.
AND TO YOU?
WE HAD SIMILAR IDEAS...

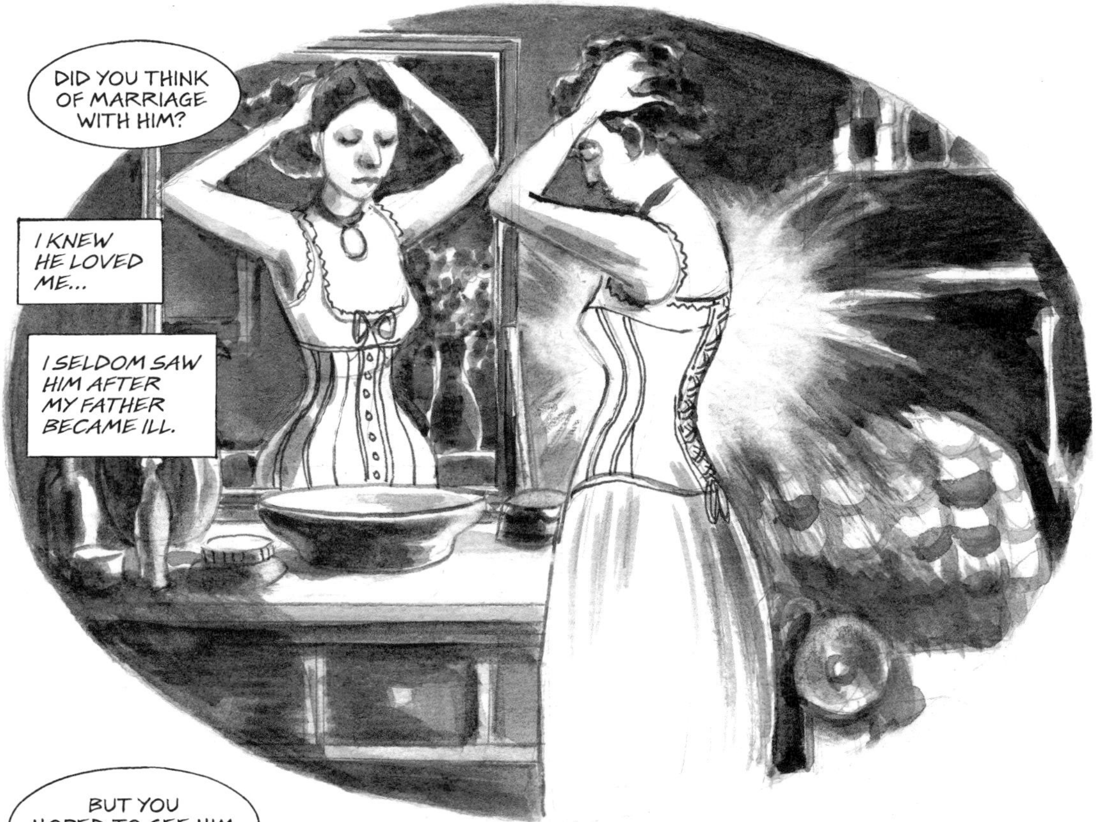
DID YOU THINK OF MARRIAGE WITH HIM?
I KNEW HE LOVED ME...
I SELDOM SAW HIM AFTER MY FATHER BECAME ILL.

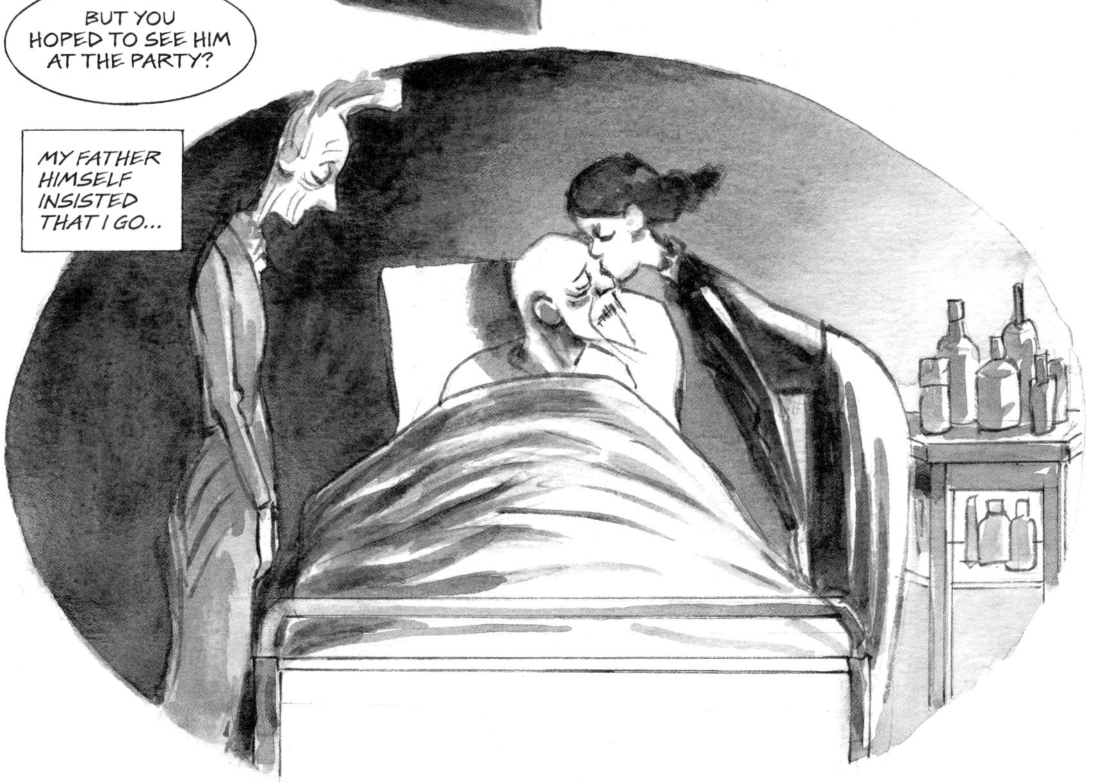
BUT YOU HOPED TO SEE HIM AT THE PARTY?
MY FATHER HIMSELF INSISTED THAT I GO...

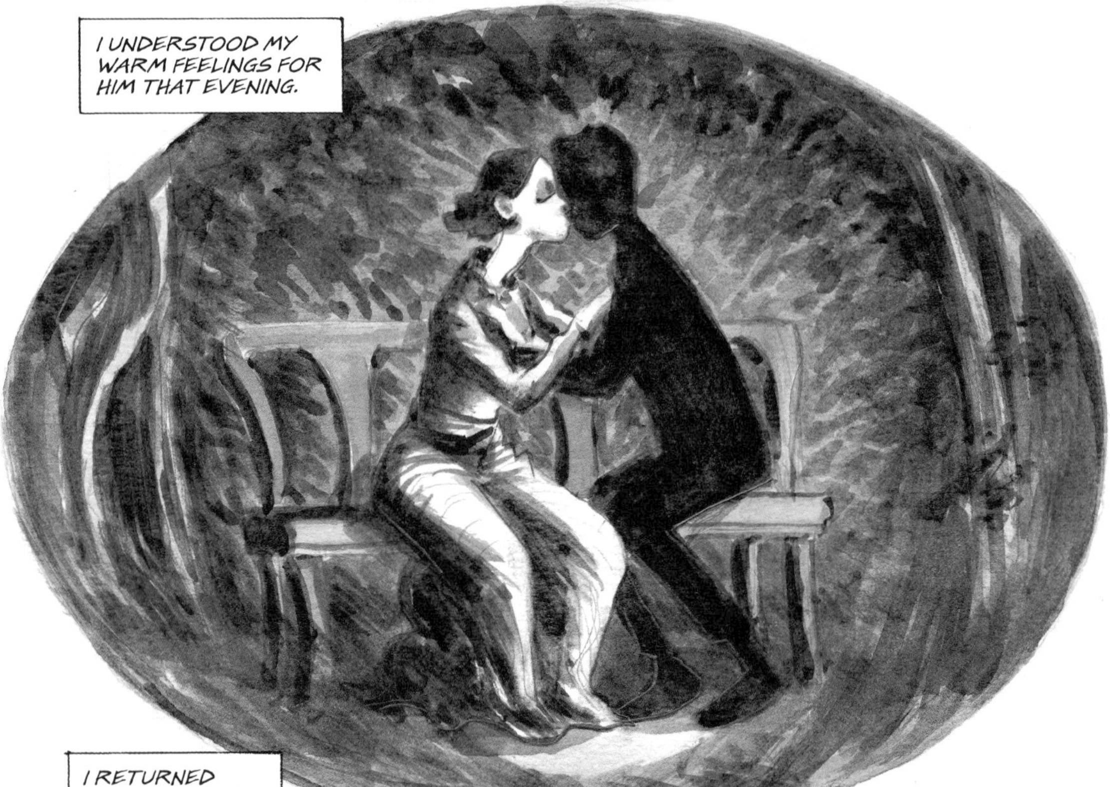
I UNDERSTOOD MY WARM FEELINGS FOR HIM THAT EVENING.

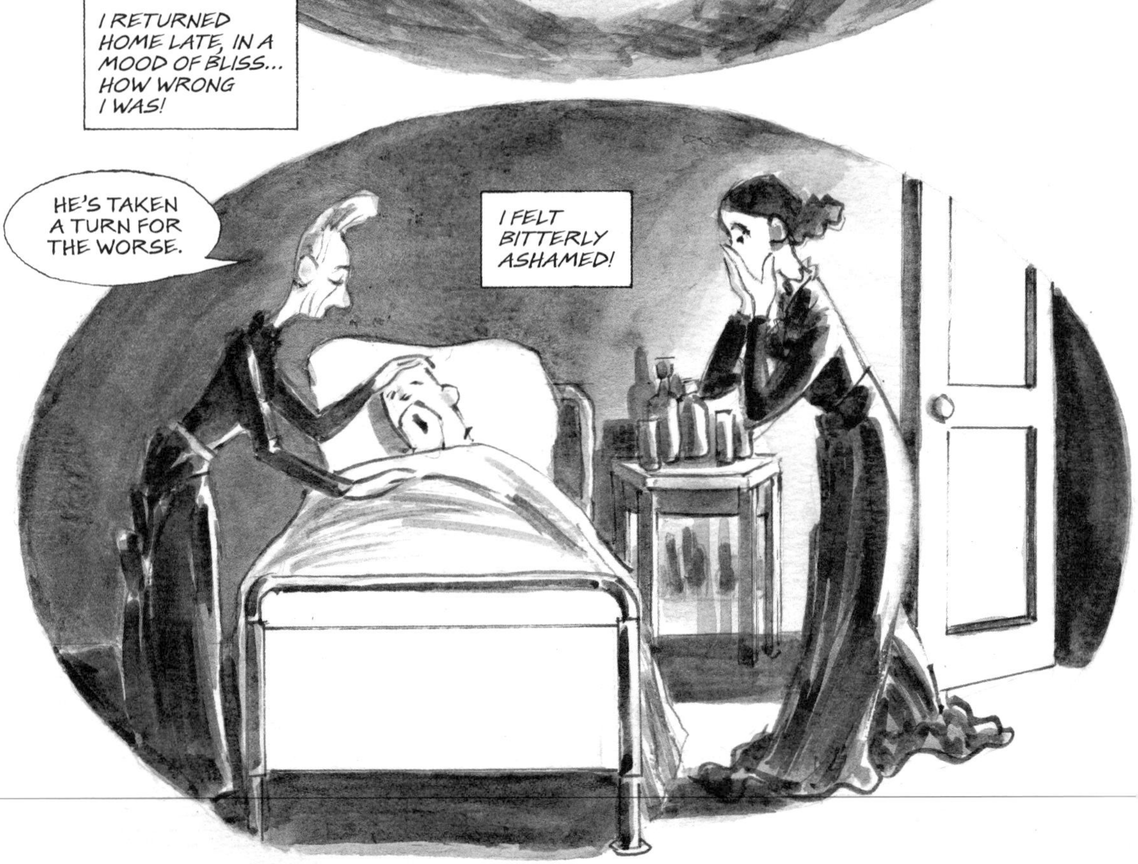
I RETURNED HOME LATE, IN A MOOD OF BLISS... HOW WRONG I WAS!
HE'S TAKEN A TURN FOR THE WORSE.
I FELT BITTERLY ASHAMED!

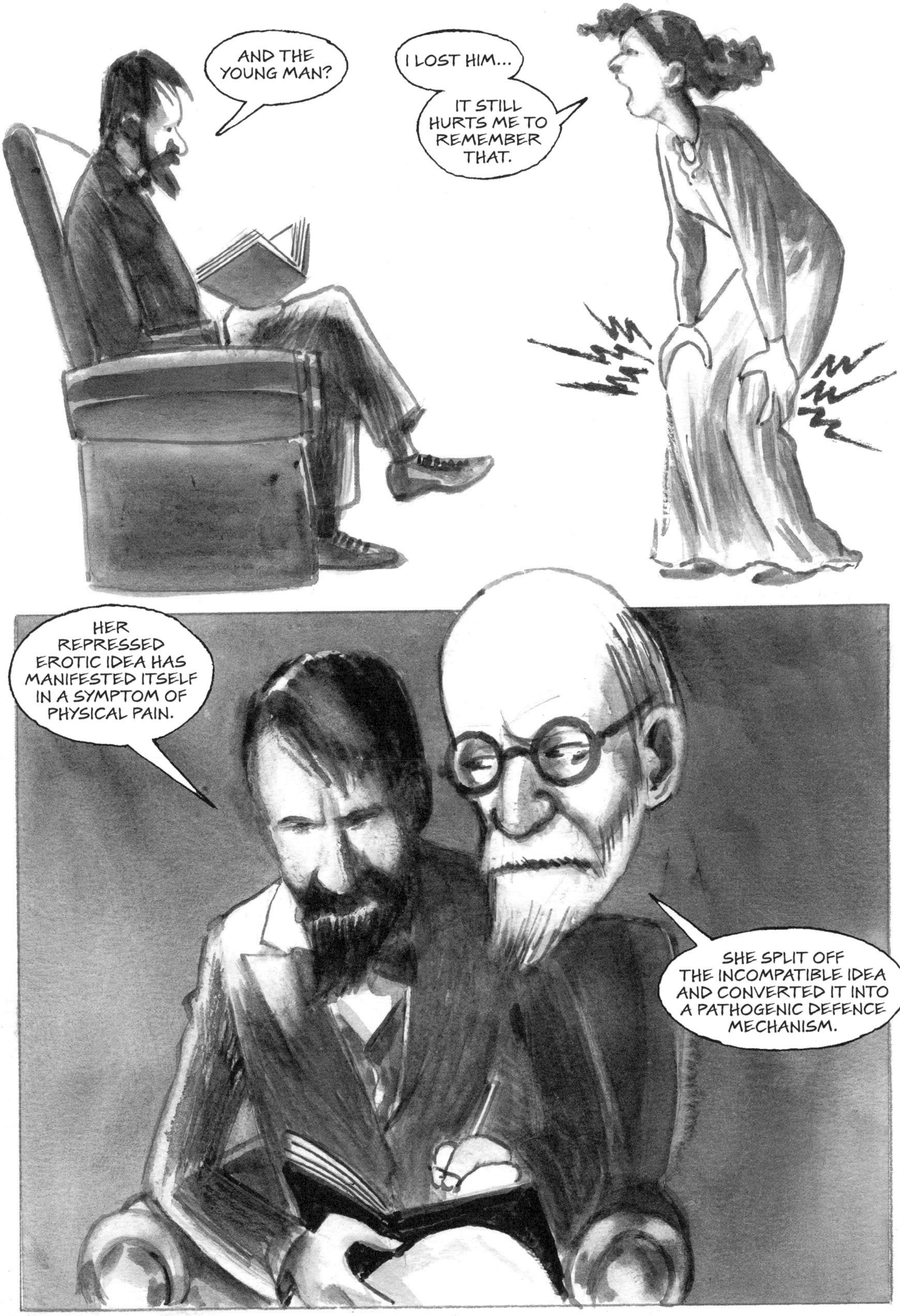
AND THE YOUNG MAN?
I LOST HIM...
IT STILL HURTS ME TO REMEMBER THAT.
HER REPRESSED EROTIC IDEA HAS MANIFESTED ITSELF IN A SYMPTOM OF PHYSICAL PAIN.
SHE SPLIT OFF THE INCOMPATIBLE IDEA AND CONVERTED IT INTO A PATHOGENIC DEFENCE MECHANISM.

HOW TO OVERCOME THE BARRIER OF DEFENCE? THE PATIENT HERSELF RESISTS AWAKENING THE FORGOTTEN MEMORY THAT MUST BE SUFFERED AGAIN IN PRESENT ABREACTION.

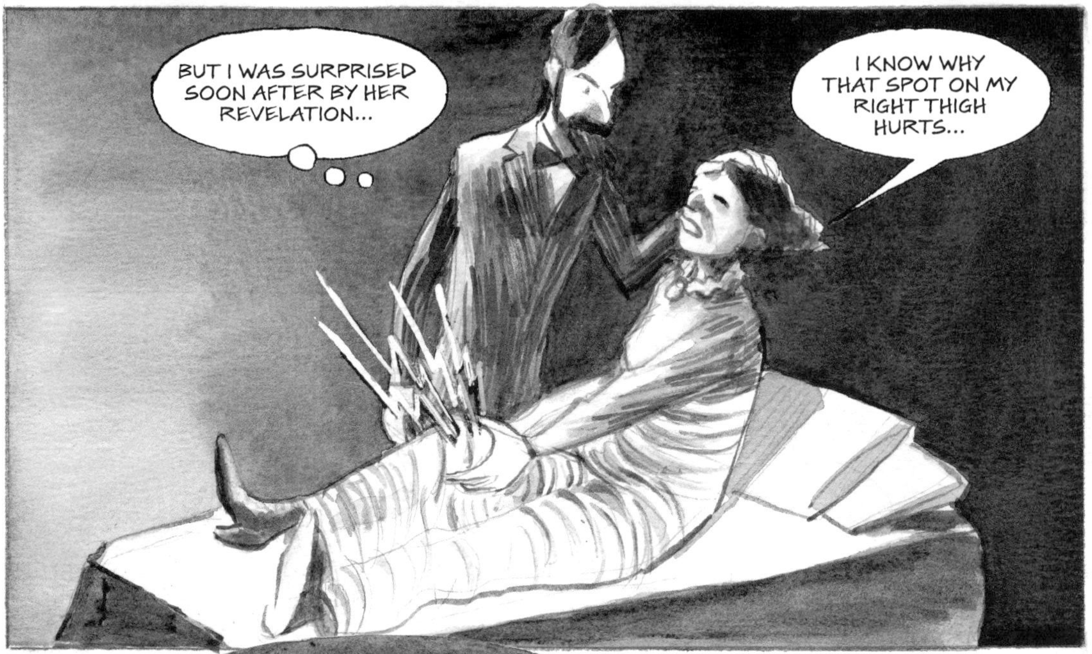
BUT I WAS SURPRISED SOON AFTER BY HER REVELATION...
I KNOW WHY THAT SPOT ON MY RIGHT THIGH HURTS...

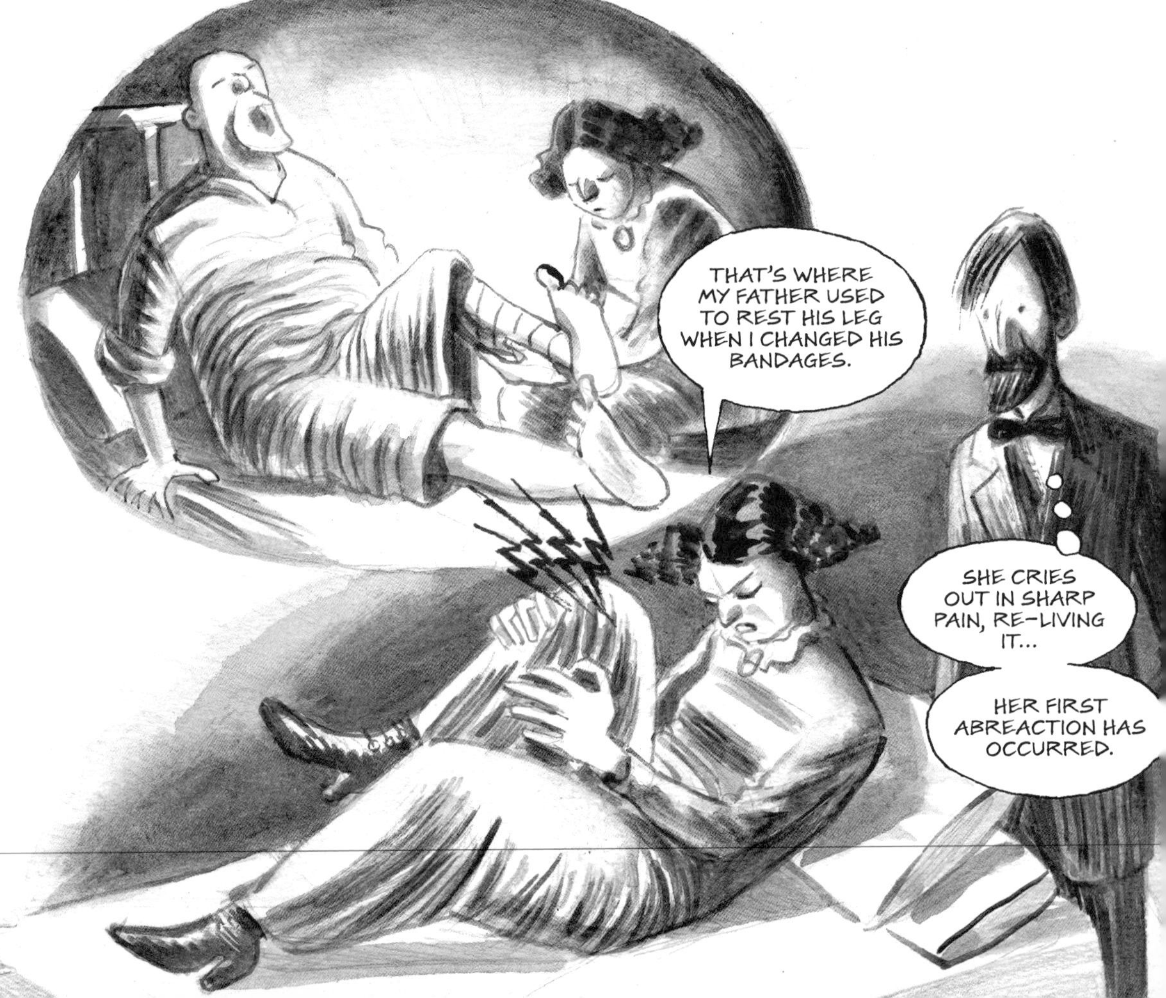
THAT'S WHERE MY FATHER USED TO REST HIS LEG WHEN I CHANGED HIS BANDAGES.
SHE CRIES OUT IN SHARP PAIN, RE-LIVING IT...
HER FIRST ABREACTION HAS OCCURRED.

AT LAST THE MYSTERIOUS PAIN IN HER RIGHT LEG BECAME CLEAR TO HER.

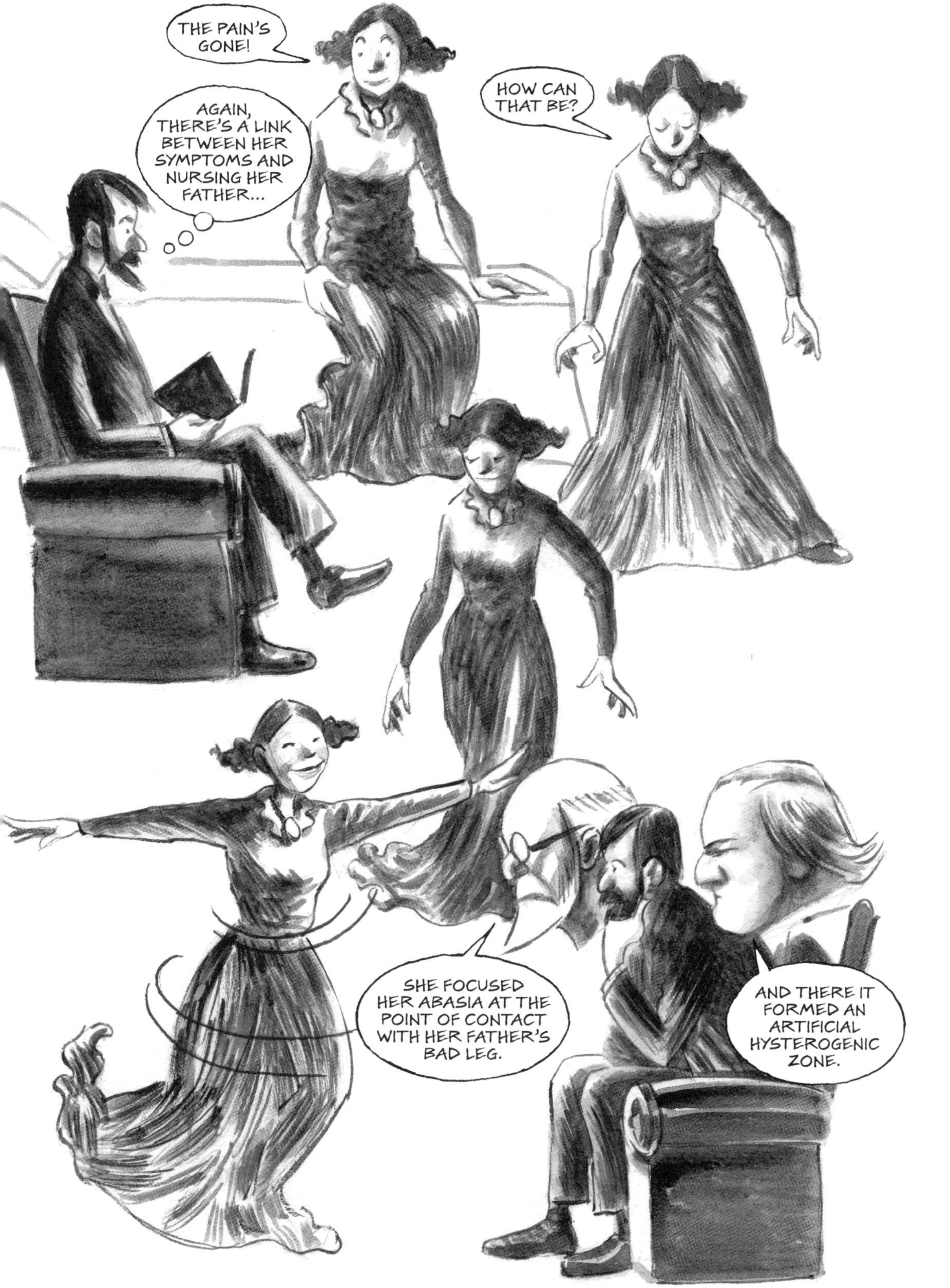

THE PAIN'S GONE!
AGAIN, THERE'S A LINK BETWEEN HER SYMPTOMS AND NURSING HER FATHER...
HOW CAN THAT BE?
SHE FOCUSED HER ABASIA AT THE POINT OF CONTACT WITH HER FATHER'S BAD LEG.
AND THERE IT FORMED AN ARTIFICIAL HYSTEROGENIC ZONE.

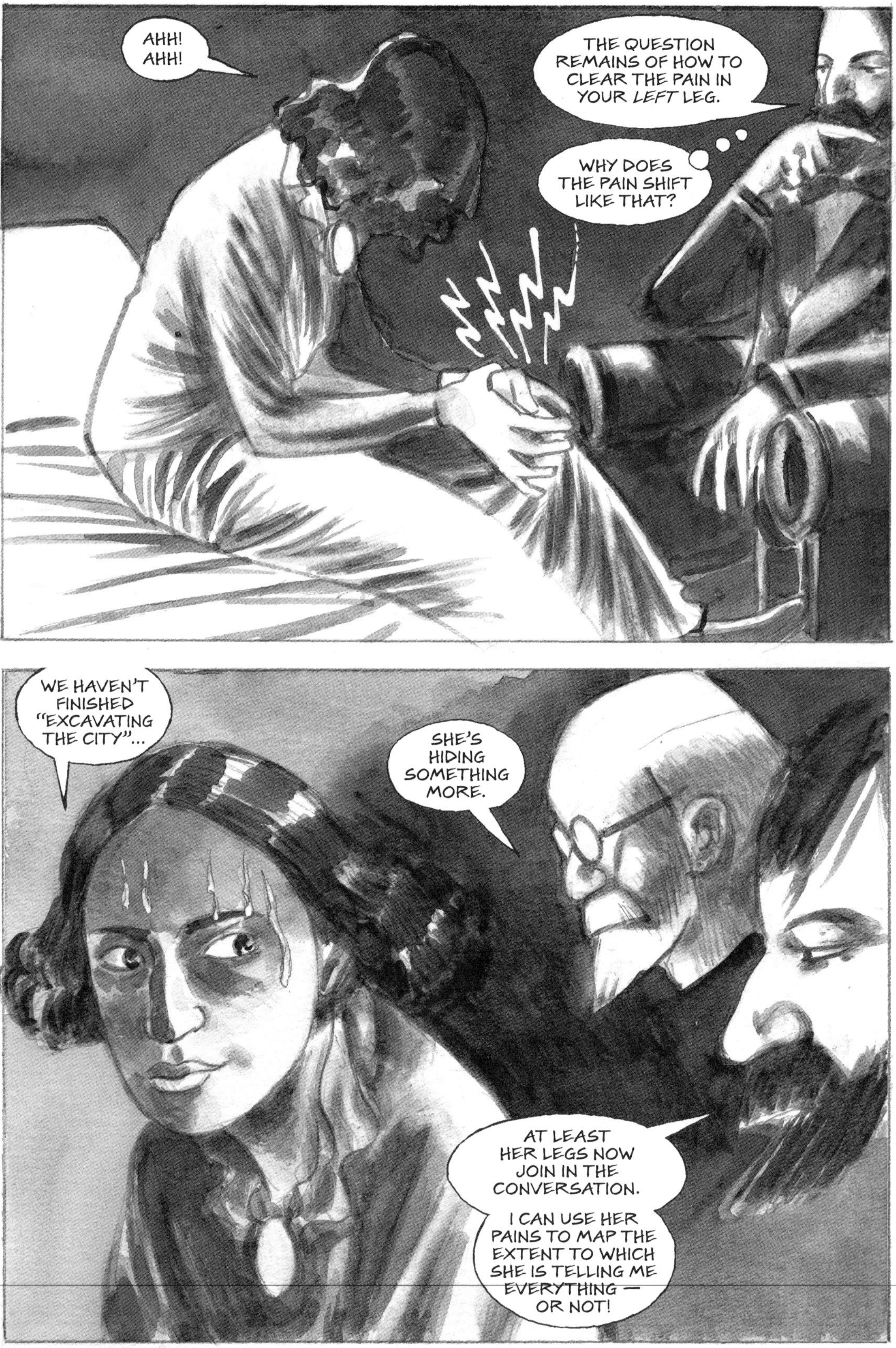
AHH! AHH!
THE QUESTION REMAINS OF HOW TO CLEAR THE PAIN IN YOUR *LEFT* LEG.
WHY DOES THE PAIN SHIFT LIKE THAT?
WE HAVEN'T FINISHED "EXCAVATING THE CITY"...
SHE'S HIDING SOMETHING MORE.
AT LEAST HER LEGS NOW JOIN IN THE CONVERSATION.
I CAN USE HER PAINS TO MAP THE EXTENT TO WHICH SHE IS TELLING ME EVERYTHING — OR NOT!

I REALIZED THAT WE WEREN'T DEALING WITH ONE SYMPTOM, BUT LAYERS OF THEM, EACH CONCEALING A "COMPASS POINT" OF ITS OWN.

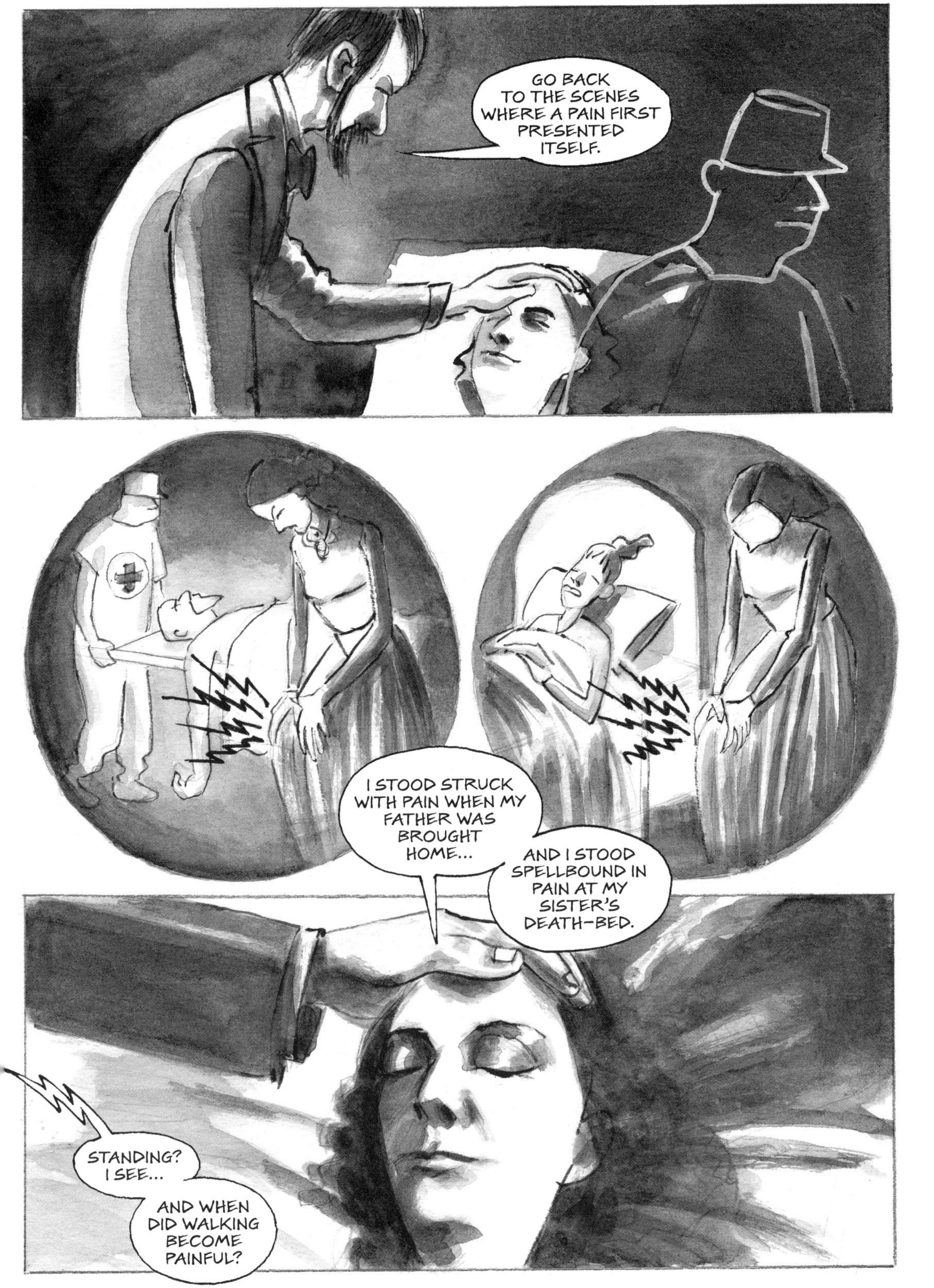
GO BACK TO THE SCENES WHERE A PAIN FIRST PRESENTED ITSELF.
I STOOD STRUCK WITH PAIN WHEN MY FATHER WAS BROUGHT HOME...
AND I STOOD SPELLBOUND IN PAIN AT MY SISTER'S DEATH-BED.
STANDING? I SEE...
AND WHEN DID WALKING BECOME PAINFUL?

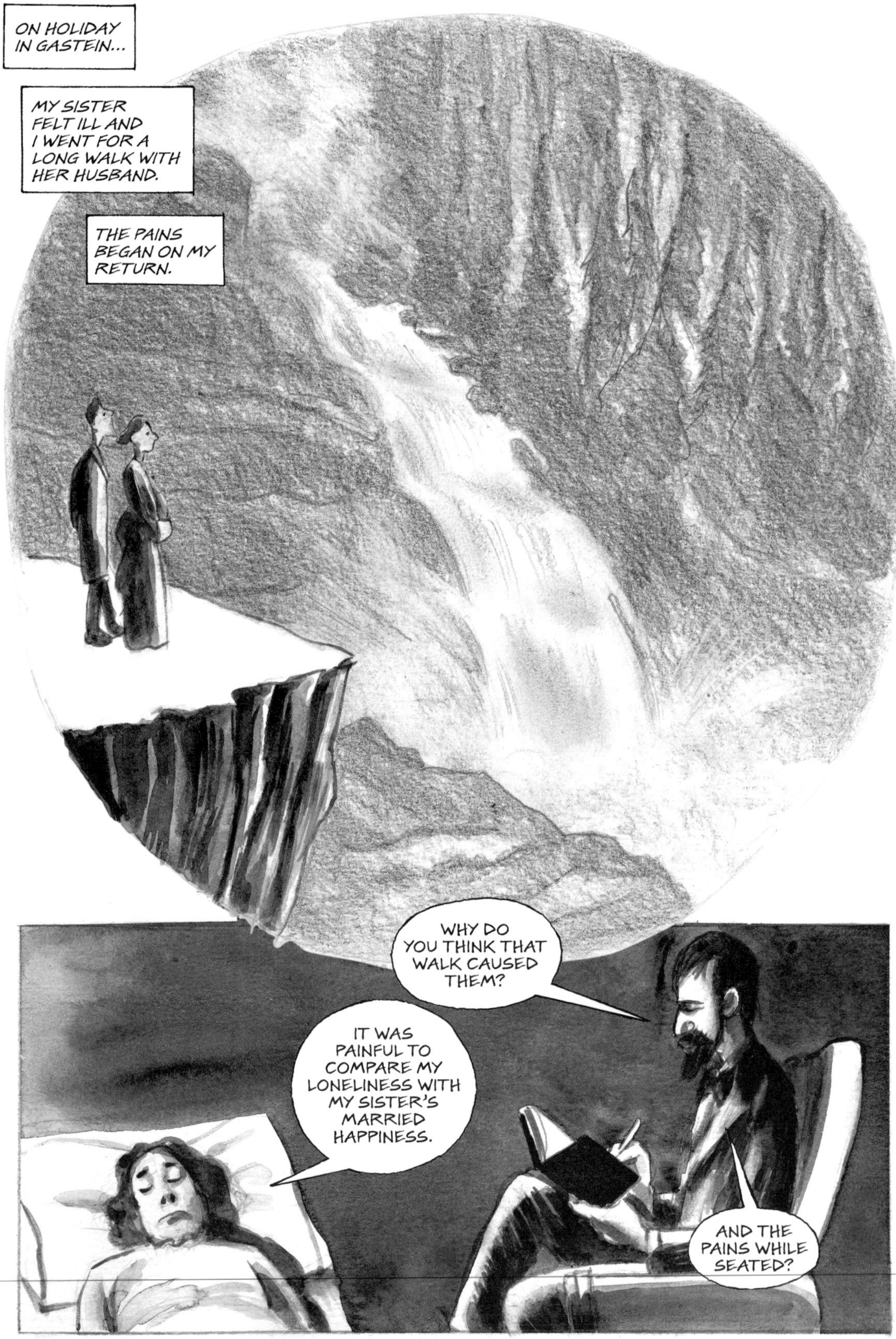
ON HOLIDAY IN GASTEIN...
MY SISTER FELT ILL AND I WENT FOR A LONG WALK WITH HER HUSBAND.
THE PAINS BEGAN ON MY RETURN.
WHY DO YOU THINK THAT WALK CAUSED THEM?
IT WAS PAINFUL TO COMPARE MY LONELINESS WITH MY SISTER'S MARRIED HAPPINESS.
AND THE PAINS WHILE SEATED?

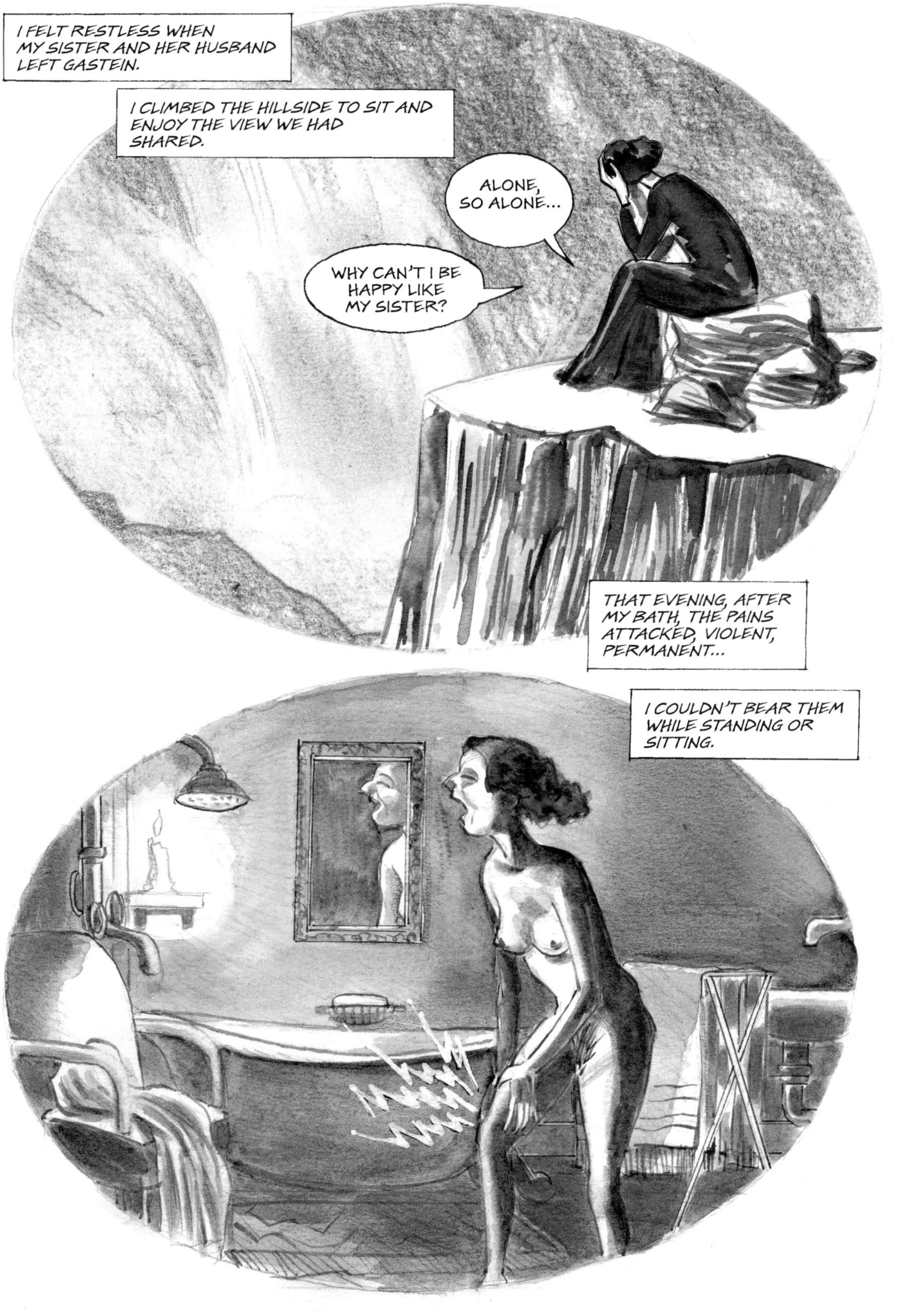
I FELT RESTLESS WHEN MY SISTER AND HER HUSBAND LEFT GASTEIN.
I CLIMBED THE HILLSIDE TO SIT AND ENJOY THE VIEW WE HAD SHARED.
ALONE, SO ALONE...
WHY CAN'T I BE HAPPY LIKE MY SISTER?
THAT EVENING, AFTER MY BATH, THE PAINS ATTACKED, VIOLENT, PERMANENT...
I COULDN'T BEAR THEM WHILE STANDING OR SITTING.

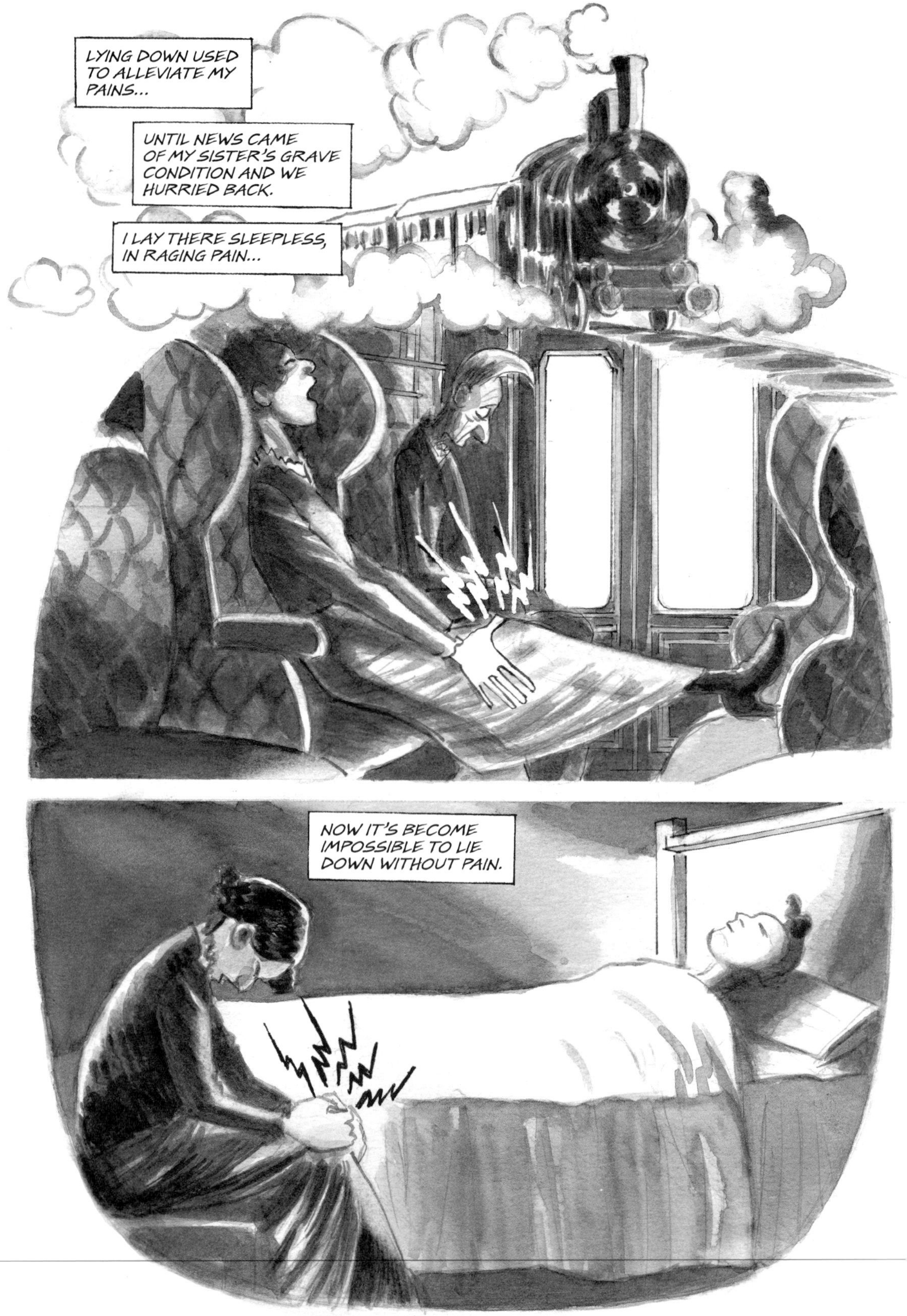
LYING DOWN USED TO ALLEVIATE MY PAINS...
UNTIL NEWS CAME OF MY SISTER'S GRAVE CONDITION AND WE HURRIED BACK.
I LAY THERE SLEEPLESS, IN RAGING PAIN...
NOW IT'S BECOME IMPOSSIBLE TO LIE DOWN WITHOUT PAIN.

STANDING, SITTING, WALKING, LYING DOWN… IN EACH INSTANCE THE FORCE OF SOME UNACCEPTABLE IDEA HAS BECOME "CATHECTED" — BLOCKED, AND CONVERTED INTO A PHYSICAL SYMPTOM.

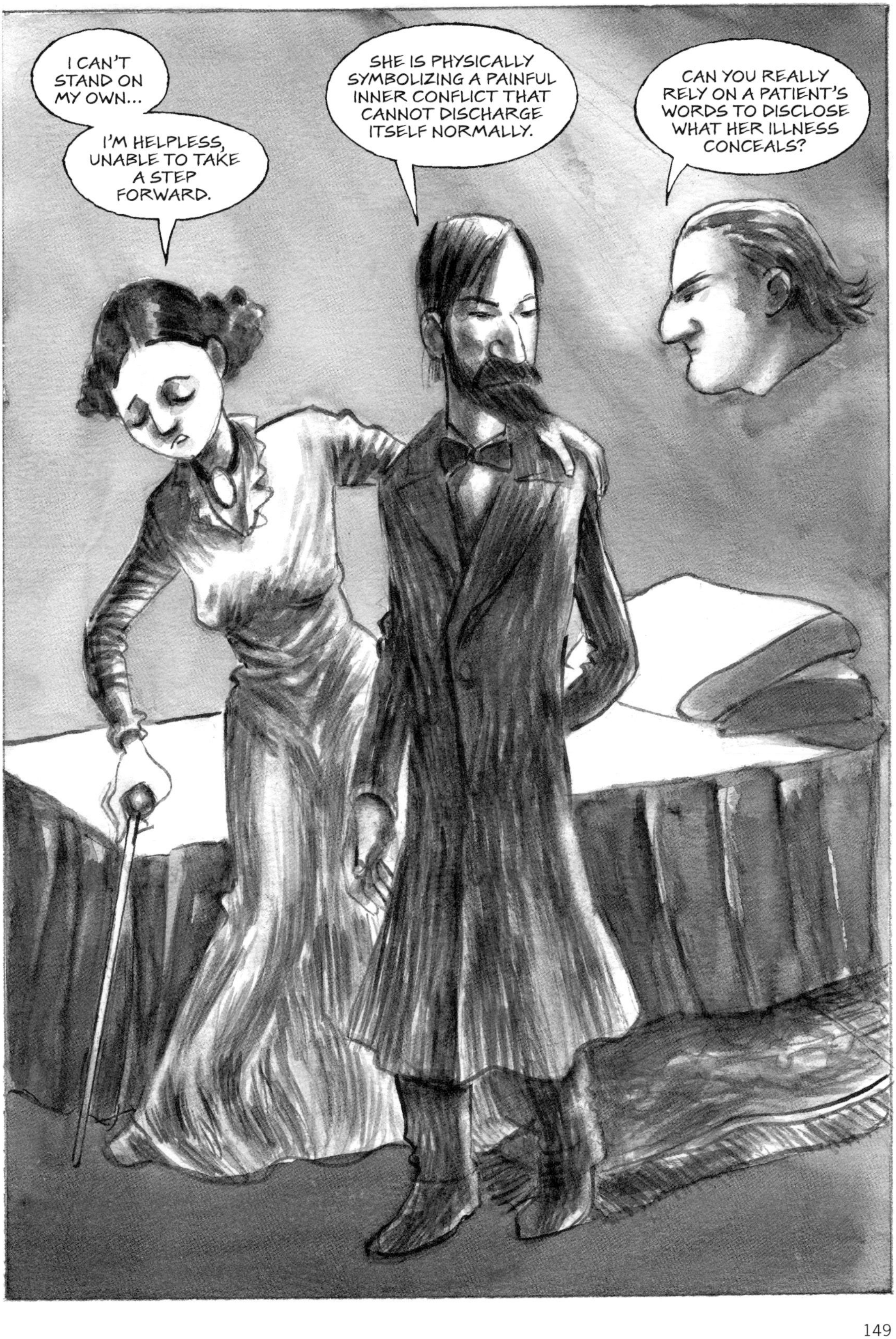
I CAN'T STAND ON MY OWN…
I'M HELPLESS, UNABLE TO TAKE A STEP FORWARD.
SHE IS PHYSICALLY SYMBOLIZING A PAINFUL INNER CONFLICT THAT CANNOT DISCHARGE ITSELF NORMALLY.
CAN YOU REALLY RELY ON A PATIENT'S WORDS TO DISCLOSE WHAT HER ILLNESS CONCEALS?

WHAT ELSE BUT WORDS DO WE HAVE? IF THE PHYSICAL APPEARANCE OF ILLNESS HAS NO ORGANIC CAUSE, THEN SURELY THE DISTURBANCE MUST BE PSYCHICAL IN ORIGIN. ELISABETH MUST HERSELF FIND THE WORDS ASSOCIATED WITH THE MEMORIES THAT RESIST MY ACCESS.

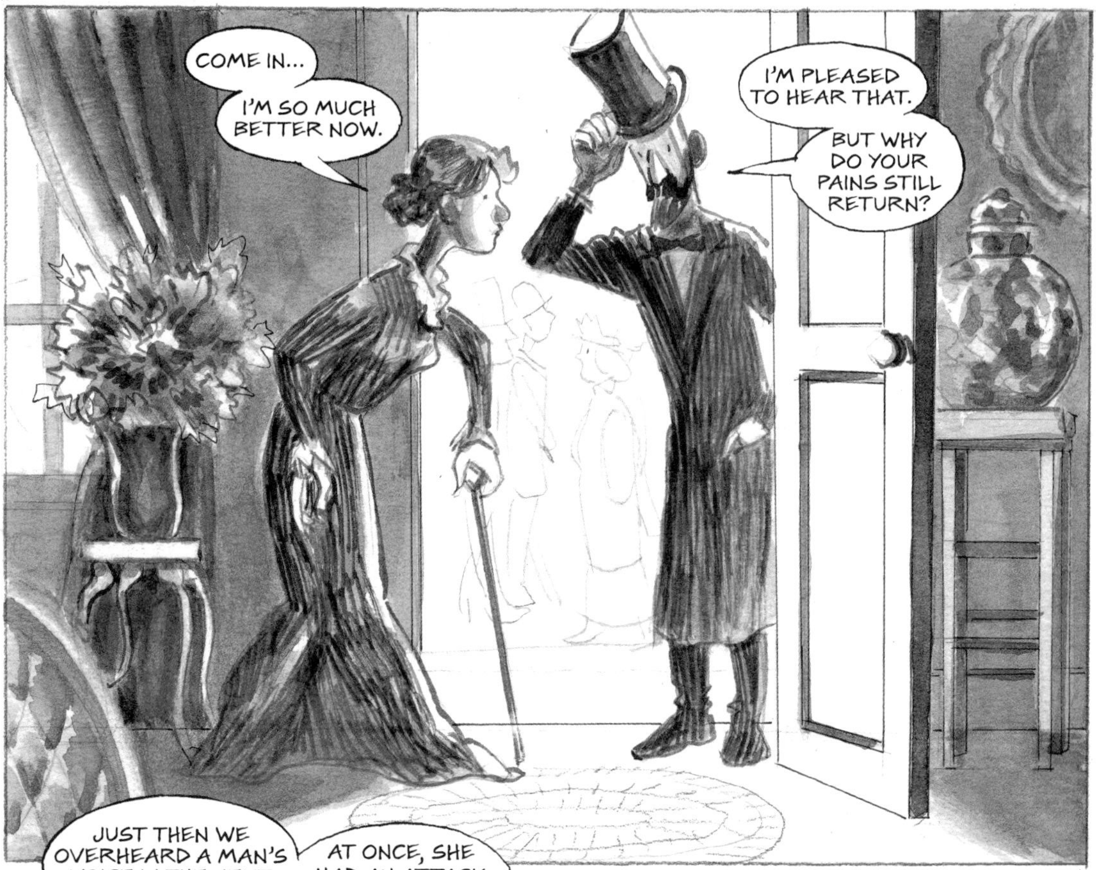

COME IN...
I'M SO MUCH BETTER NOW.
I'M PLEASED TO HEAR THAT.
BUT WHY DO YOUR PAINS STILL RETURN?

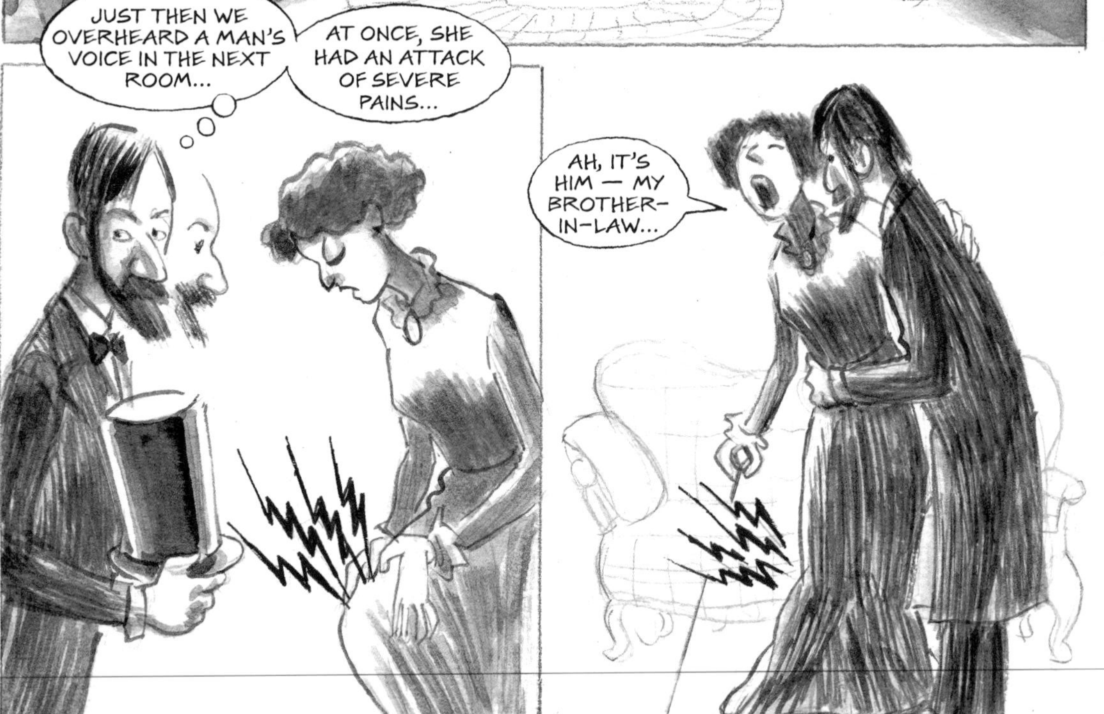

JUST THEN WE OVERHEARD A MAN'S VOICE IN THE NEXT ROOM...
AT ONCE, SHE HAD AN ATTACK OF SEVERE PAINS...
AH, IT'S HIM — MY BROTHER-IN-LAW...

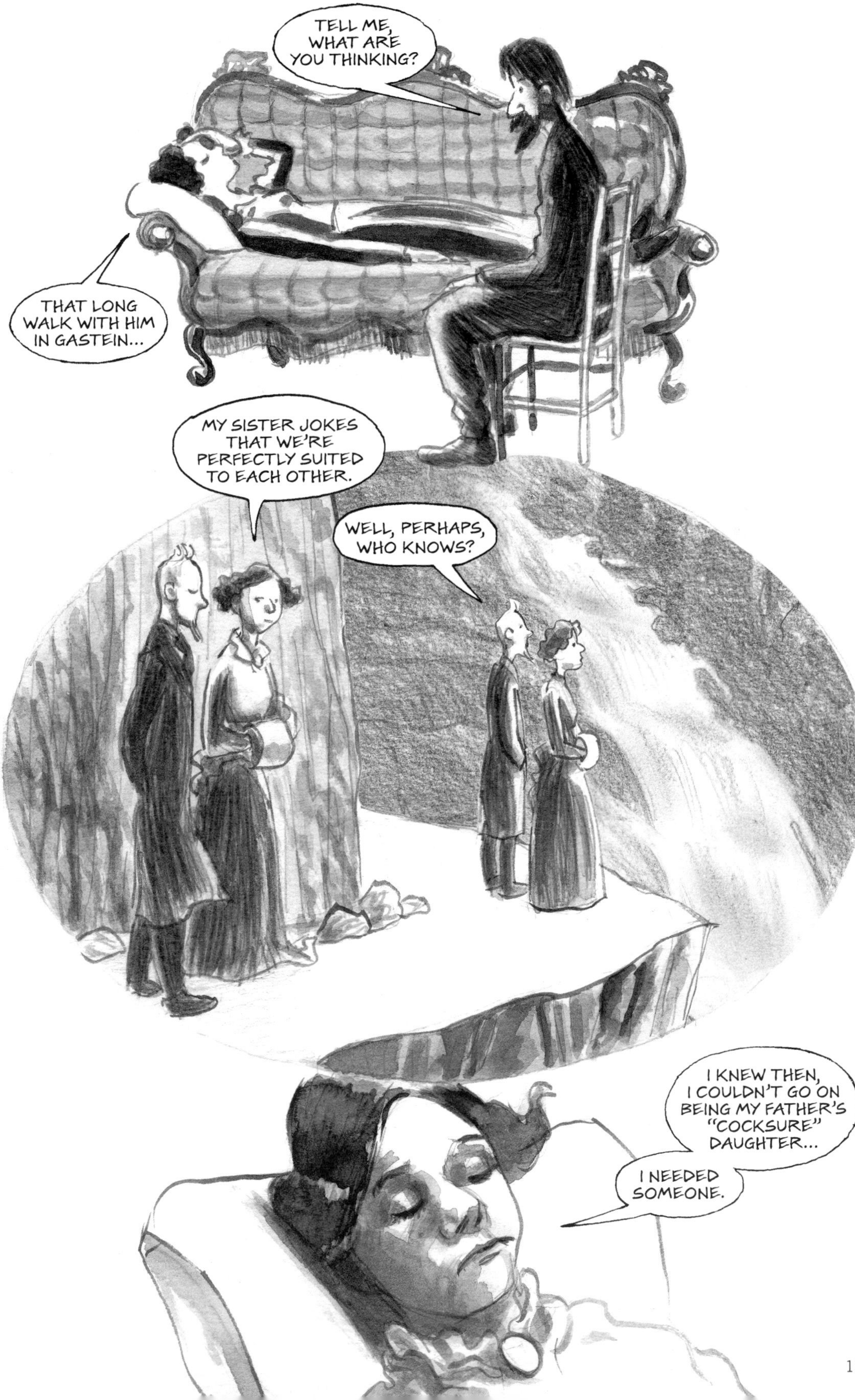
TELL ME, WHAT ARE YOU THINKING?
THAT LONG WALK WITH HIM IN GASTEIN...
MY SISTER JOKES THAT WE'RE PERFECTLY SUITED TO EACH OTHER.
WELL, PERHAPS, WHO KNOWS?
I KNEW THEN, I COULDN'T GO ON BEING MY FATHER'S "COCKSURE" DAUGHTER...
I NEEDED SOMEONE.

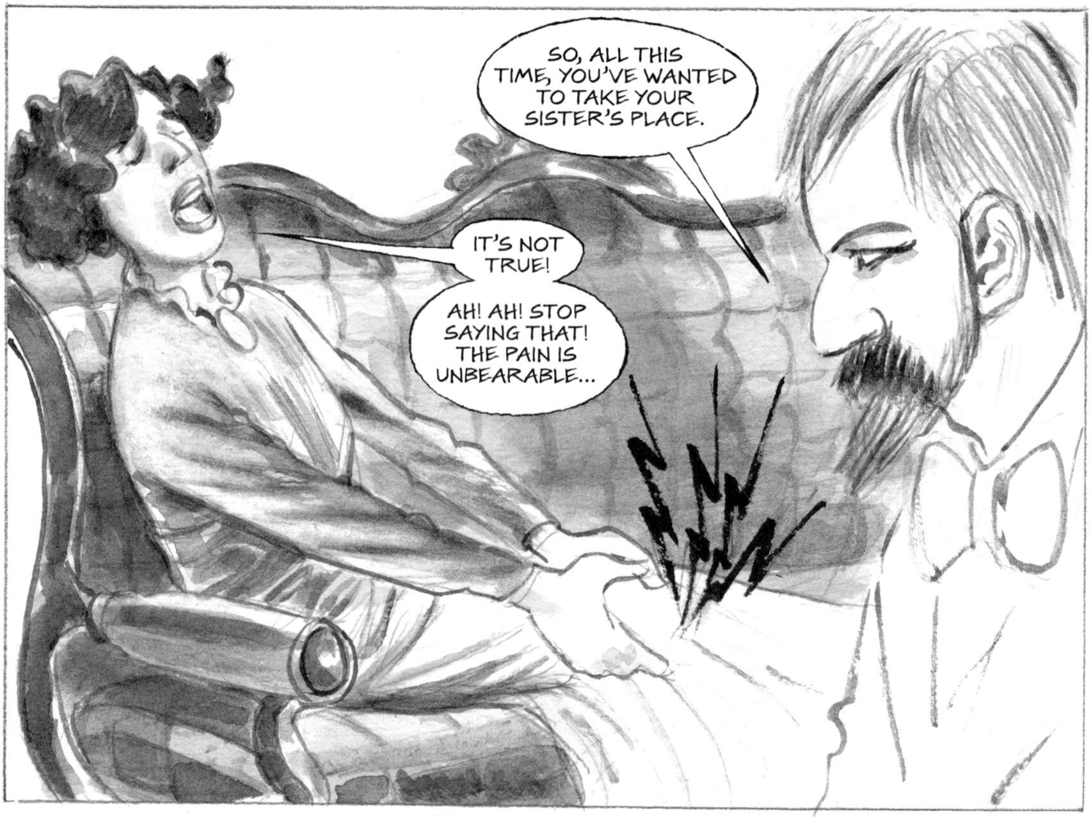
SO, ALL THIS TIME, YOU'VE WANTED TO TAKE YOUR SISTER'S PLACE.
IT'S NOT TRUE!
AH! AH! STOP SAYING THAT! THE PAIN IS UNBEARABLE...

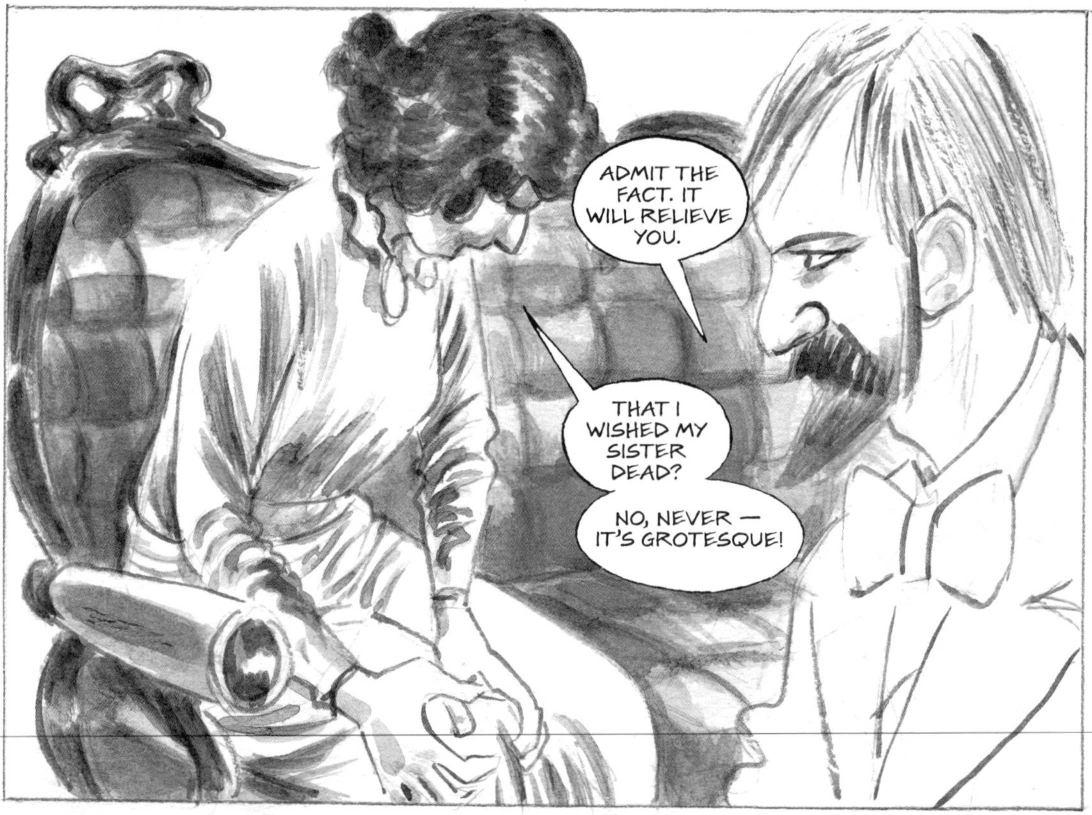
ADMIT THE FACT. IT WILL RELIEVE YOU.
THAT I WISHED MY SISTER DEAD?
NO, NEVER — IT'S GROTESQUE!

SHE COULD ONLY GAIN THE RELIEF OF ABREACTION BY RECONCILING HERSELF TO THE LOVE REPRESSED FOR SO LONG. I DECIDED IT MIGHT HELP TO RISK A CONVERSATION WITH HER MOTHER.

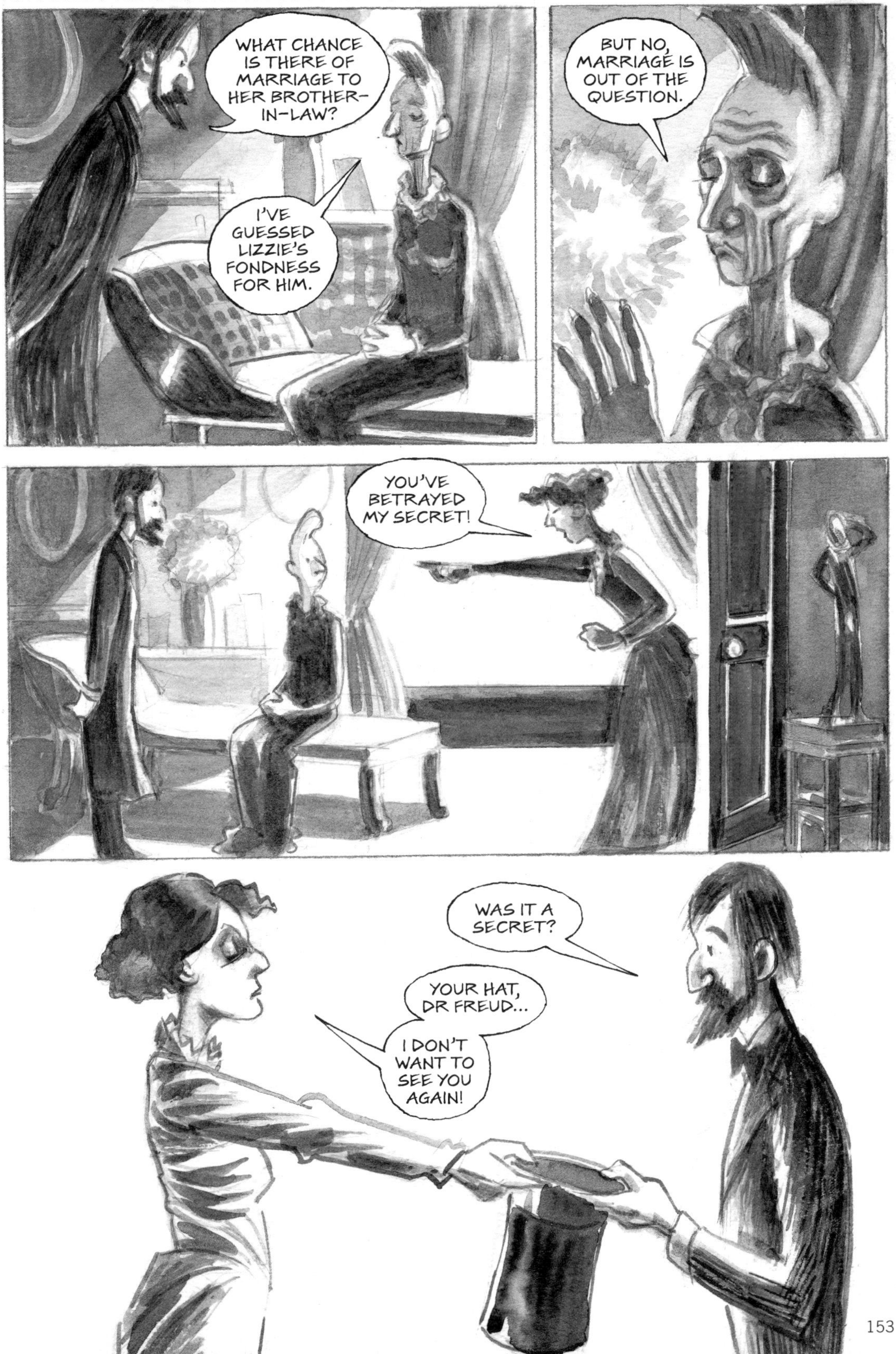

WHAT CHANCE IS THERE OF MARRIAGE TO HER BROTHER-IN-LAW?
I'VE GUESSED LIZZIE'S FONDNESS FOR HIM.
BUT NO, MARRIAGE IS OUT OF THE QUESTION.
YOU'VE BETRAYED MY SECRET!
WAS IT A SECRET?
YOUR HAT, DR FREUD...
I DON'T WANT TO SEE YOU AGAIN!

BUT I DID SEE HER AGAIN A YEAR LATER AT A PRIVATE BALL TO WHICH I'D BEEN INVITED.

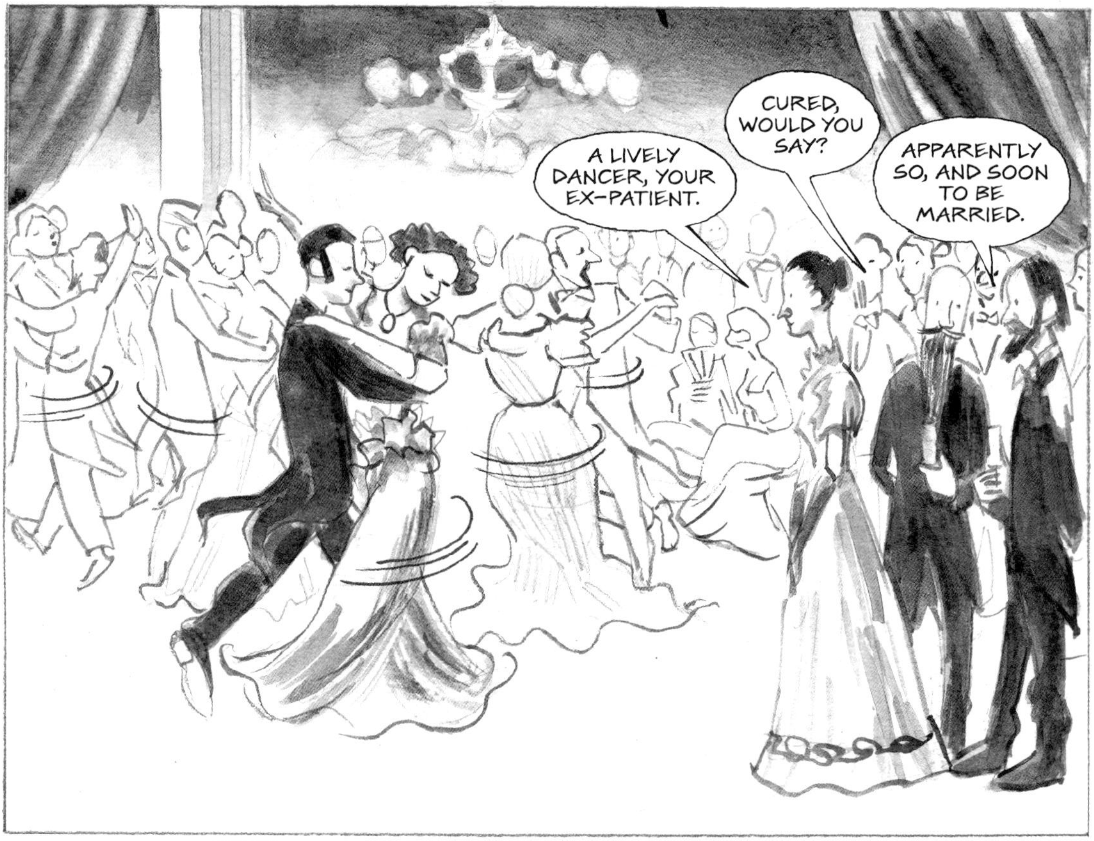
A LIVELY DANCER, YOUR EX-PATIENT.
CURED, WOULD YOU SAY?
APPARENTLY SO, AND SOON TO BE MARRIED.

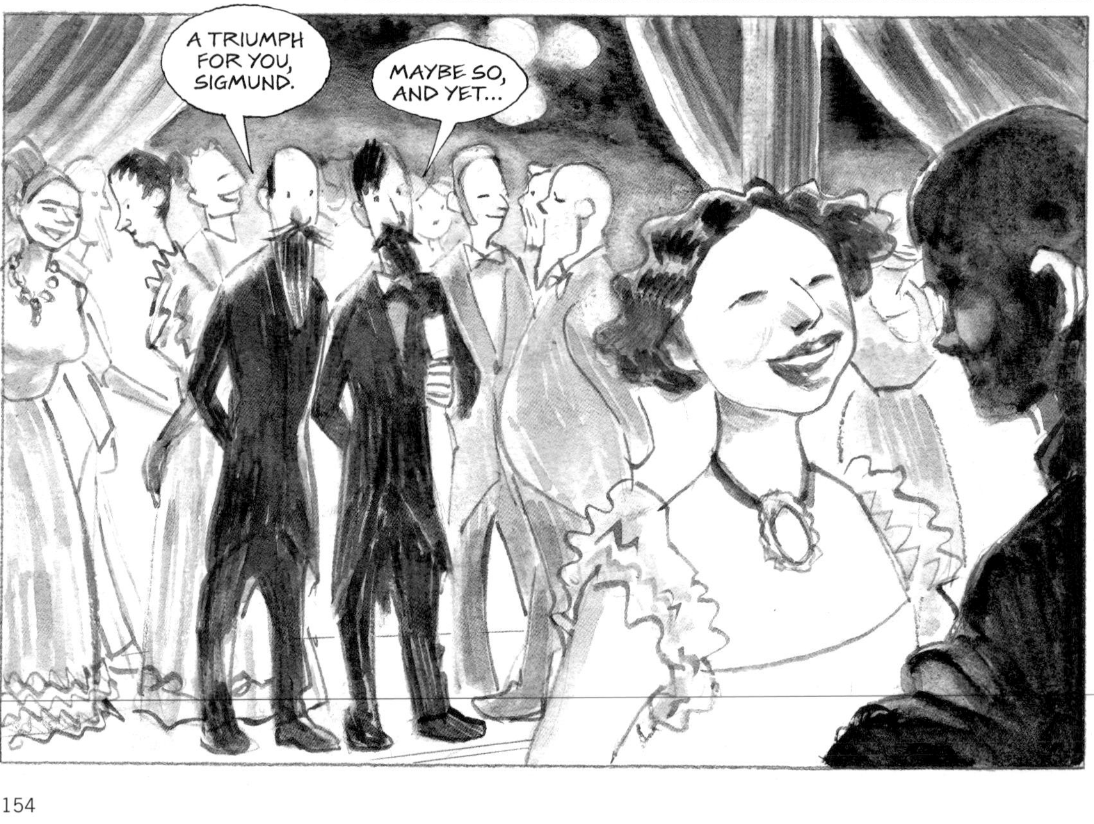
A TRIUMPH FOR YOU, SIGMUND.
MAYBE SO, AND YET...

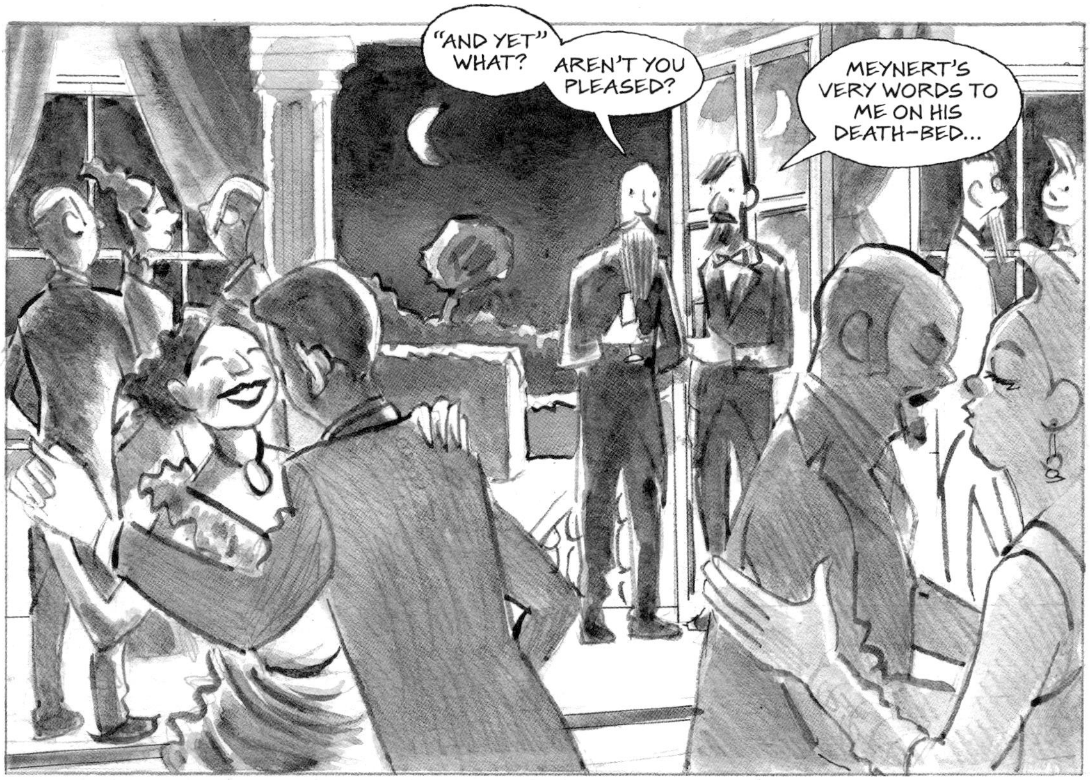
"AND YET" WHAT?
AREN'T YOU PLEASED?
MEYNERT'S VERY WORDS TO ME ON HIS DEATH-BED...

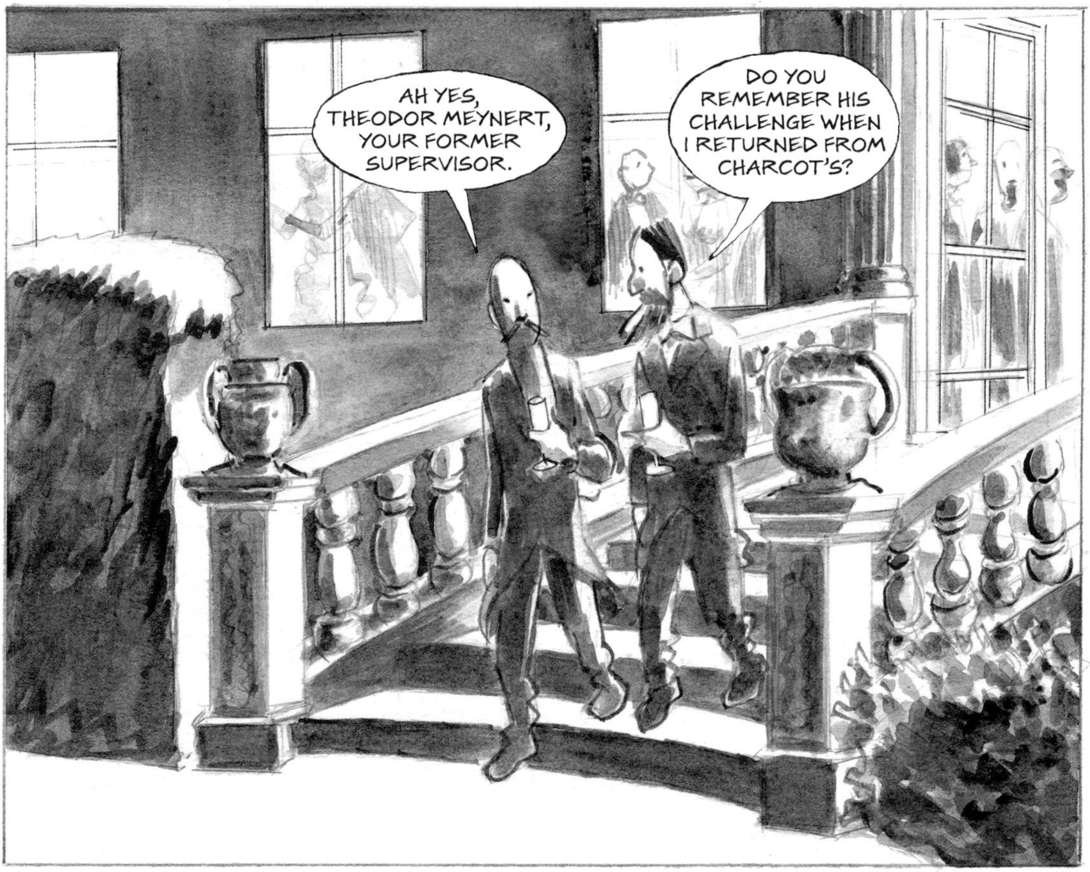
AH YES, THEODOR MEYNERT, YOUR FORMER SUPERVISOR.
DO YOU REMEMBER HIS CHALLENGE WHEN I RETURNED FROM CHARCOT'S?

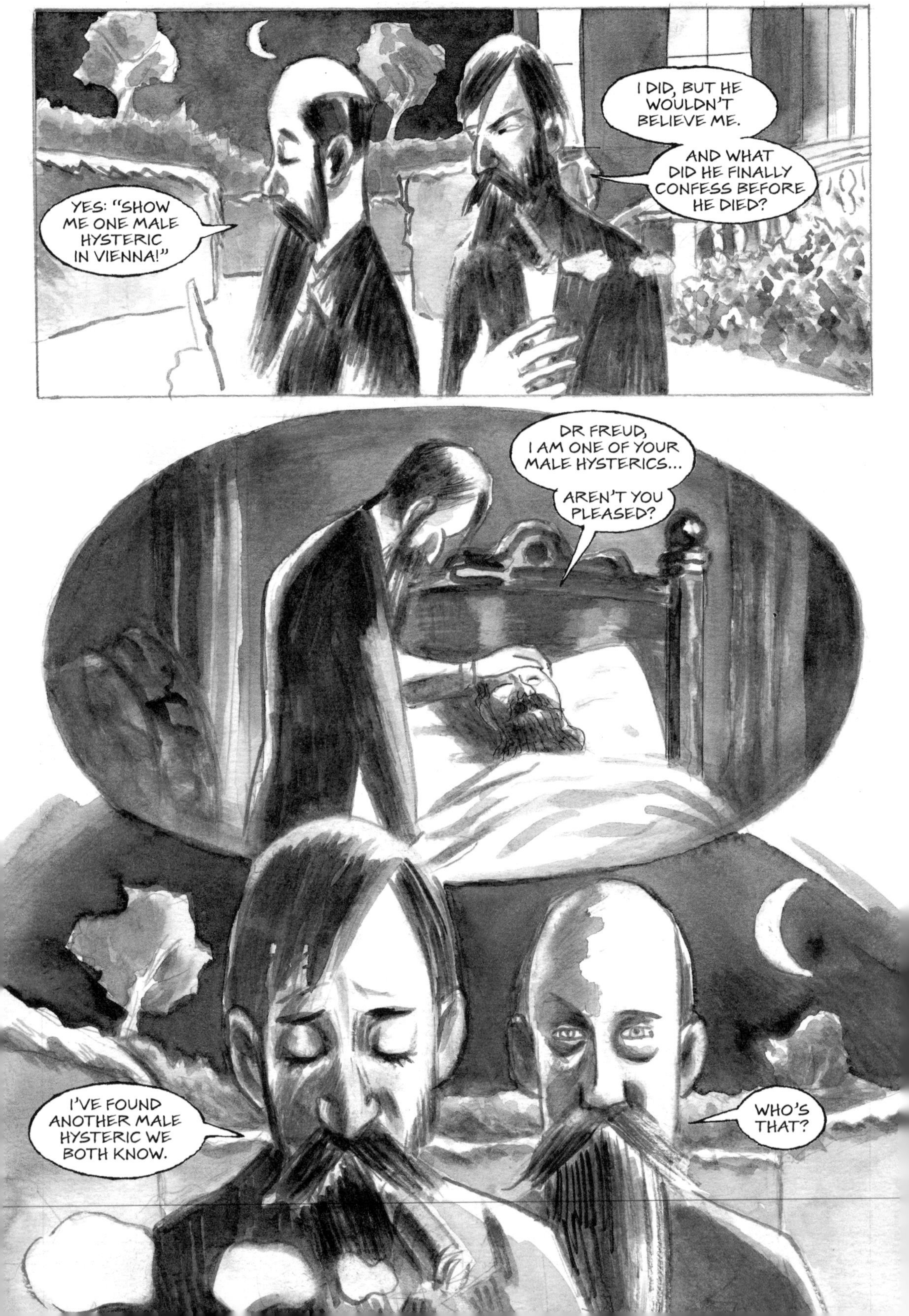
I DID, BUT HE WOULDN'T BELIEVE ME.
AND WHAT DID HE FINALLY CONFESS BEFORE HE DIED?
YES: "SHOW ME ONE MALE HYSTERIC IN VIENNA!"
DR FREUD, I AM ONE OF YOUR MALE HYSTERICS...
AREN'T YOU PLEASED?
I'VE FOUND ANOTHER MALE HYSTERIC WE BOTH KNOW.
WHO'S THAT?

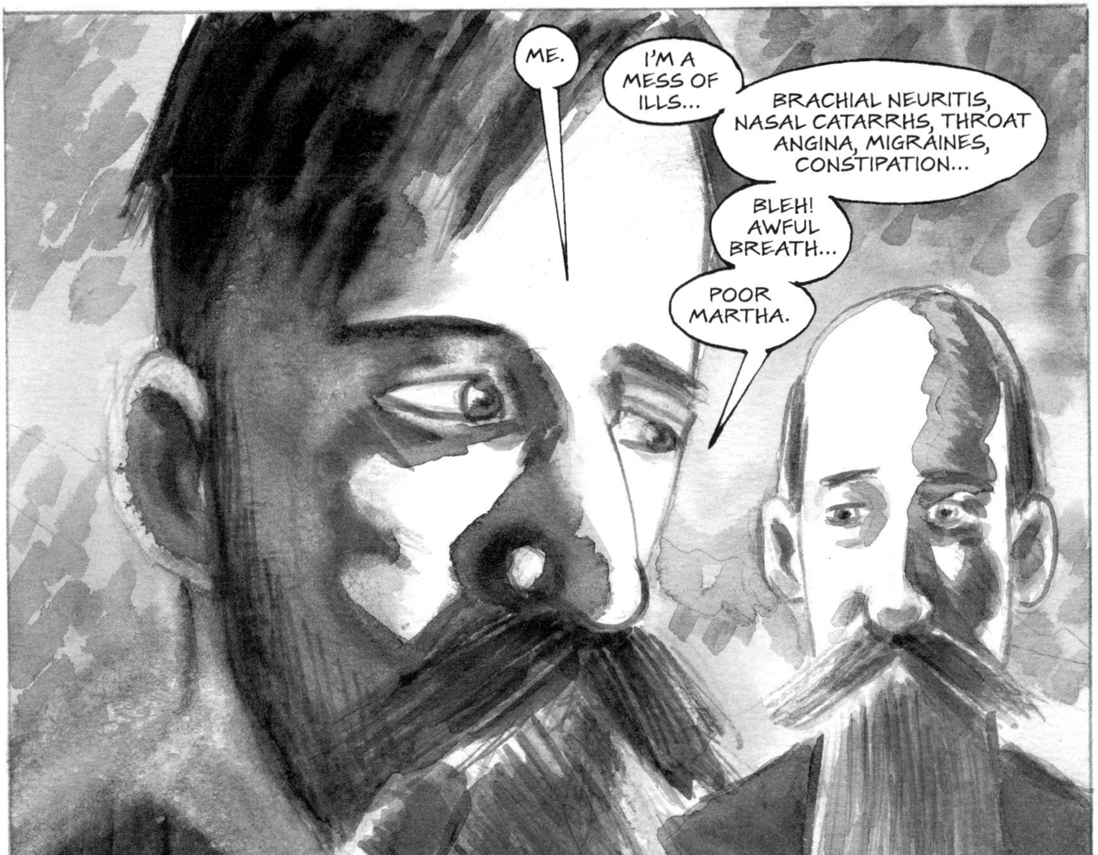
ME.
I'M A MESS OF ILLS...
BRACHIAL NEURITIS, NASAL CATARRHS, THROAT ANGINA, MIGRAINES, CONSTIPATION...
BLEH! AWFUL BREATH...
POOR MARTHA.

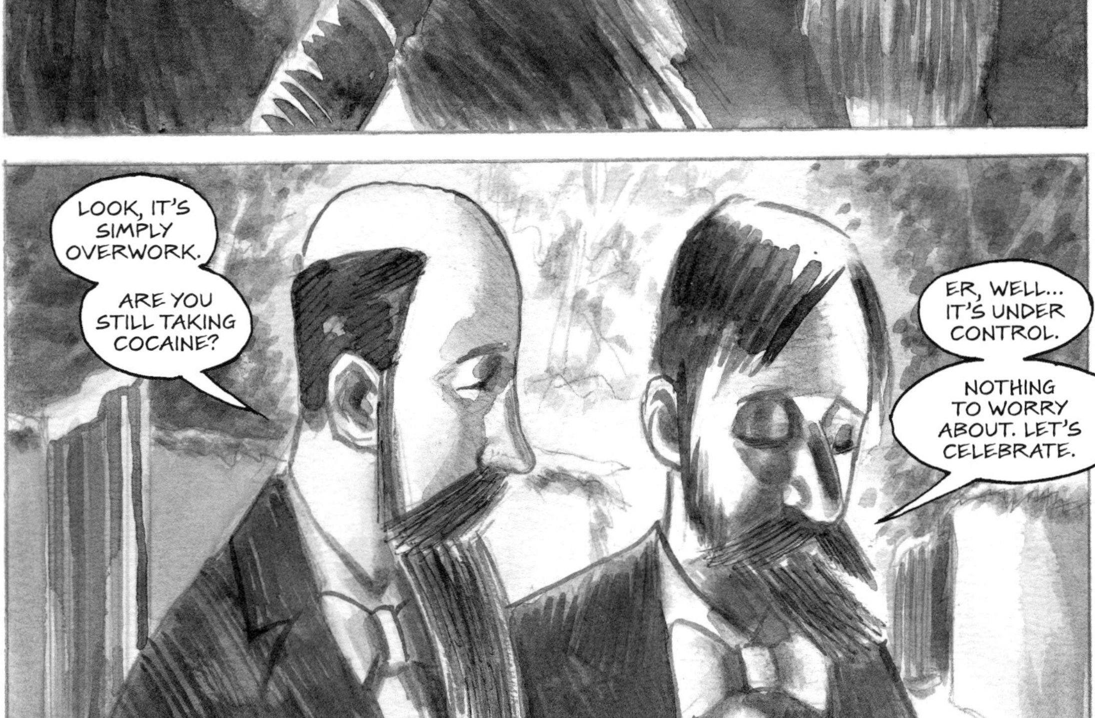
LOOK, IT'S SIMPLY OVERWORK.
ARE YOU STILL TAKING COCAINE?
ER, WELL... IT'S UNDER CONTROL.
NOTHING TO WORRY ABOUT. LET'S CELEBRATE.

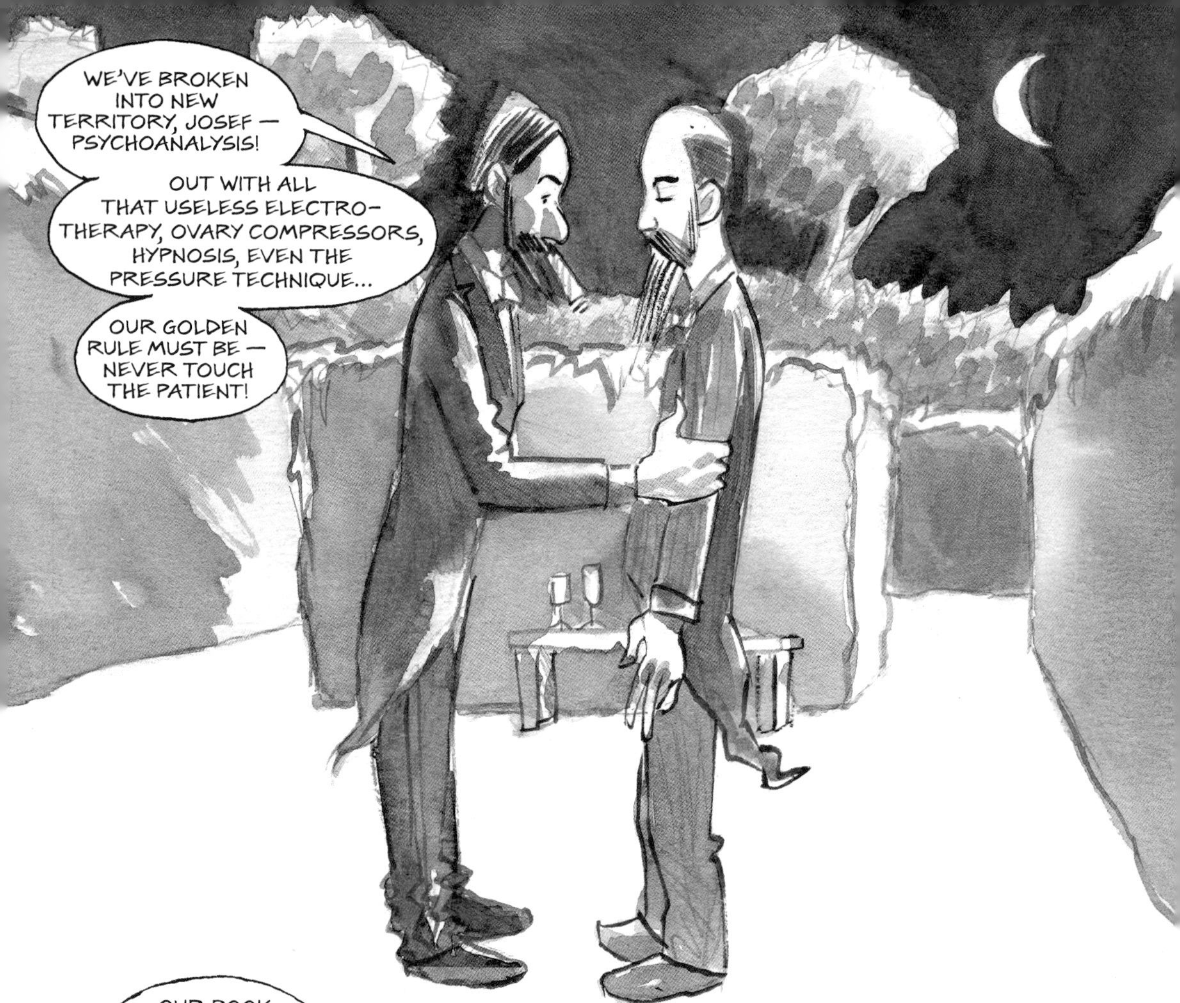
WE'VE BROKEN INTO NEW TERRITORY, JOSEF — PSYCHOANALYSIS!
OUT WITH ALL THAT USELESS ELECTRO-THERAPY, OVARY COMPRESSORS, HYPNOSIS, EVEN THE PRESSURE TECHNIQUE...
OUR GOLDEN RULE MUST BE — NEVER TOUCH THE PATIENT!

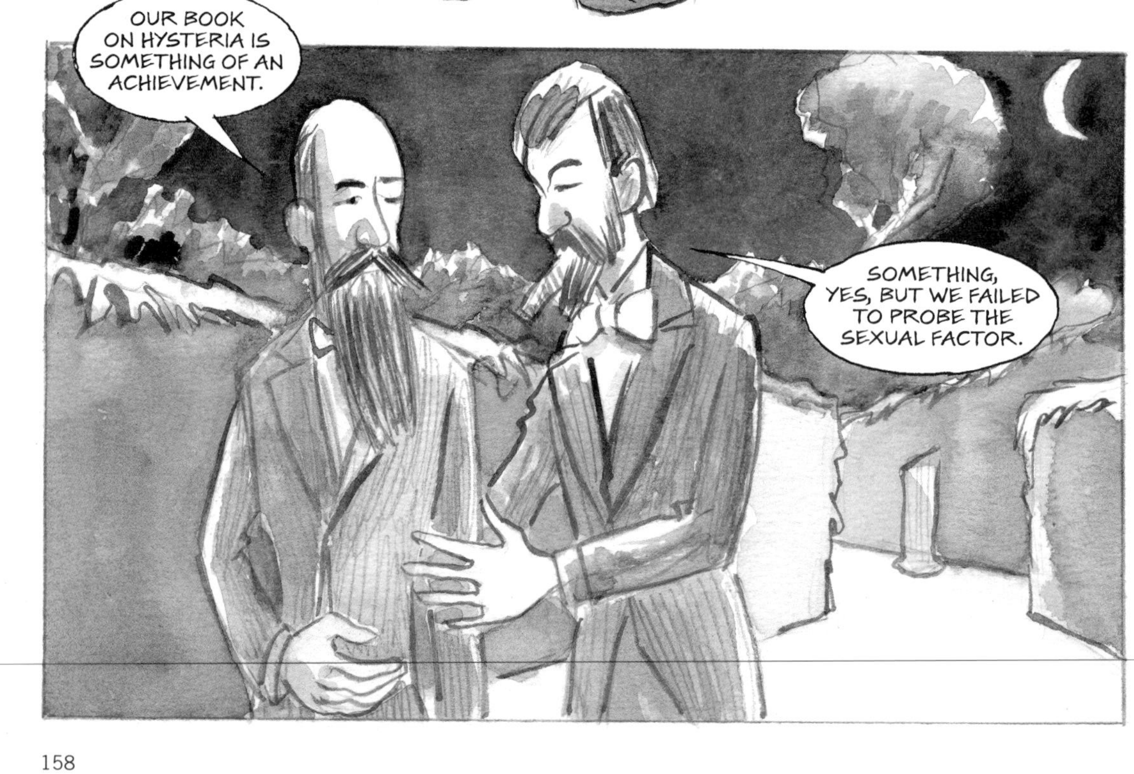
OUR BOOK ON HYSTERIA IS SOMETHING OF AN ACHIEVEMENT.
SOMETHING, YES, BUT WE FAILED TO PROBE THE SEXUAL FACTOR.

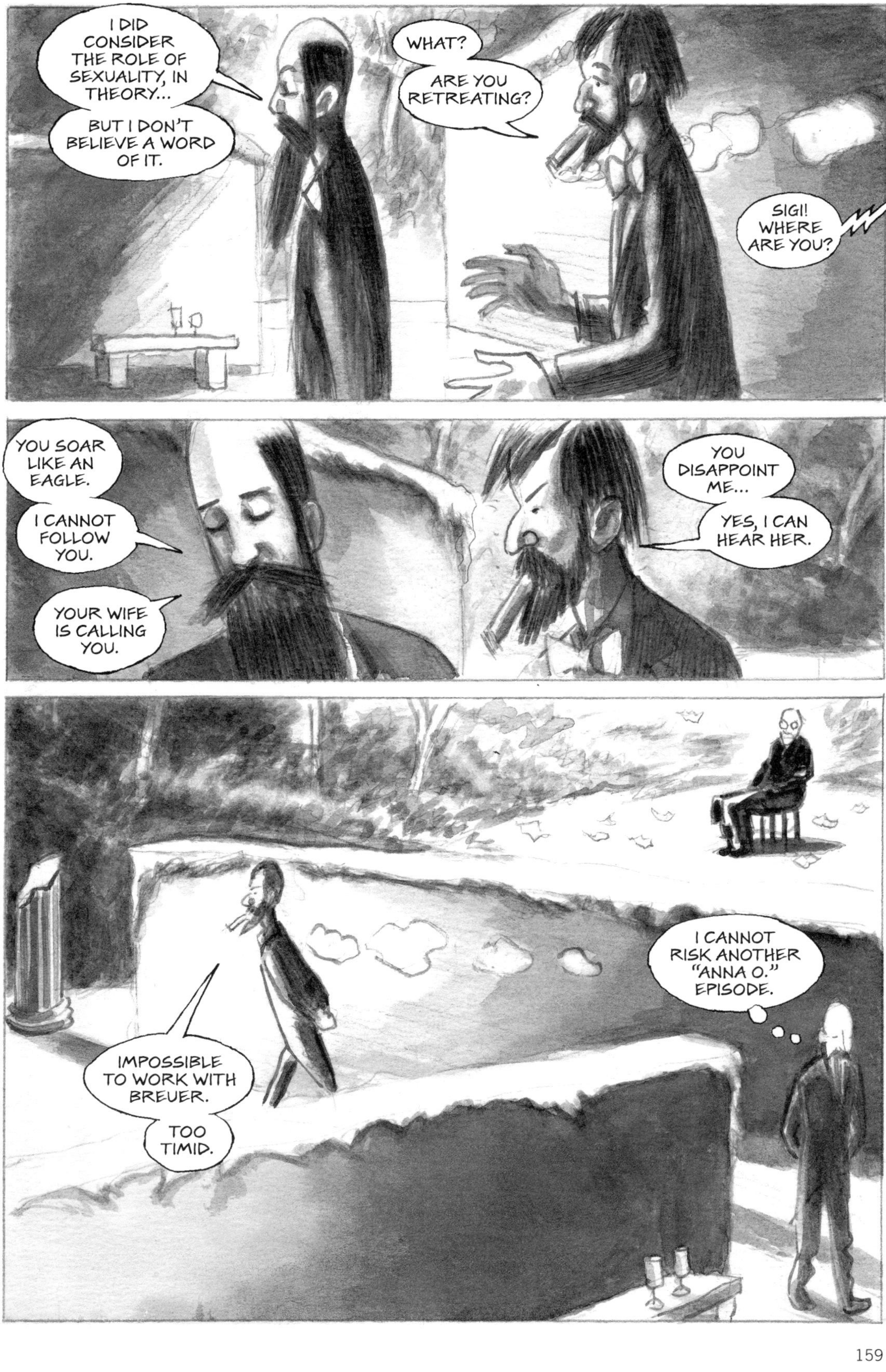
I DID CONSIDER THE ROLE OF SEXUALITY, IN THEORY...
BUT I DON'T BELIEVE A WORD OF IT.
WHAT?
ARE YOU RETREATING?
SIGI! WHERE ARE YOU?
YOU SOAR LIKE AN EAGLE.
I CANNOT FOLLOW YOU.
YOUR WIFE IS CALLING YOU.
YOU DISAPPOINT ME...
YES, I CAN HEAR HER.
I CANNOT RISK ANOTHER "ANNA O." EPISODE.
IMPOSSIBLE TO WORK WITH BREUER.
TOO TIMID.

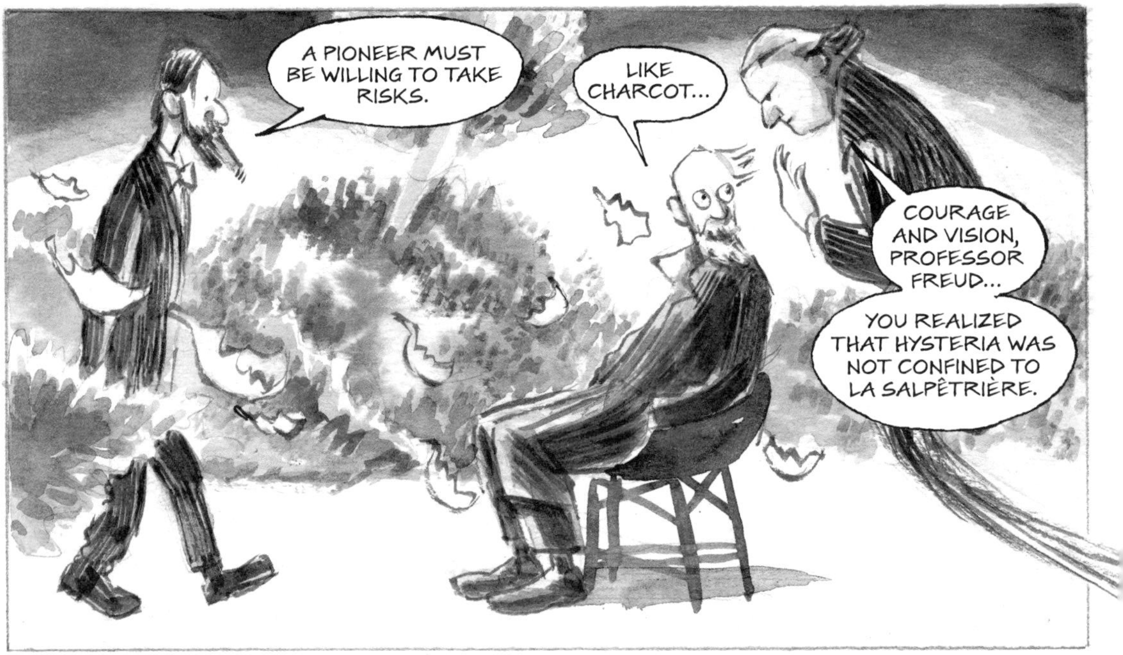
A PIONEER MUST BE WILLING TO TAKE RISKS.
LIKE CHARCOT...
COURAGE AND VISION, PROFESSOR FREUD...
YOU REALIZED THAT HYSTERIA WAS NOT CONFINED TO LA SALPÊTRIÈRE.

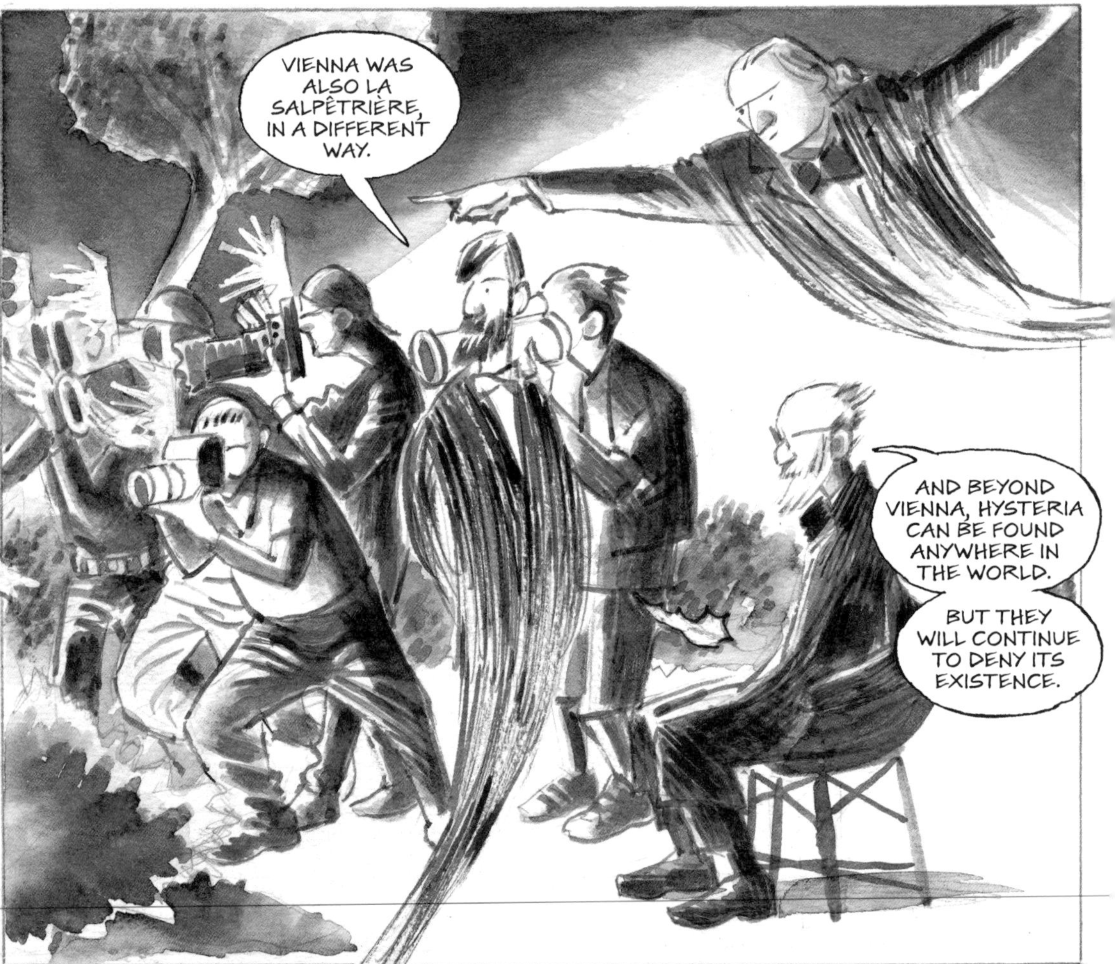
VIENNA WAS ALSO LA SALPÊTRIÈRE, IN A DIFFERENT WAY.
AND BEYOND VIENNA, HYSTERIA CAN BE FOUND ANYWHERE IN THE WORLD.
BUT THEY WILL CONTINUE TO DENY ITS EXISTENCE.

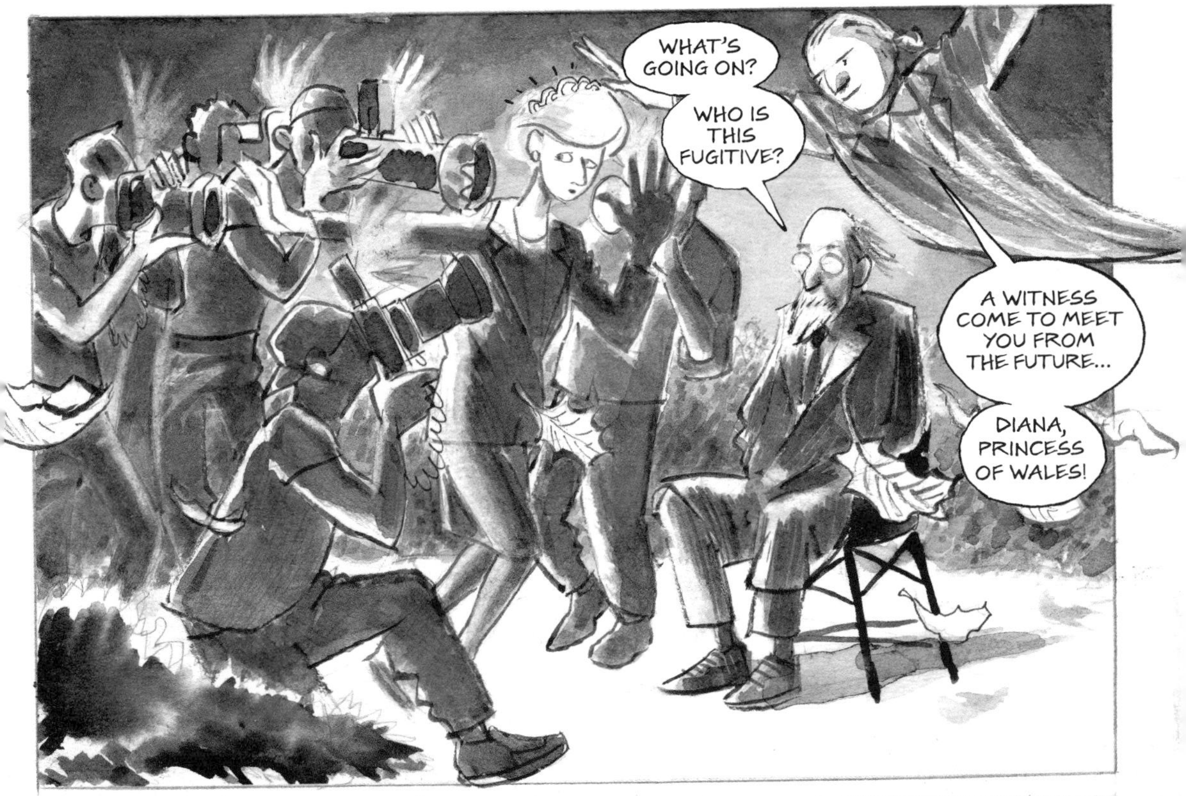
WHAT'S GOING ON?
WHO IS THIS FUGITIVE?
A WITNESS COME TO MEET YOU FROM THE FUTURE...
DIANA, PRINCESS OF WALES!

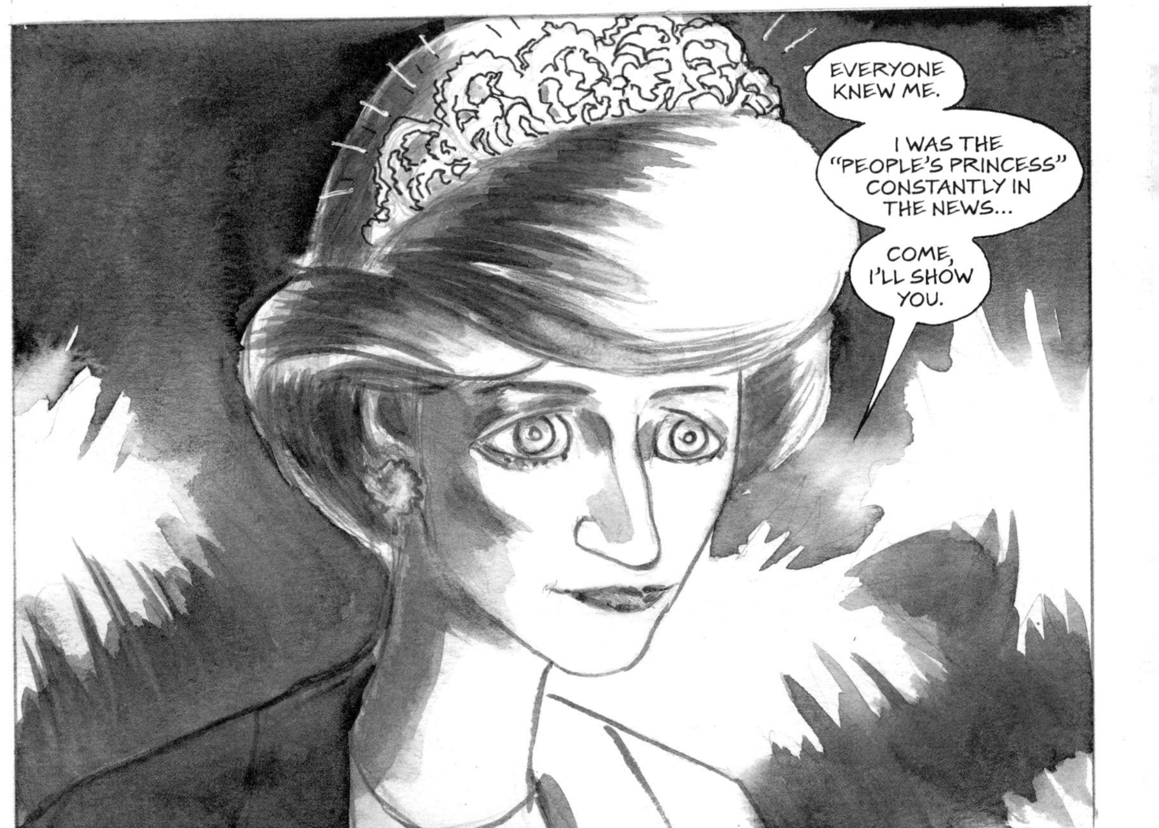
EVERYONE KNEW ME.
I WAS THE "PEOPLE'S PRINCESS" CONSTANTLY IN THE NEWS...
COME, I'LL SHOW YOU.

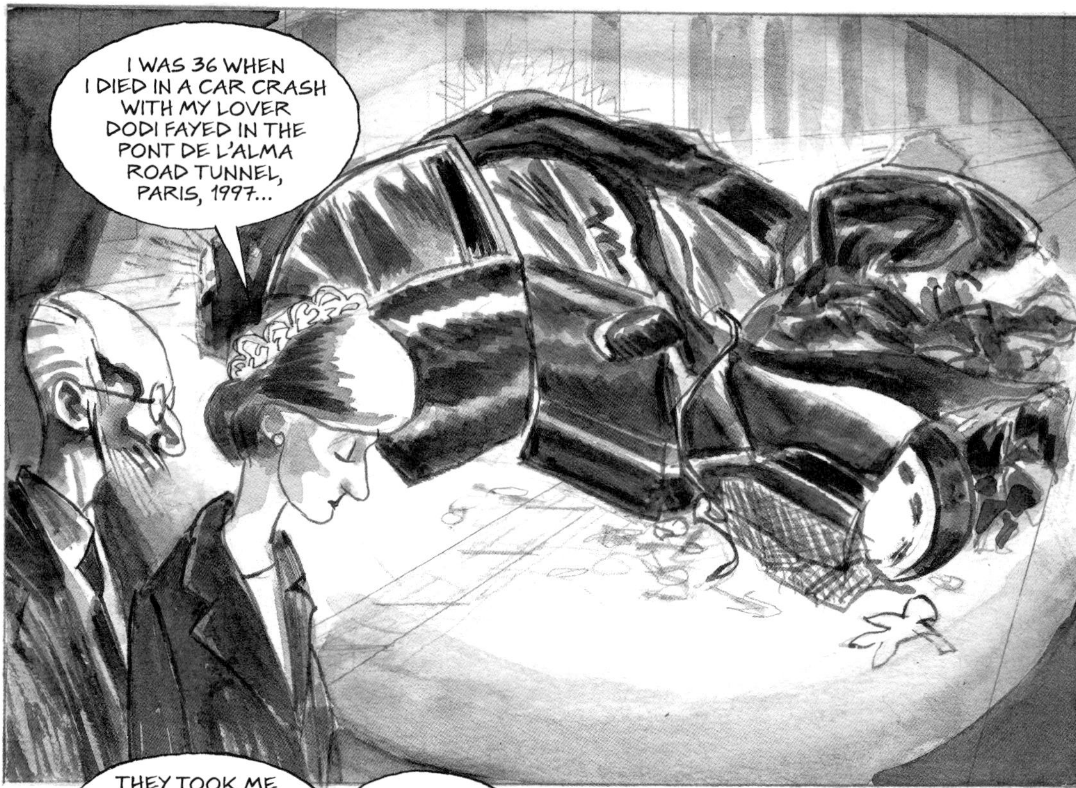
I WAS 36 WHEN I DIED IN A CAR CRASH WITH MY LOVER DODI FAYED IN THE PONT DE L'ALMA ROAD TUNNEL, PARIS, 1997...

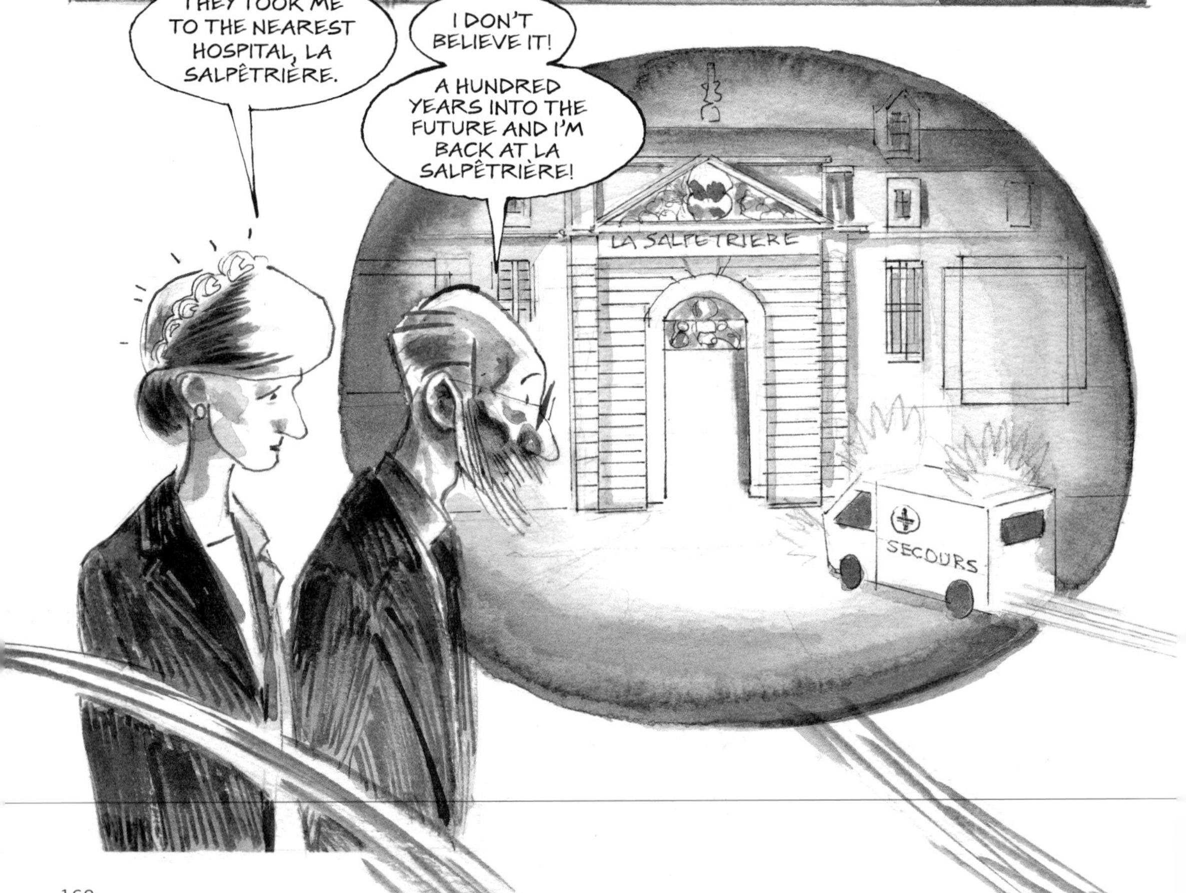
THEY TOOK ME TO THE NEAREST HOSPITAL, LA SALPÊTRIÈRE.
I DON'T BELIEVE IT!
A HUNDRED YEARS INTO THE FUTURE AND I'M BACK AT LA SALPÊTRIÈRE!
LA SALPETRIERE
SECOURS

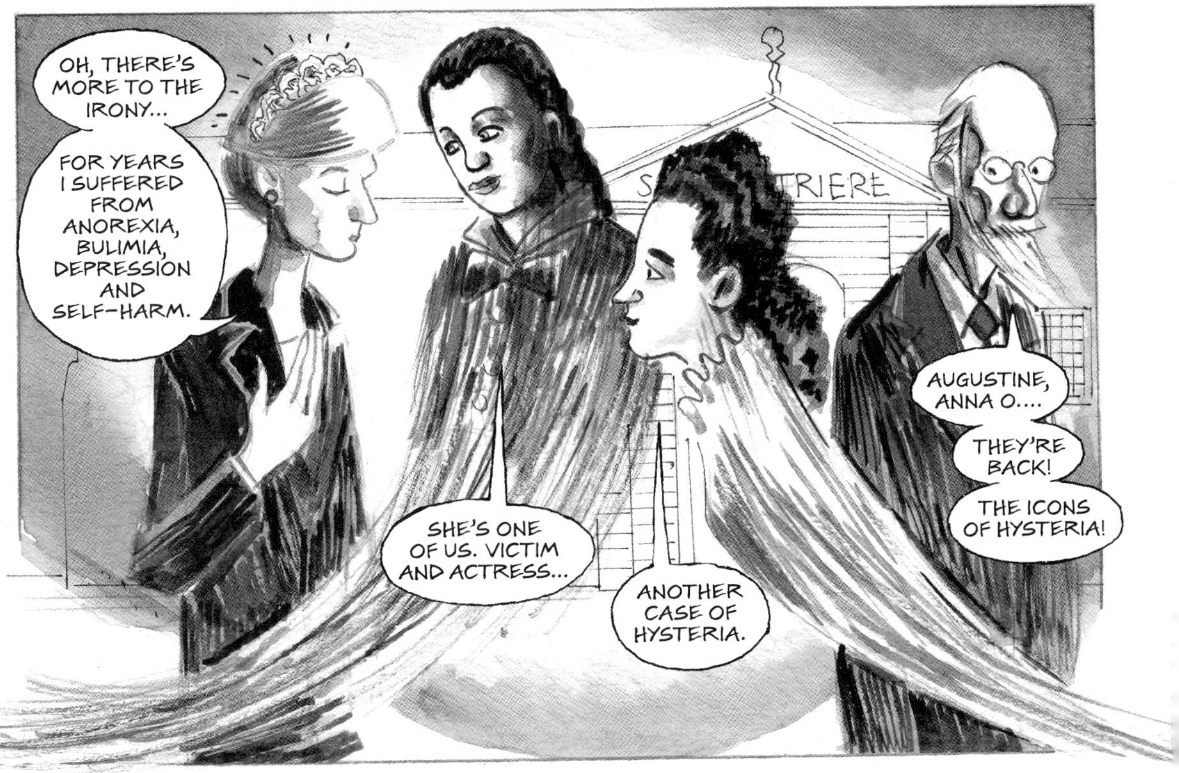
OH, THERE'S MORE TO THE IRONY...
FOR YEARS I SUFFERED FROM ANOREXIA, BULIMIA, DEPRESSION AND SELF-HARM.
SHE'S ONE OF US. VICTIM AND ACTRESS...
ANOTHER CASE OF HYSTERIA.
AUGUSTINE, ANNA O....
THEY'RE BACK!
THE ICONS OF HYSTERIA!
TRIERE

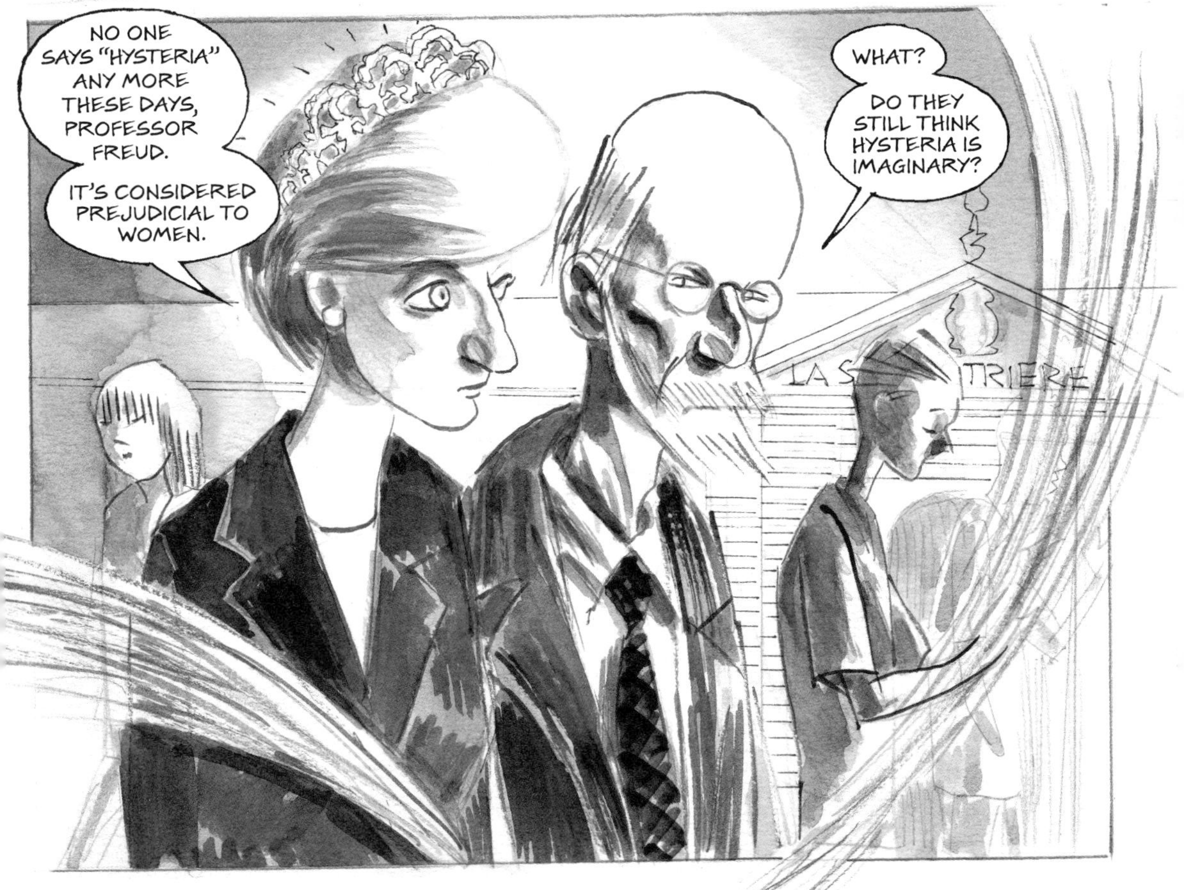
NO ONE SAYS "HYSTERIA" ANY MORE THESE DAYS, PROFESSOR FREUD.
IT'S CONSIDERED PREJUDICIAL TO WOMEN.
WHAT?
DO THEY STILL THINK HYSTERIA IS IMAGINARY?

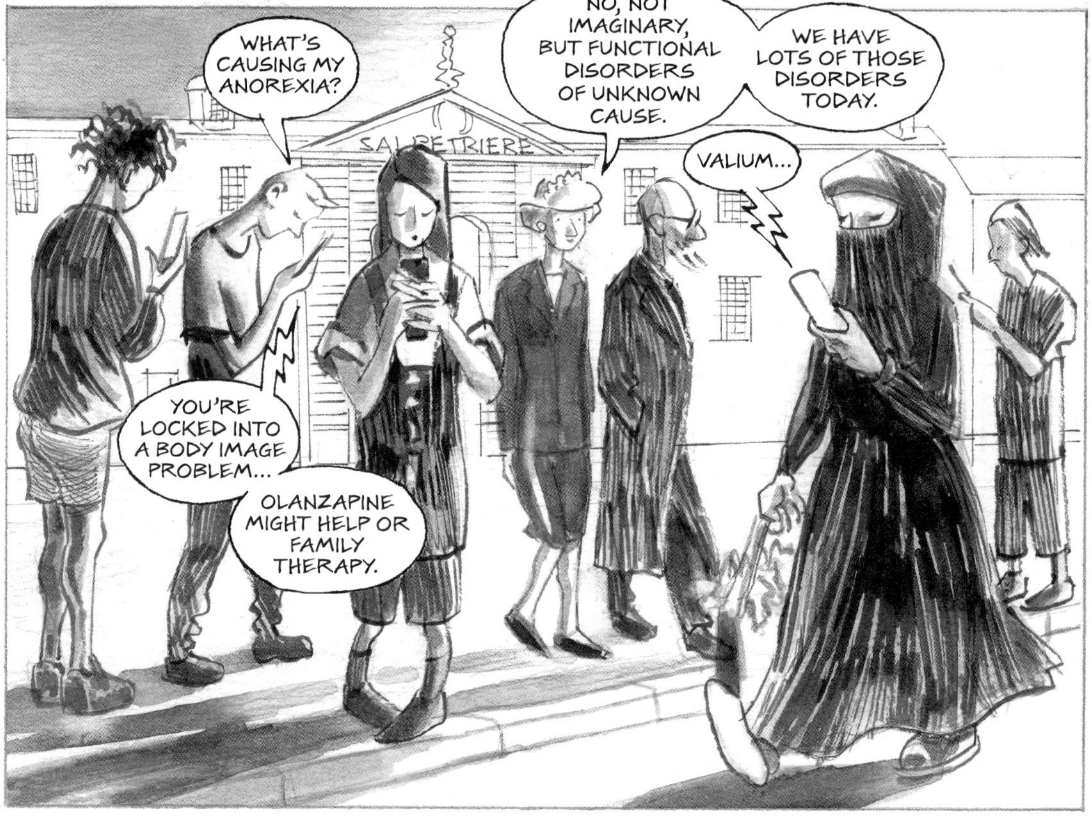
WHAT'S CAUSING MY ANOREXIA?
SALPETRIERE
NO, NOT IMAGINARY, BUT FUNCTIONAL DISORDERS OF UNKNOWN CAUSE.
WE HAVE LOTS OF THOSE DISORDERS TODAY.
VALIUM...
YOU'RE LOCKED INTO A BODY IMAGE PROBLEM...
OLANZAPINE MIGHT HELP OR FAMILY THERAPY.

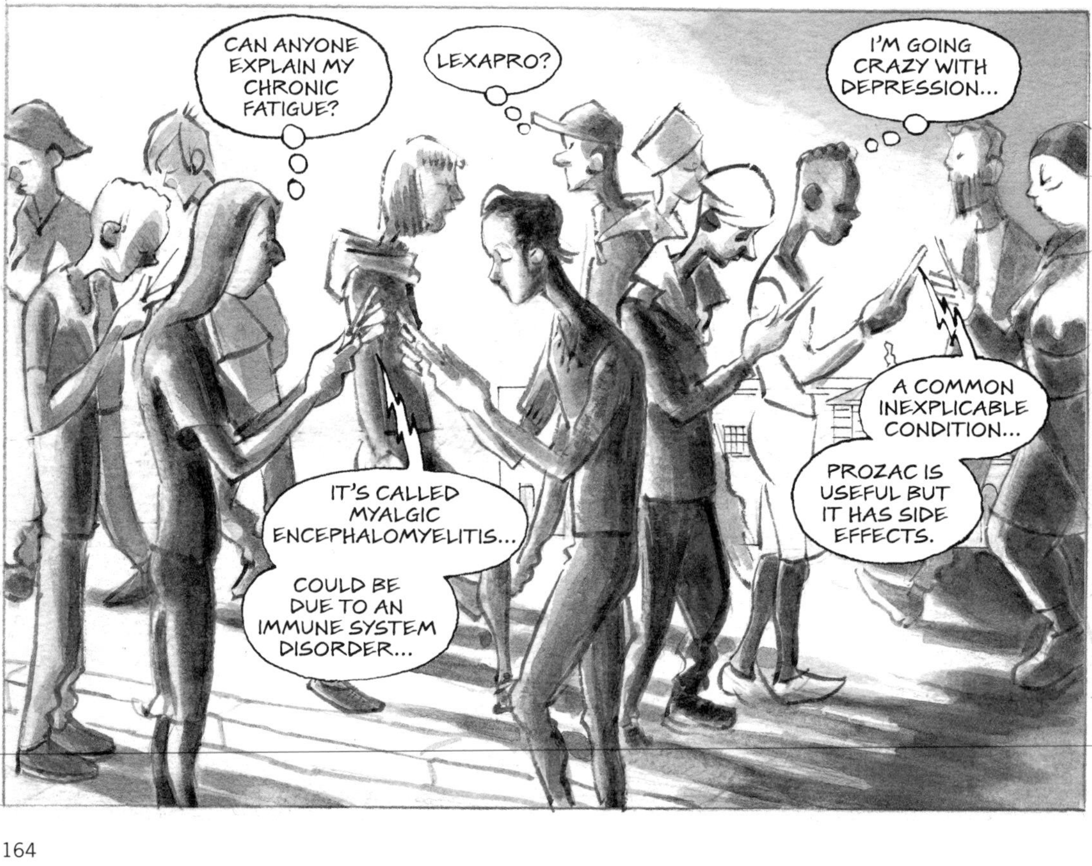
CAN ANYONE EXPLAIN MY CHRONIC FATIGUE?
LEXAPRO?
I'M GOING CRAZY WITH DEPRESSION...
A COMMON INEXPLICABLE CONDITION...
PROZAC IS USEFUL BUT IT HAS SIDE EFFECTS.
IT'S CALLED MYALGIC ENCEPHALOMYELITIS...
COULD BE DUE TO AN IMMUNE SYSTEM DISORDER...

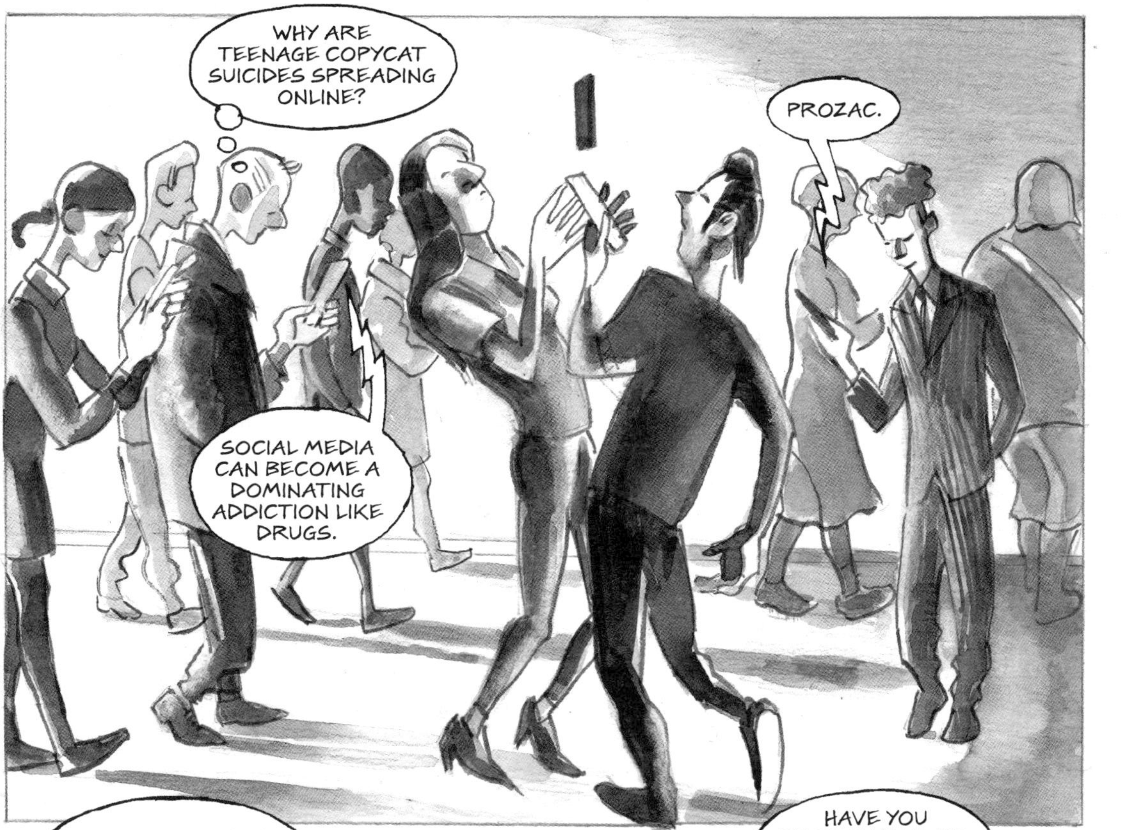
WHY ARE TEENAGE COPYCAT SUICIDES SPREADING ONLINE?
PROZAC.
SOCIAL MEDIA CAN BECOME A DOMINATING ADDICTION LIKE DRUGS.

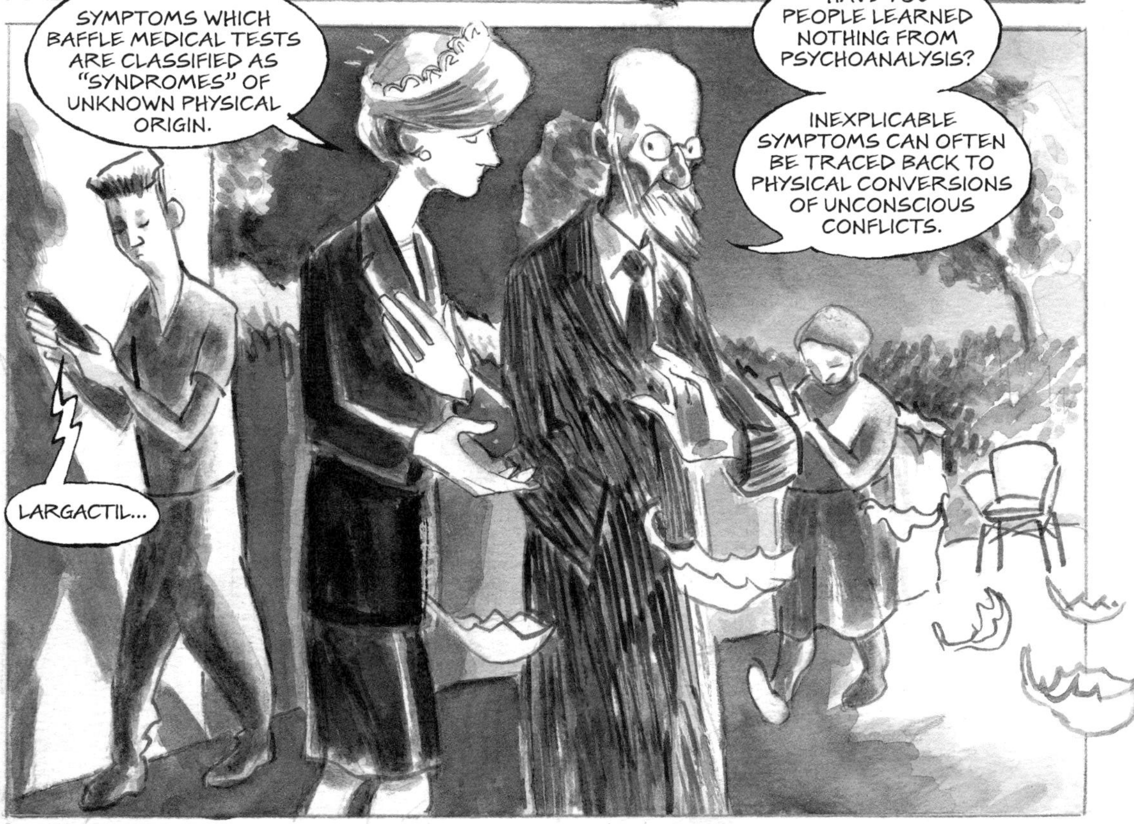
SYMPTOMS WHICH BAFFLE MEDICAL TESTS ARE CLASSIFIED AS "SYNDROMES" OF UNKNOWN PHYSICAL ORIGIN.
HAVE YOU PEOPLE LEARNED NOTHING FROM PSYCHOANALYSIS?
INEXPLICABLE SYMPTOMS CAN OFTEN BE TRACED BACK TO PHYSICAL CONVERSIONS OF UNCONSCIOUS CONFLICTS.
LARGACTIL...

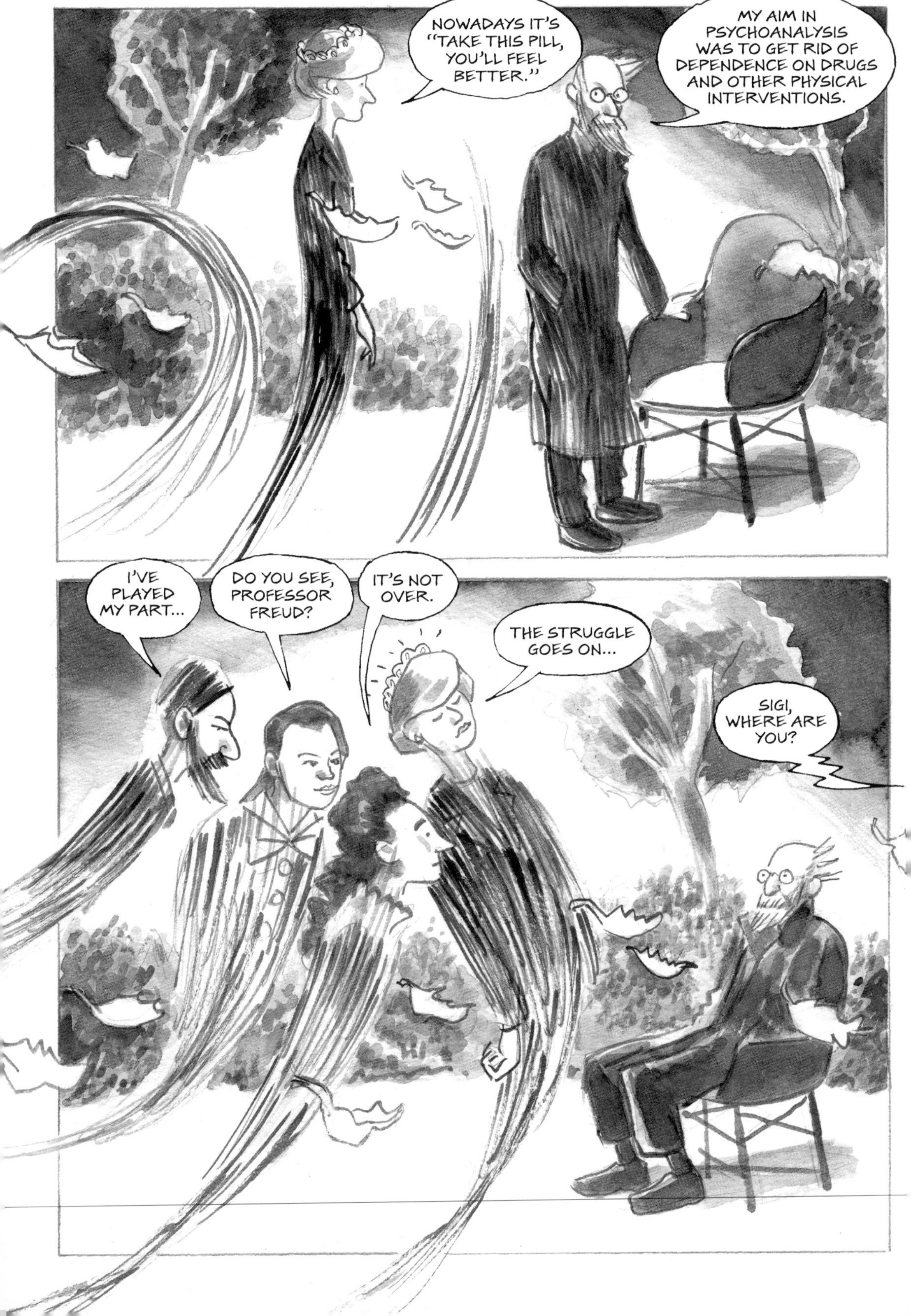
NOWADAYS IT'S "TAKE THIS PILL, YOU'LL FEEL BETTER."
MY AIM IN PSYCHOANALYSIS WAS TO GET RID OF DEPENDENCE ON DRUGS AND OTHER PHYSICAL INTERVENTIONS.
I'VE PLAYED MY PART...
DO YOU SEE, PROFESSOR FREUD?
IT'S NOT OVER.
THE STRUGGLE GOES ON...
SIGI, WHERE ARE YOU?

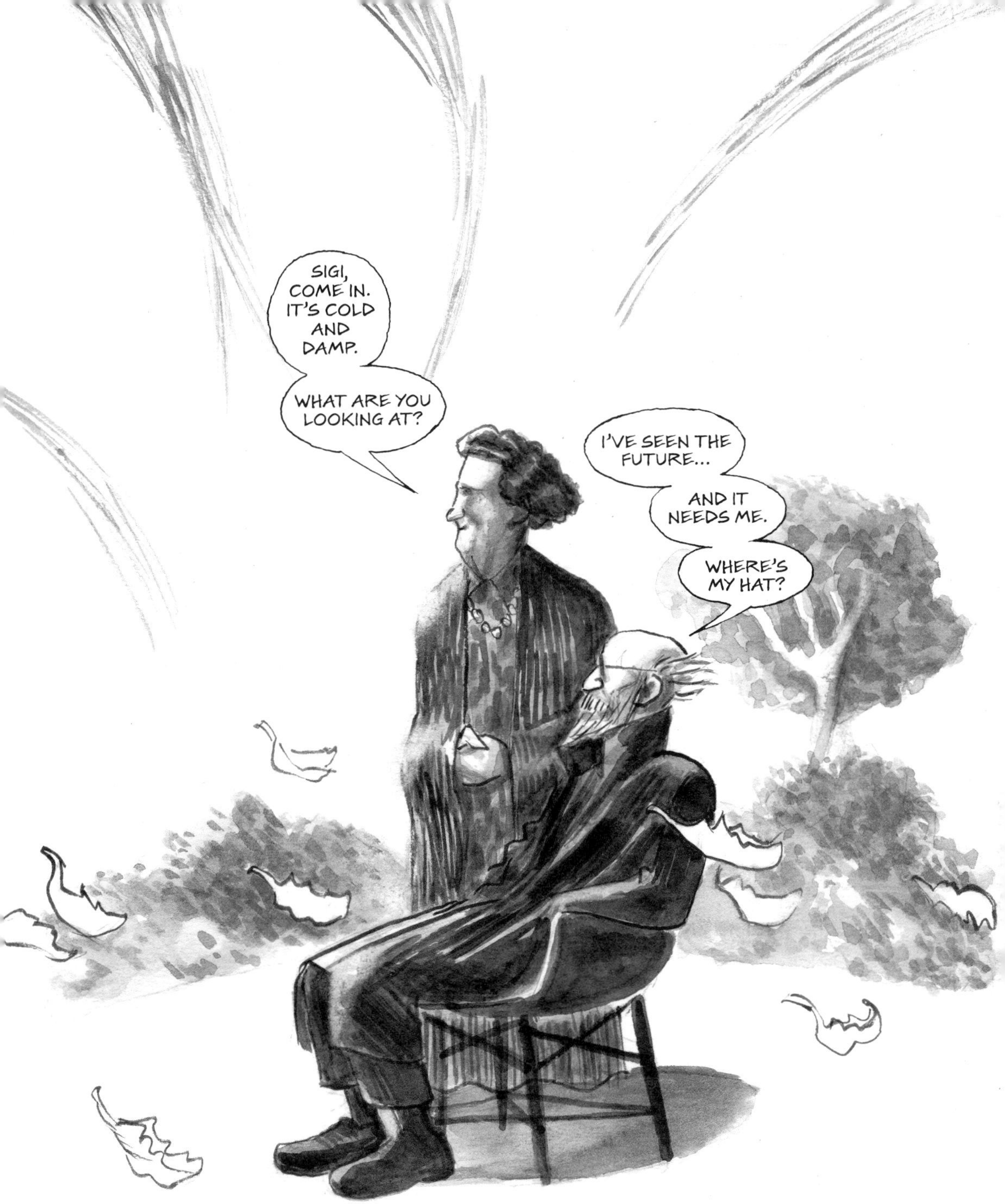
SIGI, COME IN. IT'S COLD AND DAMP.
WHAT ARE YOU LOOKING AT?
I'VE SEEN THE FUTURE...
AND IT NEEDS ME.
WHERE'S MY HAT?